ROBERT J. PENELLA is Professor of Classics at Fordham University. He is the author of *The Letters of Apollonius of Tyana: A Critical Text with Prolegomena, Translation and Commentary* and *Greek Philosophers and Sophists in the Fourth Century* A.D.*: Studies in Eunapius of Sardis.*

THE TRANSFORMATION OF THE CLASSICAL HERITAGE

Peter Brown, General Editor

I *Art and Ceremony in Late Antiquity,* by Sabine G. MacCormack

II *Synesius of Cyrene: Philosopher-Bishop,* by Jay Alan Bregman

III *Theodosian Empresses: Women and Imperial Dominion in Late Antiquity,* by Kenneth G. Holum

IV *John Chrysostom and the Jews: Rhetoric and Reality in the Late Fourth Century,* by Robert L. Wilken

V *Biography in Late Antiquity: The Quest for the Holy Man,* by Patricia Cox

VI *Pachomius: The Making of a Community in Fourth-Century Egypt,* by Philip Rousseau

VII *Change in Byzantine Culture in the Eleventh and Twelfth Centuries,* by A. P. Kazhdan and Ann Wharton Epstein

VIII *Leadership and Community in Late Antique Gaul,* by Raymond Van Dam

IX *Homer the Theologian: Neoplatonist Allegorical Reading and the Growth of the Epic Tradition,* by Robert Lamberton

X *Procopius and the Sixth Century,* by Averil Cameron

XI *Guardians of Language: The Grammarian and Society in Late Antiquity,* by Robert A. Kaster

XII *Civic Coins and Civic Politics in the Roman East, A.D. 180–275,* by Kenneth Harl

XIII *Holy Women of the Syrian Orient,* introduced and translated by Sebastian P. Brock and Susan Ashbrook Harvey

XIV *Gregory the Great: Perfection in Imperfection,* by Carole Straw

XV *"Apex Omnium": Religion in the "Res gestae" of Ammianus,* by R. L. Rike

XVI *Dioscorus of Aphrodito: His Work and His World,* by Leslie S. B. MacCoull

XVII *On Roman Time: The Codex-Calendar of 354 and the Rhythms of Urban Life in Late Antiquity,* by Michele Renee Salzman

XVIII *Asceticism and Society in Crisis: John of Ephesus and The Lives of the Eastern Saints,* by Susan Ashbrook Harvey

XIX *Barbarians and Politics at the Court of Arcadius,* by Alan Cameron and Jacqueline Long, with a contribution by Lee Sherry

XX *Basil of Caesarea,* by Philip Rousseau

XXI *In Praise of Later Roman Emperors: The "Panegyrici Latini,"* introduction, translation, and historical commentary by C. E. V. Nixon and Barbara Saylor Rodgers

XXII *Ambrose of Milan: Church and Court in a Christian Capital,* by Neil B. McLynn

XXIII *Public Disputation, Power, and Social Order in Late Antiquity,* by Richard Lim

XXIV *The Making of a Heretic: Gender, Authority, and the Priscillianist Controversy,* by Virginia Burrus

XXV *Symeon the Holy Fool: Leontius's Life and the Late Antique City,* by Derek Krueger

XXVI *The Shadows of Poetry: Vergil in the Mind of Augustine,* by Sabine MacCormack

XXVII *Paulinus of Nola: Life, Letters, and Poems,* by Dennis E. Trout

XXVIII *The Barbarian Plain: Saint Sergius between Rome and Iran,* by Elizabeth Key Fowden

XXIX *The Private Orations of Themistius,* translated, annotated, and introduced by Robert J. Penella

XXX *The Memory of the Eyes: Pilgrims to Living Saints in Christian Late Antiquity,* by Georgia Frank

The Private Orations of Themistius

The Private Orations of Themistius

Translated, Annotated, and Introduced by
Robert J. Penella

UNIVERSITY OF CALIFORNIA PRESS
Berkeley · Los Angeles · London

University of California Press

Berkeley and Los Angeles, California

University of California Press, Ltd.

London, England

Library of Congress Cataloging-in-Publication Data

Themistius.

[Orationes. English]

The private orations of Themistius / translated, annotated, and introduced by Robert J. Penella.

p. cm. — (The transformation of the classical heritage ; 29)

Includes bibliographical references (p.) and index.

ISBN 0-520-21821-3 (alk. paper)

1. Themistius Translations into English. 2. Speeches, addresses, etc., Greek Translations into English. 3. Rome—History—Theodosius I, the Great, 379–395 Sources. 4. Rome—History—Constantius II, 337–361 Sources. 5. Rome—History—Julian, 361–363 Sources. I. Penella, Robert J. II. Title. III. Series.

PA4441.T5A26 1999

185—dc21

99-30092

CIP

Manufactured in the United States of America

10 9 8 7 6 5 4 3 2 1

The paper used in this publication meets the minimum requirements of ANSI/NISO Z39.48-1992 (R 1997) (*Permanence of Paper*). ♾

For Martha

Daughter, believe
me, when you tire on the long thrash
to your island, lie up, and survive.
As you float now, where I held you
and let go, remember when fear
cramps your heart what I told you:
lie gently and wide to the light-year
stars, lie back, and the sea will hold you.

Philip Booth, "First Lesson"

Contents

Acknowledgments

The scholar needs time more than anything else. I therefore first acknowledge the two institutions that provided it. Fordham University awarded me two semestral sabbaticals, the first in the spring of 1990 and the second in the spring of 1996. In the spring semester and summer of 1993, my work was supported by a National Endowment for the Humanities Fellowship for University Teachers. I also received a research grant from Fordham University in 1997.

A number of individuals helped me with problems of detail. I acknowledge some of them in the text. Others I thank here: O. Ballériaux, Adam H. Becker, J. M. Dillon, David Konstan, Riccardo Maisano, C. E. V. Nixon, Patrick J. Ryan, S. J., John Scarborough, and Judith L. Sebesta. My Fordham colleagues Sarah Peirce and especially David Sider have unstintingly shared their knowledge of things Hellenic with me. I owe a special debt of gratitude to Thomas M. Banchich, Glen W. Bowersock, and Christopher P. Jones. They generously read the whole of my typescript and offered suggestions for its improvement.

Finally, I am grateful to Tomas Hägg and his colleagues for giving me an opportunity to air some of my observations on Themistius's private orations at a symposium on Greek biography and panegyrics in late antiquity that they organized at the University of Bergen in the summer of 1996.

Abbreviations

AC	*L'Antiquité classique*
AJA	*American Journal of Archaeology*
AJP	*American Journal of Philology*
CAH	*The Cambridge Ancient History* (edition indicated by superscript number)
CJ	*Classical Journal*
CP	*Classical Philology*
CPG	*Corpus paroemiographorum graecorum,* ed. E. L. von Leutsch and F. G. Schneidewin (2 vols., Göttingen, 1839–51)
CQ	*Classical Quarterly*
CR	*Classical Review*
FGrH	*Die Fragmente der griechischen Historiker,* ed. F. Jacoby et al. (Berlin and Leiden, 1923–)
HSCP	*Harvard Studies in Classical Philology*
HTR	*Harvard Theological Review*
JHS	*Journal of Hellenic Studies*
JRS	*Journal of Roman Studies*
LIMC	*Lexicon iconographicum mythologiae classicae* (Zurich and Munich, 1981–)

LSJ	*A Greek-English Lexicon,* comp. H. G. Liddell, R. Scott, and H. S. Jones, 9th ed. with revised supplement (Oxford, 1996)
MRR	T. R. S. Broughton, with the collaboration of Marcia L. Patterson, *The Magistrates of the Roman Republic* (3 vols.; New York: American Philological Association, 1951–52, and Atlanta: Scholars Press, 1986), American Philological Association Monograph 15 (1951–52 [vols. 1–2], 1986 [vol. 3])
PG	*Patrologia graeca,* ed. J. P. Migne (Paris, 1857–66)
PIR[2]	*Prosopographia Imperii Romani,* ed. E. Groag, A. Stein et al. (2d ed., Berlin and Leipzig, 1933–)
PLRE	*The Prosopography of the Later Roman Empire,* ed. A. H. M. Jones, J. R. Martindale, and J. Morris (3 vols. in 4; Cambridge, 1971–92)
RE	*Paulys Realencyclopädie der classischen Altertumswissenschaft*
REG	*Revue des études grecques*
RhM	*Rheinisches Museum für Philologie*
SAWW	*Sitzungsberichte der Akademie der Wissenschaften in Wien, Philosophisch-historische Kl.*
SHA	*Scriptores Historiae Augustae*
SIFC	*Studi italiani di filologia classica*
SVF	*Stoicorum veterum fragmenta,* ed. J. von Arnim and M. Adler (4 vols.; Leipzig, 1903–24)
TAPA	*Transactions of the American Philological Association*
T&MByz	*Travaux et mémoires* (Centre de recherche d'histoire et civilisation byzantines, Paris)
VChr	*Vigiliae Christianae*

Chronology of the Translated Orations

I present here an overview of the dates I have adopted for the translated orations. Arguments may be found in the Introduction.

early 340s	Oration 24
no later than early 350s?	Oration 30 (but see below)
fall 355	Oration 20
355–56?	Oration 21
late 350s?	Oration 26
ca. 360	Oration 23
ca. 360	Oration 29
360?	Oration 33
early 380s?	Oration 30 (but see above)
383–384	Oration 17
383–385	Oration 31
ca. 385	Oration 34
Undatable	Oration 22
Undatable	Oration 25
Undatable	Oration 27
Undatable	Oration 28
Undatable	Oration 32

Introduction

Themistius and His Orations

For over thirty years, from the mid 350s on, Themistius was an important figure in Constantinople.[1] He was not a native of the city and may, like his father, have been born in Paphlagonia—in Themistius's case, around 317.[2] By about 360, the date of *Oration* 23, however, Themistius asserts that he has spent "a full twenty years" of his life in Constantinople (*Orat.* 23.298b). The emperor Constantius had adlected him to the Constantinopolitan senate in 355,[3] and citizenship may have come simultaneously with adlection.[4] In the late 350s, Themistius played an important part in recruiting new senators for Constantinople. He was selected in 357 to represent the eastern city in Rome during Constantius's visit there. And it may have been during

1. On Themistius's life, see now Vanderspoel, *Themistius.* Stegemann, *RE,* 5A, 2 (1934): 1642–80, and Seeck, *Die Briefe* (1906), 291–307, were earlier treatments of importance. Themistius was amply treated in Schmid-Stählin, *Christs Geschichte,* 2.2 (1924), 1004–14. Dagron, *T&MByz* 3 (1968): 1–242, has much biographical information in it, although, as Vanderspoel points out (p. vii), he "focuses primarily on one aspect of Themistius's thought, his concept of Hellenism and its relation to the views of his contemporaries."

2. "not a native": see n. 3 to my translation of Them., *Orat.* 17. For Themistius's father's (and Themistius's own?) Paphlagonian birth, see Them., *Orat.* 2.28d. Date of birth: in *Orat.* 2.18a Themistius describes himself as a coeval (παρὰ φιλοσοφίας ἡλικιώτιδος) of Constantius II, who was born in 317 (*PLRE,* vol. 1 under "Constantius 8").

3. The dated adlecting document, the *Demegoria Constantii* (see Appendix 3), was read to the Constantinopolitan senate on September 1.

4. See Petit, *AC* 26 (1957): 355–58; Chastagnol, *Acta Antiqua Acad. Scient. Hungar.* 24 (1976): 352.

that very same year that he assumed the proconsulship of Constantinople. He retired from that office in 359, perhaps by early September.[5] Office would not come to him again (so it seems) until the reign of Theodosius,[6] when, in 383 or 384, he assumed the urban prefecture of Constantinople,[7] an office that superseded the urban proconsulship when Themistius retired from it.

Themistius's rapid rise to prominence in the late 350s brought with it a προστασία, or "position of leadership" (Them., *Orat.* 34 [XIII]), and he became a spokesman and advocate for Constantinople and its senatorial class. He apparently persuaded Constantius, when the two men were in Rome in 357, to augment Constantinople's grain dole.[8] He celebrated imperial benefactions to and love of the city, asked emperors to confirm its benefits and privileges, argued that the city enjoyed a special relationship with the emperor, and asked emperors to come to Constantinople. Constantius, Themistius noted, honored Constantinople's senate; Theodosius should do the same by granting senators public office.[9] Themistius was proud of the ten embassies he undertook on behalf of Constantinople's senate (*Orat.* 17.214b; cf. 31.352d). "My voice," he said in 383, "should be considered the senate's voice" (*Orat.* 16.200c); he could have credibly said that considerably earlier.

In addition to being a senator and officeholder, Themistius was a panegyrist and adviser of emperors. His praise and advice—and the latter could sometimes be disguised as the former—were elicited by

5. For Themistius's activities in the late 350s, see Them., *Orat.* 34 [XIII], with n. 19 to my translation. I do not accept Dagron's argument that Themistius never held the proconsulship (*T&MByz* 3 [1968]: 213–17). Vanderspoel, *Themistius,* 106–8, follows Dagron. Daly, *Byzantion* 53 (1983): 164–212, replies to Dagron, arguing that Themistius did hold the proconsulship. For the length of Themistius's term, see Daly, ibid., 187–89. For the month of his retirement—he was the last Constantinopolitan proconsul, replaced by the first urban prefect, Honoratus—see Dagron, *Naissance,* 215–17.

6. The positing of this hiatus is based on the assumptions that lemmata to *Anth. Pal.* 11.292 that claim that Julian or Valens made Themistius [urban] prefect [of Constantinople] are erroneous (see Cameron, *CQ* 15 [1965]: 221), and that the "power" (τὸ δύνασθαι) of Themistius referred to in Gregory of Nazianzus, *Epp.* 24 Gallay, written between 365 and 369, is not the power of an office then being held, but the power of influence enjoyed by a senator and ex-proconsul of Constantinople. In saying that Themistius was "nominated" (προεβλήθη) urban prefect of Constantinople by Julian, the *Suda* (Θ 122 Adler) seems to be implying that he was *only* nominated and did not actually serve (cf. Daly, *Byzantion* 53 [1983]: 204).

7. See below, p. 35.

8. See Them., *Orat.* 34 [XIII], with n. 19 to my translation.

9. Constantius: *Orat.* 3.46d–48c; 4.53a–d, 56c–d, 57d–61b. Jovian: 5.70c–71b. Valens: 6.82b–84a, 11.150d–52b, 13.167c–68c. Theodosius: 14.182a–b, 183b–84a, 18.222b–23b.

specific issues as well as by the general question of how to govern well. I have already mentioned that he acknowledged and encouraged imperial attention to Constantinople. A flexible pagan who apparently worked well with Christian emperors, he was an advocate of religious toleration. If we can believe a medieval Arabic source,[10] he urged the emperor Julian not to persecute Christians. He championed religious tolerance before Jovian (*Orat.* 5) and attempted to moderate the Arian Valens's persecution of Nicene Christians (Socr. 4.32, Sozom. 6.36.6–37.1).[11] He encouraged Valens to show clemency after the suppression of Procopius's revolt (*Orat.* 7). On the Gothic question, he supported peace, clemency, and accommodation before both Valens and Theodosius.[12] The panegyrist and adviser of emperors was also willing to educate their children, and Theodosius's son Arcadius was once briefly entrusted to Themistius's care during his father's absence from Constantinople (*Orat.* 9.123c–24b, 16.213a–b, 18.224b–25b).

In the mid 380s, Themistius says of an emperor, who might be Constantius, that "he often took advice from me in council while I was wearing my philosopher's cloak, and he also often made me his dinner guest and his traveling companion. He gently endured it when I admonished him and did not take it badly when I rebuked him" (*Orat.* 34 [XIV]; cf. Liban., *Epp.* 66.2 Foerster). Themistius here represents himself as exercising the philosopher's traditional *parrhesia,* or freedom of speech, before the man of power.[13] He suggests that he had a fairly close relationship with the emperor in question. Unfortunately, we are not in a position to write a detailed or nuanced account of his relationship with Constantius or with any other emperor in the East. The view of Themistius's most recent biographer, assessing what evidence we have, is that the "two peaks" of his political career came in the late 350s under Constantius and in the 380s under Theodosius, during both of whose reigns (in my view) he held office; that, although Themistius "did not lose official status while Julian was on the throne" (361–63), a "rift" developed between them, and Themistius's "career did not advance"; that, although under Jovian (363–64) Themistius "emerged from . . . relative seclusion," the former's reign was too short to allow the latter's career to advance; and that, although under Valens (364–78) Themistius enjoyed "continued and possibly greater political

10. Bouyges, *Archives de philosophie* 2, 3 (1924): 16–17.
11. See Daly, *GRBS* 12 (1971): 65–79.
12. See Daly, *Historia* 21 (1972): 351–79.
13. Brown, *Power and Persuasion,* 61–70.

importance," "disapproval of the emperor's approach to some issues" led to "greater distance from the court," and he did not hold office.[14] The "scholarly consensus" that there was a rift between Themistius and Julian that kept Themistius from holding office under or having a close working relationship with the Apostate has recently been challenged by Thomas Brauch, who argues that Themistius in fact was Julian's prefect of Constantinople in 362.[15]

Themistius was more than a senator, officeholder, and man about court: he began as a philosopher and teacher of philosophy. Most, if not all, of his *Paraphrases* of Aristotle's works were probably written before his adlection to the senate in 355, after which public affairs as well as philosophy would have a claim on his time; he calls the *Paraphrases* works of his youth, ἐμοὶ νέῳ.[16] In pursuing philosophy, Themistius followed in the footsteps of his father, whom he eulogizes in *Oration* 20. A grandfather and a father-in-law (presumably his first) were also philosophers (Them., *Orat.* 5.63d, 11.145b, 21.244b–c). It was as a philosopher that Themistius was adlected to the Constantinopolitan senate by Constantius (see *Demeg. Const.*). The *Codex Theodosianus* 6.4.12 from the year 361 calls him a philosopher; he is "the best of philosophers," according to Libanius in 364 (*Epp.* 1186.2 Foerster); and some time between 365 and 369, Gregory of Nazianzus refers to him as a philosopher (*Epp.* 24 Gallay). Themistius continued to the end to see himself first and foremost as a philosopher.[17] While urban prefect of Constantinople in the mid 380s, he writes that "[t]o me, the office I hold as a result of my learning [i.e., the 'office' of philosopher] is loftier than any carriages . . . or . . . loud-voiced heralds [associated with political office]. . . . It is a lofty and magnificent thing to be empowered as . . . [a] successor [to Plato and Aristotle] by tablets of office given by them" (*Orat.* 31.353c–d, 354b). But as lofty as philosophy was, it did not have to turn its back on public affairs.[18] "I

14. Vanderspoel, *Themistius,* 71–216, with quotations from pp. 113, 123–24, 154–55. Vanderspoel does not believe that Themistius held office under Constantius.

15. *Byzantion* 63 (1993): 37–78, ibid. 79–115. For the "consensus" Brauch cites, in his second article, Bouchery, *Themistius,* 204–20; Dagron, *T&MByz* 3 (1968): 230–35; Daly, *Byzantinische Zeitschrift* 73 (1980): 1–11; id., *Byzantion* 53 (1983): 164–214. Note also Maisano, *Discorsi,* 22, who writes of Themistius's "marginalization" under Julian (cf. ibid., p. 46).

16. Stegemann, *RE,* 5A, 2 (1934): 1652; Vanderspoel, *Themistius,* 37; Them., *Orat.* 23.294d.

17. His rejection of the title "philosopher" in *Oration* 21 is ironic.

18. For the two visions of philosophy at war here, see Cracco Ruggini, *Athenaeum* 49 (1971): 405–7, 410–13.

elected the kind of philosophy that operates in the public arena," Themistius asserts (*Orat.* 31.352c). This is precisely what attracted the emperor Constantius to him: "[Themistius] does not pursue a philosophy that refuses to be shared with others" (*Demeg. Constant.* 20a). There was a sharing more fundamental than the willingness to become involved in public affairs, to which Themistius was also committed: he believed that the lessons of philosophy should be broadcast, in an appropriate form, to the masses, not reserved for a few select pupils. This was why the philosopher should strive to become what Gregory of Nazianzus called Themistius: a "king of eloquence" (*Epp.* 24).[19] Rhetoric allowed the philosopher to present his teachings to the public in an attractive and persuasive manner. These three contentions—the philosopher's obligation to broadcast the teachings of philosophy to the whole of society, his need of rhetorical skill to accomplish this end, and the appropriateness of his involvement in public life—are major themes in Themistius's private orations.

Let us turn now to the orations, public and private. We have thirty-three orations in Greek by Themistius. (Two of them, however, *Orations* 23 and 33, and perhaps *Oration* 28 as well are not fully preserved, and *Oration* 25 is a brief statement, not a full oration.) Modern editions of the *Orations* have thirty-four pieces because a Latin address to Valens has been included in the collection as *Oration* 12 since the Petavius-Harduinus edition. It has been agreed now for quite some time, however, that this Latin address is a pseudo-Themistian product of the sixteenth century.[20] A Themistian work "On Virtue" that is called an "oration" by its translators survives only in Syriac; and a Themistian work "On Governing the State," addressed to Julian and preserved only in Arabic, might be an oration rather than a letter or treatise. A fragment on "The Knowledge of Knowledges" (see my Appendix 2) may be part of the lost portion of *Oration* 23 or may derive from another otherwise unknown oration. The few fragments from a Themistian work "On the Soul" that are preserved in Stobaeus may come from an oration.[21] Finally, we have some information about several of Themistius's completely lost orations.

19. For this title, see Robert, *Hellenica* 4 (1948): 95–96.

20. See Foerster, *Neue Jahrbücher für Pädagogik* 3 (1900): 74–93.

21. The pseudo-Themistian Latin address, the Syriac and Arabic works, both equipped with a Latin translation, and the fragments "On the Knowledge of Knowledges" and from "On the Soul" may all be found in the third volume of the Teubner edition of Themistius's *Orations.* There is a German translation of the Syriac oration in Gildemeister and Bücheler, *RhM* 27 (1872): 438–62. The Teubner translator of the Syriac text (R. Mach) renders its title "Oratio de virtute," and Bücheler refers to it as a

He addressed the Constantinopolitan senate concerning his embassy to Rome of the year 357 (Liban., *Epp.* 368.3, 376.4–5 Foerster). He wrote an oration in praise of Julian late in that emperor's reign (Liban., *Epp.* 1430; cf. 818).[22] In the thirteenth century, Abu 'l-Farag (Bar Hebraeus) mentions a Themistian work addressed to Julian that attempted to dissuade the emperor from persecuting Christians.[23] In 369, Themistius delivered what was probably a formal oration (or more than one?) before Valens along the Danube as head of a senatorial delegation arguing for a peace treaty with the Goths (Them., *Orat.* 10.133a–b, 11.144a [cf. 10.129a]). And he addressed the Arian Valens probably in the winter of 375/376, asking for toleration of non-Arian Christians (Socr. 4.32, Sozom. 6.36).[24]

The modern ordering of Themistius's orations has no manuscript authority.[25] It was introduced, for *Orations* 1–33, in the Petavius-

"Rede." It survives in juxtaposition to a Syriac translation of Themistius, *Orat.* 22. As for the Arabic text, its heading calls it a *risâlat,* which the Teubner translator (I. Shahid) renders "epistula"; but in the body of the text (p. 105) Themistius refers to the work as a *qaul,* which the translator renders "oratio." See the Teubner edition of Themistius's *Orations,* 3: 75–76, 83n; Vanderspoel, *Themistius,* 243. Doubts that the Arabic work is fundamentally genuine and that, as one of the two extant manuscripts maintains, it was addressed to Julian (Theodosius I being argued for instead) were probably hypercritical: see Croissant, *Serta Leodiensia,* 7–30; Dagron, *T&MByz* 3 (1968): 222–24; Teubner edition of Themistius's *Orations,* 3: 75–80; Vanderspoel, *Themistius,* 244–49.

22. Vanderspoel, *Themistius,* 127–30, has argued that this panegyric is the work "On Governing the State" extant in Arabic.

23. See Bouyges, *Archives de philosophie* 2, 3 (1924): 16–17; Dagron, *T&MByz* 3 (1968): 221–22; Brauch, *Byzantion* 63 (1993): 105. Dagron and Brauch misdate Abu 'l-Farag to the tenth century; see *The Encyclopaedia of Islam,* vol. 3 (1971), under "Ibn al-'Ibrî." Were the panegyric mentioned by Libanius in *Epp.* 1430 and the work mentioned by Abu 'l-Farag one and the same? If so, it will have combined praise with advice on religious toleration, as does Themistius's *Orat.* 5.

24. For the dates of the orations to Valens, see Vanderspoel, *Themistius,* 173, 178–79. For Themistius's lost Greek orations in general, see esp. Schenkl, *SAWW* 192, 1 (1919): 78–79; Stegemann, *RE,* 5A, 2 (1934): 1666–69; Dagron, *T&MByz* 3 (1968): 17–18, 221–29; Vanderspoel, *Themistius,* passim. Schenkl, op. cit. 79, prudently refrains from postulating on the basis of Liban., *Epp.* 1430 Foerster, a Themistian oration congratulating the newly elevated Jovian. Nor is Them., *Orat.* 9.128b, with Liban., *Epp.* 1495, explicit enough to allow us to postulate an oration in honor of Valens's (and Valentinian's) consulship of 365; note Bouchery, *Themistius,* 270, n. 12. Schenkl, op. cit., 51–52 (cf. 79), transcribes from Cod. Meteora 151 what might be a small fragment of a lost Themistian oration; and Maisano, *Discorsi,* 48, notes the existence of a fragment *Πρὸς βασιλέα* ascribed to Themistius in Cod. Venetus Marcianus 412, fols. 80v–81. It may be oratorical (*pace* Maisano), but its authenticity was questioned by E. Mioni, *Bibliothecae Divi Marci Venetiarum codd. gr. mss.,* vol. 2: *Thesaurus antiquus, Codd. 300–625* (Rome, 1985), 168–69.

25. For descriptions of the manuscripts, see Schenkl, *Wiener Studien* 20 (1898): 206–11; id., *SAWW* 192, 1 (1919): 46–68; Teubner edition of the *Orations,* 1: viii–xiii; Maisano, *Κοινωνία* 2 (1978): 100–116; id., *Κοινωνία* 5 (1981): 97–98; Bevegni, *SIFC* 80 (1987): 62–63.

Harduinus edition of 1684. When the oration "In Reply to Those Who Found Fault with Him [i.e., Themistius] for Accepting Public Office" was discovered in the early nineteenth century, it was added to the collection, in Wilhelm Dindorf's edition (1832), as item 34. Harduinus had divided the collection into two parts. The first part consisted of *Orations* 1–20, which he called *πανηγυρικοὶ λόγοι*. *Orations* 21–33 he referred to as *διάφοροι λόγοι* ("orationes variae") or, in the reader's preface and index of orations, as "declamatoriae" or "sophisticae orationes." Although Dindorf retained the Petavius-Harduinus ordering of the orations, he used no headings to mark a division of the collection into two parts. The explicitly indicated division reappeared in the Teubner edition (vols. 1–2 [1965–71]) and in Riccardo Maisano's edition (1995) but with two alterations: *Oration* 20, the only oration of Harduinus's part 1 of the collection that was not in praise of an emperor (or two) or a member of the imperial family,[26] was detached from *Orations* 1–19 and became the first oration of part 2, and the headings of the two parts of the collection became *λόγοι πολιτικοί* and *λόγοι ἰδιωτικοί*. Both of these alterations were adopted from Heinrich Schenkl.[27] The detachment of *Oration* 20 from 1–19 made the *λόγοι πολιτικοί* exclusively *imperial* panegyrics.

Although the terms *λόγοι πολιτικοί* and *λόγοι ἰδιωτικοί* have no manuscript authority as headings for Themistius's orations, the term *λόγοι πολιτικοί* does occur in Photius's remarks on Themistius (*Bibl.* 74): "Thirty-six *λόγοι πολιτικοί* were read, which include (*ὧν εἰσι*) those addressed to the emperor Constantius and to the emperors Valens and the young Valentinian [Galates][28] and also to Theodosius and contain praises and laudations of them." Photius refers to all thirty-six orations available to him as *λόγοι πολιτικοί*. It is not clear, though, whether all those orations were imperial panegyrics; if so, he had considerably more than we do. They presumably included addresses to Jovian (*Oration* 5), to Gratian (*Oration* 13) and perhaps to Julian. On the other hand, Photius's collection, like ours, may have

26. To be precise, *Orat.* 16 praises the emperor Theodosius's general and consul Fl. Saturninus as well as Theodosius himself, but it has much more praise of the emperor than of Saturninus.

27. *SAWW* 192, 1 (1919): 75–80. Although the standard arrangement and division of the *Orations* are the work of modern editors, Schenkl hypothesized that, at a stage of transmission that predates our manuscripts, Themistius's orations were in fact organized into clusters (*τόμοι*) that were almost all entirely *πολιτικοί* or entirely *ἰδιωτικοί* (*SAWW* 192, 1 [1919]: 80–89).

28. Galates, to whom Themistius addressed *Oration* 9, was never elevated to the throne.

been a mix of what we call "public" (πολιτικοί) and private orations, all of which were referred to as λόγοι πολιτικοί because Themistius was, in the words of the θεωρία to his *Oration* 4, a "πολιτικὸς φιλόσοφος, whose only goal was to procure for the city [of Constantinople] what was beneficial and, at the same time, good for it."[29] Themistius respected the early Greek philosophers' insistence that a human being is "a social and political creature," κοινωνικὸν καὶ πολιτικόν (*Orat.* 34 [III]). He hoped that he would be regarded as πολιτικός in a Platonic sense of that word (*Orat.* 26.314d–15b). He admired Aristotle's "practical and political (πολιτικήν) philosophy" (*Orat.* 34 [VI]). And he felt (*Orat.* 17.214c) that a philosopher must not resist when a philosophical emperor "selects him to serve the state" (πολιτικὴν χειροτονίαν). A *politikos* will not put self-interest above the interest of the community, and a *politikos philosophos* will not retreat from society into mere logical puzzle-solving or specialized and esoteric metaphysics.[30] Perhaps Photius and others in Byzantium or already in late antiquity were willing to regard any oration of a *politikos philosophos* as itself *politikos*.

However Photius employed the term πολιτικοί, Schenkl used it as the heading for *Orations* 1–19. By it he means orations delivered before the emperor or before official state bodies.[31] On pages 82–83 of his 1919 article in the *Sitzungsberichte* of the Viennese Academy of Sciences (*SAWW*), he reclassified *Oration* 31 and (with less certainty) *Oration* 33 as λόγοι πολιτικοί.[32] He did this apparently because *Oration* 31 was delivered before the Constantinopolitan senate and because he believed, as I do, that *Oration* 33 was delivered in the presence of an emperor. On page 80 of the same article (and inconsistently with his position on pages 82–83), Schenkl also reclassified *Orations* 25, 28, and 34 as λόγοι πολιτικοί—again, apparently because *Oration* 34 was delivered before an emperor and, in Schenkl's opinion, so were *Orations* 25 and 28. If, however, we understand λόγοι πολιτικοί not as "orations delivered before the emperor or before official state bodies,"

29. For text and discussion of the θεωρία, the so-called Φιλόπολις, see Dagron, *T&MByz* 3 (1968): 225–29.

30. When Themistius uses the term λόγοι πολιτικοί in *Orat.* 26.325c, he is clearly thinking of philosophical orations delivered to the public at large.

31. *SAWW* 192, 1 (1919): 78: "Reden . . . die vor den Herrschern oder vor staatlich eingesetzten Körperschaften bei Anlässen, die sich aus dem öffentlichen Leben ergaben, gehalten wurden."

32. Regarding *Orat.* 33, note his remark in *SAWW* 192, 1 (1919): 85, "[*Orat.* 33], der weder auf das γένος [i.e., πολιτικόν or ἰδιωτικόν] noch auf den Umfang und die Abfassungszeit sichere Schlüsse gestattet."

but more narrowly as "imperial panegyrics," no reclassifications are necessary. *Orations* 17 and 31 were both delivered before the Constantinopolitan senate. We may think of the former as *πολιτικός* because its main purpose, as a *gratiarum actio*, is to thank and laud the emperor; the latter oration is *ἰδιωτικός* because it does not laud the emperor, except in the most passing way, or even have him as its theme. While the only partially preserved *Oration* 33 did apparently praise an emperor who was present, imperial panegyric was not Themistius's principal purpose there, as it was in *Orations* 1–19. The same, it appears, can be said for *Oration* 28—if, in fact, it was an emperor whom Themistius lauded in that speech. *Oration* 34 does contain much praise of the emperor Theodosius, but its main goal is self-defense, not panegyrics, and the panegyric is part of Themistius's apologetical tactics. As for *Oration* 25, it is not an oration proper at all, but only a short statement. It has some laudatory remarks about the emperor—if, in fact, Themistius is addressing an emperor here—but only to show what a future panegyric will sound like; Themistius's main purpose here is to make a point about rhetorical practice. The vulgate arrangement of Themistius's orations, then, which persists in the Teubner and in Maisano's editions, may stand, although the term "imperial panegyrics" describes *Orations* 1–19 more precisely than *λόγοι πολιτικοί*. Not only is *πολιτικοί* vague and unsatisfying; so are its English equivalents "public" and "official."[33]

To the second part of the collection of Themistius's orations Schenkl gave the name *λόγοι ἰδιωτικοί*. This part of the collection is a miscellany; Harduinus's heading *διάφοροι λόγοι* ("orationes variae") is not a bad one. What the orations of part 2 have in common is that they are not *πολιτικοί*. But one wants something positively descriptive. Maisano's edition retains *λόγοι ἰδιωτικοί*, but adds a subheading to it: "Discorsi polemici, di scuola e d'occasione." I would suggest a description along the following lines: The private orations of Themistius are a dossier, compiled by modern editors, that consists of (1) apologetics and polemics, (2) cultural (i.e., rhetorical and philosophical) programmatics, (3) material of autobiographical interest, and (4) philosophical discourses. Only *Oration* 30, on the face of it a routine school piece, would seem to fall outside of these categories; but, as suggested below, this piece may have an autobiographical or sociopolitical significance that is no longer immediately apparent.

33. Maisano, *Discorsi,* 111, translates *πολιτικοί* as *ufficiali.*

THE PRIVATE ORATIONS

I offer in this volume annotated translations of Themistius's private orations 20–34. In the appendixes I also provide a translation of *Oration* 17, which is closely related in theme to *Orations* 31 and 34; of the fragment on "The Knowledge of Knowledges," which is either part of the lost portion of *Oration* 23 or all that remains of some otherwise fully lost oration; and of the *Demegoria Constantii,* which announces and justifies Themistius's adlection to the senate of Constantinople. The *Demegoria,* like the fragment on "The Knowledge of Knowledges," is transmitted with the thirty-three Themistian orations in Greek. There follow some comments on the Themistian orations that I have translated.

ORATION 20

This is a funeral oration (*epitaphios*) in honor of Themistius's recently deceased father, Eugenius, a philosopher like his son.[34] The *Demegoria Constantii* in praise of the newly adlected Themistius, which was read to the Constantinopolitan senate on September 1, 355, implies that Eugenius was still alive (22d–23b). He would be dead before the onset of winter.[35] He spent his last days working his land, an activity Themistius regarded as befitting a philosopher (20.236d–37b). Commentators have confidently asserted that *Oration* 20 was delivered in Eugenius's native Paphlagonia.[36] The notion is plausible, but there is no actual evidence for it.[37] Whoever the auditors were, in the θεωρία or preliminary comment to *Oration* 20 Themistius winningly calls them "the only audience . . . worthy of the dead man's virtue."

At the beginning (234a–35a) and the end (240b–d) of this funeral oration, Themistius addresses his father as a pagan "saint," whose pure soul has promptly returned to the realm of the gods, where it can

34. Recently deceased: see *Orat.* 20.234b. The name Eugenius is not given in *Orat.* 20. We know it from *Demeg. Const.* 23a and Phot., *Bibl.* 74.

35. See Vanderspoel, *Themistius,* 89–90.

36. Scholze, *De temporibus,* 71; Stegemann, *RE,* 5A, 2 (1934): 1662; Dagron, *T&MByz* 3 (1968): 24; Vanderspoel, *Themistius,* 89. Eugenius's Paphlagonian origins: Them., *Orat.* 2.28d.

37. It has also been asserted that the journey of Themistius and his children from Nicaea to his "fatherland" that is mentioned in Them., *In Arist. Phys.* 6.2 (p. 185 Schenkl), was undertaken on the occasion of his father's funeral (Scholze, *De temporibus,* 71; Stegemann, *RE,* 5A, 2 [1934]: 1662; Vanderspoel, *Themistius,* 91). But there can be no certainty about this.

consort with the souls of Socrates, Plato, and Aristotle. He prays to his father for help in his own continuing "struggle" on earth. In the rest of the oration, Themistius speaks about his father, not to him. He notes Eugenius's special devotion to Aristotle. Themistius calls Aristotle Eugenius's "favorite." Eugenius "used to strive greatly to associate with Aristotle" on earth. He was Aristotle's interpreter, and for that the Stagirite in heaven was very grateful. "The visage and shape impressed upon . . . [the] sacred mysteries" of philosophical initiation conducted by Eugenius "were almost entirely those of Aristotle" (234d–35c). But despite his special devotion to Aristotle, Eugenius was also a philosophical syncretist. If Aristotle was in first place for him, Plato came a close second. Eugenius was convinced of their essential compatibility, noting that Aristotle could serve as an excellent propaedeutic and logical support for Plato.[38] He knew Pythagoras and the Stoic Zeno and could even see some small good in Epicureanism.[39] In his view, "all [schools of philosophy] reach the same point in the end, however much they wind about" (236b). The emperor Julian would agree, affirming that "philosophy is one, and [that] virtually all philosophers have sought a single goal, though reaching it by diverse roads" (*Orat.* 9.186a Rochefort, and also see 184c–86a passim).[40]

Eugenius, Themistius tells us, had a literary as well as a philosophical breadth: Themistius notes his command of Homer, Menander, Euripides, Sophocles, Sappho, and Pindar. But the philosophical and the literary should not be seen as two disconnected spheres in Eugenius. In

38. I am not convinced by Ballériaux's attempt (*AC* 65 [1996]: 135–60) to make Eugenius a Neoplatonist. He sets the stage for his argument with the conjecture—and it is only that—that "Eugenius the philosopher," the addressee of ps.-Julian, *Epp.* 193 Bidez-Cumont, is to be identified with Themistius's father and, like his ἑταῖρος ps.-Julian, had been a pupil of Iamblichus. Even if Eugenius was somewhat influenced by Neoplatonism, Themistius makes clear that his father's primary devotion was to Aristotle. Ballériaux believes that he has already established that Themistius himself, in the noetic of his paraphrase of Aristotle's *De anima,* "n'était pas 'an Aristotelian' . . . , mais un néoplatonicien" (*AC* 61 [1992]: 466; and see *Revue de philosophie ancienne* 7 [1989]: 199–233). Yet Themistius asserts in *Orat.* 2.26d that Aristotle was his philosophical model (ὃν προὐταξάμην τοῦ βίου τε καὶ τῆς σοφίας). Schroeder and Todd judge that Ballériaux has overestimated the significance of Neoplatonic, specifically Plotinian, parallels in Themistius's paraphrase of the *De anima* (*Two Greek Aristotelian Commentators,* 34–35 and 91, n. 71; cf. Todd, *Themistius on Aristotle's "On the Soul,"* 2, 10; Blumenthal, *Aristotle and Neoplatonism,* 22–23, 144, 155). Perhaps we should think of Themistius the paraphrast as an Aristotelian who was open to some limited Neoplatonic influence.

39. See *Orat.* 20.236a with n. 10 to my translation.

40. For Julian's philosophical syncretism, see Athanassiadi, *Julian,* 138–40. In qualification of Julian, *Orat.* 9.186a, note that, in *Epp.* 89b.301c–d Bidez, Julian sees no good in Epicurus or in the Skeptic Pyrrho.

referring to his father's knowledge of Homer, Themistius calls the poet "the origin and source of Aristotle's and Plato's teachings" (236b).[41] Philosophical wisdom could be had from Homer through either a literal or an allegorical understanding of the poet's text; or Homer's narrative could provide *exempla* of the moral and the immoral.[42] And, as Themistius's own orations illustrate, Homer was not the only classical author not properly a philosopher who could nonetheless be mined for philosophical insights. Respecting literature as something not "alien to philosophy" (236c), Eugenius was broadened by it: Themistius contends that his father's wide reading made it easier for him to share his philosophical wisdom with the whole of humanity; he was not merely a narrow technical expert.[43]

After describing Eugenius's *paideia,* Themistius next points out that he was a genuine philosopher (237b ff.). Eugenius consequently insisted that discourse should aim to better the soul, not to provide pleasure and be charming. He also insisted that engaging in philosophical discourse does not in itself make a true philosopher. What is essential is commitment to philosophy's principles and acting in accordance with them, as Socrates did. Themistius not only reports Eugenius's admiration of Socrates but also goes on to compare him to the great philosopher. He then compares him, in his fight against moral evil, to Heracles—Heracles the "paradigm of virtue" (240a). Comparison of the lauded dead man to Heracles or Theseus, for example—that is, to a "man of distinction"—is recommended by Menander Rhetor in his directions on writing a funeral oration (2.421).[44] Comparison to Socrates would have been appropriate only for select subjects; Themistius awards it to himself as well as to his departed father.[45]

Menander Rhetor prescribes a range of encomiastic topics for the funeral oration (2.420): family, birth, nature (which means "physical beauty" as well as "mental endowment"), nurture, education, conduct, actions, and fortune (examples of which are "wealth, happiness of

41. Cf. the linking of Homer to Plato and Aristotle at Them., *Orat.* 33.366c.

42. See, e.g., Buffiere, *Les mythes d'Homère;* Kindstrand, *Homer in der Zweiten Sophistik,* 124–26, 168–71, for Homer as (*philo*)*sophos* in Dio Chrys. and Max. Tyr., and note also ps.-Plut., *De Homero* 2.144; Lamberton, *Homer the Theologian.*

43. On Eugenius's intellectual breadth, note the emperor Constantius's praise of him for not letting any of "the ancient teachings and subjects of study" (τῶν ἀρχαίων διδαγμάτων καὶ παιδευμάτων) escape him (*Demeg. Const.* 23a).

44. I am using the edition and translation of Menander by D. Russell and N. Wilson (Oxford, 1981).

45. See, e.g., Them., *Orat.* 23.296a, 24.300d–301a, 26.313d with n. 5 to my translation.

children, love of friends, honour from emperors, honour from cities").[46] But in *Oration* 20 Themistius restricts himself to mature *paideia,* accomplishments, character, and principles. The "missing" topics, from the viewpoint of Menander's model, are family, birth, early years and rearing, and physical and material glories. Themistius's assertion in the *θεωρία* that a brief oration was what the occasion demanded could be read as an apology for the omission of a number of expected encomiastic topics. The orator promises that he will give full details in a future biography of his father. (We have no evidence that he ever wrote this biography.) Of course, Themistius could have been brief and still touched upon the missing encomiastic topics in his funeral oration. One suspects, though, that the missing topics fell victim not so much to Themistius's desire for brevity as to his judgment that they were inappropriate or at least expendable in an encomium of a philosopher. Indeed, in his praise of non-philosophers, too, Themistius emphasizes themes of philosophical import.[47]

Several features of Eugenius's *paideia* that Themistius celebrates in *Oration* 20 are also features of Themistius's own intellectual culture: an Aristotelianism that does not close the door on other philosophical schools and is especially allied with Platonism, a literary breadth, a desire to broadcast philosophical wisdom to the whole of society, and the condemnation of a rhetoric that aims merely to please and charm (234d–36d, 237c–d). The marriage of Aristotelianism and Platonism in Eugenius and Themistius is a distinctive one, subordinating Plato to Aristotle, in contrast to Neoplatonism's subordination of Aristotle to Plato. By Themistius's literary breadth (which does not necessarily entail depth),[48] I mean his drawing on the whole of the Hellenic heritage in his orations rather than presenting himself as a narrow philosophi-

46. "conduct": Ἐπιτηδεύματα here is better translated "(habitual) conduct" or "characteristic behavior" rather than "accomplishments" (*pace* Russell and Wilson). Menander explains that the orator will laud the dead man's ἐπιτηδεύματα "by saying," for example, "that he showed himself just, humane, approachable, and gentle." Cf. the rubrics of the funeral oration given by ps.-Dionys. Hal., *On Epideictic Speeches* 6, translated in Russell's and Wilson's edition of Menander Rhetor (pp. 373–76), and the rubrics of encomium given in the *Progymnasmata* of Hermogenes, of Aphthonius and of Theon (L. Spengel, *Rhetores graeci,* vol. 2 [Leipzig, 1854], 11–14, 35–38, 109–12).

47. Cf. Vanderspoel's general comments in *Themistius,* 6–7. Note, e.g., *Orat.* 1.1a–3a in praise of Constantius (the panegyrist's business is to admire the things of the soul rather than those of the body) and *Orat.* 18.218d in praise of Theodosius (a philosophical encomium will praise what is truly worth admiring, not gifts of fortune such as power, skill or wealth.).

48. I.e., his knowledge of earlier writers is sometimes at second hand (cf. Colpi, *Die παιδεία,* 19–20, 193).

cal technician. The need for philosophy to address the whole of society rather than being an esoteric specialty is one of Themistius's central tenets. So is the rejection of a rhetoric that is not in the service of something higher than pleasure: in the *θεωρία* of *Oration* 20 itself Themistius had warned that "a philosopher should not be that concerned with beauty of language."[49] In *Oration* 20, then, Themistius can advertise his own intellectual culture while commemorating that of his deceased father.[50] The coincidence of their views points to the influence of Eugenius on his son.

ORATION 21

In this oration Themistius insists that the title "philosopher," by which people call him, does not belong to him. It is true that his father and his father-in-law were philosophers, but they "hated me," he says, and did not share their philosophical learning with him. He then quickly changes his mind: "No, they did not hate me." They did want to share their learning with him, but "by disposition I was slow to learn and hard to teach" (244c). To make clear what a true philosopher is (and, implicitly, that he himself is not one), Themistius devotes himself in the bulk of *Oration* 21 to defining a philosopher, using assertions of Plato to accomplish his task. The true philosopher (1) is of good ancestry (248a ff.), (2) genuinely possesses metaphysical knowledge and acts accordingly (250c ff.), (3) is social and free of envy in his dealings with other devotees of philosophy (254b ff.), (4) loves truth and hates falsehood and deception (257c ff.), (5) is not a lover of gain (259d ff.), and (6) is not a slanderer (262a ff.). Themistius regards each of these six features as a "touchstone" (*βασανιστήριον*)—hence the title *βασανιστής*—by which the true philosopher can be distinguished from the counterfeit.[51] *Oration* 21 ends quite abruptly after the sixth part of the definition of a philosopher; perhaps its conclusion has been lost.

49. For Plato and Aristotle in Themistius's thought, see Colpi, *Die παιδεία*, 97–98, and more generally 85–110; Vanderspoel, *Themistius*, 20–22. In *Orat.* 2, written close to the time of Eugenius's death, Themistius says that Aristotle is, in effect, his model and guide: *ὅν προὐταξάμην τοῦ βίου τε καὶ τῆς σοφίας* (26d). For Aristotle's place in Neoplatonism, see Wallis, *Neoplatonism*, 23–25. For Themistius's knowledge of Greek literature and of philosophers other than Plato and Aristotle, see Colpi, op. cit. Broadcasting wisdom to the whole of society: Them., *Orat.* 2.30b–c, 22.265b–d, 26, 28.341d–42b, 34 [XII]. Condemnation of merely pleasurable rhetoric: Them., *Orat.* 22.265b, 24.300d–301b, 26.329d–30b, 28.341b–d, 33.364b–d.

50. Vanderspoel already makes the point (*Themistius*, 91).

51. Cf. the touchstone metaphor in *Orat.* 22.266c.

Neither Themistius's refusal to accept the title "philosopher" nor his denigration of himself and, momentarily, of his father and his father-in-law should be taken at face value.[52] The tone here is ironic.[53] Although Themistius defines a philosopher seemingly in order to show that he himself is not one (246b), his real intent is to indict others, who have attacked him, and to show that it is they who lack the distinguishing features of a true philosopher. Referring to individuals who are unsocial and envious, Themistius remarks that they are "counterfeits who have wrongly been given the title 'philosopher.'" They harass the person who "is emulously engaged with Aristotle and Theophrastus"—clearly a reference to Themistius himself (255d). Themistius's philosophical opponents doubtless engaged in and encouraged criticism of him for speaking effectively to large crowds, branding this as sophistical (243a–b). Themistius objects, urging his audience to "consider *what* I say and *why* I say it. . . . When the wise Plato spoke in the Piraeus, people streamed into that place and congregated there. . . . Yet this did not prevent Plato from being wise" (245c). The vivid portraits of philosophers manqués in *Oration* 21 are surely of specific contemporaries of Themistius.[54]

Themistius refers in *Oration* 21.244b–c to his father-in-law without further specification and as someone who was in a position to have had a formative intellectual influence on him. He must be referring to his first father-in-law. His first marriage was entered into in the 340s, and his second marriage around 360.[55] *Oration* 21, then, was composed either during his first marriage or between the presumed death of his first wife and his second marriage.[56] Some have put *Oration* 21

52. Méridier, whose discussion of *Orat.* 21 is still worth reading, remarks that "[o]n ne peut l'expliquer [i.e., Themistius's refusal of the title "philosopher"] par un mouvement de modestie, puisque partout ailleurs il se fait gloire d'être philosophe . . ." (*Le philosophe Thémistios,* 1–8 at 2).

53. Reading *Orat.* 21 literally has led to chronological arguments that are invalidated by an ironic reading. Taking Themistius's reference to his father's hatred of him literally, Scholze reasons that the orator would not have spoken in this manner before his father died late in 355 (*De temporibus,* 74). Taking Themistius's rejection of the title "philosopher" literally, Seeck makes *Orat.* 21 the earliest of Themistius's extant speeches, putting it in 345 and explaining that the orator really did not yet think himself worthy of the title (*Die Briefe,* 292–93, and see the reply of Schmid-Stählin, *Christs Geschichte,* 2.2 [1924], 1005, n. 10).

54. Cf. Méridier, *Le philosophe Thémistios,* 8: "Successivement défilent devant l'auditoire toutes les contrefaçons du philosophe: le parvenu, le charlatan, l'envieux. Ce sont évidemment là des figures contemporaines, des portraits à clef sous lesquels il ne devait pas être très difficile de mettre des noms."

55. See below, p. 42.

56. Contrast Bouchery, *Themistius,* 48–49, n. 5, who associates *Orat.* 21 with *Orat.* 23 and puts them both in the 370s.

precisely in the winter of 355/56 by identifying the hostilities alluded to in Libanius, *Epp.* 402 and 407 Foerster, which are dated to 355, with the hostilities alluded to in Themistius's *Oration* 21.[57] But that identification cannot be certain. During his first marriage, Themistius was at work on his Aristotelian *Paraphrases,* to which he refers in *Oration* 21.256a.[58] It is most likely that *Oration* 21 was delivered in Constantinople.[59] Themistius was speaking in what he calls "the theater of the Muses" (243a).

ORATION 22

Oration 22 is a philosophical discourse on friendship, a subject on which Themistius's special mentor Aristotle (among others) had also written.[60] It begins by highlighting the importance of friendship and lamenting the fact that it is an undervalued and neglected topic. Both rhetors and philosophers are largely responsible for this: rhetors because they fail to speak on such serious topics, and philosophers because they fail to speak to the general public at all. Themistius, a "devotee" of "true and sincere friendship," seeks to rectify the situation. In a trifold scheme, he first provides a number of tests (*βασανιστήρια* [266c]) or criteria by which one can determine if a person has the moral makings for genuine friendship (267a–71b).[61] Next he explains how, after good candidates for friendship have been found, one chases down and captures them (271b–73c), and thirdly how, after capturing them, one safeguards and retains one's prey (273d ff.). He sustains the hunting metaphor throughout his discussion (cf. *Orat.* 23.288a). The importance of testing and forming a judgment on indi-

57. Scholze, *De temporibus,* 74–75; Stegemann, *RE,* 5A, 2 (1934): 1662–63; Vanderspoel, *Themistius,* 94–95.

58. For the time of composition of the *Paraphrases,* see Stegemann, *RE,* 5A, 2 (1934): 1652; Vanderspoel, *Themistius,* 27, 37.

59. But *καλλίπολις* at Them., *Orat.* 21.248a, refers to Plato's Utopia, not to Constantinople (*pace* Vanderspoel, *Themistius,* 94n).

60. Arist., *Eth. Nic.* 8–9, *Eth. Eudem.* 7; cf. *Rhet.* 2.4 [1380b35–81b37]. In *Orat.* 22 Themistius "si avvale d'un ampio patrimonio di luoghi comuni" (Pizzolato, *L'idea di amicizia,* 198). Bohnenblust, *Beiträge,* 26–44, ferrets out the *loci communes* in ancient discussions of friendship, including Themistius's oration among the ancient texts of which he takes account. For ancient thinking on friendship, see Fraisse, *Philia;* Pizzolato, op. cit. Note also Colpi, *Die παιδεία,* 102, 133.

61. Themistius also thinks in *Orat.* 22 in terms of the tracks (*ἴχνη*), marks (*σύμβολα*), signs (*σημεῖα*), and evidences (*γνωρίσματα*) of true friendship. Cf. Cic., *De amicit.* 17 [62], "signa quaedam et notas quibus eos qui ad amicitiam essent idonei iudicarent." For comparable use of the terms *βασανιστήρια, ἴχνη κτλ,* see Them., *Orat.* 21.248a, 250b, 254b; 23.287c–d, 288c, 292a.

viduals before entering fully into friendship with them is remarked in a number of other ancient discussions of friendship.[62] The motif of safeguarding one's friendships also occurs in Simplicius's trifold scheme: one chooses a friend (*ἐκλογή*), then forms a relationship with him (*χρῆσις*), then safeguards the friendship (*φυλακή*) through the quality of the relationship.[63]

At 276b–c, after having offered a number of suggestions on how friendship may be safeguarded, Themistius announces that he should "also say something about the mistakes that are made in the context of a friendship—both how to cut back on them and how to repair them <if> they should occur." One achieves these ends simply by frankly criticizing one's friends when they are in need of correction (276c–77c). Next comes a warning against believing slanderous statements about a friend; if one is seduced by such misrepresentations, the friendship will quickly and tragically fall apart (277c–79a). The warning against believing slander, like the remarks on the importance of frank criticism, seems to be intended as part of Themistius's discussion of how to safeguard friendship. Next and last comes a warning against villainous men who try to form friendships, for their own evil purposes, by pretending to be kind and benevolent; true friend and poseur are contrasted in the allegory with which the oration ends.

Themistius seems to be speaking to a mixed urban audience (265a–c). The city in which he is speaking is likely to be Constantinople, but another location is possible. At 266c he singles out someone, addressing him as "leader of this chorus" (*ὦ τοῦ χοροῦ τοῦδε κορυφαῖε*), and ascribes to him the same love of friendship that he himself has. Themistius's remarks at 266d suggest that the "leader of this chorus" was an official. He says there that "[a]nyone who has acquired friends has done well, even if he is merely a private citizen. But the man who oversees many cities and much territory has an even greater blessing in friendship than does a private citizen." Themistius goes on to explain precisely why it is that public officials are so blessed by friendship. Heinrich Scholze believed that at 266c Themistius was addressing the emperor Valens, who was known for his loyalty to friends (Them., *Orat.* 11.152d–53c; Amm. Marc. 31.14.2; *Epit. de*

62. Bohnenblust, *Beiträge*, 32–34. To the texts cited there add Arist., *Eth. Nic.* 8.3 [1156b25–32], and *Eth. Eudem.* 7.2 [1237b7–38a2]; Amm. Marc. 26.2.9. See also Theophrastus, frs. 538A–F, in *Theophrastus of Eresus: Sources for His Life, Writings, Thought, and Influence*, ed. W. W. Fortenbaugh et al., 2 vols. (Leiden, 1992).

63. Simplic., *In Epictet. Enchirid.* 37.155 ff., pp. 351 ff. Hadot.

Caes. 46.3).[64] But that belief was founded on the arbitrary assumption that Themistius would not have ascribed loyalty to friends to any emperor but Valens.[65] Themistius may have been addressing some other emperor here[66]—or an official below the emperor (a praetorian prefect, a vicar, or a provincial governor). Neither 266c nor any other passage in *Oration* 22 allows us to date it even roughly.[67]

ORATIONS 23 AND 29

In *Oration* 23, the philosopher Themistius is responding to opponents who have called him a "sophist" in the negative sense of that term. He is figuratively on trial. The audience are "jurors" (283b–c), Plato is the "lawgiver," and the "statute book" that defines the "crime" of sophistry is Plato's *Sophist* (286d–87d).[68] According to Plato, the sophist is (1) "a mercenary hunter of rich young men"; (2) "a merchant who sells items of knowledge for the soul"; (3) "a retailer" of such knowledge; (4) a man who is "self-employed and does the actual selling himself"; (5) "a verbal competitor, skilled in eristic"; and (6) a person who "forms opinions about the non-existent, uses appearances to imitate reality, fashions phantasms of the truth, and is a verbal wonder-worker" (288a–b). Themistius adopts the Platonic descriptions of a sophist and shows that none of them fits him.

Unfortunately, we do not have the whole of *Oration* 23. Themistius discusses Plato's first definition from 288c to 297b. From 297b to the end of what survives of *Oration* 23, he discusses Plato's second, third,

64. Scholze, *De temporibus,* 78–79. The assertion of the Teubner editors of Themistius that *Orat.* 22 is a "[d]issertatio tempore imp. Valentis" (2: 52) is based on Scholze (see Teubner edition, 1: xx).

65. Scholze's reason (*De temporibus,* 78–79) for believing that Themistius is not addressing Constantius here is no more convincing than his reason for believing that he is addressing Valens.

66. Petavius in Dindorf, *Themistii Orationes,* 665, believes that Themistius is addressing an emperor in *Orat.* 22 but does not attempt to identify him. Maisano thinks that Themistius is addressing Constantius (*Discorsi,* 735, 741n). He *may* be addressing Constantius, just as he *may* be addressing Valens. But I do not find the parallels Maisano sees between two passages in *Orat.* 22 and passages in other orations of certain Constantian date (Maisano, ibid., 740n, 764n) to be compelling evidence of a Constantian date for *Orat.* 22.

67. Dagron, *T&MByz* 3 (1968): 24, prudently regards *Orat.* 22 as undatable but puzzlingly thinks that "les différents thèmes [de ce discours entièrement rhétorique] évoquent plutôt le début de l'enseignement de Thémistios." Vanderspoel's half-hearted attempt to link *Orat.* 22 chronologically to *Orat.* 20 is not convincing (*Themistius,* 228n).

68. For the philosopher as "lawgiver," philosophy as "law," cf. Them., *Orat.* 2.31b, 32b, 35a; 21.250c; 26.314d–15a; 29.345a.

and fourth definitions. That discussion is not quite finished when the oration breaks off at 299c.[69]

At 292a–c, Themistius says that he was allowed to avail himself of 200 *medimnoi* of grain, 200 *keramia* of oil, and also a "long list [of items] of luxury and comfort that go hand in hand with the hammered tablets" (ταῖς δέλτοις ταῖς σφυρηλάτοις), but that, "though I was permitted to enjoy these prerogatives, I did not agree or consent to them." The "tablets" are probably tablets of office: in *Orations* 31.353a–b and 34 [XIV], Themistius uses the word δέλτοι (and also πινακίδες) to refer to the tablets by which he was awarded the urban prefecture. The office in question in *Oration* 23 should be the Constantinopolitan proconsulship, which Themistius held in the late 350s.[70] He accepted the office but rejected certain prerogatives that normally accompanied it.[71] Was Themistius still holding the proconsulship when he delivered *Oration* 23? Probably not. He says, ταῦτά μοι ἐξὸν [sc. παρὰ βασιλέως καρποῦσθαι] οὐχ ὑπείξα οὐδ' ὑπήκουσα (292c). Does this mean "though I [still] *am* permitted to enjoy these prerogatives [and thus still am proconsul] . . ." or "though I *was* permitted to enjoy these prerogatives [when I was proconsul] . . . "? I opt for the latter understanding.[72] But *Oration* 23 could still be Constantian in date:[73] Themistius stepped down from the proconsulship before the end of 359, but Constantius continued to rule until November of 361. Other chronological references in *Oration* 23 fit well with the supposition of a date at the end of 359 or the beginning of the next decade: Themistius's reference to a recent visit to Rome, surely that of the year 357 (298a–99a); his mention of Antioch's recent attempt to obtain his professorial services,

69. For the possibility that the fragment on "The Knowledge of Knowledges" is a piece of the lost portion of *Orat.* 23, see below, p. 45.

70. For the date of Themistius's proconsulship, see Daly, *Byzantion* 53 (1983): 187–89.

71. See esp. Daly, *Byzantion* 53 (1983): 171–77, who rightly insists against Dagron that *Orat* 23.292a–c rejects perquisites attached to the proconsulship and not the proconsulship itself. Vanderspoel, who follows Dagron both in dating *Orat.* 23 to the late 350s and in denying that Themistius held the proconsulship, believes that in *Orat.* 23.292a–c Themistius is rejecting perquisites that belonged to a public chair of philosophy (*Themistius,* 107); thus also Walden, *Universities of Ancient Greece,* 178. Perhaps it is at 23.293c that Themistius alludes to professorial perquisites; see n. 21 to my translation of the passage.

72. Against Daly, *Byzantion* 53 (1983): 175. If Themistius wanted ἐξόν to be understood as an absolute present, he might have added something like ἔτι καὶ νῦν.

73. Some scholars have put it much later, in the late 370s (or even beyond that): Méridier, *Le philosophe Thémistios,* 23–24; Scholze, *De temporibus,* 76–77; Stegemann, *RE,* 5A, 2 (1934): 1663; Teubner edition of Themistius's *Orations,* 2: 76. Seeck, *Die Briefe,* 300–301, was apparently the first to put *Orat.* 23 at the end of the 350s.

in the mid 350s (299a);[74] and his assertion that he has been among the Constantinopolitans "a full twenty years" (298b).[75] Themistius was born around 317. By 360, he was over forty years old—no longer "young" (*νέος*), as he implies in *Oration* 23.294d. "[R]aised and advanced and dwell[ing]" in Constantinople (*Orat.* 17.214c), by 360 Themistius had easily spent some twenty of those years in the eastern capital.

Those who accused Themistius of being a sophist may have been philosophers or may have included others as well. The charge seems to have been incited by Themistius's habit of addressing large audiences and by the favorable reception he received from them (282d–83b). His critics may also have been put off by his involvement in public affairs and by his holding of the Constantinopolitan proconsulship in the late 350s: was this not a sign of ambition and at odds with a philosophical vocation? (*Oration* 23 does not, however, make any explicit reference to criticism of Themistius for holding office, as do *Orations* 31 and 34 to criticism of his holding the urban prefecture.) In any case, whatever stimulated the charge and however Themistius's critics intended it, what he actually refutes in *Oration* 23 is the charge that he was a sophist in the senses in which that term is used in Plato's *Sophist* (*Orat.* 23.288a–b). Although the detailed description of a sophist is ostensibly given to show that Themistius does not have a sophist's distinguishing characteristics, it may also be intended as an oblique indictment of certain contemporaries: if the shoe fits, Themistius seems to be implying, then wear it. Themistius defends himself before an audience that he describes as "specially selected from every quarter, and . . . on trial with me" and "the first to understand . . . that my estate is some-

74. For the visit to Rome and Antioch's wooing of Themistius, see Dagron, *T&MByz* 3 (1968): 8–9, 39–40, 205–12.

75. *ἐν εἴκοσιν ὅλοις ἐνιαυτοῖς: ὅλοις* is Petavius's emendation of the manuscript's *ὀλίγοις*. Bouchery, *AC* 5 (1936): 196n, retains *ὀλίγοις* and emends *εἴκοσιν* to *εἰκόσιν* ("in the course of what seem to be only a few years"). The young Egyptian poet in Constantinople mentioned in Them., *Orat.* 29.347a–b, which was delivered soon after *Orat.* 23 (see *Orat.* 29.344c), has been identified with Andronicus, who came to Constantinople in 359 (Seeck, *Die Briefe,* 70, 300–301; Dagron, *T&MByz* 3 [1968]: 25, 45n; *PLRE,* vol. 1, under "Andronicus 5"; Maisano, *Discorsi,* 923, 930n). Vanderspoel, *Themistius,* 109, adopting a suggestion of Cameron, *Historia* 14 (1965): 487–88, suggests that the Egyptian poet of *Orat.* 29 is Harpocration, in Constantinople from 358 perhaps continuously to 363 (*PLRE,* vol. 1, under "Harpocration"). But Cameron, loc. cit., prudently warns that "there are many . . . possible candidates" for Themistius's young Egyptian poet. *PLRE,* vol. 1, and the Teubner edition of Themistius's *Orations,* both of which incline to put *Orat.* 29, along with *Orat.* 23, in the 370s, suggest Horapollon (*PLRE,* vol. 1, under "Andronicus 5," "Horapollon"; Teubner Themistius, 2: 76, 174, 178).

thing better than that of a sophist" (296c). This is a winning way of saying that his audience were admirers of his. It included a number of Galatians (299a–b).[76]

Oration 29 was delivered soon after *Oration* 23 (29.344c, *πρώην*). Themistius's purpose in *Oration* 23 was misunderstood to have been accusatory rather than defensive. It was even said that he had been targeting a specific individual in *Oration* 23 (29.346d). Themistius insists in *Oration* 29 that *Oration* 23 was not an attack on anyone. The earlier oration had, of course, contended that those who called him a sophist in the negative sense of that term were "false accusers and liars." But this contention was not made with malice, only to set the record straight about himself (29.344c–d). In *Oration* 29, Themistius explains himself sometimes to a plurality of individuals and sometimes to a single individual, all of whom apparently made up his audience: it seems that, while more than one person had misunderstood *Oration* 23, Themistius was especially interested in setting one of them straight.[77]

In correcting the misunderstanding of *Oration* 23, *Oration* 29 takes an unexpected turn. Themistius had acknowledged in *Oration* 23 that the designation "sophist" could have a favorable sense, but "[i]t is not in this spirit, of course, that these accusers of mine would so designate me; they do not wish to honor me, but to vilify me" (23.286c). Now, in *Oration* 29, although continuing to reject the designation "sophist," Themistius takes it as a high compliment that he does not deserve. The polymath Hippias of old deserved the title "sophist," but nowadays no one does. What is going on here? Is Themistius genuinely trying to wiggle his way out of *Oration* 23 to avoid giving offense to contemporary Constantinopolitan sophists (i.e., rhetorical teachers and practitioners)? He does remark that "I know that all in this city who are now called sophists are courteous and kind. . . . And so none of them is at war with me or ill-disposed towards me because of the fact that I do not declare myself to be a sophist" (29.346c). "No one finds fault with Callias," Themistius continues, "because he revered and honored . . . [the sophist] Protagoras. . . . But it was, perhaps, not a very fortunate

76. There is no positive evidence that the audience was the Constantinopolitan senate (*pace* Maisano, *Discorsi*, 778, n. 2); indeed, *Orat.* 23.282d–83b seems to me to point to a much wider audience.

77. Second person plural: 344c, 345d. Second person singular: 345a, 346a, 346b. I have marked the second person singular by interpolating the vocative "sir" into my translation.

aspect of Callias's love of instruction that he never looked to Socrates" (347c–d). Sophists and philosophers both have their proper place in the scheme of things. In rejecting the designation "sophist" in *Oration* 23, Themistius was mainly saying that he is not a false philosopher; he did not mean to denigrate contemporary sophists as a class. Still, in belittling himself vis-à-vis sophists in *Oration* 29, Themistius is surely also being ironic, as he is in *Oration* 21 with reference to the title "philosopher." Ironic, too, must be his praise of the sophist Hippias's unreachable wisdom; in fact, Themistius does refer in passing to the Platonic Socrates's marveling at Hippias as "apparent" (345d, ἀγαμένου δῆθεν Σωκράτους) and at one point speaks of Hippias's "boastfulness."[78] We are meant to think of the Socrates of the *Lesser Hippias,* to which *Oration* 29 explicitly refers; in that work Socrates discomforts the sophist while on the surface belittling himself and conceding the sophist's wisdom.[79]

ORATION 24

This oration was delivered in Nicomedia, where Themistius intended "to remain . . . and make . . . [a] contribution" (302c). He describes the kind of "chorus" he would organize there (303a). "Chorus" here refers to a teacher's body of students. When he delivered this oration, then, Themistius was attempting to establish himself as a teacher at Nicomedia.[80] In the first half of the oration (to 305c), he is advertising his educational program, hoping to attract students. If, by implicitly locating himself in philosophy's "court" (302d) and even comparing himself to Socrates (300d–301a), he lets out that his primary allegiance is to philosophy, still he insists that his soul is home to rhetoric as well. Each needs the other, just as in myth Eros needs Anteros. Without philosophy, rhetoric is merely verbal contrivance and elegance that seeks to please and charm. But without rhetoric, philosophy is grave and solemn and cannot communicate its benefits to hu-

78. In Pl., *Hipp. min.* 369d, Socrates "admits" that Hippias is wiser than he is. For the force of δῆθεν ("of apparent or pretended truth"), see Smyth, *Greek Grammar,* no. 2849; Denniston, *Greek Particles,* 265. For Hippias's boastfulness, see Pl., *Hipp. min.* 364a, 366c-d, 368b–d, and cf. Them., *Orat.* 29.346c, μεγαλαυχίας with Pl., *Hipp. min.* 368b, μεγαλαυχουμένου.

79. For an attempt fully to explicate the complex tone of *Orat.* 29, see Méridier, *Le philosophe Thémistios,* 25–32.

80. Cf. Bouchery, *AC* 5 (1936): 192–93; Maisano, *Κοινωνία* 10(1986): 30; Vanderspoel, *Themistius,* 43 ff. We have no information about how long Themistius actually remained in Nicomedia. For "chorus" meaning a group of students, see Petit, *Les étudiants,* 21.

mankind. Whatever the precise content of Themistius's Nicomedian course of study was to be, he intended to give rhetoric its proper due, blending "[verbal] pleasure with a sense of [philosophical] propriety" (304c).[81]

Themistius was competing with other teachers and speakers for the attention of the Nicomedians. Admitting that he would not be as entertaining as unphilosophical rhetors or sophists (301a–b), he had to hope that his announced educational program would be judged superior to the offerings of his rivals. While he awaited the Nicomedians' judgment, it would not hurt to cultivate their good will. He confesses his love for them, a love stirred up by an unidentified god (302c–d). In the second half of *Oration* 24, he proclaims their good qualities of soul and their claim to virtue. This second half of the oration actually begins (305c ff.) by acknowledging Nicomedia's natural and man-made wonders, in the style of an encomium of a city. But the acknowledgment is cleverly given in a kind of *praeteritio:* such wonders, the philosopher Themistius insists, however great they are, did not especially captivate him, and it is the Nicomedians' qualities of soul that are the basis of his love of them. Themistius's praise of those virtuous qualities opens into a short sermon on the importance of virtue and of the true (i.e., philosophical) learning associated with it; what begins as cultivation of good will ends as instruction.

Scholze already saw that the earthquake of 358 that destroyed Nicomedia provides a terminus ante quem for *Oration* 24: it is hard to imagine that this oration would not have alluded to that event if it postdated it.[82] We can surely move the terminus ante quem back to Constantius's adlection of Themistius to the Constantinopolitan senate in 355. Themistius would not have entertained the idea of extended employment outside of Constantinople after his adlection. Attempts were made in the mid 350s to lure the philosopher to Antioch, but a brief visit in 356 was all that the city got; and when Themistius went to Rome on an embassy in 357, the Romans tried in vain to detain him.[83] An argument advanced by H. F. Bouchery seems to allow us to move the terminus ante quem for *Oration* 24 even further back than 355. Libanius taught at Nicomedia from ca. 344 to 349. In *Epp.* 793.1

81. But contrast Them., *Orat.* 21.251a, where the superiority of philosophy to rhetoric is stressed.

82. Scholze, *De temporibus,* 73. Nicomedia was hit by a second quake during the reign of Julian. See W. Ruge, "Nikomedeia," *RE,* 17, 1 (1936): 478.

83. See Dagron, *T&MByz* 3 (1968): 8–9, 39–40, 205–6, 212. Themistius comments on his visits to Antioch and Rome in *Orat.* 23.298a–99a. He alludes to his stay in Antioch in *Orat.* 4.57b.

Foerster, probably written in 362, Libanius reveals that he has known Themistius for about twelve years. Therefore they must have met around 350 in Constantinople. If Themistius had spent some time in Nicomedia between 344 and 349, Bouchery reasons, it is likely that they would have met there and then. Therefore Libanius's arrival in Nicomedia in 344 may be taken as the terminus ante quem for *Oration* 24. Bouchery puts it in the early 340s, probably between 340 and 342.[84] That date suits the situation that *Oration* 24 shows the young Themistius facing: well aware of the academic competition he has in Nicomedia, he must woo the city's inhabitants. Some fifteen years later, it is he who will be wooed, by the cities of Antioch and Rome. It is telling to contrast the tone of *Oration* 24 and that of *Oration* 33, which I date to the year 360. In *Oration* 24, Themistius will give his hearers "a bitter potion to drink only after having smeared the cup with honey" (302b); when, securely established in Constantinople, he delivered *Oration* 33, he could afford to be more direct and even blunt.

ORATION 25

Oration 25 is a brief response to an official's request that Themistius deliver an extempore oration. A panegyric in the official's honor is what would have been called for. Themistius refuses to speak extempore, offering instead something from his repertoire of prepared orations as a specimen of his eloquence. He is willing to deliver a panegyric but needs time to prepare it. Meanwhile, he diplomatically mitigates the refusal by offering the official a few words of praise, giving him a preview of what he will say in the future panegyric.

It has been assumed that the official (*ἄρχων*) whom Themistius is addressing was an emperor. Because Themistius refers to him as *τὸν ἐμὸν ἐραστήν* (310b), which I here translate as "my admirer," W. Schmid

84. Bouchery, *AC* 5 (1936): 195–96; id., *Themistius*, 211–12. For Libanian chronology, see Martin and Petit, *Libanios, "Discours,"* vol. 1, passim, with a useful chronological table on pp. 8 ff. Bouchery, *AC* 5 (1936): 195, also will not allow Themistius to be in Constantinople with Libanius in the early 340s, again on the assumption that, if they were there together in those years, they would have met then. We do have to raise the caveat, however, that the possibility of a meeting does not entail the inevitability of a meeting. Both Dagron, *T&MByz* 3 (1968): 25, and Vanderspoel, *Themistius*, 43, 250, follow Bouchery in placing *Orat.* 24 in the early 340s. Earlier scholars had placed it between 344 and 349 (Stegemann, *RE*, 5A, 2 [1934]: 1663–64; cf. Maisano, *Discorsi*, 817, 819n). Scholze, *De temporibus*, 73, placed it in 355, at an inappropriate juncture in Themistius's life and too late (cf. below, p. 31, n. 108).

and O. Stählin thought of Constantius, who favored Themistius in the 350s. But that epithet can hardly be regarded as the exclusive property of Constantius. A passage in *Oration* 11, a panegyric delivered in honor of Valens's *decennalia* at Antioch, led Scholze to think that, in *Oration* 25, it was Valens whom Themistius was addressing. In *Oration* 11.143b–c, Themistius remarks that the ideal ruler, summoning and requisitioning true eloquence, "is impatient when it delays, does not allow it to be cautious, and says no when it requests time for preparation." As soon as Valens saw him on the present occasion, Themistius goes on to say, he requested that he speak, "and in the sequel he did not relent until I came to him with the [rhetorical] gifts that I have been able to prepare in the short time available to me." Scholze sees *Oration* 25 as Themistius's refusal, upon arriving in Antioch, to speak extempore for Valens. *Oration* 11 soon follows, quickly put together, as Themistius would have us believe, for the actual day on which the *decennalia* were celebrated (probably March 28, 373). But, while this linkage of *Orations* 11 and 25 is possible, it is not certain. It is safer, then, to regard *Oration* 25 as undatable, as does Gilbert Dagron.[85] Also, it should not be forgotten that the assumption that the *ἄρχων* addressed in *Oration* 25 is an emperor is just that, an assumption. The word *ἄρχων* can refer to various officials below the emperor. The official Themistius addresses in *Oration* 25 deals with matters of justice and law. The individual could have been a praetorian prefect, a vicar, or a provincial governor rather than an emperor.[86] But having been adlected to the senate of Constantinople in 355, Themistius was acquiring more and more status there, making it increasingly less likely, I suspect, that an *ἄρχων* who expected a panegyric from him would have been anyone less than the emperor himself. Therefore, if

85. Schmid-Stählin, *Christs Geschichte*, 2.2 (1924), 1010 (cf. Maisano, *Discorsi*, 839, "per le espressioni usate e per il tipo di rapporti che esse presuppongono, [the official addressed] può essere identificato con Costanzo, meno probabilmente con Valente o con Teodosio"); Scholze, *De temporibus*, 41–42 (followed by the Teubner edition of Themistius's *Orations*, 2: 114, and by Vanderspoel, *Themistius*, 177–78); Dagron, *T&MByz* 3 (1968): 25. With regard to the supposedly hurried composition of *Orat.* 11, Vanderspoel well notes that "[t]hat is fiction, since the philosopher is unlikely to have traveled to Antioch completely oblivious to the fact that he was to deliver a speech."

86. For the wide application of *ἀρχ-* words, see Mason, *Greek Terms*, 26 (s.v. ἀρχή), 27 (s.v. ἄρχω), 110 ff. For *ἄρχων* applied to a praetorian prefect, note Liban., *Epp.* 840.5 Foerster, with *PLRE*, vol. 1, under "Tatianus 5"; applied to a vicar, Theodoret, *Hist. eccl.* 3.7.5 Parmentier, with *PLRE*, vol. 1, under "Capitolinus 2"; applied to a provincial governor, Liban., *Epp.* 308.2. For the jurisdictional functions of these officials, see Jones, *Later Rom. Emp.*, 1: 481–82.

the *ἄρχων* of *Oration* 25 is an official lower than the emperor, I would be inclined to regard it as a relatively early piece.

Extempore oratory, whether for practical ends (such as winning a case in court) or as mere rhetorical display, was a highly regarded skill in the Roman imperial world. For Quintilian, the acquisition of this skill is "the greatest fruit of one's studies and a most splendid reward for a long stretch of work" (*Inst.* 10.7.1). One after another of Philostratus's sophists strives for extempore fluency or displays his skill at it. The regard in which this kind of fluency was held is again confirmed in Eunapius's account of the sophist Prohaeresius.[87] Audiences took extraordinary delight in extempore performances. No wonder that speakers sometimes misrepresented prepared orations as genuine improvisations. Extempore speakers were thought to display bravado and divine inspiration, to have a store of readily available knowledge. There was a freshness to their oratory that might make prepared speeches seem stale.[88]

Not everyone applauded extempore speaking, however, and Themistius was one of the dissidents. "I am not so clever and glib as to be able to improvise portraits [i.e., panegyrics] at random, as the remarkable sophists do," he says at *Oration* 25.310c. By frankly admitting that he is not adept at speaking extempore, Themistius seems to want to disarm the objection that he is opposed to improvisation out of envy of a skill he does not himself possess. The admission makes it more likely that he will be taken to be speaking on principle.[89] But he is being ironic, of course. The sophists are not "remarkable"; and, skill or no skill, he would not choose to speak extempore. Improvisation, he implies, is theatricality, mere tour de force.[90] He himself is a "Socratic

87. Philostr., *Vitae soph.* 491, 521, 527, 528, 535, 536, 565, 569–70, 576, 577, 586, 594, 595, 598, 607, 614, 621, 628. Eunap., *Vitae phil. et soph.* IX 2.8–20 [483–85] Giangrande, with Penella, *Greek Philosophers,* 82; X 4.5 [488] ff.; X 7.7–8 [492].

88. Delight: Tac., *Dial.* 6.6; Lucian, *Rhet. praec.* 20; Philostr., *Vitae soph.* 577. Misrepresentation: Lucian, *Pseudolog.* 5–7; Philostr., ibid. 579. Bravado, etc.: Tac., loc. cit.; Philostr., ibid. 482 *τὸ κινδύνευμα*, 521 *ἐθάρρει*, 482 *πάντα μὲν εἰδέναι*, 509 *θεοφορήτῳ ὁρμῇ*, 483 *ἕωλά τε καὶ πολλάκις εἰρημένα*, 579; Lucian, *Pseudolog.* 5 *ἕωλα*.

89. Assumption that criticism of an extempore speaker, using all of rhetoric's devices, arises from envy: Lucian, *Rhet. praec.* 20. Critics of Scopelian, who was skilled at extempore oratory, motivated by envy: Philostr., *Vitae soph.* 515. Eunapius surely implies at *Vitae phil. et soph.* X 4.7 [488] Giangrande that Prohaeresius's rivals refrained from speaking extempore because they lacked the skill, not on pure principle.

90. Quintilian warns against theatricality (*scenicum*) when one is speaking extempore in court (*Inst.* 10.7.21). Perhaps theatricality is what *Pan. Lat.* 6.1.1 Mynors has in mind: "neque mediae aetatis hominem ostentare debere subitam dicendi facultatem."

portraitist" (310c); he does employ rhetoric, but in ways that befit a philosopher.

The main and obvious objection to a rhetorical improvisation is that it necessarily lacks the precision and craftsmanship of a prepared oration.[91] Aelius Aristides's formulation of this objection is of special interest here. When the emperor Marcus Aurelius met Aristides at Smyrna and asked him to declaim, the rhetor told the emperor that he would have to wait a full day after proposing a theme, "for I am not one of those who vomit their orations; I am one of those who meticulously prepare them [before delivering them] (*τῶν ἀκριβούντων*)."[92] In a version of this story that must be independent of Philostratus, the Aristides Prolegomena locate the incident in Athens and report a fuller version of the second half of Aristides's remark: " . . . I am one of those who meticulously prepare orations and [thereby] satisfy my audience" (*τῶν ἀκριβούντων καὶ τῶν ἀρεσκόντων*).[93] In the fourth century, rivals of the sophist Prohaeresius quoted the saying of Aristides, in its Philostratean version, when they shied away from competing with him in extempore speaking (Eunap., *Vitae phil. et soph.* X 4.7 [488] Giangrande). Apparently, it had become common to appeal to the authority of the "divine" Aristides, as Eunapius calls him (ibid. XIV 2 [494]), against the practice of extempore oratory.[94] I would therefore suggest that it is significant that there is no mention of Aristides in Themistius's *Oration* 25. If Themistius is addressing an emperor here, then his failure even to allude to Aristides, who was also addressing an emperor when he made his well-known remark in a comparable situation, is more apparent. There is only one reference to Aristides in the whole Themistian corpus, at *Oration* 26.330c, and it is not laudatory: the "descendants of Aristides" are contrasted to those of Plato, the former being practitioners of a misleading and unphilosophical rhetoric. Aristides had criticized Plato for the slurs he had cast on rhetoric. For taking on Plato, he in turn was attacked by contemporaries and, many

91. See Cic., *De orat.* 1.33 [150]; Plut., *De lib. educ.* 6c–7a; Lucian, *Rhet. praec.* 18, 20. The younger Pliny represents Isaeus as one who has avoided the distinctive weakness of improvisation: "He always speaks extempore, but one would think that he had spent much time writing the oration out beforehand" (*Epp.* 2.3.1).

92. Philostr., *Vitae soph.* 582–83; cf. 581–82. Aristides was not untried in extempore speaking (Aristid., *Orat.* 50.14–18, 22, 29 Keil). But his strength lay elsewhere (Philostr., ibid. 585). According to Philostratus's informant Damianus, Aristides practiced extempore speaking privately, although he disparaged it publicly.

93. Lenz, *The Aristeides Prolegomena,* 59–60, 113–14 (Treatise B 9); Behr, *Aelius Aristides,* 142–47.

94. For Aristides's renown, see W. Schmid, "Aristeides 24," *RE,* 2 (1896): 891–92.

years later, by the Neoplatonist Porphyry. This controversy surely played an important part in shaping Themistius's view of Aristides as an opponent of Plato and a practitioner of a debased form of rhetoric—despite the fact that Aristides actually respected Plato and philosophy and was a critic of the sophistic culture of his own day.[95] Because of his view of Aristides, Themistius refrained from referring to him and to his well-known dictum against extempore oratory in *Oration* 25. Themistius speaks here independently of Aristides on an important issue of rhetorical practice, hoping to be cited by future readers in his own right.[96]

ORATIONS 26 AND 28

Oration 26 is addressed to "a few discriminating men" (ἔμφρονες).[97] In the προθεωρία or preface to this oration, Themistius contrasts them favorably to the "large audience in the theater" whom he had recently addressed. "Discriminating" here probably means "more educated"; that is suggested by 326a, where Themistius remarks that "[m]any of you, no doubt, share in the madness and frenzy of philosophy." His audience is listening to him respond to critics who advise philosophers "to be silent, to keep what they know to themselves and . . . neither to make it public nor to share it" (312d). These critics have accused Themistius of the "crime" of speaking publicly in the heart of the city before large, heterogeneous audiences. In light of this behavior, they regard Themistius as an innovator—"introducing new deities" like Socrates—and a sophist. Themistius hurls the two epithets back at his accusers. He is a statesman, not a sophist. As for the charge of innova-

95. For details on Aristides's critique of Plato and reactions to it, see Behr, *Aelius Aristides,* 54–55, 59–60, 94–95; id., *AJP* 89 (1968): 186–99. For Aristides's respect for Plato and philosophy and for his criticism of contemporary sophistic, see Aristid., *Orat.* 3.686–94; 4.1, 6–7 Behr; Behr, *Aelius Aristides,* 106–7.

96. The unfriendly allusion to Aristides in Themistius's *Orat.* 26 does not disallow that Aristides influenced Themistius. Jones, *CP* 92 (1997): 149–52, has revealed unquestionable borrowings from Aristides (?), *Orat.* 35 Keil, in Themistius, *Orat.* 16. For less compelling (or uncompelling) claims of Aristidean influence on Themistius, see Dagron, *T&MByz* 3 (1968): 90, n. 40 *bis;* Colpi, *Die παιδεία,* 165–68; Vanderspoel, *Themistius,* 9–11.

97. Kesters did not succeed in his attempt to establish that *Oration* 26 is an adaptation of a work by Antisthenes (*Antisthène,* 1935) or by another, anonymous Socratic of the fourth century B.C. (*Plaidoyer,* 1959). De Strycker, in his response to Kester's *Antisthène,* remarks that "on regrette de devoir constater l'échec d'un effort aussi vaste et aussi consciencieux" (*Archives de philosophie* 12 [1936]: 206). He could not know that Kesters would be arguing essentially the same thesis in a second monograph twenty-three years later!

tion, did not Socrates speak "to everyone without reserve" (318b)? Did Plato "confine himself quietly to his couch and room" (318c)? Did not Plato and Aristotle write for the general public (319a, 319b–d, 325c)? In any case, innovation is not wrong provided that what is introduced is good: all the arts and philosophy itself have advanced through innovations, as Themistius explains in a digression mainly on the history of philosophy (315d–20a).[98]

Themistius insists that, far from being a crime, it is his social duty to disseminate the lessons of philosophy as widely as possible. Philosophy, he explains, can benefit large numbers of people simultaneously. Its general assertions apply to everyone. And philosophical admonition and censure are easier to take en masse than when dispensed individually. What his opponents see as cultivating the crowd and building a reputation, Themistius sees as an essential aspect of his role as a philosopher.

The critics to whom Themistius is responding as *Oration* 26 opens are laymen (311d–12d). But laymen who, for whatever motives, insist that a philosopher should "sit quietly in his room and converse solely with his pupils" (313d) are only part of the problem. The other part are philosophers who do shun the public and thereby, in Themistius's view, discredit philosophy. Themistius is thinking mainly here of contemporary Neoplatonists, who tended to retreat from the world.[99] The last quarter of *Oration* 26 concerns them. It consists of a direct speech put into the mouth of representatives of "the city" and aimed at a personified Philosophy who "does not value keeping company with the general public and is even ashamed to do so because she regards such behavior as deserving of censure" (326a). She will not address the masses, let alone actively serve the state. Themistius urges her to change her ways and share her wisdom with the public. She claims the art of rhetoric as her own and teaches that it can be beneficial; it remains for her only to use it to broadcast her teachings and persuade the whole community to accept them.[100]

Oration 28, which I suspect has been preserved only in part, also criticizes contemporary philosophers, again surely Neoplatonists. They have become "nonentities . . . fearful . . . and wary of public assem-

98. There is another "history of philosophy" in *Orat.* 34 [II–VI]. Each serves the rhetorical needs of its own oration.

99. See Fowden, *JHS* 102 (1982), esp. 54–59; cf. Dagron, *T&MByz* 3 (1968): 43–44; Cracco Ruggini, *Athenaeum* 49 (1971): 406, n. 14.

100. For philosophy's need of rhetoric (and vice versa), cf. *Orat.* 24.301d–305c.

blies" (341d). Hidden away in their "secluded corners" (ibid.), they have developed unsocial and arrogant dispositions. Themistius wants "to restore Socrates's descendants to their ancient condition" (342b), that is, to a public role. He sees himself engaged in an act of restoration (ἐπανάγειν), not of innovation. Philosophers who have something worthwhile to say to the public and refuse to say it are just as troublesome to Themistius as loquacious rhetors who merely give their audiences pleasure (341b–d).[101]

Several passages in *Oration* 26 bear on the question of its date. At 326d, "the city" asks personified Philosophy, "Didn't they [my senators] make you their equal in status precisely so that they might hear you address them?" This is surely an allusion to Themistius's senatorial status. (And we can also infer from it that *Oration* 26 was delivered at Constantinople.) Much earlier in the speech, Themistius says in his own person, "I have access to both the senate and the assembly" (313c). *Oration* 26's terminus post quem, then, is Themistius's adlection to the senate in 355. Many scholars have taken the allusion to "my previous ordeal" at 313c to be a reference to Themistius's defense of himself in *Oration* 23 against the charge of sophistry.[102] If that is correct, then on my dating of *Oration* 23 the terminus post quem for *Oration* 26 becomes Themistius's stepping down from the Constantinopolitan proconsulship late in 359. "My previous ordeal," though, could refer to something earlier than *Oration* 23. If so, then Otto Seeck and L. J. Daly may be right in dating *Oration* 26 to Themistius's proconsulship, which Daly suggests he may have assumed as early as the middle of 357.[103] Their textual arguments, however, are invalid. They both argue that 26.326c—"But my people are docile and compliant, the most easily managed of all and most readily won over by rational discourse"—implies that Themistius was holding office when he

101. For criticism of philosophers who refuse to address the public, cf. Them., *Orat.* 2.30b–c, 22.265b–d, 34 [XII]; Dio Chrys. 15 (32).8, 20 and 18 (35).4. For Themistius's "public" philosophy, *Orat.* 31.352b–c; cf. *Demeg. Const.* 20a, 22b. He does once point to a frustrating side of addressing the masses: *Orat.* 33.366b–c.

102. Petavius in Dindorf's edition of the *Orations* ad loc.; Méridier, *Le philosophe Thémistios,* 36; Scholze, *De temporibus,* 77; Maisano, *Discorsi,* 850, n. 8; Vanderspoel, *Themistius,* 109.

103. Seeck, *Die Briefe,* 300; Daly, *Byzantion* 53 (1983): 178, 187–89. When the city berates philosophers who "are unwilling to hold office, bear arms or serve in the senate" (26.326b), one thinks of Themistius as a counterexample—a senator who either had held or was holding the office of the proconsulship. Scholze, *De temporibus,* 75–78, put *Orat.* 26 in the late 370s along with *Orats.* 23 and 29. More recently, scholars have favored Seeck's 358–59 for *Orat.* 26: Seeck, *Die Briefe,* 300; Dagron, *T&MByz* 3 (1968): 25; Vanderspoel, *Themistius,* 109; Maisano, *Discorsi,* 845.

delivered *Oration* 26. But it is the city of Constantinople, not Themistius, that is speaking here. Daly further argues that at 26.314a—"What other indications and evidence could you possibly need that the gentleman [Themistius] is a sophist, since you see the chair (*τὸν θρόνον*) and platform, the stolen goods that are proof of his crime?"—Themistius is referring to "the chair of state" (i.e., the proconsul's chair). Surely what he is referring to here is simply the sophist's chair (cf., e.g., Them., *Orat.* 21.243a–b).

Oration 28 cannot be dated.[104] Scholars have assumed that the *ἄρχων* whom Themistius praises in the last paragraph of the oration is an emperor and have suggested either Constantius or Theodosius.[105] They are probably right in assuming the presence of an emperor in Themistius's audience, although it must not be forgotten that the term *ἄρχων* can be applied to officials below the emperor.[106] It is likely that *Oration* 28 was delivered in Constantinople, but we cannot be certain of that.

ORATION 27

Themistius probably delivered this oration in Paphlagonia, perhaps in his father's native city there, where he himself may have been born.[107] Scholze's suggestion that it was delivered around the time of Eugenius's funeral, which presumably was held in his native Paphlagonia, is sheer conjecture. With Dagron, we should regard *Oration* 27 as undatable.[108]

Although Themistius is speaking before a plurality of auditors (332c), he directs his remarks to a young man (332d, *νεανία*), apparently a Paphlagonian and present in the audience.[109] The young man,

104. Cf. Dagron, *T&MByz* 3 (1968): 25.

105. See Vanderspoel, *Themistius*, 233–34; Maisano, *Discorsi*, 915.

106. Cf. above, p. 25.

107. Neighbors (*γειτόνων*) of the city in which Themistius is speaking are explicitly identified as Paphlagonians (333c–d). For the Paphlagonian provenance of Themistius's father (and of Themistius?), see Them., *Orat.* 2.28d.

108. Scholze, *De temporibus*, 71–72, offers a "coniectura, licet vana, quae tamen non displiceat." That conjecture has gained the status of fact in the Teubner edition of Themistius's *Orations*, 2: 154, and in Vanderspoel, *Themistius*, 37–38. (Scholze, op. cit. 73, also inappropriately placed *Orat.* 24 around the time of Eugenius's funeral, for which see p. 10 above; Bouchery, *AC* 5 [1936]: 194, objected.) While Dagron, *T&MByz* 3 (1968): 25, wisely regards *Orat.* 27 as undatable, he then too narrowly describes it as an "exercice rhétorique qui évoquerait plutôt la période de formation de Thémistios" (cf. Maisano, *Discorsi*, 891). It is an oration that could have been delivered, I think, at any time during Themistius's career.

109. I have added the vocatives "young man" or "my friend" in a number of places where there is no vocative in the Greek to alert the reader to the sustained addressing of the one individual.

who may already have spent some time studying in a more distinguished place,[110] has belittled the rhetorical schools of the locale merely because they are not prestigious. At one point in his oration (336c–d), Themistius challenges him with a question: "Do you think that the city where eloquence first made its appearance"—that is, Athens—"is the only fitting place to be educated?"[111] Themistius's answer is no. Eloquence is bound to no place. Eloquence (*οἱ λόγοι*), like reason (*λόγος*), belongs to the human soul (338d). If a teacher of rhetoric is truly in command of his subject, it does not matter where he teaches. Therefore, in selecting a school of rhetoric, one should "look to men, not to places" (338a).[112] Themistius adduces his own experience: he studied rhetoric in Pontus, in a place "far more obscure" (332d) than the city in which he is speaking. His teacher was excellent, and—what is left for his auditors to note—study in Pontus has not proved to be a liability for him. Appealing to Homer, Themistius even suggests that "the eloquence that flourishes in an isolated area is perhaps more honored than that found in big cities" (334c). Although Themistius directs his remarks to one young man, there were clearly other Paphlagonians who also needed to hear his message (332b). Indeed, in the years immediately following his rhetorical studies in Pontus, Themistius may have needed to assure himself, too, that place did not matter.

Philosopher that he was, Themistius could not broach his subject without differentiating between good and defective eloquence (338d ff.). The latter is superficial, aiming merely at ornament and delight, or is in pursuit of gain. The former is grounded in virtue; that is the kind of rhetoric one would want a teacher to champion, wherever he might set up his school.[113]

110. Suggested by the word "again" at 340c: "do you have to travel far again . . . ?" Cf. also 337c: "If . . . you have a strong desire for tales about foreign places, then you should not only sail about the Greek world, but also . . . ," which may be taken to imply that the young man has already sailed about in the Greek world.

111. Libanius, *Orat.* 1.53, speaks of "the flow of students to Athens" as "something of long standing and as old as the business of rhetoric itself" (trans. A. F. Norman). Note also a telling remark of Eunapius of Sardis: he judges Nymphidianus of Smyrna to have been a worthy sophist, even though "he did not share in the education and training enjoyed at Athens." One should be aware that Eunapius himself had studied rhetoric in Athens. See Eunap., *Vitae phil. et soph.* X 8.3, 493; XVIII 1, 497 Giangrande. There were many other cities besides Athens, of course, whose schools of rhetoric, like the cities themselves, were more prestigious than those of Paphlagonia.

112. Cf. the belittling of place in contexts such as Sen., *Epp.* 28.1 ff., 66.3; Plut., *De exil.* 607e.

113. For a close analysis of *Orat.* 27, see Wilhelm, *Byzantinisch-neugriechische Jahrbücher* 6 (1927–28): 451–89, and *Philologische Wochenschrift* 50 (1930): 1003–4.

ORATION 30

This short progymnasmatic piece is wrongly titled *Θέσις εἰ γεωργητέον* in the manuscripts: it is an encomium, not a *thesis*.[114] Drawing on what had become *topoi* on the subject, it lauds agriculture as the sine qua non of human civilization, as, in Xenophon's words, "the mother and nurse of the other arts" (*Oeconom.* 5.17).[115] A similar encomium survives among the Libanian *progymnasmata* (*Progymn.* 8.7 Foerster).[116] Commentators have argued (or rather affirmed) that *Oration* 30 is an early work of Themistius, and at least two of them make 355, the year of his adlection to the Constantinopolitan senate, its terminus ante quem.[117] Some have thought that they could detect something youthful in the language of this oration.[118] A more fundamental assumption undoubtedly underlies the unanimity on chronology: that, as Themistius moved further and further away from the period of his own higher education and from the purely academic phase of his career to a period more and more given to public affairs, he would have been less and less likely to produce a routine rhetorical exercise such as *Oration* 30.[119] The fact remains, though, that there is no solid evidence on the basis of which *Oration* 30 can be dated.

Nor is there any evidence that will allow us confidently to answer the question why this progymnasmatic piece was deemed worth preserving among Themistius's private orations. Themistius was not a teacher of rhetoric, and the other private orations contain weightier stuff. But by linking *Oration* 30 to a passage in *Oration* 20, one may hypothesize that the former oration does in fact have an autobiographical significance.[120] In the latter oration (20.236d–37b), we learn that Themistius's father, Eugenius, who died in the fall of 355, enjoyed

114. The point was already made by Harduinus in his opening note to this oration. Encomium and *thesis* are two of the progymnasmatic modes, on which see Kennedy, *Greek Rhetoric,* 54–73. The error in the title is surely not Themistius's.

115. For the conceptual background and *topoi,* Kier's dissertation *De laudibus vitae rusticae* is still a valuable resource.

116. Farming and farmers are also praised in Liban., *Progymn.* 10.4, but in a different progymnasmatic mode, the *synkrisis.*

117. Scholze, *De temporibus,* 70 ("Themistio iuveni"); Dagron, *T&MByz* 3 (1968): 26 ("les débuts de la carrière de Thémistios"). Before 355: Stegemann, *RE,* 5A, 2 (1934): 1665; Teubner edition of Themistius's *Orations,* 2: 182.

118. Scholze, *De temporibus,* 70 ("sermone quodam tenero et simplici"); Stegemann, *RE,* 5A, 2 (1934): 1665 ("daher [i.e., because of the presumed early date] auch der zierliche und einfache Stil").

119. Note the language of Dagron, *T&MByz* 3 (1968): 25–26: "par sa manière il [cet éloge] évoque plutôt les débuts de la carrière de Thémistios."

120. Thus Vanderspoel, *Themistius,* 84; cf. Maisano, *Discorsi,* 935.

farming in his old age. He "praised agriculture highly and loved it," declaring it a suitable endeavor for a philosopher in retirement. We might well imagine Themistius composing *Oration* 30 in the early 350s as a rhetorical gift for his father. Or it may have been composed earlier and without reference to his father and presented to him at a later time, after its theme had acquired a relevance to his activity in retirement.

Maisano suggests that *Oration* 30 had a sociopolitical purpose: to encourage agricultural productivity.[121] In a not dissimilar vein, I would propose that this oration may be celebrating as much as encouraging agricultural productivity. In pointing out that agriculture tames the wildness in human beings, in noting that some lawmakers have "safeguarded peace so that the digger and the plowman would be free from fear," and in remarking that kings "put their hopes . . . in the blessings of agriculture" and are at a loss "unless the interests of those who nourish the community take precedence over the whole military establishment" (349c–d, 350c, 351c), *Oration* 30 may be alluding to Theodosius's Visigothic treaty of 382, to the peace it secured for the farmers of the Balkans, and to the Visigoths settled within the empire who themselves became farmers.[122] At *Oration* 30.349d, Themistius says that "[i]f some inhospitable Scythian, who lives an uncultivated life, has chosen to be a vagrant instead of a farmer, then he pays the price for his mistake—he is without hearth, a vagrant, patterning his life on that of the wild beasts." In classicizing late Greek prose, "Scythian" can mean "Goth," as in *Oration* 34 [XX] ff. But if one thinks of the Goth at *Oration* 30.349d, it is the Goth beyond the pale, not the Goth settled by Theodosius within the empire.

If *Oration* 30 is more than a mere *progymnasma,* if it had a significance or context that today we can only guess at, it is easier to understand why Themistius (and his knowing posthumous editors?) wanted to see it preserved.

ORATIONS 17, 31, AND 34

I have provided a translation of *Oration* 17 in Appendix 1. That "public" oration forms a set with "private" *Orations* 31 and 34, all three of

121. *Discorsi,* 935.

122. Note Them., *Orat.* 34 [XXII], "[Y]ou [Theodosius] have acquired [through the treaty of 382] more farmers for us"; [XXIV], "[Y]ou Thracians and Macedonians, . . . [i]t is time to sharpen your sickles instead of your swords." Cf. Them., *Orat.* 16.211a–b, 212b.

which bear on Themistius's holding of the urban prefecture of Constantinople.[123] He held this office under Theodosius, when he was "old" (*Orat.* 17.214b, ἐν γήρᾳ; 34 [XII], εἰς τουτὶ τὸ γῆρας). His tenure was brief. In a passage of *Oration* 34 that defensively minimizes the importance of a long tenure and even recommends a short one, Themistius describes his prefecture as lasting "<a few> months" ([XI], μῆνας <ὀλίγους>): "I did not make <a few> months any the less honorable than many years."[124] There has been general agreement that at least some portion of Themistius's prefecture is to be placed in calendar year 384. But whether it fell completely in 384 or included a part of 383 or of 385 has been much debated; and we cannot know, of course, how many months Themistius means by "a few."[125] Themistius had already held office some twenty-five years earlier: he had been the last holder of the Constantinopolitan proconsulship, which was replaced by the urban prefecture in 359.[126]

Orations 17, 31, and 34 were delivered in the order in which they appear in our editions. *Oration* 17 is Themistius's official acceptance of the urban prefecture.[127] Delivered before the Constantinopolitan senate upon his appointment to office, it appropriately includes, in the manner of a consular *gratiarum actio,* a laudation of the emperor who appointed him. Theodosius, a philosophical emperor, has called the philosopher Themistius to serve the state in office; Themistius explains that the emperor's offer and his own willingness to accept are proper and in line with the best of Hellenic and Roman tradition. Exercising the urban prefect's role as head of the senate,[128] Themistius asks that august body to support him (and Theodosius) and to hold him to a high standard of leadership, and he exhorts his fellow senators to honor philosophy and virtue.

123. *Orats.* 31 and 17 are juxtaposed, in that order, in codices A and *Π*. *Π* does not have *Orat.* 34. Codex A does have 34 but does not juxtapose it to 31 and 17. See the Teubner edition of the *Orations,* 1: viii–ix, x.

124. The conjectural supplement, producing a nice contrast between "a few months" and "many years," is virtually certain in light of the phrase μῆνες ὀλίγοι καὶ ἡμέραι a few lines below—unless what dropped out was a numeral giving the precise number of months. For the length of Constantinopolitan prefectures, see Dagron, *Naissance,* 284.

125. Méridier, *Le philosophe Thémistios,* 88, 101; Seeck, *Die Briefe,* 305–6; Schemmel, *Neue Jahrbücher* 11 (1908): 155; Scholze, *De temporibus,* 54–58; Stegemann, *RE,* 5A, 2 (1934): 1646; Bouchery, *AC* 5 (1936): 204–5; Schneider, *Die 34. Rede,* 44–51; Dagron, *T&MByz* 3 (1968): 11–12, 23, 26; Vanderspoel, *Themistius,* 209–14. Schemmel puts Themistius's prefecture entirely in 385, but without giving any reason. Stegemann erroneously makes Themistius's prefecture last longer than a year.

126. See above, pp. 1–2.

127. See Chastagnol, *La préfecture urbaine,* 192–93.

128. See Dagron, *Naissance,* 230–31, 283.

The private *Orations* 31 and 34 respond to criticism directed against Themistius. *Oration* 31 was delivered before the Constantinopolitan senate. Themistius appears still to be holding the urban prefecture.[129] His critics here are fellow senators: he tells them that, if they do not amend their judgment of him, he wants no part in the senate and will console himself with the accolades he has received from the city of Rome and from various emperors.[130] The critical senators have claimed that Themistius betrays philosophy by being active in public affairs. He replies by insisting, as he has already done in *Oration* 17, that "the kind of philosophy that operates in the public arena" (352c) has a venerable pedigree. He did not accept the public honors offered to him (including but not restricted to the urban prefecture) on the mistaken assumption that office leads to virtue or for self-advancement or on a quid pro quo basis, nor did he actively seek out such honors. Rather, all was done for the public good.[131] Virtue and learning already achieved grounded everything. Philosophy, he says, remains his primary "office." If this sounds too good to be true, the same should be said for the high moral ground that Themistius's critics took: they were undoubtedly his political rivals and opponents.

There seem to be oblique allusions already in *Oration* 17 to the senatorial criticism that is explicitly countered in *Oration* 31. In the earlier oration, Themistius says that "it would have been wrong for me to refuse to accept" the urban prefecture (214c), implying that some had maintained that it was wrong for him to have accepted it. Themistius insists in *Oration* 17 that the senate's support of him is "essential"; each senator should be content to play his part and to follow him as leader of the senate (215c, 216b–c). The implication here is that some senators are in fact obstructing Themistius. It has been suggested that, in *Oration* 17, Themistius is anticipating criticism that was voiced only later.[132] But we can easily imagine that criticism of Themistius's assumption of the urban prefecture and, more generally, of his role in public affairs was already being expressed at the very beginning of his prefecture.[133] Since *Oration* 17 is a speech of acceptance and of praise

129. Bouchery, *AC* 5 (1936): 207–8, judged differently.

130. Cf. his telling the Constantinopolitans in *Orat.* 34 [XXIX] how much the Romans admire him.

131. Contrast the judgment of Geffcken, who has no sympathy for Themistius: "[Themistius] was filled only with the consuming fire of ambition. . . . The ambition of Themistius . . . repels us far more than Libanius's naïve vanity" (*Last Days,* 181–82).

132. Méridier, *Le philosophe Thémistios,* 91–92, 100.

133. We can also easily imagine that criticism of his role in public affairs predated his prefecture. Therefore, when Themistius says in *Orat.* 31.352a–b that "I have often wished to speak . . . about the grievances that certain individuals are expressing against

of the emperor who appointed him, and not an apologetic piece, Themistius would have regarded it as inappropriate to refer to his critics in that oration in any but an oblique way.

The title of *Oration* 31 is *Περὶ προεδρίας*, and the word *προεδρία* also occurs once in the oration itself, at the very end (355c), where Themistius refers to the senate as a place where "Calliope [presides] (*ἐν ᾧ . . . ἡ προεδρία*) and any man 'whom the daughters of great Zeus will honor.'" The term *προεδρία* needs to be considered in connection with the term *προστασία*, which occurs twice in *Oration* 34. In section XIII of that oration, Themistius says that he "first attained this position of leadership (*τῆς προστασίας ταύτης*)" when Constantinople selected him to go to Rome as her ambassador in 357. In section XVI he says that he could not have refused "when I was summoned to lead the city (*καλούμενος εἰς προστασίαν*)" by Theodosius. John Vanderspoel believes that the *προστασία* of section XIII is the *principatus senatus*, which Themistius would still have been holding in the 380s.[134] But if the word *προστασία* is employed consistently in *Oration* 34, how can Theodosius be said in section XVI to be summoning Themistius to a *principatus* that he was already holding? *Προστασία* in *Oration* 34 seems, then, to mean nothing as precise as *principatus senatus*, but to be a general term for "a position of leadership," a position Themistius first enjoyed in 357 as Constantinople's ambassador. What, then, of the *προεδρία* of *Oration* 31? Some have thought that this is the *principatus senatus*. Others understand it to be the presidency of the senate. There is further disagreement on whether the *προεδρία* was something Themistius had from his assumption of the urban prefecture or whether he became a candidate for the *προεδρία* after having been in office for a while as prefect. Vanderspoel understands *προεδρία* as a presidency of the senate that "was held by the urban prefect ex officio," and here I am inclined to agree with him.[135] *Oration* 31 (*περὶ προεδρίας*), then, is an oration on the urban prefecture, or more precisely on a specific aspect of the prefecture: in it, Themistius defends his suitability to preside.

---

me" without specifying what grievances he has in mind, one should not interpret "often" narrowly to mean "often since my assumption of the prefecture."

134. *Themistius*, 68–69, 105–6, 209.

135. See Méridier, *Le philosophe Thémistios*, 98–100; Dagron, *T&MByz* 3 (1968): 49–50; id., *Naissance*, 232, 253; Vanderspoel, *Themistius*, 105–6, 209. For the distinction between the presidency and the *principatus senatus*, see Chastagnol, *La préfecture urbaine*, 68–72. *Orat.* 31.355a ("If you should . . . welcome philosophy . . . , then no decree [*ψῆφος*] would make me happier than one issued by you") *could* refer to an impending vote on *προεδρία*, but it need not have such a precise sense. If *προεδρία* is an ex officio presidency of the urban prefect, it could still, of course, have been formally granted by the senate, but presumably at the very beginning of the prefect's term.

Oration 34 continues the apologetic of *Oration* 31.[136] Themistius has now stepped down from the urban prefecture (see section XI). He speaks this time not to the senate, but to a mixed group of Constantinopolitans.[137] The emperor Theodosius is in the audience (I, XXI, XXII). So is one particular critic of Themistius. The orator sometimes addresses his remarks specifically to this individual.[138] The critic of *Oration* 34 has employed "up / down," "ascend / descend" and "lift up / cast down" metaphors against Themistius: in accepting the urban prefecture, Themistius "descended" from the heights of philosophy and "cast her down" (I, IX, X, XIX, XXVII–XXX). The Alexandrian poet Palladas used precisely such language in an epigram that criticized Themistius for accepting the prefecture: "Come and ascend to the depths," he wrote, "for now you have descended to the heights" (*Anth. gr.* 11.292). That is, Themistius has actually descended to what he imagines to be the heights of office; he should ascend to what he wrongly thinks are the depths of philosophy without office. It is not surprising that Angelo Mai, who discovered the text of *Oration* 34 early in the nineteenth century, already proposed that the individual critic whom Themistius addressed in this oration was none other than Palladas, and that the oration is, in part, a response to Palladas's epigram.[139] Alan Cameron, turning Mai's notion on its head, has suggested that it was Palladas who was "picking up the words" of Themistius.[140] But Mai's view is not implausible. I would only warn that we not too confidently assume that it was Palladas who introduced the "up / down," "ascend / descend," "lift up / cast down" metaphors into the debate. These metaphors may have been used by any number of Themistius's critics, both inside and outside of the senate, and may have entered the debate early in Themistius's urban prefecture.

136. Schneider, *Die 34. Rede,* 28–42, undertakes an investigation of the sources of *Orat.* 34.

137. Note the second person plural in sections I, II, X, XIII, XXV, XXIX. The audience included some orphans whom Theodosius had helped (XVIII). There are no grounds for making this speech an address to the senate (*pace* Maisano, *Discorsi,* 990, n. 5).

138. Note sections IX, XII, XVI, XXVII, XXVIII, XXX. In some passages, I add a vocative "[sir]" or "[my good man]" to show that the text has a second person singular. Sometimes the second person singular seems to be used indefinitely, like English "one" (III, VIII, IX *init.*) The alternation between second person singular and plural is also a feature of *Orat.* 27 (cf. above, p. 31).

139. See Mai in Dindorf, *Themistii Orationes,* 444, 471–72, 482. The supposition has general support in subsequent Themistian scholarship.

140. Cameron, *CQ* 15 (1965): 222.

In arguing in *Oration* 34 that it is appropriate for a philosopher to be active in public affairs and even to accept office, that such behavior is "keeping within ancestral bounds" (section I) and that he did not accept the urban prefecture out of ambition (IX), Themistius reiterates what he had already stated in *Orations* 17 and 31. But there is a new concern in *Oration* 34. Themistius is no longer in office. Looking back over his tenure, he affirms that it was meritorious despite its brevity (X–XI). The tone is perhaps defensive rather than smug. Themistius may have been forced to resign from office. Dagron suggests that the philosopher may have fitted badly into an urban prefecture that had become more and more bureaucratic.[141]

If *Oration* 34 has a new concern, it also has a new apologetic tactic. Nearly half of it consists of a panegyric on the emperor Theodosius.[142] He is a philosopher in the purple, Plato's ideal ruler, a source of good and a bulwark against evil. Past governmental abuses are absent from his reign. His *philanthropia* manifests itself in his foreign as well as in his domestic policy: in 382, he made peace in the Balkans, not by destroying the Visigoths, but by sparing them and admitting them into the empire. Themistius himself senses that, from a formal point of view, his panegyric of Theodosius is disproportionately long in what purports to be a speech of self-defense: "one point after another gets hold of me and diverts me from the theme of my oration. I have not come here intending to enumerate all the praiseworthy actions of our ruler" (section XIX). Yet even if the panegyric is overly long, it is not alien to Themistius's theme, because, as he immediately explains, "[m]y purpose in praising [Theodosius] is to show that I myself am a man of good judgment, that in associating with [him by accepting the urban prefecture] I did not bring philosophy down, but lifted her up." The panegyric does, of course, honor the emperor, who is present. It also serves to disarm the charge that the emperor himself was wrong in offering an office to a philosopher (I). But its main purpose in this "private" oration is to assist Themistius in his self-defense by changing the question "How could a philosopher have accepted public office?" to "Who could have failed to come to the aid of such an ideal ruler?" (XIV). Themistius played

141. Schneider, *Die 34. Rede,* 15; Dagron, *T&MByz* 3 (1968): 49; id., *Naissance,* 253, 276–77.

142. For a detailed analysis of the structure of *Orat.* 34, see Schneider, *Die 34. Rede,* 18–27. Schneider regards the "Lobrede" as extending from section XVI through section XXVII, but panegyrical material actually occurs before section XVI.

Iolaus to Theodosius's Heracles, and who could have refused Heracles? (XXVIII).

ORATION 32

Oration 32 begins (and ends) with a reference to the two kinds of human offspring, psychic (insights, convictions, the spoken and written word, etc.) and bodily (children). Misfortunes suffered by our bodily offspring will inevitably cause us emotional pain; but if the soul is in good condition, our psychic offspring (here, our insights and convictions), shaped in part by the teachings of Plato and Aristotle, will help us endure that pain. The oration soon moves on, from 358a ("All philosophers admit . . . "), to a more general and abstract discussion of pain and other human emotions. Themistius insists that the emotions are natural and useful to us. It is a mistake to try to eradicate them. One should only control them through reason, ensuring that each emotion remains in a measured or moderated state. This, in a nutshell, is the doctrine of *metriopatheia.* Having set it forth in abstracto, Themistius comes back to "the issue at hand" (360d), which is now defined, not as the pain that our children's misfortunes cause us, but more fundamentally as our love of and attachment to our children; it is, after all, that love that causes us to feel the pain. Love of children is philosophic as well as natural; in fact, Themistius contends that philosophers have a greater or better love of their children than nonphilosophers do. Love of children presumably must be moderated, like any other emotion. Themistius alludes only to cases in which this emotion is too weak, leaving us to assume that it is also possible that there are cases in which it is too strong.

One can see from this brief summary that the double title of *Oration* 32, *Μετριοπαθὴς ἢ Φιλότεκνος*, preserved in Stobaeus's extracts from Themistius as well as in the Themistian manuscripts themselves, aptly alludes to the two major segments of the oration: the presentation of the doctrine of metriopatheia, which insists that the emotions are natural even if in need of control, and the discussion of one of these natural emotions, love of children.[143] The oration's argument is

143. For the double title in Stobaeus, see *Anth.* 2.15.29, 3.1.122, 3.12.21, 4.5.27 Wachsmuth-Hense. In all but the second case, the double title of *Orat.* 32 is erroneously given to extracts from other Themistian orations. At *Anth.* 4.26.24 the title of *Orat.* 32 is given only as *Μετριοπαθής*. Ballériaux, *Byzantion* 58 (1988): 24–31, analyzes *Orat.* 32 into four parts and a brief peroration.

not developed as clearly as it might have been, but Scholze perhaps went too far in judging its structure to be "perturbata."[144] And even if Scholze's judgment is accepted, one should not assume too quickly that a poorly ordered oration necessarily belongs to the early stages of an orator's career.[145] Writers do improve with time, but backsliding is always possible.

The doctrine of metriopatheia was held by both Academics and Peripatetics. It is also found in pseudo-Pythagorean texts. The Aristotelian Themistius insists, though, that followers of the Stagirite have a special claim to it: all philosophers accept it in practice—and who could fail to do so if it is true to human nature?—but only Peripatetics accept it in theory (358a).[146] Themistius, like other ancient advocates of metriopatheia, polemically contrasts this doctrine to Stoic *apatheia,* understood to mean that human beings should ideally be utterly impassive. Utter impassivity, however, does not appear to be what Stoics actually meant by apatheia. Their view of the human soul as unitary rather than bipartite or tripartite may have made it a theoretical challenge for them to find a way to give psychic citizenship to irrational feelings. But they did find a way. Their unitary rational soul included healthy, natural emotional states, *eupatheiai,* which could oxymoronically be called "rational emotions." Apatheia meant not freedom from all emotions, but only from those that are excessive, unnatural or contrary to reason. "[A] Stoic *eupatheia,*" writes John Dillon, "comes out in practice as being very similar to a properly moderated Platonic-Aristotelian pathos."[147] Themistius, then, misrepresents or even cari-

144. *De temporibus,* 70. He complains specifically that "[c]omparatio liberorum, unde oratio XXXII proficiscitur, sermone progrediente plane neglegitur. iam orationis clausula ad hoc exordium recurrit." Stegemann replied that "[d]ie Disposition ist zwar locker, aber nicht so zerfahren, wie Scholze meint"; and he explained that the topic μετριοπάθεια does not turn its back on children, with whom the oration begins, but prepares for their readmission into the oration under the topic φιλοτεκνία (*RE,* 5A, 2 [1934]: 1666).

145. Scholze writes: "Denique Themistii iuvenis defensionem [i.e., *Orat.* 32] esse dispositione, quae plane perturbata sit, probatur" (*De temporibus,* 70). Dagron, *T&MByz* 3 (1968): 26, would put *Orat.* 32 "aux débuts de la carrière de Thémistios," apparently because he sees it as a mere "exercice oratoire" in which Themistius would not have engaged later. Cf. Maisano, *Discorsi,* 957, 960n.

146. On *metriopatheia* and the Stoic matters discussed in this paragraph, see Lloyd in *Stoics,* ed. Rist, 233–46 passim; Rist, in ibid. 259–72; Rist, *Stoic Philosophy,* 22–36; Dillon in Anton and Preus, *Essays,* 2: 508–17; Moraux, *Der Aristotelismus,* 2: 282–84, n. 197; Becchi, *Prometheus* 18 (1992): 102–20. The term *metriopatheia* and its cognates occur neither in Aristotle nor in the text of Themistius, *Orat.* 32. One wonders whether μετριοπαθής in the title of *Orat.* 32 is genuinely Themistian.

147. In Anton and Preus, *Essays,* 2: 515–16.

catures the Stoics on the emotions, but such misrepresentation seems to have been common in antiquity.[148]

It is hard to imagine that Themistius was not already a parent when he wrote *Oration* 32. His first marriage produced at least two children, one of whom was the son named Themistius who died in 357, probably in the second decade of his life. Themistius remarried after the presumed death of his first wife. In a letter to Libanius from the late 350s or the beginning of the next decade, he hopes for more children from this second marriage, which he says he has recently entered into. We do not know whether those hopes were fulfilled.[149]

Omer Ballériaux has suggested that *Oration* 32 was occasioned by the death of the younger Themistius. The notion is highly improbable.[150] It is true that, in discussing the misfortunes inflicted on children by fate, Themistius does allude, in the opening section of the oration, to the premature death of Socrates's son and, in a later section of the oration, to Zeus's reaction to the slaying of his son Sarpedon. But he also alludes to other misfortunes suffered by the children that people have brought into this world: blindness, infertility, unspecified impairments (*οὐδένεια*, "worthlessness"), and, in a later section of the oration, sickness (356b–d, 361b, 363c). Furthermore, as has already been pointed out, Themistius is more fundamentally concerned in *Oration* 32 with human love of and attachment to children than he is with pain caused by children's misfortunes. But, regardless of the relative importance of the latter theme, one finds it hard to understand why, if *Oration* 32 was occasioned by the death of his son, Themistius nowhere

148. The emotionless Stoic sage is a picture that "[i]n some respects . . . is accurate, but in a number of others . . . is an influential caricature" (Rist in *Stoics,* ed. id., 259).

149. For Themistius's marriages and children, see Seeck, *Die Briefe,* 292, 296–97, 301; Bouchery, *Themistius,* 101–4, 124–27; Stegemann, *RE,* 5A, 2 (1934): 1644–45. Chronological precision is impossible. "[A]t least two children": I am assuming that the *παῖδες* mentioned in Them., *In Arist. Phys.* 6.2 (p. 185 Schenkl), are children of his first marriage. In this passage, Themistius reveals that he is making use of the *cursus publicus.* It has been assumed (Scholze, *De temporibus,* 84; Stegemann, ibid., 1654) that he would not have had that prerogative before he was adlected to the senate in 355, which therefore should be regarded as the terminus post quem of the *In Arist. Phys.* But Themistius will have been known to and well regarded by Constantius in the early 350s (Dagron, *T&MByz* 3 [1968]: 8; and on the date of *Orat.* 1, see below, p. 238, n. 3), and that emperor readily granted warrants for the use of the *cursus publicus* (Jones, *Later Rom. Emp.*, 1: 130). Themistius might have been granted a warrant, then, before 355. "In a letter to Libanius": A few lines of Themistius's letter survive in a scholion to Liban., *Epp.* 241 Foerster, which is a reply to it; the scholion puts Themistius's letter in the reign of Julian, but that date was challenged and the letter placed in 359 by Bouchery, ibid., 125–26.

150. Ballériaux, *Byzantion* 58 (1988): 22–35; his suggestion is also rejected by Vanderspoel, *Themistius,* 41.

clearly refers to it.[151] Philosophers may be expected to bear misfortune with emotional reserve, but this does not require that mention of a misfortune be suppressed. Indeed, I would argue that the absence of any clear reference to the death of the younger Themistius in *Oration* 32 suggests that it was delivered either before he died or well after the period of grieving that would have immediately followed his death.[152] If the oration was delivered after the son's death, Themistius would certainly have had him in mind; but the son's death, I contend, did not elicit the oration. If anything specific elicited *Oration* 32, it may have been a contemporary attack on Themistius or on philosophers in general for siring children—an attack to which Themistius felt the need to respond.[153] "The philosopher," he concludes, "is not ashamed of loving his children any more than he is ashamed of loving wisdom or the written and spoken word." Siring children is "the same sort of legitimate productivity" as is writing or orating (363d–64a). For Themistius, the philosopher no more divorces himself from family life than he does from civic life. That view won Constantius's favor: in his *Demegoria* of 355, the emperor not only acknowledges Themistius's philosophic contributions to society at large, but also praises him for his marriage and procreation of children (22a–b).[154]

ORATION 33

Only the opening of *Oration* 33 survives, the text breaking off in mid paragraph (and mid sentence) after a few pages. *Oration* 33 was a philosophical sermon, and in the extant opening pages Themistius underscores how unpopular and discomforting such sermonizing could be. The philosopher might, for example, have to disabuse people of the belief that happiness consists in the possession of material wealth. If by "happiness" we mean "wealth," then we are using the word "happi-

151. Ballériaux is not troubled by this aspect of his thesis. Themistius's audience "comprenait à *demi-mot* les allusions de l'orateur." Themistius "célèbre *discrètement* la mémoire de son fils" (*Byzantion* 58 [1988]: 31–32). The italics are mine.

152. Vanderspoel, *Themistius*, 42, tentatively puts it in 349 or 350.

153. Note 361b: "I have expatiated on these matters . . . because I suspect that, whenever you see philosophers just as attached to their sons and daughters as the masses are, you ridicule and look down on them." What is represented here as a hypothetical or "suspected" criticism may actually have been a real and recent one.

154. Constantius alludes to the preservation of the human race through procreation (*παιδοποιίας τὴν διαδοχὴν σωζούσης τοῦ γένους*), just as Themistius speaks of how procreation ensures the immortality of the human race (32.355d, 361c, 363d). But one need not assume that Constantius is referring to *Orat.* 32 here (*pace* Vanderspoel, *Themistius*, 41–42).

ness" in an inappropriate and degenerate way. It is just this kind of linguistic critique that Themistius is engaged in here: to "put some very ... well-known words to the test and show you what meaning they had when they first gained currency ... and then how most people ... put false ... usages of them into circulation" (366d). Words—for example, the words *βασιλεύς* and *ὕπατος*—lose their original value just as coins do. It is at this point, as Themistius is about to explain the original and true sense of the words *βασιλεύς* and *ὕπατος*, that *Oration* 33 breaks off. The manuscript preserves no title for this oration. Harduinus titled it *Περὶ τῶν ὀνομάτων τοῦ βασιλέως καὶ τοῦ ὑπάτου*, which is adopted in the Teubner edition. Better to leave it untitled, since we cannot know how central the discussion of *βασιλεύς* and *ὕπατος* was or precisely what course the argument took.

Themistius delivered *Oration* 33 before a large audience at Constantinople. On the basis of his understanding of Themistius's reference in 367b–c to certain coins that were withdrawn from circulation "a short time ago" (*ἔναγχος*), Seeck dated the oration to 348 or 349.[155] Themistian scholars have followed him. The additional notion that *Oration* 33 was an inaugural lecture given by Themistius upon accepting an imperial appointment ca. 348 to teach philosophy in Constantinople[156] is groundless. One might wonder whether Themistius would have thought an inaugural lecture to be the right moment to underscore the discomforting role of philosophy or to tell an audience that "if your intention ... is anything other than to submit yourselves quietly to my oration ..., then I shall abandon the whole lot of you" (367a). In any case, Jean-Pierre Callu, on numismatic grounds, would put the terminus post quem of *Oration* 33 in 354, the year, in his view, of the demonetization to which Themistius refers as happening "a short time ago."[157] In the notes to my translation of *Oration* 33, I suggest that, in the lost part of the oration, Themistius lauded the current emperor, and that that emperor was holding the consulship when *Oration* 33 was delivered.[158] The laudation of the emperor would have been prompted by his presence in the audience in Constantinople. What we are looking for, then, if Callu is correct, is an emperor who

155. *Die Briefe*, 293.

156. Thus Dagron, *T&MByz* 3 (1968): 7, 26.

157. In *Les "dévaluations,"* 117–19; see also Callu and Barrandon in *Società romana*, ed. Giardina, 1: 577, 579, 581, and Callu in *Hommes et richesses*, 227–28. Maisano, *Discorsi*, and Vanderspoel, *Themistius*, are apparently unaware of Callu's discussions.

158. See below, p. 208, n. 9.

was consul and in Constantinople soon after (ἔναγχος) the demonetization of 354. Constantius appears to be our man. He was consul in 354, 356, 357, and 360, but during these years a presence in Constantinople is attested only for late 359 and early 360. *Oration* 33, then, should belong in the opening months of 360.[159]

FRAGMENT ON "THE KNOWLEDGE OF KNOWLEDGES" (APPENDIX 2)

This fragment is transmitted at the end of *Oration* 23 but is clearly discontinuous with what precedes it. It has been thought to derive from a lost work, presumably an oration. But *Oration* 23 itself breaks off before reaching its end, so one might speculate that the fragment on "The Knowledge of Knowledges" is part of the lost portion of *Oration* 23. It might have been part of Themistius's lost argument there that he was not a person who "forms opinions about the non-existent, uses appearances to imitate reality, fashions phantasms of the truth, and is a verbal wonderworker" (288b). Instead, he would have argued, he was a philosopher, equipped with "the knowledge of knowledges."

Scholze groundlessly asserted that the putative lost oration from which this fragment derived was entitled *Περὶ φρονήσεως*, "On Good Judgment," and *Περὶ φρονήσεως* has persisted as a convenient title for the fragment. It is true that the term *φρόνησις* occurs towards its end (see the penultimate paragraph of my translation), and that the opening word of the fragment is the cognate participle *φρονοῦσα*. But the title I have supplied better represents its overall content.[160]

TRANSLATIONS OF THEMISTIUS'S ORATIONS

The earliest extant translations of Themistian orations are into Syriac: we have a Syriac version of *Oration* 22 and an otherwise unpreserved

159. For Constantius's attested whereabouts from 354 to 360, see Barnes, *Athanasius*, 221–24. I am grateful for correspondence in 1995 and 1996 from J.-P. Callu and J. P. C. Kent on Them., *Orat.* 33.367b–c. In a letter to me of February 12, 1996, Kent "strongly" favors the date 360 for *Orat.* 33. Julian was consul in 363, but he had left Constantinople midway through the year 362, never to return there again (Bowersock, *Julian*, 83–85). Jovian was consul in 364, but he never reached Constantinople (Amm. Marc. 25.5–10, Zos. 3.30–35). It is probably not necessary to look to Valens, since we want a date close to 354.

160. The fragment can be found in the Teubner edition of Themistius's *Orations*, 3: 4–5; see also the Teubner apparatus criticus to *Orat.* 23.299c, where "or. 27" is a typographical error for "or. 23." See Petavius's comment on *Orat.* 23.299d; Scholze, *De temporibus*, 79–80; Stegemann, *RE*, 5A, 2 (1934): 1663; Dagron, *T&MByz* 3 (1968): 17.

Syriac version of a Themistian work, likely another oration, "On Virtue." The two pieces are preserved together in a ninth-century manuscript; the translations themselves have been ascribed to Sergius Resaïnensis, who died in 536.[161] We also have two Arabic versions of a work "On Governing the State" that is ascribed to Themistius and (according to one of the two manuscripts) was addressed to the emperor Julian. The work does not survive in Greek. Each of the two versions, despite their closeness, is signed by a different translator, both of whom flourished in the tenth century. One of the translators tells us that he worked not from the Greek original, but from a Syriac translation. This Themistian work in Arabic might be an oration rather than a letter or treatise.[162]

In sixteenth- and seventeenth-century Europe, Themistius's Greek orations were gradually discovered and translated into Latin. This activity culminated in the nearly complete Greek text and Latin version of the public and private orations by Petavius and Harduinus (Denys Petau, S.J., and Jean Hardouin, S.J.), published in 1684.[163] The 1684 edition was only "nearly complete" because *Oration* 34 and the *θεωρία* to *Oration* 20 were not included. When Angelo Mai published the *editio princeps* of these two pieces in 1816, he equipped it with a Latin translation. Meanwhile, an Italian translation of some of the public orations by M. Cesarotti had appeared in 1805 (*Orats.* 5–7, 9 and portions of 1–4).[164] Many years would pass before Glanville Downey published an English translation of *Oration* 1 in 1958.[165] More recently D. Moncur has translated a portion of *Oration* 8 and

161. See the Teubner edition of Themistius's *Orations,* 3: 8–9.

162. See above, p. 5. Not surprisingly, translators were attracted early to Themistius's Aristotelian *Paraphrases.* Already Themistius's contemporary Vettius Agorius Praetextatus translated his paraphrases of Aristotle's *Prior* and *Posterior Analytics* into Latin (see *PLRE,* vol. 1, under "Praetextatus 1," p. 723). We have a number of medieval translations of Themistian paraphrases into Arabic, Hebrew, and Latin: see, e.g., Stegemann, *RE,* 5A, 2 (1934): 1653–55; 'A. Badawi, *La transmission de la philosophie grecque au monde arabe* (Paris, 1968), 100–102 (and note 166 ff.); Dagron, *T&MByz* 3 (1968): 14–16; Zonta, *Athenaeum* 82 (1994): 403–7.

163. Petavius's 1613 and 1618 editions, with Latin translations, contain fewer orations than the edition of 1684. For the sixteenth- and seventeenth-century printed editions and Latin translations of Themistius's orations, see Maisano, *Archivum Historicum Societatis Jesu* 43 (1974): 277–89.

164. For this translation, see Maisano, *Discorsi,* 84–86. Cesarotti also translated the *Demegoria Constantii.* Maisano found a reference to an anonymous sixteenth-century Italian translation of fourteen unspecified Themistian orations in an eighteenth-century source, but he has been unable to locate the translation or to discover anything else about it (*Archivum Historicum Societatis Jesu* 43 [1974]: 280; *Discorsi,* 70n).

165. Downey, *Greek and Byzantine Studies* 1 (1958): 49–69.

the whole of *Oration* 10 into English,[166] and J. Mark Sugars's unpublished 1997 University of California at Irvine dissertation includes an English translation of *Oration* 7.[167] As for the private orations, we have none in a modern language until 1959; in that year, H. Kesters published a French translation of *Oration* 26. A German translation of *Orations* 20 and 21 by Siemer Oppermann appeared in 1962, and Hugo Schneider translated *Oration* 34 into German in 1966. An English translation of *Oration* 23 forms part of James Smeal's unpublished 1989 Vanderbilt dissertation. My own translations were completed but not yet published when, in 1995, Maisano's Greek text and Italian translation of Themistius's public and private orations appeared. A selection of Themistius's orations in English translation has been announced as forthcoming in the series Translated Texts for Historians (Liverpool University Press). It will offer public orations 1, 3, 5, 6, 14–16, and private oration 34. Finally, Ballériaux is preparing a new edition of Themistius's orations with French translation for the Budé series.[168]

The unpublished translation left behind by Glanville Downey, the first North American to devote himself to Themistius, merits comment. This translation, in typescript, is in the possession of Walter E. Kaegi, Jr., of the University of Chicago. He kindly made it available for my inspection during a brief stay in that city. Almost all of Downey's translations are dated; they range from 1948 to 1954. They are equipped with some notes, most of them brief, many of them merely short glosses. Many references to ancient sources and parallels are noted in the margins. The typescript has some corrections and additions in pen and pencil. Downey prepared this translation both to gain mastery over the meaning of the Greek text and as a first draft of an English version that he hoped would eventually be published. His original project was to publish a critical Greek text with translation and commentary.[169] But when he agreed to publish his critical text in the Teub-

166. Moncur in P. Heather and J. Matthews, *The Goths in the Fourth Century,* Translated Texts for Historians 11 (Liverpool, 1991), 26–50.

167. Sugars, "Themistius' Seventh Oration: Text, Translation, and Commentary."

168. My survey of translations does not take account of the select passages from Themistius that one can find translated here and there: e.g., a few passages from *Orat.* 5 in English in E. Barker, *From Alexander to Constantine: Passages and Documents Illustrating the History of Social and Political Ideas 336* B.C.–A.D. *337* (Oxford, 1956), 378–80, or passages from *Orats.* 5 and 34 in French in Dagron, *T&MByz* 3 (1968): 55–57, 168–72.

169. See Downey, *HTR* 50 (1957): 259n; *Classical Bulletin* 34 (1958): 49, 51n; *Greek and Byzantine Studies* 1 (1958): 49.

ner series, he then announced "an annotated English translation" that would appear separately from the Greek text.[170] Downey published only the first volume of the Teubner Themistius (with H. Schenkl posthumously). He was afflicted by a "morbo gravissimo oculorum," and the work was turned over to A. F. Norman.[171] Of Downey's English translations, only that of *Oration* 1 ever went into print.[172] In the preface to the first volume of the Teubner Themistius, which carries the date 1961, Downey writes that he is about to send his English translation to press: "Orationum versionem Anglicam cum commentario perfeci quam mox typis mandatum iri spero" (p. xix). The word *perfeci* was apparently an exaggeration: the unpublished Chicago translation does not appear to be ready for a publisher, and Professor Kaegi knows of the existence of no other typescript.

The translations I offer here are based on the Greek text of the Teubner edition of the *Orations* by Schenkl, Downey, and Norman (1965–74). When I cannot accept the reading of that edition, I so indicate in the footnotes.[173] The standard page numbers of the Petavius-Harduinus edition are given in square brackets in the text of my translations. (In the Petavius-Harduinus edition, each page is subdivided into four sections with the letters *a* through *d*. I do not mark these subdivisions in my translations.) I also use square brackets to identify quotations or allusions, for short glosses, and when I want the reader to see immediately how I am fleshing out the Greek text. Angular brackets indicate conjectural supplements. The paragraphing is mine. I have closely examined the translations of Petavius-Harduinus, Mai (1831 ed.), Kesters, Oppermann, Schneider, Smeal, and Maisano.

170. *Studia Patristica* 5 (1962): 480n.

171. See the Teubner edition of Themistius's *Orations,* 2: vii.

172. Downey, *Greek and Byzantine Studies* 1 (1958): 49–69. The published translation is a slightly revised version of the Chicago typescript.

173. I considered inter alia, of course, Maisano's 1995 Greek text. For criticism of the Teubner edition, directed mainly at Downey and the first volume, which contains the public orations, see Hansen, *Gnomon* 38 (1966): 662–66; id., *Philologus* 111 (1967): 110–18; Maisano, *Archivum Historicum Societatis Jesu* 43 (1974): 291; id., *Κοινωνία* 2 (1978): 93–100 passim.

The Orations

ORATION 20

A Funeral Oration in Honor of His Father

PRELIMINARY COMMENT ON THE ORATION
(*Θεωρία τοῦ λόγου*)

This oration of mine does not have as its goal the winning of honor or the display of oratorical talent; its aim is to express a sense of reverence towards my father, and its assumption was that this reverence would be greater and more solemn if given utterance in your presence. For this is the only audience that it regards as worthy of the dead man's virtue.

An oration such as this one generally tends to eschew verbosity. Besides, the only choice I had was to refrain from speaking at length, since the <present> occasion did not permit me to prepare a long oration. What it required was a shorter rather than a lengthier panegyric. For any funeral oration written long after the death of its subject seems stale; and, [in any case], I have reserved all the particulars of the life of the deceased for a biography.[1]

If you should find that, in its style, this oration does not fully measure up to the ancient models, there would be nothing astonishing about that. It is difficult to achieve that level of precision in one's writing if one does not work at it constantly, but instead gives much more attention to other things. Also, a philosopher should not be that concerned with beauty of

1. "for a biography": see Balleriaux's reservations about this understanding of the Greek (*AC* 65 [1996]: 145, n. 56).

language. Rather, you should mainly pay heed to whether or not he has, on all occasions, been true to his sense of what befits a [philosopher's] son and one who is himself trying to be a philosopher.[2]

[233] You [who are my audience] say that you will not allow me to sing dirges and lamentations. Nor does philosophy permit this. Whenever she sees me overwhelmed by grief and brought to tears, she becomes angry and threatens to do dreadful and pernicious things to me. She threatens to deprive me straightway of what my father left me—and I do not mean land and fields and flocks. I mean the thing that I strive for and lay claim to above all else, the thing that I alone among my brothers am trying to inherit.[3] Philosophy threatens [234], if I am overwhelmed by grief, to strike my name off the list of her attendants. I must therefore keep my eyes as steady as iron or horn, just as Homer made the eyes of Laertes's son [Odysseus] stay fixed while he was concealing the pity he felt for his wife [*Od.* 19.209–12]. Odysseus, though, did not need much endurance, for he was soon to have his Penelope and speak freely to her. But you, once gentlest of fathers and now gentlest of gods, when will I be reunited with you?

Philosophy has just now carried you across on that blessed journey. Having returned from there, she brings us the news—if we are to believe her—that, as soon as you were freed from the bond of nature, you immediately darted high up towards the aether and heaven. You did not have to break or pull away from that bond while it continued to hold you down; rather, it released you and let you go on its own. Philosophy tells us that you yoked together the pair of immortal horses that you raised and reared together over such a long period of time. These are the horses that you habituated to run in unison and to hasten upwards together, so that one of them does not force the yoke up while the other drags it down. It is because of the training you gave them, I suppose, that you did not just now have to use goads or reins on the pretentious and arrogant horse. No, that horse was gentle and kind to his fellow steed and cooperated in pulling your chariot upwards.[4]

2. With Deichgräber in Oppermann's edition, I have deleted the last three words of the *θεωρία*, (viz., *καὶ εἰς φιλόσοφον*). On this and other (*προ*)*θεωρίαι* that have survived in the Themistian corpus, see Seeck and Schenkl, *RhM* 61 (1906): 560–66.

3. "dirges and lamentations": cf. Pl., *Rep.* 3.398d. "the thing that I . . . am trying to inherit": i.e., philosophy.

4. For the two horses of the soul, see Pl., *Phaedr.* 246a–b, 247b.

The holy gathering of gods and the assembly of benevolent spirits [*daimones*] received you. They blessed you, went forth to meet you and welcomed you because you had fulfilled the task for which they had sent you to the earth and then returned promptly in an unblemished and holy state. Neither before nor after your return did Rhadamanthys or Minos find any imprint or mark of defilement on your soul. Those two men sit you next to Socrates and Plato, having also brought out your favorite, the divine Aristotle. Even during your sojourn here [on earth] you used to strive greatly to associate with Aristotle. Your physical body was unable to bar you from associating with him, even though your favorite was then so very far away.[5]

O divine person, I imagine that the famous Aristotle now honors you and loves you more than he loves anyone else and is so full of joy that he does not know what to do with himself. He renders thanks to you [235] for having been his interpreter, a more lucid one than a Bacis or an Amphilytus was for Loxias [Apollo]. He is grateful to you for having explained the wisdom that he had discovered and cultivated but then concealed in darkness and wrapped in abstruseness. His intention had not been to grudge good men this wisdom; but he did not want to cast it out onto the streets either.[6] You would determine who were worthy of his wisdom. You would remove the darkness and uncover Aristotle's handiwork [ἀγάλματα] for them.

Just as a person approached the inner sanctuary [of Aristotle's works], he would be filled with awe and anxiety. He would be in distress and gripped by a sense of utter helplessness, unable to take a step, unable to embark on any path that would lead him into the sanctuary. Then that interpreter [Eugenius] would open the gateway of the temple, clothe the god's statue [ἀγάλματος], and make it beautiful and clean on all sides. He would show the statue, now all sparkling and shining with a heavenly light, to the initiate. That fog and cloud would be completely broken up without delay. From the depths, meaning would emerge, full of light and splendor instead of the original dark-

5. Rhadamanthys and Minos were judges in the next world (e.g., Pl., *Apol.* 41a, *Gorg.* 523e–24a). The Greek for "associate" (ξυνεῖναι, συνουσίαν) in the last two sentences of this paragraph is commonly used of a pupil's relation to a teacher.

6. "O divine person": ὦ θεία κεφαλή as at Them., *Orat.* 3.46b, 9.128a, 14.183d; cf. Pl., *Phaedr.* 234d, *Tim.* 44d. "a Bacis or an Amphilytus": famous prophets (interpreters of the god's will). Cf. Pl., *Theag.* 124d; Ael. Aristid., *Orat.* 5.40 Lenz-Behr; Liban., *Orat.* 56.11; Them., *Orat.* 2.26c, 3.46b. Bacis was originally a title; several well-known prophets bore the name (Kern, "Bakis 1," *RE,* 2 [1896]: 2801–2). "He is grateful . . . onto the streets either": cf., for this and the next paragraph, Them., *Orat.* 23.294d, 26.319b–d.

ness. And Aphrodite would be at the torch-bearer's [i.e., Eugenius's] side, and the Graces would also attach themselves to the sacred rite.[7]

To be sure, the visage and shape impressed upon these sacred mysteries were almost entirely those of Aristotle. Nevertheless, my father helped to open up all the shrines of the sages. He was one of those who were fully initiated in the sacred knowledge that Pythagoras of Samos brought back to Greece from Egypt[8] and in what Zeno of Citium later taught in the Painted Stoa. He always displayed the works of the great Plato right at the door [of Aristotle's "temple"] and in the very temple precinct.

When passing from the Academy to the Lyceum, he did not change his clothes; he would often first make a sacrifice to Aristotle and then end by worshiping Plato. He always got angry at those who actually tried to build a dividing wall between the two [sacred] enclosures and to separate them. For he felt that Aristotle's philosophy is an excellent preliminary rite to Plato's frenzy and, at the same time, a defensive wall and safeguard for it. Plato's philosophy is still too accessible, still assailable by sophists, he thought; Aristotle provided fortifications for him, fenced him in on all sides, and kept his teachings from being assailed by plots. Many people, he felt, because of their own inaction and laxity, are unprotected and enter the contest before being rubbed with oil.[9] Hence, they are often unable to defend a view that is defensible **[236]**—a good and strong position gets tripped up and thrown by a weak and inferior one.

My father, then, never quarreled with the wise Plato, nor did he think that Aristotle ever did so lightly. As for Epicurus, the son of Neocles, he considered him to be a clever fellow, no divider of the indivisible. He would often haul Epicurus in, at least to show him to people

7. For the play on the two senses of ἄγαλμα in this and the previous paragraph, cf. Them., *Orat.* 25.310b, 27.332b. For the revelation of a cult statue as a metaphor for the revelation of philosophical truth, cf. Them., *Orat.* 23.298c–d. The presence of Aphrodite and the Graces meant that Eugenius's words of explication had a beauty and charm to them; cf. Them., *Orat.* 26.319d. Neither what is said here nor Themistius's remarks at *Orat.* 23.294d necessarily imply that Eugenius produced written commentaries (*pace* Seeck, *Die Briefe,* 133; *PLRE,* vol. 1, under "Eugenius 2"; Maisano, *Discorsi,* ad loc.).

8. For Pythagoras in Egypt, cf., e.g., Diog. Laert. 8.3; Porph., *Vita Pyth.* 6–8; Iambl., *Vita Pyth.* 3–4 [14–19].

9. "Plato's frenzy": cf. Pl., *Symp.* 218b; Them., *Orat.* 26.326a. "a defensive wall and safeguard": Themistius is thinking of Aristotle's logical works; see Ballériaux, *AC* 65 (1996): 148–49. "before being rubbed with oil": i.e., before studying Aristotle's logical works.

who were unacquainted with him; but then he would very quickly strike him off of his list, having poured perfume on his head since he was a lover of pleasure. This hauling in of Epicurus was not something to wonder at.[10] For no philosophical school has settled far off from the others or keeps a great distance between itself and another school. The schools of philosophy are like side roads that, though they break away and deviate from a wide and long highway, nonetheless all reach the same point in the end, however much they wind about.

When my father would invite the poet Homer in and entertain him as the origin and source of Aristotle's and Plato's teachings—well, on those occasions you really would have needed a Homeric utterance so that you could say, in the poet's own words, "Heavens, how beloved and honored this man [Eugenius] is by everyone!" [*Od.* 10.38]. My father did not keep away from the ancient stage or the theater, nor did he regard them as places utterly impure and alien to philosophy. The golden Menander frequently joined him in chorus and celebrated the mysteries with him, and so did Euripides, Sophocles, the beautiful Sappho and the excellent Pindar. Consequently, he was not a man of only one tongue. He was not made just for an audience of philosophers and unintelligible to rhetors or schoolteachers. Whenever other [devotees of philosophy] tried to say something philosophical—well, you would have a harder time grasping what they mean than understanding someone speaking Persian. But when my father spoke, even a vine-dresser or a smith had something he could take home with him. He would talk about government with an officeholder, about statesmanship with a statesman, and about any aspect of agriculture with a farmer.

My father praised agriculture highly and loved it. He declared that in agriculture one could find the only kind of rest that is suitable for a philosopher—the kind that comes after hard work. Agriculture, he said, provides good exercise even for a person who is very old and has become frail with the passing of time [237], and it is full of temperate pleasure. If you went to visit him in his old age, you would have frequently found him planting or cleaning things up or moving something from one place to another or feeding water into conduits so that his plants would be irrigated. He would have given you some of his pro-

10. "no divider of the indivisible" (*τῶν ἀτόμων οὐκ εἶναι τομόν*): wittily alluding to Epicurus's atomism and also affirming that he was not a hairsplitter, obstinate or an extremist? "having poured perfume on his head": cf. Pl., *Rep.* 3.398a. Cf. Themistius's comments on Epicurus in *Orat.* 26.324a, 34 [XXX].

duce. He would have taken you through his rows of grapevines and shown you his unusually beautiful and large grapes. Like writers on genealogy, he would have told you what "cities" his colonist grapes had come from. His piece of land was one that he had put in good order himself. He exposed springs of water there, where they had not previously been seen, and tended to everything else in such a way that the place was a beautiful residence and one suited to a philosopher. And even though this piece of land did not have a very Hellenic name, nonetheless one often hears that name uttered by those who are Hellenes through and through.[11]

Now, since Odysseus's father was wearing rags and had poorly made and patched shoes on his feet, his son tells him that his plants have been quite well tended, but that he himself is not well cared for [Hom., *Od.* 24.226–50]. But I know that my father made himself beautiful and decked himself out before his plants received any such attention—and I describe him in these terms, not because he wore a fine, well-woven garment, but because he had a soul that was well ordered and not full of rustic crudeness.[12] His cultivated and fruitful vines and garden were not the property of a man who had a blind and uncultivated mind.

Nor could you have made any comparison of even a brief remark or admonition of his to the fruit that grew without interruption for Alcinous or to the golden apples of the Hesperides; for my father's intention was not to achieve beauty alone in his words. He said that those who, in working the soil, plant only groves of lush plane trees and cypresses and have no interest in wheat and grapevines aim more at enjoyment than at nourishment. He used to compare such tree-planters to those who, in their discourse, are in search only of pleasure and of how to charm their audience, but neither know how, nor even try, to speak of the things from which the soul derives nourishment and by which it is bettered. Such men, he would say, are not yet philosophers any more than those tree-planters are farmers. They are flatterers,

11. "[the rest] that comes after hard work": Themistius has Hes., *Op.* 289–92, in mind here; cf. Them., *Orat.* 27.340d. For the appropriateness of agriculture for the philosopher, see Muson. Rufus, fr. 11 Lutz; for its appropriateness for the wise old man, see Cic., *De senect.* 15–17 [51–60], with Powell's commentary. Cicero mentions Odysseus's father Laertes, whom Themistius also has in mind (see next paragraph in the text). "his colonist grapes": with the manuscript group O and Oppermann, I read *σταφυλῶν* ("bunches of grapes") instead of *στεμφύλων* ("pressed grapes"). Eugenius would have told you where he got his vines. "this piece of land . . . Hellenic name": was this land in Eugenius's native Paphlagonia (see Them., *Orat.* 2.28d)?

12. "a soul that was well ordered": cf. Pl., *Gorg.* 506e.

fawners, and cooks instead of physicians; they are beautifiers instead of athletic trainers [**238**].[13]

My father had a simile that he applied to people who were quite good at stringing together and mouthing the pronouncements prescribed by philosophy but neglected the actions that are the concern of those pronouncements. He pointed out that such individuals resembled a person who, since he wanted a healthy body, would collect drugs and herbs—enough to be of use in sickness when ground up and mixed together—and would zealously get himself a physician's instruments and could tell you what Hippocrates of Cos, Erasistratus [of Ceos], and Diocles [of Carystus] all prescribe in their writings for good health. But when such a person became ill and should have been deriving benefit from all those preparations, he would kiss those drugs and instruments and Hippocrates goodbye. He would recline on a couch that was covered with purple carpets and set a Sicilian table for himself.[14] Then he would drink and feast to his heart's content, as a Corinthian girl or an Ionian boy served him. Such a person, my father used to say, derives no benefit from the mere acquisition of drugs, just as there is nothing to be gained by someone who adopts and learns well the pronouncements of the philosophers but is unwilling to make them his own through application. The latter has no more of a claim to philosophy than the former does to the art of medicine.

My father also observed that an athlete who has weak and undeveloped shoulder and upper arm muscles and cannot hold his head up straight[15] because of soft living and intemperance is just as ridiculous [as our would-be medical expert], if, in that condition, he shows you his weights and tells you all about his exercises. He is ridiculous, indeed, if he then enters the racecourse to compete but has neither the ability nor the desire to do so, or if he sits down in the baths or in a corner of the boys' wrestling school and tells them, while they are washing themselves, about feats of wrestling. Similarly, my father would say, in philosophy it is not necessary to make a show of words. He used to say

13. Alcinous's garden: see Hom., *Od.* 7.112 ff. "lush plane trees": cf. Them., *Orat.* 27.339b. "flatterers, fawners . . . athletic trainers": for these metaphors, cf. Pl., *Gorg.* 462b–66a.

14. "a Sicilian table": i.e., a lavish one. Cf. Them., *Orat.* 24.301b, with n. 1 to my translation; Pl., *Rep.* 3.404d, which mentions Corinthian girls as well as Syracusan tables.

15. *τὸν αὐχένα λυγίζοιτο*: Greg. Nyss., *In Ecclesiasten Orat.* 3.660M., p. 329 Alexander, also mentions, among the consequences of excessive drinking, a crooked neck "that can no longer support itself on the shoulders."

that we do not judge that a person is well advanced in wisdom because we have observed, for example, that he can skillfully distinguish the various things that are good and says that virtue is greater than and far superior to everything else—superior to what people call the things of the body and to what fortune rules over without our having any say in the matter. No, it is not on any such basis that we would judge a person to be well advanced in wisdom; rather, we would try to determine whether the person's thinking is in line with his words [239], whether he is really committed to his principles, whether he always prefers the morally good action to the action that brings wealth or fame. It was my father's contention that anyone not so disposed would be a philosopher only in word, not in his heart.

My father used to point to Socrates the Athenian as one who exemplified all these qualities of the true philosopher. Socrates was rebuked at home by Xanthippe and also by Critias and the Thirty Tyrants, who threatened to kill him and drive him out and do horrible things to him if he did not change his mind and be of service to the regime that was in power. Nonetheless, he never succumbed to fear. He was never frightened, nor did he think that there was any danger so terrible and formidable that evil should win out over good or impiety over piety. So he refused to apprehend Leon of Salamis, and he could not be forced into accepting a motion against the generals associated with Pericles, Erasinides, and Diomedon, although the people themselves were pressuring him to do so as they shouted down at him from their seats in the assembly.[16]

Not even when the Athenians condemned Socrates, not even when he was in confinement, did he do anything ignoble or base. Nor did he say anything ignoble to his friends, who gathered in the prison. Instead, he conducted a philosophical discussion about the soul and explained what was to be found in Hades, all the good things there that await virtue and all the punishments and penalties that await vice. So

16. "Socrates . . . who exemplified": with Gasda, "Kritische Bemerkungen," 6, and Oppermann, I would correct παραδείγματα here to παράδειγμα. For Socrates' wife Xanthippe's bad temper and scoldings, see Xen., *Symp.* 2.10; Plut., *De cap. ex inim. util.* 90d–e; Diog. Laert. 2.36–37. The Athenian regime of 404–403 B.C. known as the Thirty Tyrants, one of whose leading members was Critias, tried to pressure Socrates into taking part in the arrest of Leon; see Pl., *Apol.* 32c–d. Pericles, Erasinides, and Diomedon were three of the eight commanding Athenian generals at Arginusae in 406 who were condemned in the wake of the Athenian victory there (Kagan, *Fall of the Athenian Empire,* 354 ff.). For the motion referred to by Themistius, see Pl., *Apol.* 32b; Xen., *Hell.* 1.7.14–15. Socrates was the only one of the presiding *prytaneis* to persist, in vain, in his resistance to it.

not much time passed before the Athenians repented of what they had done to him. They punished Meletus for having brought Socrates to trial. <Anytus> fled from Athens on his own, and because of Socrates the people of Heraclea in Pontus stoned him to death. One is now shown Anytus's grave there, in the outskirts of the city, not far from the sea, where the people of Heraclea pelted him.[17]

My father showed the world actions of his own that were very similar to those of Socrates. He showed the world that he had many public struggles in the civic arena and no lesser domestic ones in his own household,[18] and that he was enduring and holding up against all these struggles easily, because one must elect to be a philosopher in deed, not in word.

Men of old gave Heracles, son of Zeus and Alcmene, his due when they deified him, established special religious rites for him, and offered him not merely the sacrifices that one would have appropriately made to a hero, but those that one made to a *daimon* or to a god as well [240]. For Heracles was a paradigm of virtue. He visited all parts of the earth, ridding it of cruel tyrants and strange beasts. Yet I think that moral evil is more violent than boars, more overpowering than lions, more reckless than a multiform dog, and it has more heads than a hydra.[19] Those who have defeated the beast of moral evil and have revealed its weakness also deserve, I believe, to have sacred precincts established at public expense and priests appointed in their honor. For it is not unfitting that these individuals, after they have been freed from the body, have a share in divinity, as "good men, averters of evil, guardians of the articulate human race" [Hes., *Op.* 123, with Pl., *Rep.* 5.469a]. And it seems to me that the gods, wanting to show and remind the human race once again that the virtue of the human soul can reach great heights, brought you, father, to earth and made you

17. Socrates's "philosophical discussion": one thinks, of course, of Plato's *Phaedo,* in which the condemned Socrates, in his last hours, discusses the immortality of the soul and (113d ff.) the fate of souls after death. For the conflicting ancient notices on what happened to Socrates's accusers Meletus and Anytus, see Schenkl, *Wiener Studien* 21 (1899): 233–35.

18. What these "struggles" were we do not know.

19. Themistius is alluding to four of the famous twelve labors of Heracles: the catching of the Erymanthian boar and the "multiform" dog Cerberus, and the killing of the Nemean lion and the Lernaean hydra. "Multiform" (πολυμόρφου) could easily be understood as "multiheaded" if the heads are those of various animals (see Michaelis, *JHS* 6 [1885]: 292–94). Otherwise, "composite" in a broader sense (cf. Apollod., *Bibl.* 2.5.12)? Or "multibodied" (cf. Eur., *Herc. fur.* 24)? For the hydra's heads, see J. Boardman et al., "Herakles," *LIMC* 5:1 (1990): 34.

appear here in the recent past, after a long lapse of time, just as they had brought Heracles here long ago and, after him, Socrates.

For you, the contest has been blessed and happy. You have returned to those fortunate and happy beings who sent you down to this place, and you have left us in this rough sea, in this meadow of infatuation. We have no one who will extend a helping hand. We are trying to keep our heads above water, to emerge in the end from the slime and the mud. In the future we must follow in your footsteps—if, that is, we can ever put our feet where yours have gone. Yet you did frequently put me to the test, just as eagles test their young, to see if my eyes could endure and hold up against the bright light of truth. And often, when you dismissed me, you would fill me with a wonderful sense of hope, rejoicing and glad that I was proving, by not blinking in the face of the sun, that your offspring was genuinely yours.[20]

Having kept my eyes open in those days, I must not now close them. Because of your effort on my behalf and your vote of confidence in me, I must engage in the struggle, so that I do not at all appear to be the son of an unphilosophical father. Please come to the assistance of your son from on high; in answer to his prayers, instill in him, O blessed one, the strength and courage he needs for the struggle.

20. "in this rough sea": cf. Pl., *Alc. II* 151b (with Eur., *Phoen.* 859–60)? "in this meadow of infatuation": Empedocles B 121 Diels-Kranz. Cf. Them., *Orat.* 13.178a–b, where the Empedoclean origin of the phrase is acknowledged, but where the rhetorical context requires that Themistius question the phrase's belittlement of the sense world. "from . . . the mud": cf. Pl., *Rep.* 8.533d. "you . . . put me to the test": cf. Them., *Orat.* 27.333b. "the bright light . . . the sun": cf. Pl., *Rep.* 7.515e–516b. For eagles so testing their young, cf. Arist., *Hist. animal.* 8(9).34.620a; Plin., *HN* 10.3 [10]; Ael., *De nat. animal.* 2.26, 9.3; ps.-Jul., *Epp.* 184.418d Bidez; Jul. (?), *Epp.* 191.383c; Greg. Naz., *De se ipso et de episc.* 371–74 [*PG* 37.1193]; Claudian, *Panegyr. Honor. III Cos.*, praef.

ORATION 21

The Examiner [Βασανιστής], or, The Philosopher

[243] All you gentlemen whom I have brought together today in the theater of the Muses, why do you sit here in a state of shock?[1] Why are you so amazed? Surely, now, it does not seem peculiar and strange to you that a man who is considered worthy of being called a philosopher was seen yesterday gathering an audience![2] Surely it does not seem strange to you that today he is seen seated in a very sophistical and pompous manner on a lofty chair, intending to elicit from you, by what he says, the shouts of approval and applause that the marvelous sophists often enjoy from you! Well, if you *are* astonished by this, be assured that your astonishment is justified! For no philosopher actually behaves this way or desires to do so.

But I am not the one who debases and trespasses against the title "philosopher"; the guilty party is he who originally bestowed that title on me and taught you to think of me as a philosopher. That title does not reflect the truth [244]. I know that I am the son of a trueborn and genuine philosopher; I do not doubt my mother's word about this, as

1. "The examiner" of the oration's title, or "the one who applies a touchstone" (cf. below 247c, 248a), determines whether a person who claims to be a philosopher is a true one. The oration will set forth the marks of a true philosopher.

2. I.e., engaging in sophistical behavior, like that mentioned in the next sentence. But Themistius would not consider the mere gathering of an audience necessarily sophistical; and, if he suggests, in the next sentence, that he is behaving sophistically and pompously, he does not mean what he says seriously. For the irony of the whole oration, see above, p. 15.

Telemachus doubted Penelope [cf. Hom., *Od.* 1.213 ff.]. But I do not consider myself a philosopher, and I think that those who do so deceive themselves. Why are they in this predicament? Why do they draw others into it as well?

Look, I am speaking to you expressly against myself in a public theater and am saying that this title does not befit me! I tell you that he who first applied it to me apparently did not take into account that it is not enough to have a father who is a philosopher. One must also be reared and educated by philosophical teachers and trainers, and one's soul must be molded while it is still young and tender. For this is how an imprint really gets into the soul and can become deeply fixed there and escapes being merely superficial. Somehow or other I have been deprived of such teachers, even though I had two fathers who were leading [philosophers], the one who begot me and the one who chose me to be his son-in-law.[3] Now Aristippus, reared only by his philosopher mother, was content to be referred to as "taught by his mother." You know, of course, which Aristippus I mean—not the very famous one, the pupil of Socrates, but the son of his daughter. This Aristippus, it seems, was loved by his mother, and she imparted her teachings to him, eager to make him worthy of herself and of his grandfather. But these two fathers of mine hated me and were at odds with me! No, they did not hate me—for it is not right, I think, for wise and blessed men to detest their offspring. Rather, by disposition I was slow to learn and hard to teach. Although they very much wanted to imprint their teachings on me, they were unable to do so, for that part of me that should have received the imprint was too hard to be receptive of it.[4]

So if this is the case, put an end, my good men, put an end, I say, to your error. Put an end to it now, by the Muses, and give me no share at all in the title "philosopher." Instead, drive me—if you can drive me anywhere—and push me in the direction of the reality you intend to

3. Themistius's father, Eugenius, is the subject of *Orat.* 20. Themistius is most likely referring here to the father of his first wife (cf. above, p. 42). Vanderspoel conjectures that this individual was the philosopher Maximus of Byzantium; see Vanderspoel, *Ancient History Bulletin* 1.3 (1987): 73, where however he misunderstands Them., *Orat.* 21.244b–45a; id., *Themistius,* 41.

4. "and one's soul must be molded ... merely superficial": cf. Pl., *Rep.* 2.377a–b. "leading [philosophers]": *κορυφαίων*, for which cf. Pl., *Theaet.* 173c; Them., *Orat.* 2.37c, 21.250a, 21.251c. The emperor Constantius called Themistius's father *ὁ πάντων κορυφαιότατος* (*Demeg. Constantii* 23b). For this term applied to philosophers, see Athanassiadi, *Julian,* 139. For the "Cyrenaic" Aristippuses, see, e.g., Guthrie, *History of Greek Philosophy,* 3: 490 ff.; for the younger Aristippus's being "taught by his mother," see the testimonia in Giannantoni, *Socraticorum reliquiae,* 1: 287–88. "Although they very much wanted ... receptive of it": cf. Pl., *Theaet.* 191c; Them., *Orat.* 8.105a, 11.144b.

indicate by this title, for there is no other good you will do me that would be as great as that. And if you must live in a place where that appellation is used, give it to others, not to me. Otherwise I shall be a laughingstock, like a person wearing a coat that belongs to someone else and is much too big for him. Only a few will know the truth, that you love to give titles to people [245]; most will assume that I took the title by force, usurped it, snatched it from you against your will. And I would not want to acquire a bad reputation among men.

Be aware that I am the first one to ridicule those afflicted by this kind of disease [i.e., the use of unmerited titles]. I think that they differ little from a charcoal-maker or a smith, covered with soot and dust, who at some point decides that he should not be called a charcoal-maker <or a smith>. He gets very angry at those who so designate him and, if he gets hold of any of them, is ready to make mincemeat of them. He now thinks that he should be known as a seer or a physician or as some other kind of expert who is more respectable than a charcoal-maker or a smith.[5] I am also indignant at Aesop's ass when I hear that, although an ass, the animal dressed up in a lion's skin. (So a group of children beat the ass with clubs and deprive him both of his lion's skin and his presumption [Aesop, *Fab.* 199, *Fab. Aphth.* 10 Hausrath-Hunger].) But what I am saying is this: if I should agree to be your philosopher, you would have quite a monstrosity in me!

Anyone else who so desires has permission, it seems, to come before you at a public gathering and address you with considerable scope, because this is a fortunate and free city. Consequently, there is nothing surprising in the fact that I too shall avail myself of this open atmosphere. You should not get stirred up when you hear me speak.[6] For it is not a philosopher whom you will hear, but only a man who is taking his fill of a bounteous and lavish feast that is laid out before him.

And yet, even if I were to lay claim to the thing at issue [i.e., philosophy] and apply that title [philosopher] to myself as something that belongs to me, you should not become agitated through focusing merely on my speaking to you publicly; you should consider *what* I say and *why* I say it. Is what I say useful and beneficial to the audience? Is

5. "<or a smith>": I add these words (i.e., *ἢ σιδηρέως*) after *ἀνθρακέως μέν*. "ready to make mincemeat": cf. Pl., *Rep.* 6.488b. "as a seer . . . other kind of expert": cf. Hom., *Od.* 17.383–84.

6. In *Aristotelis opera,* ed. O. Gigon, vol. 3: *Librorum deperditorum fragmenta* (Berlin and New York, 1987), 334, the passage that begins with this sentence and extends two paragraphs forward through " . . . class myself among philosophers" appears as a fragment (84.2) of Aristotle's *Περὶ τἀγαθοῦ.*

my goal to win admiration? When the wise Plato spoke in the Piraeus, people streamed into that place and congregated there, and they came not only from the city, but also from the fields and vineyards and silver mines. Yet this did not prevent Plato from being wise. And when he discoursed on the Good, the huge crowd became dizzy and drifted away from his band of auditors, and in the end Plato was left with an audience consisting only of his customary pupils. Now, if a person is in search of praise, Plato's experience would be very painful for him. It would be a sophist's misfortune [246]. But a philosopher's discourse is not at all diminished even if he speaks under a lone plane tree and only the cicadas are listening. If he needs praise too, he is not in want of it: it will be enough for him that one man, Phaedrus of Myrrhinus, praise him. The cicadas, of course, will sing and sing again under the noonday sun.[7]

But what does this have to do with me? For I have just been telling you over and over that I do not class myself among philosophers. That status is difficult to achieve, quite difficult, gentlemen. Hesiod makes that rough and steep path the way to philosophy; Pindar prescribes toils and heavy costs for it; and the famous Socrates, son of Sophroniscus, says that human beings achieve it only through divine apportionment.[8]

So that you may better understand that Hesiod, Pindar, and Socrates tell the truth and that, in turning away from the title "philosopher" and standing in awe of it, I am not acting unreasonably, listen as I tell you how many and what kinds of qualities a person must have by natural disposition, as a gift from the gods, and also what qualities he must acquire later in life through instruction, if he is not to do dishonor to that title. I shall not be setting forth my own criteria—for I would once again be a sophist if I had personal knowledge of the criteria on the basis of which I were coyly to reject the title "philosopher." Rather, I shall report Socrates's and Plato's remarks and tell how *they* defined a philosopher when they were refuting the accusations brought against philosophy and showing that the pure and guileless race of philosophers is understandably small and consists of few human beings.

7. "you should not become agitated . . . publicly": i.e., you should not assume that all public speaking is sophistical. For Plato's loss of his large audience upon discoursing on the Good, see Riginos, *Platonica,* 124–26. "cicadas": In Plato's *Phaedrus,* Socrates converses under a plane tree with Phaedrus alone, the cicadas singing as the two men talk (*Phaedr.* 229a–30c, 236e, 258e ff.).

8. Hes., *Op.* 289–92 (cf. Pl., *Rep.* 2.364d); Pind., *Ol.* 5.15. For Socrates, see Pl., *Meno* 99e, 100b; ps.-Pl., *Virt.* 379d.

What there are many of, according to Socrates and Plato, are counterfeit philosophers, men who wrongly enroll themselves in that corps, men who force their way into a greater and more majestic calling from lowly and trifling fields. It is because of such men that philosophy has been the recipient of so many grave reproaches in the past and still is. These reproaches are elicited when, from time to time, individuals who have been reared in a base and slavish way learn a skill on their own or are taught it by their master and then, having escaped from slavery by means of this skill, become discontented with it and yearn for the honor that philosophy brings. By Zeus, isn't this just the sort of person that that little, bald-headed smith [in Plato] is, the one who, just after being freed from his bonds, dressed himself up in fancy clothes as he was about to lay hands on his mistress?[9] When such people try to consort with philosophy, what do we imagine that those who see and hear about it will think about her [247]? Won't they blame philosophy for all the evils that these men have in their souls? When they discover that these men are base, money-loving and rapacious, quarrelsome and abusive, deceitful and plotting quacks, they will not assume that these blemishes are caused by their natural dispositions or their earlier base employment; they will assume that men get these blemishes from philosophy.[10]

But it is not right, my excellent sirs, that you should share their thinking. Your various blessings exceed those of other men, and the most valuable blessing of all is that you not be deceived in matters of the greatest importance. By Zeus, if someone should intentionally bring into your marketplace debased gold or a garment colored with imitation purple dye or a counterfeit stone, you will get angry and not put up with it. You will deliver such a person to your official flogger to be punished as a criminal and a deceiver. To guarantee the punishment of such deceivers, you have devised many tests for the purity of gold, of purple dye and of aquamarines. You have a committee of examiners to do the testing. Whenever you make a purchase, you summon them to be at your side and to get their approval of the transaction.

But suppose someone goes about in your city adulterating, dishonoring and hawking the most divine of human blessings [i.e., philosophy].[11] Suppose this person claims a privileged position and regards

9. Cf. Pl., *Rep.* 6.495c–e; Them., *Orat.* 5.64c.
10. Cf. Pl., *Rep.* 6.486b, 500b.
11. Cf. the remarks on the sophist's hawking of knowledge in Pl., *Protag.* 313c ff.

himself as a human being in the midst of a herd of cattle because he knows (or does not know!) about "things equivocally named" [τὰ ὁμώνυμα] and what the difference is between "the why" and "the how" and other such truly obscure and ambiguous terms in Aristotelian logic.[12] Will you be unable to administer any test of genuineness to him? Will you be unable to apply a straightedge to him that would show, if it does not align with him, that he is curved and bent? You do not lack men who could administer such a test, but you fail to trust or employ them. I would have told you the names of individuals here who possess this knowledge if I had been convinced that you would make use of their experience. But, as it is, you seem to me to prefer to act on your own rather than to have need of others to explain things to you.

So let us all, both me and you, ask the wise Plato, as I said, to disperse the mist from our eyes in order that we may truly be able to distinguish between gods and men on our own [248]. The companion of Zeus [i.e., Plato] will hear us; in fact, he already has heard us. Look, my good sirs! I feel my heart being filled! Suddenly, on this side and that, thoughts of the touchstones devised by Plato are flowing into my mind, touchstones by which he purged the race of philosophers in the fair city and brought it to a more complete state of perfection than Phidias did his statues.[13]

First of all, he says, let philosophers be the fruit of sacred marriages [*Rep.* 5.458e]. A sacred marriage is a union and joining of the best man with the best woman [ibid. 5.459d]. Think about this Platonic model first, gentlemen; and after you have carefully reflected upon it, safeguard it and keep it at hand if it seems compelling to you.

Think about it in the following terms. You have many horses and many dogs, I suppose, in your homesteads, and herds of cattle and

12. Petavius and Cobet (*Mnemosyne* 11 [1862]: 230) deleted "or does not know" (ἢ οὐκ ἐπίσταται), but I would defend it. The false philosopher "does not know" in two senses. First, he has only a superficial grasp of what he pretends to have mastered (cf. Themistius below, 21.251–53); secondly, he blunders even at that superficial level, "the why" and "the how" (τὸ διότι καὶ τὸ καθότι) being a mistake for "the what" and "the why" (τὸ ὅτι καὶ τὸ διότι). See, e.g., Arist., *Anal. post.* 78b33, 89b24, 93a17; id., *Metaph.* 1.1 [981a29]; Them., *In Arist. Anal. post.* A6, A13, B2 (pp. 16, 27–28, 43 Wallies). The term τὸ καθότι ("the how") occurs nowhere in Aristotle or, except here, in Themistius's orations or *Paraphrases*. For "things equivocally named," see Arist., *Cat.* 1a1; cf. Them., *Orat.* 23.291a.

13. "to disperse . . . from our eyes": a Homeric metaphor (*Il.* 5.127). Cf. Pl., *Alc. II* 150d–e; Them., *Orat.* 22.267d. The need to distinguish between gods and men on the Homeric battlefield is paralleled by the present need to distinguish between true and counterfeit philosophers. "The companion of Zeus": cf. Pl., *Phaedr.* 248c, *Soph.* 216b. "I feel . . . filled!": cf. Pl., *Phaedr.* 235c. "the fair city": cf. Pl., *Rep.* 7.527c.

flocks of sheep in your fields. Now whenever you want to produce fine calves, purebred foals and pups that will make good hunting dogs, do you breed from all your animals indiscriminately or do you try as much as possible to breed from the best ones? I see, in fact, how you examine the stallion who will mount the mare to determine whether he is proud of bearing, carries his neck high and is free-spirited. You examine the bitch from whom you intend to produce puppies to see if she really is a true-bred Laconian and not a worthless hound, to determine whether she is a vulpine from somewhere or other or a Maltese. In like manner, you examine your bull and your ram. And when you sow wheat and barley and plant a grapevine or an olive tree, do you, by Demeter and Dionysus, pay no heed to the plants and the seeds?[14] Aren't you, rather, fully convinced that excellent and productive trees and leguminous plants will grow from the seeds and plantlings of excellent and cultivated stock as surely as the seeds and plantlings of poor and uncultivated stock will produce trees and leguminous plants that are also poor and uncultivated?

Surely Theognis [1.183–92] was not being foolish when he indignantly complained that we bear these principles in mind for all living things except human beings, but that, when it comes to humankind, we ignore them and think they make no sense. We think that the son of a cook, perhaps, or of a baker, someone brought up on fetters and hard knuckles, can reach the majestic and high-minded level of philosophy. We are ignorant of the fact that such a person's soul is thoroughly smeared with the baseness and slavishness of the seed from which he sprang [249], that that seed does not allow him to see anything pure and unadulterated beyond his roots. No, the seed that produced him draws him to his original nature. It knows how to turn him in that direction. He is like sinuous branches: you can never make them straight by softening them with your hands and bending them into shape, for they take on again the twisted shapes that are innately theirs.[15]

14. "You have many . . . from the best ones?": cf. Pl., *Rep.* 5.459a. "a vulpine": ἀλωπεκίς, thought to be a hybrid between a dog and a fox. Cf. Them., *Orat.* 27.335d with n. 9 to my translation. "a Maltese": see Strabo 6.2.11 [277]; but Callimachus, and others, thought that this dog came, not from Malta, but from the island in the Adriatric Sea that had the same Greek name, Μελίτη (Call., fr. 579 Pfeiffer, with the editor's note). "by Demeter and Dionysus": appropriately here, Themistius swears by the grain goddess and the god of wine.

15. "brought up on . . . hard knuckles": like the sausage-seller in Aristoph., *Eq.* 411, 1236. "pure and unadulterated": cf. Pl., *Phileb.* 52d, 59c; *Symp.* 211e. "like sinuous branches" etc.: cf. Pl., *Theaet.* 173a (?), and see Kertsch, *VChr* 30 (1976): 241–57.

It is really inevitable, because of the milieu in which he was raised, that such a person will turn his eyes downwards, in the direction of servile employments. For the slavery that has been his since childhood has cut him off from higher, upright, and free-spirited work. It compels him to desire the clandestine, the deceitful, and what is shrouded in darkness, because that is what accords with his character. Such people are always ready to act as they do, and they are shrewd, for they learned and practiced in their childhood how to flatter their master by what they said and win his favor by what they did, and how to slander their fellow slaves and drive them from the house. They suffer their condition because their useless cunning has bent and twisted them all out of shape: whether they lower or raise their eyebrows, they abase themselves before the expedient and are disdainful of gods and men. Thus, such individuals, raised in an uninterruptedly servile manner, have in themselves a hatred that is hard to wash away, an immutable hatred; and for this reason they are readily filled with malice and ill will towards anyone at all.[16] There could never be another human condition worse than this one or more alien to philosophy.

The people of Elis and Pisa honor the Olympic wild olive so much that they do not permit anyone to strip for the games unless he can prove who his father and mother are and show that he sprang up from an undefiled root. They demand this proof even though it was a contest of physical strength that they established. In such a contest it would be enough to ensure that the participants have strong and well-built bodies. Yet they would never have allowed the famous Philammon to roll around in the dust by the banks of the Alpheus if Aristotle had not vouched for his lineage and adopted him.[17] Now isn't it disgraceful that the people of Elis and Pisa are so minded about a contest of physical strength, while we will admit anyone at all to the contest of virtue? We will very carefully inspect a person and meticulously examine him to make sure that he is not in any way maimed or in less than perfect shape, without having first stripped his soul bare of the cover-

16. "servile employments": cf. Pl., *Theaet.* 175e. "For the slavery . . . free-spirited work": cf. ibid. 173a. "Such people are . . . what they did": cf. ibid. "hard to wash away . . . immutable": cf. Pl., *Rep.* 2.378d. "filled with malice and ill will": cf. ibid. 6.500c.

17. An Olympic victor was crowned with a wreath of wild olive. One had to be Greek and free-born to compete in the Olympic Games. See J. Wiesner, "Olympia," *RE,* 18, 1 (1939): 6, 31–33. Philammon was an Olympic victor (Aeschin. 3.189; Dem. 18.319). So far as I know, no other extant ancient text sheds light on any connection Aristotle may have had with him. (The scholion 429a Dilts to Aeschines, loc. cit., is irrelevant; see Schaefer, *Jahrbücher für classische Philologie* 93 [1866]: 29.)

ings that have been put on it [250]! I understand that, in addition to the other ways in which the Lacedaemonians dishonor Lycurgus, they lead up to the altar of [Artemis] Orthia both slaves and free men indiscriminately—a helot, if he should happen to be at hand, along with a Eurypontid or an Agiad. Or maybe this is not improper after all; for they do have the ordeal of flagellation and the crown.[18]

I must now provide a means by which one could factually demonstrate what I am contending: you would find, if you investigate their forebears, that all those who are most distinguished in philosophy are, to use Homer's words, "fostered by" and "sprung from Zeus," and that the proverbial saying involving Codrus can be applied to all of them—just as, I think, by tracing and exposing clear and pure streams we discover that they emanate from ancient sources.[19] Suppose, though, that someone should try to mislead us by adducing just one counterexample. In response, let us concede, if you will, that nature does produce individuals who are possessed of virtue even though they are blemished by the defect of ignoble ancestry; but let us also point out that such a combination of traits is not something that occurs easily.

We must now look for the remaining marks and features that absolutely must be stamped on the philosopher's mind, characteristics that are even more essential for him to have than an ivory shoulder is for the descendants of Pelops. What, then, does the all-wise Plato next say is an indication that souls are noble? I shall read to you from his own words, one passage after another, just as pleaders in court read from legal texts. "Let it be agreed that the philosophical disposition must have knowledge—not all knowledge, but the kind that can reveal

18. The Lacedaemonian helots can be thought of as state slaves (Jones, *Sparta,* 9). The Eurypontids and Agiads were the two royal houses of Sparta. Themistius feels that the Spartans dishonor their lawgiver Lycurgus by admitting anyone at all to Artemis Orthia's altar. But then he remembers the ritual flagellation of their youth, a ceremony that took place at the same goddess's altar. He means either that only the Spartiate elite could participate in the ceremony (Cic., *Tusc.* 5.27 [77]; Tertull., *Ad martyr.* 4; Simplic., *In Epictet. Enchirid.* 14.233, p. 266 Hadot; cf. Philostr., *Vita Apoll.* 6.20) or that the ceremony, a contest of endurance, allowed the acknowledgment of an elite of victors. For the "crowning" of the victors, cf. Nic. Damasc., *FGrH* 90 F 103z. For the flagellation ceremony, see e.g. Michell, *Sparta,* 175–77; Tigerstedt, *Legend of Sparta,* 2: 165–66 with n. 43 for bibliography; and now esp. Kennell, *Gymnasium of Virtue,* 70–83, 149–61.

19. "'fostered by . . . from Zeus'": διοτρεφεῖς καὶ διογενεῖς, frequently occurring epithets in Homer that imply kingliness or nobility. The proverbial saying involving the legendary Athenian king Codrus was "more noble than Codrus" or "older [ἀρχαιότερος, πρεσβύτερος] than Codrus" (see Scherling, "Kodros," *RE,* 11, 1 [1921]: 993–94; Bühler, *Zenobii proverbia,* 4: 80–85). The "ancient" (ἀρχαίων) sources of streams are implicitly noble (and therefore clear and pure); ἀρχαίων here is textually sound (see apparatus criticus of the Teubner edition).

eternal being, being that is not set a-wandering by the process of generation and of decay" [cf. Pl., *Rep.* 6.485a–b]. Listen to this lawgiver, then, as he prescribes the areas of knowledge that philosophers should passionately desire to master, and note that he does not permit them to mix and combine all areas of knowledge together into one Myconus. For he showed that one man cannot perform well in many areas of competence.[20] The metalworker, for example, cannot make a good pair of shoes, nor can the shoemaker work metal well. If some weavers or vine-dressers are brought together to build a house, the house that they have built, Plato would say, is most likely to prove defective, not the one built by an architect; and if a woman who is skilled in music but ignorant of weaving has woven a garment, that is the garment that will annoy seamstresses.[21] A helmsman, Plato would insist, will not be both a common sailor and a helmsman at one and the same time, nor will a physician be simultaneously an athletic trainer and a physician [251]. The former must supervise and direct the rowers but not be a rower, the latter must supervise and direct gymnastic trainers but not be one. So too, I think, philosophers should supervise certain teachers (rhetors, for example, and grammarians) and what they teach but should not themselves do the work of rhetors or grammarians. For it would really be quite ridiculous for someone who lays claim to pure and incorporeal Being and is contemptuous of the merely human to devote himself to syllables, to spend his life mastering verbal contractions and elisions and planing down phrases. Yes, it would be ridiculous for such a person to give young students a thrashing, to bear down on their wretched pedagogues, to be filled with arrogance and proudly to exalt himself because of his exercise of such power. The true philosopher, the wings of whose soul are in excellent condition, could hardly endure even the sight of stakes and whips. For do you think that, if a person were able to do both something better and something baser, he would give himself over to the pursuit of the baser? Do you think that he would give up the better and put the baser in the very forefront of his life?[22]

20. For the mythological Pelops's ivory shoulder (Pind., *Ol.* 1.27; Dio Chrys., *Orat.* 7 [8].28) as a mark of his descendants, cf. Greg. Naz., *Orat.* 4.70; Them., *Orat.* 6.77b. The proverbial expression involving the Cycladic island Myconus was applied to the indiscriminate bringing together of diverse entities (Bühler, *Zenobii proverbia,* 4: 183–89). "one man cannot . . . of competence": Pl., *Rep.* 2.374a.

21. Because it will need frequent mending.

22. "grammarians": the word is *γραμματισταῖς*, on which see Kaster, *Guardians of Language,* 447. For the student's slave pedagogue, see Walden, *Universities of Ancient*

Whenever you see someone who prides himself on his prominence and distinction as a philosopher but is absorbed in the [base] activities I was just speaking of, someone who persists in such activities and never gives them up, not even in the face of dire necessity, know well, gentlemen, that such a person is deceiving you; he plays the part of an Agamemnon, but inside he is a Mithaecus or a Thearion. Do not go along with him. Do not be taken in by his small repertoire of clever sayings. He takes those same sayings around with him everywhere, and they do not even belong to him. He has stolen them, taken them from someone else and then altered them, just as Autolycus altered what he stole. He is proud and self-satisfied before audiences that do not know who the real author of his clever sayings is.[23]

Inform yourselves about such a person, questioning him in the following way. Sir, you should say, since you claim to be a philosopher of the highest order, we would like you, of course, to make this bounteous blessing of yours available to us in our own city. Now if we saw you practicing medicine, it surely would not have made sense for us to refer the members of our households, our women and children, to you [252] unless you had first shown us that you had made many sick people well and had restored many lame people to a sound condition. We also would have wanted you to show us medicines that you had compounded skillfully and effectively and potions similarly prepared, and to let us see that you had some pupils who would eventually take over your practice. For these are the actions and evidences of the practice of medicine, and knowledge in any field is judged on the basis of such actions and evidences.

So first tell us now, my good man, about some action of your own along these lines, some one of those many kinds of action that are characteristic of a philosopher. When have you made clear that you cannot be bought by an offer of money, as did the famous Xenocrates when Alexander [the Great] offered him fifty talents? When have you forgiven a debtor, as Zeno of Citium did? What sort of verbal abuse

---

Greece, 327n. "to be filled with arrogance . . . of such power": cf. Pl., *Rep.* 6.494d. "stakes and whips": i.e., stakes (*παττάλους*) or posts to which students being whipped would be tied? Cf. Dion. Hal., *Ant. Rom.* 20.16.2. "For do you think . . . of his life?": cf. Pl., *Rep.* 10.599a.

23. "dire necessity": "dire" is literally *Διομήδεια*(*per conj.*); for this proverbial expression, cf. Pl., *Rep.* 6.493d, with Adam's note. "Agamemnon . . . Thearion": i.e., he plays a royal role, but is actually a slavish caterer to base appetites. The reference is to Pl., *Gorg.* 518b; Mithaecus was the author of a cookbook and Thearion a baker. On Autolycus, see Them., *Orat.* 29.344a, with n. 1 to my translation.

have you endured, like that which Socrates endured from Thrasymachus? When have you refused a monetary token of appreciation from public officials, as Theophrastus did from [Demetrius] of Phalerum? Maybe you have never done any of these things. Well, then, do you scorn pleasures, have you refused to lay out money for prostitutes, have you avoided the enticements of courtesans, have you refused to blur the distinction between sons and household slaves?[24] Or have you written any long or short books—and how many books there are that give evidence of the wisdom of the philosophers [who wrote them], both ancient philosophers and those of recent times!—have you written any books, I say, on virtue and vice, on the nature of things, or on the difference between truth and falsity? No? Well what, then, by the Muses? If you have not written anything, have you at least trained some pupils, four or three or two or even one, someone who credits you for what he knows about philosophy?

If a person has difficulty pointing to and showing you all or any of these signs [of the true philosopher] and can only keep repeating [his repertoire of sayings] like a babbler or a barking dog, do not marvel at him any longer. Do not believe that he is Zeus's son Hermes[25] who, having left his father and heaven and having clothed himself in bits of human flesh, is now wandering around in our city. Do not believe this even if he can tell you the titles of tens of thousands of books and the names of that many writers; for this is something that I think even philosophers' secretaries can do, and they know how to excel in wisdom no better than other slaves do.

Suppose that an individual spends some time with a philosopher who genuinely understands what he is doing, sitting at his side as he writes and reads. Imagine this individual then culling out a few sayings from the philosopher's writings and trying to glue and sew them all together. This collection of sayings would not at all resemble <what> the

24. Xenocrates: cf. Them., *Orat.* 2.26a; see, in addition to Diog. Laert. 4.8, the ancient testimonia collected and commented on in Isnardi Parente, *Senocrate-Ermodoro,* 65–68 (frs. 23–32), where however the Themistian passages have been overlooked. The ancient sources disagree on whether Xenocrates rejected the whole of Alexander's gift or kept a portion of it; they also differ on Alexander's motives in offering it. For Zeno's lending activities, see Sen., *De ben.* 4.39.1; Diog. Laert. 7.13. Socrates: see Pl., *Rep.* 1.336b–38d, 340d, 341a–c, 343a. Demetrius, a pupil of Theophrastus (Strabo 9.1.20 [398]; Diog. Laert. 5.75), was Macedonian governor of Athens, 317–307 B.C. On the action of Theophrastus reported by Themistius, see the comment of Colpi, *Die παιδεία,* 128, n. 213. "to blur . . . household slaves?": i.e., "to treat your sons like slaves" or vice versa.

25. Hermes *logios,* the god of *genuine* eloquence.

philosopher actually says [253]; it would be like those cloaks that beggars pin together from both unused and well-worn pieces of fabric. So if a person is madly ecstatic over such a collection of sayings [that he has scraped together], we should pity him for being a beggar and deranged. We should realize that we do not consider a person to be wealthy just because he struts around the agora wearing a gold ring and deliberately holding it out for everyone who meets him to see. Such a person's poverty is immediately apparent in how he cherishes and shows off his possession—since, of course, he has no other more valuable treasure at home. If he did, he would not be parading around with his ring in the vulgar manner in which he does so.

Why is it that men like him do not deceive us, that we do not call a person who cannot strike clear and varied postures a [pantomimic] dancer, that we do not call a person who does not know how to play the lyre a lyre-player—and yet we are persuaded that a person who is not wise is wise? The reason, I think, is that the sounds of music and the movements of [pantomimic] dance are appraised by our ears and eyes, and these sense organs are capable by themselves of distinguishing what pleases them from what rankles them in music and dance, but a person cannot judge wisdom unless he possesses it.

Now, since most of us have ears and eyes but not wisdom, that same guile that I was just alluding to takes full advantage of our ignorance. She sees that a more learned kind of Greek is foreign to us. So she gathers up some nice little antiquated words, words that are obscure because of their age, and deafens us with them. She threatens us with the odd *πευθήν* ["inquisitor"] and *ἀμυντήριον* ["bulwark"] and other such terrors, with the result that those who hear her speaking shudder and are distressed and almost become speechless, as they say happens to people who are seen by a wolf before [they see him].[26] If you do not understand what guile has said and consequently try to question her

26. "words that are obscure": Pl., *Theaet.* 180a. "She threatens us," etc.: the Teubner edition prints the transmitted text, *τὸν ἄτοπον πευθῆνα ἔπεισι καὶ τἀμυντήριον καὶ τοιαῦτα ἄττα μορμολυκεῖα*, which I believe is corrupt. I have adopted Gasda's correction of *ἔπεισι* to *ἐπισείει*("Kritische Bemerkungen," 7–8). I would also emend *τὸν* to *τὸ* [sc. *ὄνομα*]. Another possible emendation is *τὸ ἄτοπον πευθὴν ἔπεισι κτλ*("The odd word *πευθήν* occurs to her" etc.). What is odd about the two words adduced by Themistius is not apparent (*pace* Maisano, *Discorsi*, ad loc.). He himself seems to have used the word *πευθῆνας* (emended from *πεφθῆνας*) in *Orat.* 34 [XVII]. And if Themistius intends "odd" to mean "obscure because of their age," it should be noted that *πευθήν* is not attested before Arr., *Epict. Diss.* 2.23.10, and Lucian, *Phal.* 1.10, *Alex.* 23, 37. Gasda suggested that the two words in our text are intrusive explanatory glosses that ousted the original readings. For the belief about the wolf, see Gow on Theocr. 14.22.

about her utterances, you will be hit with another expression, one that is even more confounding. You will never accomplish anything, and neither will the fellow who is uttering this stuff. He will just keep merrily repeating his *δήπουθεν* ["doubtless"] and his *κἄπειτα* ["and thereupon"] and his invocations of the "pair" of Dioscuri [*τὼ Διοσκόρω*], and then he will run off in utter scorn of your ignorance and thickheadedness.[27] One who has not had the eye of his soul cleansed by the process of education is more easily fooled, I think, about these sophists, just as people who do not have very sharp vision are more easily fooled about the colors of things **[254]**.

Now if someone should come to the city claiming to be skilled in rhetoric, why is it, by Zeus, that it will not take many years for us to find out for certain whether he speaks the truth about his knowledge of rhetoric or is nothing but a deceiver and a fraud? The reason, I think, is that there are many among us who are steeped in this kind of learning; they can easily determine the truth about such a person and convince the rest of us that they are right. But when it comes to wisdom [i.e., philosophy], even though we do not yet possess it ourselves, we refuse to believe the critic who does possess it. We think that jealousy and resentment have caused him to treat like dirt, and spit upon, some self-styled philosopher whom we, because of the impression he has made on us, are almost carrying around on our shoulders. So far are we from understanding that no wise man would be so ill-disposed towards someone like himself! In any case, the mysteries [of Dionysus] do allow the wand-bearing devotee of the god to lead the way for the person who has not been lawfully initiated.[28]

Next my oration appropriately takes up another sign, [the presence or absence of which] is also quite a good gauge of "whether or not a soul is philosophical": "you will observe whether a soul" in its dealings with those who have a desire for learning "is social and gentle" or

27. "If you . . . try to question . . . neither will the fellow": cf. Pl., *Theaet.* 180a. In writing "neither will the fellow," which is patterned on "neither will the fellows" in the Platonic passage, Themistius shifts abruptly from guile personified to an individual motivated by guile. Themistius's false philosopher is fond of the Atticizing *δήπουθεν* (cf. Lucian, *Lexiph.* 21, *Rhet. praec.* 18; Moeris, *Lex.* s.v. *δήπουθεν*[p. 120 Pierson-Koch]) and of *κἄπειτα* (cf. Lucian, *Lexiph.* 21, where the similar *κᾆτα* is branded as another Atticist favorite), and he likes to invoke the Dioscuri (Castor and Pollux) in the Attic dual. "he will run off in utter scorn": cf. Pl., *Symp.* 181d?

28. "are almost carrying . . . shoulders": Pl., *Rep.* 10.600d. "So far are we . . . ill-disposed": cf. Pl., *Theaet.* 151d. The philosopher, Themistius says, would be well disposed towards a genuine fellow philosopher. "In any case" etc.: i.e., those ignorant of a subject should follow the lead of a person who is genuinely steeped in it. For the Bacchic wand (here *narthex*), see Dodds on Eur., *Bacch.* 113.

"unsocial and savage" [cf. Pl., *Rep.* 6.486b]. Now let us agree that metalworkers, carpenters, and, if you wish, poets and all other craftsmen are quarrelsome and hostile towards one another whenever any one of them gets up and speaks. They are rewarded for what they do, in some cases with money, in others with praise as well as with money; and the worsted craftsman simply cannot obtain as great a reward [as his more fortunate colleague]. So the craftsman who gets the lesser portion inevitably feels anger and irritation at fellow craftsmen who successfully carry off the greater portion. But the feelings of those who are genuinely and truly competing to understand Being and who keep this toilsome project alive in their souls [i.e., philosophers] are very different: these individuals are delighted, happy, and filled with joy in proportion to the number of partners and helpers they can get in their pursuit of the object of their passion. For they observe that, even in hunting, it is difficult for a single tracker to find his prey; it is easier to uncover an animal's lair if a group of hunters work together. So too in the hunt for truth, there is much that is hard to get access to, much that is shadowy and hard to ferret out if you go after it by yourself. One has to call in many fellow hunters and assistants in this quest [255], more than the number of men, the best of the Greeks in their day, who long ago were brought together against the boar that was destroying and devastating the Aetolian king's lands [Hom., *Il.* 9.529 ff.]. It is true that, once the beast was caught, the huntsmen began to fight and contend over its best parts, and, as a result, war broke out between the Acarnanians and the Aetolians "over the head and shaggy hide of a boar" [Hom., *Il.* 9.548]. In philosophy, however, once the truth has appeared and shone forth, all who have assisted in the task of discovering it enjoy it with no bloodshed.[29]

This is why Ariston welcomed Cleanthes and shared his pupils with him, this is why Crates welcomed Crantor, and this is why Speusippus sent for Xenocrates from Chalcedon. Lycon and Ariston of the Lyceum were both devoted to the teachings of Aristotle. It was Lycon, however, who had a reputation for great learning, so much so that, because of that fame, his enemies at sea kept their hands off of his ships, as if they were sacred objects. Yet Lycon was not unfriendly to this Ariston, nor

29. "Now let us agree . . . and speaks": cf. Hes., *Op.* 25–26. "those who are . . . competing . . . Being": cf. Pl., *Rep.* 6.490a. "this toilsome . . . souls": cf. Pl., *Epp.* 2.313a. "even in hunting. . . .": cf. Pl., *Rep.* 4.432b–d; Them., *Orat.* 1.3b. "the Acarnanians and the Aetolians": Homer has "the Curetes and the Aetolians." For the Curetes as Acarnanians, cf. Strabo 10.3.1 [462] ff., Pausan. 8.24.9.

was he irritated by the fact that Ariston, because of his perseverance [in his studies], was overtaking him. Instead, he agreed, with good humor and graciously, that "the cripple is outrunning the man whose limbs are healthy." (Ariston happened to be lame in one leg.)[30]

So too the Muses, although they are nine in number, join with one another and with Apollo in a united chorus. None of them gets angry at the others over the fact that she does not have a monopoly on wisdom and is not the exclusive recipient of the poets' invocations. Calliope does not lay personal claim to the *cithara,* nor Thalia to the flute, nor Terpsichore to the *lyra.* Rather, each of the Muses is content to make her own donation and contribution to the whole chorus. The Muses sing in response to one another, says the poet [Hom., *Il.* 1.604, *Od.* 24.60]; they do not impede or malign each other or shout one another down.[31]

But aren't these men [of ill will] counterfeits who have wrongly been given the title "philosopher"?[32] If a person is emulously engaged with Aristotle and Theophrastus on a couch in his room and there succumbs to their charms, having nothing else to be inquisitive about, isn't this something these men have managed to learn about very quickly? Don't they then get the whole city stirred up about it, and call in the king's eyes to find out if the fellow still breathes and beholds the sun—this murderer and sinner and parricide and poisoner **[256]**? And the most serious accusation they bring against such a person, as he tells us, is that he applied himself to the categories and discussed what is "in a subject" with some foreigner. If he should turn his attention to

30. Themistius adduces four pairs of philosophers. They are, in his order of presentation, two Stoics, two Academics, two more Academics, and two Peripatetics. The Stoic Ariston was from Chios, the Peripatetic Ariston from Ceos. Crates and Crantor were messmates (Diog. Laert. 4.22). On Speusippus and Xenocrates, see Isnardi Parente, *Speusippo,* fr. 20 with her comment; Tarán, *Speusippus of Athens,* T11 with his comment. On Lycon and Ariston "of the Lyceum," one of the individuals to whom Lycon bequeathed the Peripatos and one of the witnesses to his will (Diog. Laert. 5.70, 74), see Capelle, "Lykon 14," *RE,* 13, 2 (1927): 2307–8; Wehrli, *Die Schule des Aristoteles,* 6: 22–23 (on Lycon fr. 9).

31. For the harmony and cooperation of the Muses, cf. Plut., *De frat. am.* 480e; Iambl., *Vita Pyth.* 9 [45]; Synes., *Dio* 4.42c–d Terzaghi. For *cithara* and *lyra,* both words commonly translated as "lyre," see Maas and Snyder, *Stringed Instruments.* The ancient sources are not in accord in assigning instruments to individual Muses: Roscher, *Ausführl. Lex.* 2:2 (1894–97): 3293–95, 5 (1916–24) 389–90; M. Mayer, "Musai 1," *RE,* 16, 1 (1933): 725–30.

32. I reject Jacobs's *οὐχ οἱ παράξενοι* and restore the transmitted *οὐχὶ παράξενοι,* putting a question mark after *ψευδώνυμοι.* After Oppermann, I also put question marks at the end of the first three sentences. The counterfeit philosophers do not necessarily include Christians (*pace* Schlange-Schöningen, *Kaisertum und Bildungswesen,* 74).

syllogistic argument and write something on nature, why, this would be an act of rebellion! The acropolis would have to be delivered from this tyranny![33]

Now if you lay any claim to the truth or to wisdom and really have something in common with Plato or Socrates or Pythagoras, you should not injure or destroy a person who shares their enthusiasms; rather you should honor and exalt him, you should help to encourage him and to urge him on. Whenever such a person has someone to praise and applaud him, someone before whom he will feel honored because of his labors, he is most likely to make progress, not to lose his edge, and not to turn away from what he passionately desires.[34] But as things are now, you seem to be trying to ensure, through extraordinary efforts, that you do not, by praising someone else, appear to be withdrawing your own claim to wisdom for his sake. You apparently want to avoid admiring some other person yourself so that you do not prepare the way for him to be admired by yet someone else. The consequence you fear is that people may stop looking to and admiring you alone. So, whenever you see that someone is a laughingstock and completely off the mark, you are kind and benevolent to him and do not hesitate to marvel at his wisdom both privately and publicly. But whenever people admire someone [who deserves admiration]—and deep in your heart your own sentiments are the same as theirs—on those occasions, ill will swells up in you, a cloud covers your face, and you look with hostility both upon the man who is praised and upon those who are praising him. Surely you know that the soul does not generate any other disease that is more serious than envy and jealousy; and the more intently someone afflicted by this disease gazes not only at what is at hand and in his vicinity, but also at what is distant and far removed from himself, the more envious he becomes.

33. The "person ... engaged with Aristotle and Theophrastus" is, of course, Themistius himself. "to be inquisitive about" (περιεργάζεσθαι): it is the counterfeit philosophers, of course, who have much else to be "inquisitive" about (i.e., they are meddlesome). "the king's eyes": the Persian king's informers were so called (Xen., *Cyropaed.* 8.2.10–12). "discussed ... with some foreigner": apparently a reference to some incident in Themistius's life about which we know nothing more. "what is 'in a subject'" (ἐν ὑποκειμένῳ): cf. Arist., *Cat.* 1a–3a *passim.* For an acropolis (in Latin, *arx*) as the seat of tyranny, see Mayor on Juv. 10.307. Themistius wrote a (lost) commentary on or "paraphrase" of Aristotle's *Categories* (see Them., *In Arist. Phys. 1* 2.110, p. 4 Schenkl). He wrote "on nature" in his extant paraphrase of Aristotle's *Physics.* The reference here to "his attention to syllogistic argument" has been taken as evidence of a now lost Themistian commentary on Aristotle's *Prior Analytics.* (His commentary on the *Posterior Analytics* is extant.)

34. "to make progress ... desires": cf. Pl., *Rep.* 6.490b.

I used to pay heed to what the poet Hesiod says, that a potter harbors a grudge against a fellow potter and an ovenworker against a fellow ovenworker [cf. Hes., *Op.* 25–26]. But now some [footsoldiers] are boldly leaving their ranks and are engaging with men on horseback.[35] Restore them to their original positions; do not allow those who are exposed and on foot to fight against men who are mounted and well protected [257]. But if they do passionately desire to engage in serious combat, they should lay down their hide shields and their skin helmets and all that useless equipment and take up a genuine shield, the kind of shield that Homer says belonged to Nestor—unassailable, made of gold and fitted with staves [*Il.* 8.192–93]. Or they should take up the kind of shield that Hephaestus fashioned for Achilles. On it were depicted the earth, the ocean and the heavens; the great sun and, opposite it, the moon, and all the other heavenly bodies; and also human affairs—people fighting, farming, dancing, marrying, tending flocks, pleading their causes [Hom., *Il.* 18.478 ff.].[36]

You do see, however, that it is not for every man to carry such a great shield, any more than it is for every man, for example, to sail to Corinth.[37] Carrying such a shield is something to be done by the son of Peleus, the descendant of Aeacus, the one reared by the wise Chiron [i.e., Achilles]. Suppose that a man who has deserted his own station and is not strong enough to bear the arms he has taken up still ambitiously tries to bear them. When he first appears on the battlefield, he does startle and confuse the enemy, and in the confusion some of them do fall upon one another. But after the battle has reached its peak and the fighting then subsides, his limitations are revealed, and he is stripped of the defensive arms that do not belong to him. Because of these and even worse misfortunes that may ensue, we must reject and guard against feelings of envy. If you find that a person is assaulted by this plague, then drive him away and expel him from sacred places, as if he had a disease even more terrible than leprosy.

Plato says that the fourth mark [of the true philosopher] is "the absence of falsehood, the determination to hate what is false and never

35. I give what I judge to be the approximate required sense of a corrupt sentence; see Petavius's note ad loc. in Dindorf's edition. Counterfeit philosophers who attack their betters are like foot soldiers engaging with cavalrymen against whom they are unequipped to fight.

36. For Achilles's shield, cf. Them., *Orat.* 22.266a–b.

37. The saying that it is not for every man to sail to Corinth was proverbial. The sense is that not everyone has the resources required in a given situation. Cf. Hor., *Epp.* 1.17.36, with scholia; Strabo 8.6.20 [378]; Aul. Gell. 1.8.4; *CPG* 1.135, 289 and 2.591.

under any circumstances to embrace it, and love of the truth" [*Rep.* 6.485c]. Here too, then, I marvel at the wall our legislator [Plato] builds around a wisdom that is faithful to the truth in every respect. Let us take up this fourth mark of the philosopher and spend some time analyzing it.

One finds, no doubt, much truth and also much falsity in the various fields of learning, just as one does in business dealings and transactions. Now surely it is hard to believe—don't you agree?—that a person who does not let falsehood in under any circumstances would make partial concessions to it. Surely such a person, while speaking truthfully about even and odd numbers and, let us say, about the sides and diameters of geometrical figures, does not act fraudulently when it comes to buying or selling or other such transactions involving business partners. Such a person does not deceive his business partners, does he [258]? Surely he does not agree in writing to pay one hundred minas for something and then cheat the seller of twenty-five, does he? Consider, though, that, in the various fields of learning, falsity harms only the person who is making the false statement, whereas in this matter of deceit in business dealings something else is also going on: an injustice is being done to another person. What difference does it make to us, by the gods, if someone deceives himself with the pronouncement that Aristotle says that things that are "in a place" are not each in some [one] place, or with the assertion that Plato requires punishments inflicted on individuals to be visited on their descendants too, down to the fourth generation, or with any other such nonsense?[38] These deceptions, my good men, have no effect on us, unless we send our children to study under a person so deceived. On the other hand, if a person swears to have heard what he never heard, and if he should violate his oaths more readily than the Spartan Lysander[39] and always misrepresents what he is really thinking, shall we assert that his deceptions harm only schoolboys—or that they now harm all who, since they belong to the same community as this deceiver, necessarily talk to or engage in action with him?

38. Aristotle *would* say that a thing that is "in a place" must be "somewhere" or "in some [one] place": Arist., *Phys.* 206a1 ff.; Them., *In Arist. Phys. III* 5, p. 91 Schenkl. For Plato's general opposition to inherited punishment, see Pl., *Laws* 9.856c–d, with Morrow, *Plato's Cretan City*, 466–67.

39. It was said that the policy of this commander and statesman of the fifth and opening years of the fourth centuries was "to cheat boys with dice and men with oaths" (Diod. Sic. 10.9.1; Plut., *Lysand.* 8.5; Polyaen., *Strateg.* 1.45.3; Ael., *Var. hist.* 7.12).

No vice, you know, has a worse effect on the human community than untrustworthiness. It is the only evil against which we lack the means to protect ourselves. For our deceiver makes an utter mockery of the only protective device we have contrived against it—I mean swearing an oath and invoking the gods. He behaves in this manner so that he may more easily avoid having his fraud detected. Whenever an untrustworthy man has done some evil and then must deny it, the water of the Styx is a joke to him, as is the Styx itself, and neither the gods of Tartarus nor Tartarus itself means a thing to him.[40] Because of this duplicity, human beings are harder to manage and wilder than beasts. We hear the poets complaining that:

If a hunter hears and sees a snake or lion
In the mountains, he can steer clear of the beast;
For he knows the designs of those animals,
And he knows what they are thinking.
But a man keeps one thing concealed in his mind and says another.
His words are soothing and gentle,[41]

but he and his fellows plot "hostile actions" against other human beings while they live together with those others in a single community and say flattering things to them. The license to say whatever one wants is a terrible thing. It is terrible, too, how brazenly a man will stand by all the sly written agreements he concocted right in the middle of the agora and in the presence of both Greek and non-Greek witnesses [259]. This malicious deceit must be completely driven out of a philosophical soul.

There is another kind of deception, one that is not really injurious to others but does bring disgrace upon the individual who engages in it. It is found not in something one says or does to the detriment of another person, but in something one says about himself and his own condition. It comes in two forms, which can be distinguished from one another: one encounters it when a person represents what is truly his as less and of lesser value, or as more and of greater import, than it actually is. The understating is called self-depreciation [εἰρωνεία], and the overstating is called false pretension [ἀλαζονεία].[42]

Underrepresenting the truth is a clever and tricky device, and there are times when it is useful to the philosopher. That is why even Socrates

40. I.e., he is not deterred by fear of punishment in the underworld.

41. The author of these hexametrical verses cannot be identified, but cf. Hom., *Il.* 9.312–13. The words "hostile actions," which I incorporate into the prose text, actually belong to the last verse.

42. The terms and definitions come from Arist., *Eth. Nic.* 2.7 [1108a22].

would employ <it in> his conversations when he had to make fun of a sophist who was full of conceit and brimming over with madness.[43] For such men become more aware of their own worthlessness when they are shown to know less than the person who is feigning ignorance.

The other kind of deception, overrepresenting the truth, is annoying and offensive. There is nothing harder to tolerate than hearing a person praise himself, especially if he praises his own learning; for those who are truly learned cannot help blushing even when others praise them on that score. It is also difficult to be in the company of a businessman who wants to do nothing but sing the praises of his own wealth, of his goblets and drinking horns [*rhyta*], of his purple garments and his gold. A braggart soldier, too, the kind who appears in comedy, would test your patience.[44] But nothing gives you such a bloated feeling and makes you so very nauseous as the person who admires—and admires to excess—his own cleverness and sharpness of mind, who marvels at how easily he learns, at how much he has learned, and at how good his memory is. No, there is nothing more sickening than someone who is a living catalogue of the many works of Aristotle and Plato, who plays this role constantly and on every occasion, whether you invite him to go to the baths with you, or take him to dinner, or ask him something about Aeschylus, or inquire about the nature of the lyric poet Simonides's island [i.e., Ceos]. It is impossible to address such individuals without having this sick feeling to which I was just alluding. As soon as they open their mouths, Dodona's bronze resounds. They will tell you about the two affirmative premises and explain that [a syllogism of] the second figure with such premises is not valid.[45]

43. Themistius himself is "underrepresenting the truth" in this oration in denying that he merits the title "philosopher." For Socrates's famous *εἰρωνεία* cf., e.g., Pl., *Rep.* 1.337a; Cic., *Acad.* 2.5 [15]. "madness": I read *παραφροσύνης* (cf. Pl., *Soph.* 228d) with Oppermann instead of *περισσοφροσύνης* with the Teubner edition.

44. "There is nothing harder . . . on that score": cf. Dem., 18.128. For the braggart soldier as a comic type, see Legrand, *New Greek Comedy,* 95–97; Webster, *Studies in Later Greek Comedy,* 64.

45. "Dodona's bronze": the resounding bronze of the shrine of Zeus at Dodona was proverbial for loquacity; see Cook, *JHS* 22 (1902): 5–6. "They will tell you" etc.: I accept the transmitted text (*αἱ δύο καταφάσεις* [sc., *ὑπηχοῦσι*], *καὶ ὅτι οὐ συνάγει οὕτω τὸ δεύτερον σχῆμα*), as does Maisano, *Discorsi,* ad loc. Oppermann misunderstood and corrupted the passage through his conjectural emendation of *ὅτι οὐ* to *ὁτιοῦν*. He translates: "die Verdoppelung der Aussage, und jedwedes führt so den zweiten Ausdruck herbei." The Teubner text adopted Oppermann's emendation. Themistius's braggart is showing off his knowledge of Aristotelian logic. Cf., e.g., Alex. Aphrodis., *In Arist. Analyt. prior. I* 6, p. 95 Wallies, *ἴδιον γὰρ τοῦ δευτέρου* [sc.,*σχήματος*] *τὸ ἐκ δύο καταφατικῶν μηδὲν συνάγειν*; [Them.], *In Arist. Analyt. prior. I* 17, p. 50 Wallies; Kneale and Kneale, *Development of Logic,* 74.

"We certainly cannot admit [into the ranks of true philosophers] the man who takes bribes or the lover of" gain and "money" [260], otherwise all the desires of his soul will be diverted from learning to profit, like a stream diverted downhill [cf. Pl., *Rep.* 3.390d, 6.485d]. Whatever men rightfully inherit from their fathers they must take care of and "safeguard, thereby acquiring the habit of serving philosophy" [Pl., *Rep.* 6.498b]. They should not work to make money themselves, nor should they welcome into their houses a person who is ready for and brimming over with the marketplace. For it is contrary to nature that springs that flow from the marketplace be pure and just, since open channels have not been dug for them with a spade or fork; rather, their waters are collected as they emerge from gloomy and pestilential passageways after flowing underground and in darkness.

If we adhere to this rule [i.e., that lovers of gain cannot be given our approval], we shall not allow those who claim to be philosophers to prepare legal briefs and, having shut down the schools, to strut around on the speaker's platform, sparring with and railing at rhetors and soldiers alike.[46] We shall not allow them to subject themselves to all the many things to which men who are engaged in these activities all day and night in the courts are subjected—men who, when their clients decide on a peaceful [out-of-court] settlement, sometimes demand a fee for future services! We shall hardly permit would-be philosophers to turn these schools of ours into law courts, to turn the shrines of the Muses into a place where justice is sold, and to blur the difference between pupils and people pleading causes. We cannot allow them to fail to be put to shame by the fact that even the Persians had a law that set off the tumultuous marketplace from areas fit for free men![47]

We shall not allow men who claim to be philosophers to build a house for which they have hired neither metalworkers nor carpenters nor architects; [there can be no building projects in which,]

> Instead, everything springs up with no sowing and plowing,
> Bronze and gold and iron laboriously wrought.[48]

We shall not allow such men to cause craftsmen to suffer from hunger or to turn painters away because the latter do not paint free of charge.

46. The word "soldiers" (στρατιώταις) could also be translated as "civil servants." See Lampe, *Patristic Greek Lex.*, s.v.; MacMullen, *Soldier and Civilian,* 49–50, 159–60, 164.

47. For the Persian law, see Xen., *Cyropaed.* 1.2.3.

48. The next sentence makes the point clearer: philosophers should not be so attached to their money that they refuse to employ craftsmen. The quotation is a conflation of Hom., *Od.* 9.109, with a recurring Homeric line (e.g., *Il.* 6.48).

We shall not let would-be philosophers accept a piece of land as a gift from someone only to fight with the donor over its boundaries. Nor shall we let them measure out a *kyathos* and call it an *amphoreus,* thereby constantly defrauding their neighbors. They say that the Carthaginians once did something of this sort [261]. Having asked the Libyans for a piece of land equal in measure to an oxhide, they proceeded to cut the hide into a [long], narrow strip and to turn the gift of land into something much larger [than had been intended]. The Carthaginians still call that area of Carthage "Oxhide," chuckling at the irony of how the smallness of what is normally designated by the term "oxhide" contrasts with the size of the piece of land so named.[49]

My friends, if our "philosopher" zealously endorses such acts of acquisitiveness and contends with his neighbors over a single clod of soil, when will his vision be able to encompass the whole earth? When will he be able to open his eyes up to the earth in its entirety? When will our "philosopher," if he does such terribly bad things <for the sake of> three or four cubits of land, understand that the whole earth itself, along with the ocean, is a small thing? All this unmanly behavior to which I have been alluding is the mark of a small and servile soul, of a soul that gives undue honor to this purple dye of ours and to all the other things that [lovers of gain] pride themselves on in their cleverness, cunning, and deceit: how they get as high a price as possible [when they sell]; how they pay as little as they can [when they buy]; how they rob people of all they have; how, to escape paying what they owe to people who have sold them something, they restrain them in nets from which there is no escape![50]

If pupils, caught like fish by a few [animal] hairs, should come to study under someone who is so in love with money, they will end up even more speechless than fish, but this teacher of speechlessness will

49. "*kyathos . . . amphoreus*": an absurdly hyperbolic example of fraud. The *kyathos* is .045 of a liter. The *amphoreus,* if it is the Attic μετρητής, is ca. 39 liters; even if it is the lesser Roman *amphora,* it will amount to ca. 26 liters. See Hultsch, *Griechische und römische Metrologie,* 101, 703, 704; Nissen, "Griechische und römische Metrologie," 843–44, 868. For the Carthaginian ruse, cf. App., *Pun.* 1 [1]; Huss, *Klio* 64 (1982): 403. The area referred to is Byrsa, also the Greek word for oxhide. The Carthaginians used the long, narrow strip of oxhide that they had cut to measure off the perimeter of a large area instead of only claiming a piece of land equal in area to that of the uncut oxhide.

50. "to encompass the whole earth . . . the earth in its entirety": cf. Pl., *Theaet.* 174e. "this purple dye": cf. Themistius's allusion above (21.259c) to the businessman who boasts of his purple garments. For the transmitted κομψοῖς καὶ δεινοῖς καὶ πανούργοις, I read Oppermann's conjecture κομψοί τε καὶ δεινοὶ καὶ πανοῦργοι ("in their cleverness, cunning and deceit").

still demand a fee from them. He will roar with indignation, shaking his aegis again and again. He will turn over the coins [his pupils give him,] examining both sides of them to make sure that they are not counterfeit or debased. He will tie down those unfortunate youngsters who often have difficulty paying his fee because they are poor or their parents are dead. Then, having put down his strap, he will lecture them on how all the gold on and under the earth does not equal the value of virtue. "For what is wealth?" he will ask. "It is something earthly and perishable." And maybe he will say these things while there are still some boys standing around whom he mercilessly made mincemeat of during his examination [of their money] because there was a speck of dirt on it![51]

This lover of gain will not understand that, if one's words do not accord with one's character, then they belong to someone else and not to the person who utters them. This was the case with Thersites when he spoke to the Achaeans about [some Trojan prisoner] "whom I may have bound and be leading off into captivity" [Hom., *Il.* 2.231 ff.]. For these words belonged to Achilles and Ajax. The hunchbacked Thersites represented as his own words that did not belong to him **[262]**.[52] Consequently, this "nobleman," this "speaker of lofty words," this "doer of brave deeds" weeps. The wisest of the Achaeans [i.e., Odysseus] whips him so that he will not babble and meddle in things and speak rashly,[53] so that he will not vent his hostility on the excellent Greek warriors and disrupt their assemblies.

But Thersites has opportunely slipped into my oration on his own, I know not from where, and has allowed it to move on without ado to another mark [of the true philosopher]: we shall not permit the follow-

51. "If pupils . . . a fee from them": cf. Pl., *Soph.* 221b–23b, for the sophist as angler (or hunter) who seeks a fee. "animal hairs": The reference is apparently to the fishing line or at least to a leader (cf. *Anth. Pal.* 6.23.7, 6.192.3; Plut., *Terrestr. an aquatil.* 976e–f; Opp., *Hal.* 3.75). "more speechless than fish": the word is normally ἀφωνότερος, not Themistius's ἀναυδότερος. Cf. Lucian, *Gall.* 1, *Adv. indoct.* 16; Galen 7.514 Kühn; Sext. Emp., *Adv. rhet.* 18; Didym. Caec., *De trin.* II 7.8.4 (p. 228 Seiler); Johan. Chrys., *Expos. in Psalm.* 8.2 (*PG* 55.108), *In Epist. ad Ephes.* 1.3.2 (*PG* 62.25). "teacher of speechlessness": cf. Them., *Orat.* 26.313c, "artificers of silence." "shaking his aegis": like a formidable Homeric god (*Il.* 4.167, 15.229). "having put down his strap" (ἀπὸ τοῦ ῥυτῆρος ἐξελθών): i.e., after whipping them. The teacher ties students down (προσπατταλεύων) to whip them; cf. Them., *Orat.* 21.251b, παττάλους τε καὶ ἱμάντας. Or does ἀπὸ τοῦ ῥυτῆρος ἐξελθών mean "once he has got going at full gallop"? See *LSJ*, s.v. ῥυτήρ (A) 2. "all the gold . . . value of virtue": Pl., *Laws* 5.728a; cf. Them., *Orat.* 27.340a.

52. I.e., Thersites did not have the character of one who would have succeeded at capturing Trojan prisoners.

53. The Greek word I represent as "speak rashly" (ἐπέσβολος) is from the Homeric passage (*Il.* 2.275).

ers of philosophers to be meddlesome and interfering slanderers. We shall require them, far more than everyone else, to learn and to be versed in those teachings found in Plato's works: for "whether anyone in the city is of low birth or has some evil trait that has been inherited from his ancestors, male or female—these are matters of which the true philosopher has no more knowledge than he does of the proverbial number of gallons of water in the ocean" [Pl., *Theaet.* 173d].[54]

Aesop the story-writer was a wise man. He said that every human being carries two sacks, one on his front side and one on his back. Each sack, he said, is full of vices; but the sack on one's front side is filled with the vices of others, whereas the sack on one's back is filled with the vices of the person carrying it. Consequently, human beings do not see their own vices, but they do get a very close look at those of others [Aesop, *Fab.* 229 Hausrath-Hunger]. Well, would that my sacks were reversed so that I would see only my own vices and be unable to see the vices of others! There is nothing sweeter, they say, than to know everything [about people]—yes, all the *good* things [about them]![55]

The information [on cookery] provided by the cook [Carion] in comedy was of no benefit to <the> person who heard it from him. In fact, [when it came to the actual act of cooking], Carion caused grief to the dinner guests by using the wrong spices. His great vice, though, was not that his cooking was bad or strange, but that he was not a well-meaning person. He went into people's houses <not> to do his job, but to gossip, to whisper things, and to slander people. He did not intend to carry out [valuables], as a roguish cook might well have done after concealing them in a basket. (Such a thief does deserve to be hanged, if it comes to that, for his consummate inquisitiveness.) No, our Carion's purpose was to carry out the family secrets. And he did not merely broadcast what he heard; he added many details [that he himself invented] and exaggerated the negative.[56]

54. Cf. Themistius's remarks on slander in *Orat.* 22.277c ff. "gallons": the Greek actually has χόες. The Attic χοῦς is 3.2–3.3 liters (Hultsch, *Griechische und römische Metrologie,* 703; Nissen, "Griechische und römische Metrologie," 843). For the proverbial thought, cf. Aristid., *Orat.* 3.18 [33] Dindorf; Basil, *Sermon. de mor.* 22.1 [*PG* 32.1365]; Liban., *Orat.* 11.126; Them., *Orat.* 7.97c.

55. The Greek for "there is nothing sweeter than to know everything" is a slight variant on Menand., *Epitrep.*, fr. 2 Sandbach.

56. Themistius is referring in this paragraph to Menander's lacunose *Epitrepontes,* from which he quotes at the end of the previous paragraph. There has been some disagreement over the constitution and interpretation of the Themistian text. See Wilamowitz, *Menander, "Das Schiedsgericht,"* 48–50; Gomme and Sandbach, *Menander: A Commentary,* 291–93; Masaracchia, *Helikon* 8 (1968): 364–69; Primmer, *Wiener Studien* 20 (1986): 123–41. "Consummate inquisitiveness" is what drives a thieving cook to ferret out the valuables in the house where he is employed.

So, my malicious and deranged Carion, you have heard that so-and-so offered some frankincense to the gods. Then say that he offered some frankincense [263]. This is all you heard. You did not hear that he offered them all-black bulls or castrated rams. Yet, after overpowering Plato with your witchcraft, you even give a full report on all the phantoms so-and-so has conjured up! Then, if you learn something good about a person, you are close-mouthed and more taciturn than an Areopagite; whereas, if you latch on to something bad about someone, you make a whole *Iliad* and *Odyssey* out of it.[57] In the latter case, much of what you say is not even information that you heard directly or indirectly; you invent it and make it up yourself.

Next, you get quite irritated at the person who has passed some information on to you. You refer to him as someone possessed by an evil spirit, as someone hateful to the gods. You claim that you do not believe him, you get angry at him and complain about him. Yet you pass on that unbelievable, abominable trash, which fully deserved to be the object of your anger. What is more, when you retell what he told you, you do so in a very dramatic way. You almost go as far as to fill the ears of cobblers and bath attendants with that stuff!

But as for that fellow "possessed by an evil spirit" and "hateful to the gods," that person at whom you are so angry and enraged—if someone asks and presses for information about him, you would be less likely to bring him out into the light of day than you would Priam's mother. Why? Because you *are* that person, I think; you are both playwright and actor in your dramas. Reluctant to contend for the dramatic prize unmasked, you have recourse to masks of anonymous characters, such as we find in tragedies whenever dramatic poets fail to come up with names for their characters. And often, after installing all the required theatrical machinery, you even bring gods and spirits [*daimones*] into the drama![58]

57. "you have heard," etc.: is the example random? Or is Themistius thinking of someone informing against a person for ignoring Constantine's and Constantius's prohibitions of sacrifice (*Cod. Theod.* 16.10.1–2, 4–6)? "all-black bulls" (*παμμέλανας ταύρους*): is Themistius thinking of Hom., *Od.* 3.6? "after overpowering Plato": Carion uses "magic" against Plato's criticism of slander. "more taciturn . . . Areopagite": a proverbial expression. Cf. Alciphr., *Epp.* 1.16 Schepers; *CPG* 1.181, 2.146; Wallace, *Areopagos,* 110–11.

58. "you have recourse" etc.: cf. Pl., *Cratyl.* 425d. The person Themistius berates is both playwright (inventor of slander) and actor (reporter of slander). But this person refuses to report slander on his own authority (unmasked) and instead appeals to anonymous sources. He is very theatrical in his reports, even bringing divine beings into them on figurative stage machinery.

By Zeus, calumny that originates in dreams is not any different from what I have just been talking about, is it? Sleep, which relaxes the limbs and subdues all, lulls other evildoers into a state of rest, it seems; but the slanderer's malice is actually incited by it. If a good dream, one that speaks well of someone, should stand by the slanderer's head, it is truly fleeting and passes through the gates of ivory. But for calumniating and defamatory dreams, it is the gates of horn that are thrown wide open. (It would be better to say not that defamatory dreams pass through or wish to pass through the gates of horn, but that slanderers themselves drag and lead them through.) At the break of dawn you will hear a slanderer, in his sullen and gloomy mood, say that during the night he was troubled by spirits, that [in his dream] he was walking along with such-and-such a person and had dinner with a wicked and sinful man who does this and that, and that he fears that the whole city will suffer some evil from this person. Now does such a person, whether awake or asleep, seem to you to be the type who could ever free himself from his mischievous and perverse manner and become the embodiment of proper standards **[264]**? Could he ever acquire a true harmony in his words and hymn the life of gods and men, just as Homer's Achilles sings after he has withdrawn from battle [Hom., *Il.* 9.189]—or I should say just as Homer himself does?[59]

For you all know, I am sure, that whatever Homer names, he also praises, that he does not regard even very ordinary things as undeserving of favorable mention. For Homer, sandals are "beautiful," and whips are all "radiant." He is all full of wonder at the tree that had sprouted up at Delos. In Homer's verses, even the good swineherd [Eumaeus] has some nice things said about him; in fact, the poet tries to convince you that the keeper of swine was a leader of men. It was Thersites alone, you see, whom Homer reproached. The reason he did so, I think, was that Thersites himself reproached people and was insolent and had many unseemly words in his repertoire and did not use them in a disciplined or appropriate way.[60]

59. "sleep, which relaxes . . . and subdues all": Themistius uses two Homeric epithets (cf. Hom., *Il.* 24.5, *Od.* 20.57). Dreams that pass through gates of ivory are unfulfilled, whereas those that pass through gates of horn find fulfillment (cf. Hom., *Od.* 19.560 ff.). "the whole city will suffer . . . person": cf. Hes., *Op.* 240. "and become the embodiment . . . gods and men": cf. Pl., *Theaet.* 175e–76a. The phrase I translate "become the embodiment of proper standards" literally refers to proper standards of dress.

60. "sandals": e.g., Hom., *Il.* 2.44. "whips": e.g., *Il.* 10.500. "the tree": *Od.* 6.162 ff. Eumaeus: e.g., *Od.* 14.2–4, 421, 437–41, 526–27. Eumaeus as "leader of men": e.g., *Od.* 14.22. For Homer's praise and Thersites's failure to receive it, cf. Dio Chrys. 16 (33).11.

ORATION 22

On Friendship

[264] Why is it, my good men, that, if someone tells you how the Trojans and Achaeans fought one another or gives an account of the assault that Xerxes launched across the Hellespont against Greece or tells of all the woes that Greeks had to endure from fellow Greeks because of civil strife, you enjoy these stories and are held spellbound by them? Why do you think that your sons should learn them, beginning with the wrath of Achilles? Why do you think that it is enough to teach them about Achilles's wrath, convinced that they will grow in wisdom if they learn about the wars and enmities of cities and individuals and about the misfortunes that resulted from such strife? How can you be so interested in conflict without ever having given thought to stories of friendship and to how much friendship benefits human beings? You do not want to learn about this yourselves, nor do you urge your children to learn about it. Yet the poet of strife himself [i.e., Homer] prays that strife may perish from among human beings; and no one would choose to live without friendship [265], even if he possessed all of life's other good things.[1] So let anyone who thinks that friendship is a thing of little worth know that he is worth very little himself. On the other hand, let anyone who believes that friendship is easy to come by listen to the words of Theognis [79–80]:

1. "the poet of strife prays": *Il.* 18.107. The sentiment is actually Achilles's. "no one would choose . . . good things": a slightly altered version of Arist., *Eth. Nic.* 8.1 [1155a5–6].

Few companions will you find, O son of Polypas,
Who can be relied upon when things get bad.

Why then do you fail to pay heed to what is said about friendship? Or is it the case that you do heed it? You are, after all, eager to listen; you gladly pay attention to every word spoken to you. But those who speak to you employ various modes of discourse. Some of them bring you together to praise you. Others practice their rhetorical skills before you. Others sing and sing again, pouring down upon you their sweet and delicate sounds. What you do not seem to me to have many opportunities to hear, however, are orations that can improve people's lives. This is no fault of yours; it is the fault of those so-called philosophers, who have assumed that it was enough for them to whisper their words to the young in some isolated corner. They thought, as Callicles put it in his criticism [of Socrates], that they could avoid the center of the city and those gathering places wherein the poet [Homer] says that men gain distinction [*Il.* 9.441]. Well, we must let those philosophers stay where they want to stay; it will be my duty to bring speech out into the light and to accustom it to tolerate the crowd and to put up with noise and with the clamor of the seated assembly. If speech is capable of benefiting people individually, it certainly will be able to benefit many individuals at once. For orations, one might say, are not like servings of food that are enough for one or two diners but cannot satisfy more than that number; rather they are more like the rays of the great god [the Sun], which shine down on thousands of eyes no less than on any two.[2]

But I must bring the argument back to the point at which I digressed from its forward course. It is certainly good for a lover of horses to be skilled at distinguishing horses of high quality from those of lesser quality and for a lover of gold to possess the touchstone by which gold is tested [**266**]. A person who has considered what makes cattle excellent will have better cattle himself; and if a seaman and a hunter have thought about what makes the best ship or the best dog, they will have, respectively, a better ship and better dogs. I myself am unaccomplished and unskilled in all such matters; I do not particularly like to pass judgment on such things and am unable to do so. But there is one thing of which I am a devotee, and that is true and sincere friendship. I

2. "those so-called philosophers . . . distinction": cf. Pl., *Gorg.* 485d, where Callicles is the speaker; Them., *Orat.* 28.341d. "orations . . . not like servings of food": cf. Them., *Orat.* 26.327a. "like the rays of . . . [the Sun]": cf. Them., *Orat.* 26.330d-31c.

would choose to have true friendship over a Nisaean horse, a Celtic hound, Darius's gold, the bull in Crete, and Achilles's shield. Yes, I would choose friendship over the shield that Homer described as having on it the whole of heaven, the sun and the moon, and, opposite the sun, the ocean and the earth, with people farming, marrying, pleading their causes and fighting. There is no question that that object was inferior to friendship—so much so that Achilles's grief over Patroclus was not a bit diminished when his mother got him that shield. He had given up one shield so that his friend might not be grieved, and then he refitted himself with that other marvelous one so that his friend might not go unavenged.[3]

Since I am so passionately devoted to acquiring friends, I have collected for myself many tests for genuine friendship and have been searching around in the hope of learning of someone who has the same passionate devotion to friendship that I do. And I see that you, leader of this chorus, do have the same zealous yearning for it that I have—so much so that, if friendship were not what we desired, I would have been jealous of you, just as one is of his rivals in love. As it is, men who desire a beautiful woman have decided which of them will love her through the shedding of blood, and the ambitious do not stop fighting with each other over the object of their ambition. How could we even begin to tell what sorts of warfare much-desired wealth presides over? Only lovers of friendship do not fight each other over what they seek to acquire; they straightway find the object of their yearning in one another.

Anyone who has acquired friends has done well, even if he is merely a private citizen. But the man who oversees many cities and much territory has an even greater blessing in friendship than does a private citizen [267]. Two ears, two eyes, one body, and the one soul that is in that body are quite meager for a person who must listen to and observe many things and attend to many matters simultaneously. But if he is rich in friends, he will see things happening far away, hear those

3. "the touchstone . . . tested": cf. Pl., *Gorg.* 486d? For the prized Nisaean horse, see my n. 9 on Median horses at Them., *Orat.* 27.335d. For Celtic hounds, prized as hunting dogs, see Keller, *Die antike Tierwelt,* 1: 101–3; Merlen, *De Canibus,* 49–51, 54–57. "the bull in Crete": presumably the Minotaur. Or could Themistius be thinking of the extraordinarily fine bull who fathered the Minotaur (Diod. Sic. 4.77.1–3; Apollod., *Bibl.* 3.1.3)? Achilles's shield: When Patroclus leads the Myrmidons into battle, Achilles lends him his armor (*Il.* 16.124 ff.). After Hector kills Patroclus and strips him of this armor, Achilles's mother Thetis gets her son new armor from Hephaestus. Themistius describes the new shield (*Il.* 18.478 ff.) at *Orat.* 21.257a–b as well as here.

who are not close to him, know the future just as seers do, and be in the presence of a number of individuals at once, just as the gods are.[4]

How, then, can one find this great good that friendship is? How, having found it, can one chase it down and, having done that, hold on to it firmly? Must we not, like hunters, be taught first of all to recognize the tracks of our prey? Must we not have a precise knowledge of its marks and signs and ponder over them? With their help we shall avoid unwittingly ending up at the edge of some precipitous cliff—as happens, I think, to those who are tracking down wild animals—instead of finding our most excellent prey. For you can be certain that in this hunt many wily beasts mimic blessed friendship; and it is the most scheming and savage beast, the one people nowadays call pretense [*ὑπόκρισις*], who especially does this. So great is pretense's villainous ability to mimic true friendship that one could repeatedly be deceived by her tracks all the way to her lair. But it is not enough for pretense to walk alongside of friendship; you might also hear her speak with a voice resembling friendship's voice, uttering sounds that have the seductive power to deceive you.[5]

It really does seem that every human good is overlaid with danger, that nothing is uncontaminated by its opposite. One of the poets of laughter rightly says that there is no good in life that springs up, like a tree, from a single root; evil always springs up along with good [Menander, fr. 337 Koerte]. This fact is what utterly destroys most people, for they are unable readily to pick out the better over the inferior. So let us all, me along with you, acknowledge our need of Homer's Athena, in the hope that somehow she will disperse this heavy mist from our eyes, so that we may be able to distinguish, not a god from a man in battle, but true friendship from feigned friendship.[6]

I must tell you, then, about all the various evidences of true friendship that are to be looked for in a person who is to be given the stamp of approval. For my oration says that, along with asking for Athena's assistance, it is also setting its own hand to the task [**268**].[7]

4. "Two ears, two eyes" etc.: cf. the virtually identical phraseology in Them., *Orat.* 1.17c; see also 15.196d. For the thought, cf. Arist., *Pol.* 3.16 [1287b30]; Xen., *Cyropaed.* 8.2.10–12; Dio Chrys., *Orat.* 1.32; Synes., *De regno* 11.11d–12a Terzaghi.

5. This oration will end with an allegory in which friendship and pretense are personified and contrasted (280a ff.).

6. "this heavy mist": cf. Them., *Orat.* 21.247d, with n. 13 to my translation.

7. "[A]long with asking . . . the task" is proverbial: *CPG* 1.157–58, 306; cf. Eurip., fr. 432 Nauck.

First of all, let the individual being put to the test be very affectionate and very loving of those close to him. Let him be possessed by nature of this stimulus [to friendship], a quality that contributes to the forming of attachments.

Now if anyone should say, on the basis of these introductory remarks, that I am talking nonsense in demanding that, before having any experience of a person, one know what can be known only after such experience,[8] let him fully understand that he will not need to be a prophet. For, as the poets tell us, none of us "is sprung from an oak of ancient fame or from a rock" [cf. Homer, *Od.* 19.163]; each of us has a father, a mother, a brother, perhaps also a [more distant] relative. Whenever you want to know how this person who is being put to the test will treat you as a friend, learn first how he treated his father or mother, or how he treats his brother, or how he gets along with his wife. If he is gentle and well-disposed towards these relatives, you ought to expect even better treatment for yourself; if he is difficult and ill-disposed towards them, you should stay far away from him. For a person who mistreats those close to him cannot be kind to those outside that circle.

Next you must make sure that the person under investigation does not utterly lack a sense of gratitude.[9] For just as some fields are unproductive, whereas others can be relied upon to give a return to the sower, so too some souls are barren of acts of kindness, thoughtless, and unfit for friendship, whereas in other souls there blossoms forth an eagerness to repay kind deeds. You should not demand that an act of kindness be paid back in full. Just examine how people are inclined. See if they will give back as much as they can. At least they can commend and remember kindness. For nothing at all cements a friendship more than gratitude, and nothing destroys it more than ingratitude. Persian law actually demands that ingratitude be punished, because, however it arises, it more than anything else causes hatred.[10] Where the law does not punish ingratitude, there people hate each other because of it but cannot get legal redress; instead, they keep their hostility hidden.

We must also consider how our "prey" handles pleasures and hardships [269]. For in the struggles one undergoes on behalf of friendship,

8. For this apparent dilemma, cf. Cic., *De amicit.* 17 [62].

9. Themistius resumes his listing of the qualities one should look for in a friend after the digressionary (and disruptive) remarks of the previous paragraph.

10. For the Persian law see Xen., *Cyropaed.* 1.2.7; Amm. Marc. 23.6.81.

it is necessary <to tolerate many hardships> and to forgo many pleasures. What makes the son of Strophius [i.e., Pylades] renowned other than the fact that he valued the sufferings shared with Orestes more than royal power in his native land?[11]

We certainly must consider whether a potential friend is a jealous person, or whether he can keep envy at bay. Envy instinctively fights against what is closest at hand and lays claim to what does not belong to it.[12] <Do you> really <think> that someone who has this disease within him could love a friend well?

And there is something else you certainly will not overlook, I think, when you are going to judge whether or not a person has a friendly nature: if he is at all stingy, do not fail to note that. For to the soul that will yearn for true friendship, nothing presents a greater obstacle than miserliness. There are so-called friends, as we see, who clasp each others' hands, stroll around and spend time together, behaving this way for a period of time; but once chance drops a few coins between them, they jump on each other, biting and tearing like little dogs.[13]

What, then, of the person who is gentle, gracious, no lover of money, and not jealous? If, [despite all these qualities], he is a lover of fame and addicted to being first, could he ever be a good companion? Who does not know that love of distinction has very little tolerance of the equality that is part of friendship? Let us never recommend a pretentious or arrogant person to someone seeking a very egalitarian relationship. Nor should we recommend a person who is easily irritated or inclined to anger. For how could a madman be a suitable candidate for a close relationship? I do think that anger is a temporary madness.[14]

Next we must make sure that the person we are examining is not excessively given to the pursuit of something that is not unconditionally good for him. I am thinking of activities such as dice-playing,

11. "<to tolerate many hardships>": some such words are required in this conjectured lacuna, left unfilled in the Teubner edition; see the Teubner apparatus criticus. Pylades and Orestes were remembered for their exemplary friendship (see G. Radke, "Pylades 1," *RE*, 23, 2 [1959]: 2080). Euripides, *Orestes* 763–67, has Pylades announce that his father banished him from his native Phocis because of his role in Orestes's matricide.

12. I.e., an envious person is not content with what he has and wants what his friend has.

13. "And there is something . . . miserliness": cf. Pl., *Rep.* 6.486a. "like little dogs": cf. Arr., *Epict. Diss.* 2.22.9–10; Lucian, *Pisc.* 35–36.

14. "What, then" etc.: cf. Pl., *Rep.* 6.486b. "anger is a temporary madness": cf. Them., *Orat.* 1.7b; Seneca, *De ira* 1.1.2, "iram . . . brevem insaniam." See also Philemon, fr. 184 Kock; Hor., *Epp.* 1.2.62; Plut., *Reg. et imperat. apophthegm.* 199a (Cato the Elder).

checkers, or playing the lyre or the flute. If all a man's desires, diverted downhill like a stream [270], incline to one such pursuit, then his friendships cannot be strong enough to nurture the better things [that otherwise would be expected of friendships].[15]

It will not be easy, then, will it, to find a man of such purity? But couldn't one also say that virtue is rarer than gold, that you must be content if even one such person should pass the test? Clearly, a man who knows how to select true friends will not have many friends, will not have countless friends.[16]

Next, it is essential that your potential friend, while not himself resting content with [too] few friends, also avoid having too many. Think about this point. It is impossible that the majority of people are going to be delighted or distressed by the same things. Nor is it possible for them to be treated similarly by fortune. What is pleasant or painful to one is not so to another, and chance sometimes treats one person well and another badly. So let the potential friend who himself has so many friends whom he honors tell us this: when some of his many friends are delighted by the very same things that are troubling others, with which group will he sympathize? When one of his friends wants him to share in his pain and another wants him to join him in feasting, to which of the two will he go? Isn't it true that, if he honors some of his friends, he necessarily incurs the ill will of those who are not honored? Homer's remark is not as applicable to spoils of war as it would be a fitting remark about friends: the discerning keep what is dear to them truly circumscribed.[17]

Now since fine things are not easy to come by, and neither we ourselves nor those upon whom we are passing judgment will be free of moral blemish, we should not utterly reject a person who has some small defect in his soul. All we need to determine in such cases is that

15. "If all a man's desires" etc.: cf. Pl., *Rep.* 6.485d. With Reiske (see Teubner apparatus criticus), I move the phrase "diverted downhill like a stream" so that it refers to "desires" and not to "friendships."

16. This paragraph makes, for the second time in this part of the oration (cf. n. 9 above), a digressionary observation before Themistius continues with his list of qualities one should look for in a friend.

17. Plutarch wrote a treatise on the problems caused by *polyphilia* (*Mor.* 93a–97b); cf. Arist., *Eth. Nic.* 8.6 [1158a10–15], 9.10 [1170b20–71a20]; *Eth. Eudem.* 7.2 [1238a8–10], 7.12 [1245b19–25]. For other ancient positions on *polyphilia,* see Bohnenblust, *Beiträge,* 37–38. "the discerning" etc.: Themistius has τοῖς φρονίμοις ὄντως ὀλίγον τὸ φίλον. He is apparently thinking of Homer, *Il.* 1.167, where Achilles says that he, unlike Agamemnon, goes off with "some small part of the booty for myself" (ὀλίγον τε φίλον τε). Homeric φίλος can mean "one's own" as well as "friendly, dear."

we have not fallen in with someone who has a kind of moral failing similar to our own. For while virtue in all its forms is in harmony with itself, vice is neither well-disposed towards virtue nor is it self-content.[18] Consequently, he who is easily stirred to anger cannot be a friend to one similarly disposed, nor can the languid befriend the languid or <the stubborn> the stubborn. But if these traits are matched so that they are complementary, they would be able to brook each other and form a union fairly well. A person who is insensible to maltreatment will fit well with someone who is insulting, the humble soul will be well suited to the boastful, the browbeaten to the contemptuous, the languid to the energetic. The spendthrift can put up with the miser, and the person who desires nothing more than to escape notice is a good match for the lover of fame [271]. Such were the friendships of the past that won glorious remembrance; in them there was a stable union. For example, the friendship of Chabrias and Iphicrates is celebrated. Now one of them [Iphicrates] was intense and active. Chabrias, on the other hand, could not easily be stirred to action. As a result, since one needed a bridle and the other a goad, the two of them inevitably fit together. Homer, you know, knew how to depict friendship as well as war. He represented Patroclus as Achilles's friend, gentle Patroclus and pompous Achilles. He also wrote about Sthenelus and Diomedes, one [Diomedes] long-suffering and the other unable to bear up against an act of insolence.[19] Where does Homer give evidence of these two traits of the men? [In the book] in which he has depicted the king of the Achaeans [Agamemnon] directing his army after the man of Zeleia [Pandarus] had shot his arrow [*Il.* 4.85 ff.]. When Sthenelus and Diomedes are angrily chided by Agamemnon, the former does not endure it, but the latter keeps quiet [*Il.* 4.364–418].

It seems, then, that one who knows how to select true friends must approve and disapprove of the above-mentioned and other such traits.[20]

18. "fine things . . . not easy to come by": see Pl., *Cratyl.* 384b; id., *Rep.* 6.497d; *CPG* 1.172, 462; ibid. 2.89, 717. "vice is [not] . . . self-content": this is explained in the next sentence of the oration.

19. Chabrias and Iphicrates: Athenian generals of the fourth century B.C. Cf. with Themistius's remarks the similar but more nuanced representation of Chabrias and Phocion (not Iphicrates) in Plut., *Phoc.* 6. "Homer, you know, knew how" etc.: cf. what Themistius says about Homer in the first paragraph of this oration (264d). "gentle Patroclus": Themistius's adjective, *μείλιχον*, is Homer's actual word for Patroclus at *Il.* 17.671, 19.300. Homer also uses the adjective *ἐνηείς* to describe Patroclus's gentleness (*Il.* 17.204, 21.96). "unable to bear up": I read the manuscript's *οὐ στέγοντα*, not the Teubner conjecture *οὐ στέργοντα*.

20. I.e., approve of the good traits and disapprove of the bad.

Now how shall we chase down and capture these men [who meet our approval]? One must not let them go when they have been found. They should be encircled at a rapid pace, with more eagerness than hunters display in encircling thickets. For this beast of ours is a tame one, not wild; and we are expending effort not for the sake of a few slices of meat, but to share our whole life with someone. What kind of nets shall we set up around these prospective friends? What kind of bait shall we put out—something that will neither harm them when they taste it nor be falsely and deceitfully pleasurable, but that will get hold of them without doing any harm and will beguile them to their advantage? Well, anglers and hunters catch animals and fish by dangling various kinds of bait before them, but the hunter himself is the bait by which a friend is caught—and a friend is the *only* creature caught in this way. So the hunter must be a decent and good human being; if he is, his prey, having got a taste of him, will be caught and no longer be able to get away easily. Being decent and good will allow the process of selecting a true friend to proceed automatically. If a person approaches us and is delighted by our goodness, then he is the one we were long searching for [272]. If, however, a person either fails to marvel at our virtue or actually shuns it, then he must, in the first case, be avoided because of his indifference to virtue or, in the second case, be despised as morally worthless.

Let us make a list of the various kinds of hook to be used in our hunt. First, in approaching our prey we must not get too close. We must tame them gently, as if we were approaching foals. We should begin with what might seem to be small and very insignificant steps—casting kind glances at our prey, conversing with him in a winning manner, sitting and walking with him, [letting it] become apparent that he enjoys it when we cast our eyes on him. We must hunt down a place in the agora where we shall often be in his company. We must also be with him at banquets, in the baths, at the theater or on military campaign, on the road, or anywhere else where we can associate with each other. I would not say that these are great occasions; but the smallest things are always the beginnings of the greatest things. If I had not been intimidated [on previous occasions] by those who are ready to ridicule me for beating a topic to death, I would have also mentioned snares that are even more trivial than the ones I just referred to. As it is, if I say that extending your right hand, tightly clasping the hand of the person you are hunting down, and squeezing his fingers leave a sting behind that will goad him on to becoming your friend, they surely will ridicule me, as I well know, and will say that I have become a victim of petty detail. Yet I observe that even fathers, when they are very fond of their youngsters, are induced to give them a little smack or bite because of their natural feelings for them.[21] All such behavior seems to point to a heart that is driven to be united with the soul of someone it loves; since such spiritual adhesion of soul to soul is impossible, the heart resorts to a physical gesture to express its desire to implant itself in the other person's soul.

Praise should be considered the most effective drug that can be used in hunting down a friend, even though flatterers have made it very suspect, just as perfumers have done to olive oil.[22] For in applying olive oil to those near at hand, perfumers spoil it, just as flatterers do to praise. Therefore, one should use these things, like wine, in moderation [273], neither exceeding the limits of temperance in the case of olive oil nor those of truth in the case of praise. Someone actually in your company is the last person in the world who should be praised. For praise is the only drug that takes greater effect and penetrates more vigorously when it is not [directly] applied to the individual being drugged. It is this direct application of praise that people disapprove of as suspect and treacherous. So those who praise others are no different, I think, from archers; their arrows are more forceful when they shoot them from a distance than at very close range.

We should bring up siege engines not only against the person being hunted down, but also against those who will make our goal reachable if they are captured first. So we should be obliging and amiable in our dealings with the children, siblings, and parents of the one we are hunting down. For if even a dog, as the proverb says, fawns on a person who is well-disposed towards him, how much more gentle and tame are human beings in response to someone who treats them well. The contest is a great one; it is not a hare or a boar or a deer that is being hunted down, but the most docile and gentle creature of all. In chasing down a true friend, then, we should imitate lightly equipped hunters. Just as they tame pigeons and doves and then use those tamed birds to beguile their fellow birds and to lead them, with no resistance from them, right to the birdlime or the snares, so too we should first capture the friends of those whom we have not yet caught and then

21. "natural feelings": with Maisano, *Discorsi,* ad loc., I restore codex Δ's ἀπλάστου ("natural") for the editions' ἀπλήστου ("insatiable").

22. Olive oil was commonly used as a base for perfume in antiquity (Amouretti, *Le pain et l'huile,* 185–89).

employ the former in our pursuit of the latter. For if tame pigeons often win over even other varieties of bird, <surely human beings we befriend will win over their friends for us.>[23]

So much for that. Next I must discuss how to safeguard and retain what has been hunted down. For what would we gain from the hunt if, after getting hold of our prey, we could not keep that hold on it? We must safeguard it by setting a goal for ourselves from the very start, the pursuit of which will unquestionably ensure our success. This goal is the common good, just as it is in a household, a city, and all other social groups; none of these groups can be preserved unless each of their members refers all his actions[24] to this one governing principle.

All things that have care bestowed upon them [274] become better and are of more use both to themselves and to their owners. If a groom tends to his horse, a farmer to his cow, a hunter to his dog, each of these animals is better for it. Conversely, lack of care ruins not only a horse and a dog, but also a shield, a lyre, and a sickle. So too care keeps friendship in good order, but carelessness makes it unsteady and weak. Do not think that a household you manage needs constant attention if it is not to deteriorate very quickly, whereas a friend you have acquired does not need preservative care. If your house has suffered any damage at all because a storm has hit it or a wind has assaulted it or heavy rain has inundated it, you certainly will not leave it unattended to; but will you casually neglect a friend whom grief or disease or some other misfortune has attacked? If water has got into a wall, the only thing you would suffer is water damage. If a person has failed to take care of some other possession or tool, the only pain inflicted on him would be that his possession or tool would be ruined. But when a friendship has been neglected, its destruction is not the only result; hatred also arises. And whenever hatred arises, the human race is most greatly afflicted by troubles. After hatred has made its appearance, you will find yourself at war with a fine and honorable gentleman, the sort of person I just endorsed for friendship with you.

Therefore, put aside delay on every front. Share your friend's sufferings, be with him during his sleepness nights. Join with him when he is

23. "a dog . . . fawns on a [well-disposed] person": cf. Hom., *Od.* 10.216–17; Sext. Emp., *Pyrrh.* 1.67; Diog. Laert. 6.60; *Menandr. et Philist. Sent.* III 61–62, in *Menandri Sententiae,* ed. S. Jaekel (Leipzig, 1964). "<surely . . . for us>": some such supplement seems necessary; see the Teubner's apparatus criticus.

24. "all his actions": for *παντὸς τῶν πραττομένων* I adopt Reiske's conjecture *πάντα τῶν πραττομένων.*

in danger, incurs expenses, and suffers disgrace. Do not wait to be invited to join with him. Rush to do it on your own. Keep anticipating what a given situation demands. Try, in response to each need your friend has, to keep changing the role you play: play the part of a physician when he is ill, of a lawyer when he is involved in a lawsuit, of an adviser on all occasions, of a helper when he has come to a decision.

Since there is much inequality and disparity in life, and absolute uniformity of condition is something that is simply not found [275], I shall no longer speak with reference to "roles played"—for I do not now need this embellishment—but with reference to chance, which is out of our control, chance that brings wealth and poverty, renown and obscurity. It is inevitable that friends, however close they are, will not have an equal share of any of these things; and, in friendship, being favored by fortune often causes a person to look down upon the less favored party.[25] Therefore, if fortune advances you beyond your less favored fellows, you must be sure to bring your friend along with you. For if he has been left behind, you will find it difficult to look upon him as you did before fortune favored you. If you should take your friend in tow but some necessity pulls him in the opposite direction, keep trying to look upon him just as you always have. For if pretentiousness slips in unnoticed and gets hold of you, it will lift you high above your friend and quickly break all those bonds that link you together. What happens is that a balance is not maintained in the relationship, weight having been removed, so to speak, from one side of the scales.

The tragic poet [Euripides] praises even the man he does not know, if only he is a good man, and he considers such a person to be his friend [fr. 902 Nauck]. I accept this idea and consider it to be very well put; but I would advise those who want to preserve a friendship to form as binding a relationship as possible and to realize that being together is an invaluable way to create a bond. For if "exercise is everything" in every area of life, we should consider spending time together to be the exercise proper to friendship.[26]

We must put aside rivalry, contentiousness and all <competitiveness>, guarding against such behavior because it sows seeds of hatred; for friendship is not found among those who struggle against one an-

25. "this embellishment": i.e., this metaphor. "of these things": I read Reiske's *τούτων* instead of the transmitted *τούτου*.

26. "exercise is everything": this saying was ascribed to Periander (Diog. Laert. 1.99).

other, but among those who aid one another in struggle. Consequently, it is likely that those who will safely preserve their relationships are not people who enjoy a reputation in the same fields or professions. For pursuit of similar goals is dangerous; it implants in those concerned a desire for identical accolades and gently coaxes them to contend with one another. So if you are a rhetor or a physician or a schoolteacher, and fate should couple you with another rhetor or physician or schoolteacher [276], do not become your friend's rival. Instead, become Hesiod's rival. Do not try to show that your friend is inferior to you. Instead, show that the poet [Hesiod] fell short of the truth, that he always yields the higher reputation to you if your understanding should prove to be wiser than his, that he always comes in second if it is more fitting that you take first honors. If you do this, we shall no longer marvel at those verses of his [*Op.* 24–26]. No, we shall say to him who fathered those lines: O wonderful and self-taught poet, it is not the pursuit of [common] professions that causes ill will and strife; it is human character that is responsible for them. If people are temperate and good-natured, even their pursuit of a [common] profession will goad them on only moderately; but if <they lack those qualities>, then it is difficult for them to have a friendly relationship with another person, [common] profession or not.[27]

To make no mistakes lies beyond human nature. Let me say that I am not persuaded by the Stoics that there ever appeared among human beings individuals who, as they imagine, were wise and good and no longer [fallible] human beings themselves. The epitaph inscribed at Athens on the public tomb was probably closer to the truth; it ascribes perfection in everything to the gods alone. So since all human beings are imperfect, I should also say something about the mistakes that are made in the context of a friendship—both how to cut back on them and how to repair them <if> they should occur.[28]

27. "<competitiveness>": some such supplement is needed for the unfilled conjectured lacuna in the Teubner edition; see that edition's apparatus criticus. "become Hesiod's rival": i.e., take issue with Hesiod, who comments on the "good strife" that drives individuals who share the same goal or profession (*Op.* 24–26). "self-taught poet": cf. Them., *Orat.* 13.170c. The adjective is not meant to deny divine inspiration. Cf. Hom., *Od.* 22.347; Kaster, *Guardians of Language,* 49–50. "it is not the pursuit . . . profession or not": cf. Pl., *Rep.* 1.329d. Themistius seems to take a stronger position against pursuit of common goals at the beginning of the paragraph than he does at its end.

28. Themistius regards the perfect, infallible Stoic sage as an unrealizable ideal. For that ideal see, e.g., Cic., *Pro Mur.* 29–30 [61–63]; Diog. Laert. 7.121–23; *SVF* 3.548, 557. Cf. Them., *Orat.* 22.270c, "neither we ourselves nor those upon whom we are passing judgment will be free of moral blemish." For the tomb and inscription, see Dem. 18.289.

Now there is a big difference between a friend and a flatterer.[29] What really puts them worlds apart is that a flatterer praises everything in his associate, whereas a friend would not let you off if you go wrong. What is foremost in a flatterer's mind is to profit or to get a big meal from what he does. It is not you by whom he has been taken, but your money or your power. Therefore he does not care about your condition. His concern is that you *not* be in the best condition so that he can work his will on you as easily as possible.

In contrast, a friend's attention is riveted on you alone. He has succumbed to you alone and would not wish any bad condition upon you. Thus we must gently free our friends from their [moral] diseases, not causing them much pain but not letting them go untreated either. Physicians often leave the knife aside and cure an ailment painlessly by administering drugs [277]. This is also how you should treat a friend.[30] You too can heal your friend by using drugs instead of cautery and surgery. The drugs I refer to are words—not sweet words intended to charm, but words brimming with goodwill and frankness. Sweet words only give food and water to a disease. But words that are stern and truthful and brimming with frankness are not insulting. There is a big difference between admonition and verbal abuse, between criticism and insult, not only in the speaker's intent, but also in what he actually says. Stern, truthful, and frank words admonish rather than abuse, correct rather than insult. In giving such admonition, you must be careful not to apply to the patient biting words that have not been tempered. You must mix into those words something soothing and mild, just as honey is used in a potion that is good for a patient but bitter.[31]

A person who is disposed to admonish in this way will not allow his friend to refuse a drug because it is unpleasant or permit him to shut out his [metaphorical] physician. To allow such behavior, to procure for the patient the very things that encourage disease so that the procurer actually promotes the malady—this, I say, is what constitutes

29. The contrast between friend and flatterer is common (Bohnenblust, *Beiträge*, 31–32). Both Plutarch (*Mor.* 48e–74e) and Maximus of Tyre (*Diss.* 14 Koniaris) wrote pieces on how to distinguish them. See Fitzgerald, *Friendship, Flattery, and Frankness*, in which Konstan (pp. 16–19) comments on Them., *Orat.* 22.

30. "Thus we must gently free": because true friends wish us well and deserve our well-meaning correction. "how you should treat a friend": the "you" is now not the ailing party, who could not expect to be corrected by a flatterer, but the party who is doing the correcting.

31. On the importance of frankness in true friendship, see Bohnenblust, *Beiträge*, 35–36. On tempering frankness and avoiding verbal abuse, cf. Cic., *De amicit.* 24–25 [89–91]; Plut., *Quomodo adulator* 66d, 70d–e, 74d–e.

vice in a [literal] physician. Thus I do not applaud the physician who agrees to give his patient every kind of food and drink that intensifies and complicates the disease; he is a wine-pourer or table-setter instead of a healer. Clearly, excess [of any kind] should be avoided in friendship as well as in medicine. For either <route>, [excessive leniency or excessive harshness], leads somewhere other than where one should end up; one route terminates in flattery, the other in alienation.[32]

Slander is a harmful thing wherever she appears, and she stirs up war wherever she slips in—between father and son, and between brother and brother. The *Hippolytus* is her drama. She does injustice both to the person she plots against and to the person she deceives—to the former because she forces him to suffer undeservedly, to the latter because she forces him to act against the one slandered.[33] But, [though harmful in any context], slander is by its very nature the worst enemy of friendship and more subversive of it than anything else is. Wherever she sees a flourishing friendship [278], she quietly gets a footing there and then gradually undermines and gets the better of the unprotected and weak party.

So we must wall out slander. We must drive her away by refusing to believe her. We must, in the midst of everything we hear, build ourselves a strong fort to keep slander's plots far away, to shut her out and repel her completely when she approaches. If slander escapes your notice and gets in, do not admit her and conceal her. Do not keep her unexposed and work on her in those circumstances. What you should do is to bring her out into the open and confute her there. Then you will see her quickly become dizzy, you will see her writhe, stutter and not know what to do. Even if slander should endure this once, she will never bother you afterwards; she would not try it again or come near you again.

As for those fools who have delighted to have slander approach them and have gladly opened their doors to her, they do not benefit whatsoever from their kind reception of her; for slander has caused them to lose their wits, and they are no different from madmen. Consider how alike all their actions and experiences are. They fear and are

32. "a wine-pourer . . . healer": the contrast is of Platonic origin (*Gorg.* 464b ff.). "excess [of any kind]" etc.: cf. Aristotle's assertion that friendship is a mean between flattery and hostility (*Eth. Eudem.* 2.3 [1221a7], 3.7 [1233b30]).

33. Cf. Themistius's remarks on slander in *Orat.* 21.262a ff. In Euripides's *Hippolytus,* Hippolytus is slandered, and his father Theseus believes the slander and acts against his son.

suspicious of those whom they should have least feared. They are like people who take precautions at the banks of insignificant streams. They remind you of the manic Orestes of tragedy, shouting to his sister as she tends to his illness.[34] The most pitiful thing of all, though, is that they take up arms against their closest friends and would most gladly kill them. But this is the doing of yet another madman and the theme for yet another tragedy!

It is helpful on many occasions to call to mind the storyteller Aesop. Here one thinks of the excellent tales he has left us that pertain to slander. He always puts the garb of slander on the fox, a crafty and cowardly animal; and in his tales he shows the mightiest of animals falling victim to the fox. I would like to tell you the story I have at hand, as long as you calmly tolerate my being compared to the sophists.[35]

Two bulls were the leaders of a single herd. They were close associates and on the friendliest of terms. Now a lion feared their partnership and did not feel that he could take any bold action against them or, because of them, against the herd. In bad condition because of hunger, the lion goes to the wily one [i.e., the fox], and they agree to form an alliance. The fox was so unmatched in villainy and cleverness [279] that, by bringing up the engine [of slander], she managed to alienate the two bulls and got them to attack each other madly. With the bulls at odds with each other, she handed them over to the lion, and they were a prey that was docile and ready for him.

This was Aesop's wily fox. But there are also foxes in the ranks of human beings—no, I should say that there are puny and mean specimens of humanity who drag foxes in their train. In fact, it is not foxes that some people drag along with them, but serpents full of a bitter and foul poison. These are serpents that crawl along stealthily and conceal themselves behind curtains of kindness and benevolence.[36] They should be driven away and scared as far off as possible. For we are often beguiled and gladdened by their bite; we see only the tips of their tongues and do not wish to take a good look at what is inside their mouths.

34. See Eurip., *Orestes* 251–65.

35. "compared to the sophists": Themistius is alluding to the common use of Aesopic material in the schools of rhetoric and in rhetors' and sophists' orations (Perry, *Aesopica,* 1: 295–97; Chambry, *Esope,* xxxv). For the fable that follows, cf. Aesop, *Fab. Aphth.* 16, *Fab. synt.* 13 Hausrath-Hunger, and Perry, ibid., 1: 475 (*Fab. gr.* 372), but in all of these versions the lion acts on his own, without the aid of the fox. The third version alone has the lion use slander to alienate the bulls.

36. Themistius moves now from the issue of slander to the more general theme of villains who pose hypocritically as friends.

I wish to compare these serpents to what I think they resemble, if you are willing to hear me out. I have seen in many places, I believe, a representation of Scylla that does not conform to Homer's description of her. For Homer says nothing more about her form than that she was a creature living in a cave who had six heads and twelve hands, but sculptors go beyond Homer in their representations of her. They make her a young woman from head to midriff, but from the waist down she ends up consisting of frightening and awful dogs. These dogs have three rows of teeth. Their heads are raised high, each one in search of its own prey.[37] Now I surmise that what Homer means is that the wise and shrewd [Odysseus] had precise knowledge of Scylla in her entirety; that the upper part of this creature did not enchant him; that, on the contrary, he was prepared, armed and ready to fight her; and that it is the undefended who fall prey to her. If a person does not think that this is what Homer says but sees only the apparent sense of the story, then it seems to me that, upon beholding Scylla, he sees the human female but will be unable to see the dogs.

How then shall we defend ourselves? How shall we tell whether we are looking at the genuine face of friendship or at the face of villainy wearing a mask of kindness? I do not want to bore you to death. Do you just want me, by undergirding my oration with a myth, to give you some additional symbols and signs of the truth and then to leave it up to you yourselves to discern what is manifested in those symbols and signs [280]?[38]

As Prodicus tells the story, when the days of Heracles's youth were past, he was once sitting quietly and thinking about what kind of person he should be and what path he should take to lead his life as best as he could. Two women appeared to him, one of whom Prodicus names Virtue and the other Vice. When each of the women had told

37. For ancient representations of Scylla, see Roscher, *Ausführl. Lex.*, 4 (1909–15): 1035 ff.; J. Schmidt, "Skylla 1," *RE*, 3A, 1 (1927): 654–55. "I have seen in many places": possibly one place was the Constantinopolitan hippodrome. See Cameron, *Porphyrius*, 185; Dagron, *Naissance*, 325–26; Hebert, *Schriftquellen*, 6–8. "heads and ... hands": Homer, *Od.* 12.85 ff., actually uses the word "feet," not "hands." "frightening ... dogs": Themistius uses Homer's adjective, σμερδαλέος, but in Homer it describes Scylla's six upper heads. "These dogs ... rows of teeth": τρίστοιχοι ... ὀδόντες, as in Homer, but in the latter with reference to Scylla's upper heads. Although Homer says nothing about Scylla's consisting partially of dogs, he does compare her voice, in lines whose authenticity was suspected in antiquity, to that of a puppy (σκύλακος), apparently seeing an etymological link between her name and the word σκύλαξ.

38. I.e., Themistius will end with an allegory and no further comment. Petavius wrongly suggested, at the end of his Latin translation of this oration, that "desunt multa."

Heracles what she had to offer, and he had decided to make Virtue his leader, she took him and said, "Come with me, so that you may see even better that you are right in choosing me."[39]

She led him to a lofty place that rose up from a broad and open plain. There were two peaks there, although they appeared to form a single crest if you looked at them from a distance. Virtue brought Heracles near to that lofty place and showed him that the mountain tops were quite separate from each other. "<This> peak on the right," she said, "is known as the sacred place of Friendship, who is my companion and sister; this one on the other side is the sacred place of Pretense, a divine partner of Vice. Come near and examine the nature of each place, so that, looking at them from a distance, you do not regard them as one and the same peak."

At the same time, Virtue ordered Good Judgment, who was also present, to point out and explain every feature of the locale. So Good Judgment showed Heracles the spurs of both mountain crests. They were very similar and resembled one another. They were both lush with the same flowers and trees, except that on one spur the flora were always flourishing, whereas on the other spur they shot up and died quickly. A stream of cold, clear water flowed from each peak. But in one case the water was sweet and pleasant throughout the whole course of the stream; in the other case it seemed rather sweet if one tasted it downstream, but as you approached the source it got bitter and tasted poisoned. This bitter-tasting water would cause convulsions and dizziness in those who were misled by its appearance into drinking it.

Good Judgment noted that the peaks themselves no longer seemed similar, but were utterly different from one another. She pointed out the one on the right first. It was well shaded by a grove of evergreens (the cypress and the laurel), and it was full of fruit-bearing trees. Gentle breezes wafted through the trees, the kind that support and encourage their growth [281], not the kind that break limbs off and rip trees up. An utterly undisturbed tranquillity and joy held sway over the place. A very small number of people came into view; whether going

39. For Prodicus's famous tale of the "Choice of Heracles" alluded to here, see esp. Xen., *Mem.* 2.1.21–34 (= Prodicus B 2 Diels-Kranz). The allegory that follows is indebted to Dio Chrys., *Orat.* 1.66 ff. Cf. also Max. Tyr., *Diss.* 14.1 Koniaris, where the Prodican choice between Virtue and Vice is transformed into a choice between Friendship and Flattery. Discussion in Bohnenblust, *Beiträge,* 16–21; Scharold, *Dio,* 32–40; Mesk, *Philologische Wochenschrift* 54 (1934): 556–58.

towards the peak or walking away from it, they had the same look of pleasure on their faces.

At the very top of the mountain peak a maiden [i.e., Friendship] was seated. She was in the bloom of youth, not physically stunning, but abounding in genuine and old-fashioned beauty, the kind that one finds in statues of ancient craftsmanship, which require time and more than ordinarily keen eyes to be appreciated. She was bedecked in white, in delicate and translucent clothing, so that in many places her body showed through. She had a soul that was more visible than her body. Her glance was unaffected and dignified, her smile steady and unchanging. If a person approached her in awe and admiration, she would not offer him gold or silver but would <make> him more handsome and of larger stature, oftentimes two or three times larger than he had been.[40]

Now Heracles marveled at her and prayed that she would show favor to him. "And who are these women near her?" he asked Good Judgment; "they are such beautiful and fitting companions for the goddess." "This one here," she said, "who possesses so much light and whose seat is unbreakable, is Truth, a daughter of Zeus. This one, resting on [the goddess] and with her head turned [towards her], is called Kindness; the goddess employs her services in everything she does. That young man there, more solemn than you would expect for his age, the one who is carrying gold chains in his hands, is Desire, one of Friendship's assistants. He has neither wings nor arrows, for he does not desire to fly, and he does his work without shedding blood.[41] When he sees people who are decent and good and thus well suited to each other, he joins and binds them together. His bonds cannot be undone, they are utterly unbreakable, and they are the sole source of delight for those so bound. But come here," she said, "and look at the other woman, into whose clutches the masses fall."

Good Judgment first pointed out to him the approach to the second peak [i.e., its spur], which, as I said, looked like the approach to the first peak. Then she showed him the highest point of elevation itself

40. "bedecked in white"(*ἠμφίεστο δὲ λευκόν τινα κόσμον ἰκέον*): the Teubner edition prints the transmitted *ἰκέον* but marks it as corrupt, and I have ignored it in my translation. For emendations, see, in addition to the Teubner apparatus criticus, Romano, *Κοινωνία* 2 (1978): 340–41; Albini, *SIFC* 4 (1986): 272. "but would <make> him more handsome" etc.: I tentatively accept Jacobs's supplement *ἔθηκε: οὐ χρυσίον...προέτεινεν, ἀλλ᾽ αὐτὸν καλλίω...<ἔθηκε>.*

41. For the ascription of wings and (bow and) arrows to Desire, i.e., Eros, see Roscher, *Ausführl. Lex.*, 1. 1 (1884–86): 1346 ff.; Fasce, *Eros,* 136–39, 163–64, 173, 193.

[on the left side], a steep and precipitous summit, its top hidden by a bluish cloud. It was surrounded by cliffs, chasms, and heaps and piles of human bones [282]. The whole place was full of animals whose bite is deadly and venomous. Then Good Judgment showed Heracles Pretense herself, who claimed to be Friendship and likened herself to that goddess. But Pretense had a painted face, not a genuine beauty; and instead of a peaceful smile she had a deceitful grin. In order to appear desirable, she pretended to feel desire for those who came to her. Since no one would come any distance to her on his own, she would run out and kowtow to people, go meet them herself and take them back with her—and she would not take no for an answer!

Pretense also had a group of women in attendance on her, but they were nothing like the first group [i.e., those who attended on Friendship]. Deceit was there and Treachery and sordid Trickery. Instead of Truth, it was Perjury who attended on Pretense. Perjury is reckless, bold, and implacable, and she more than anyone else helped and worked with Pretense. When Heracles saw a woman who was apparently lying in ambush at the approach to Pretense's mountain peak, he asked Good Judgment who she was. "Flattery," she said, "who goes in advance of Pretense. This divinity, as you see, lies in wait for those who are approaching and engages with them. She does amazing things to enchant them, persuading them to be bold and go to the top of the mountain." "And who is that sullen and pensive woman who is leading a few smitten and wailing souls down the mountain?" "That is Repentance," Good Judgment said. "She is a slow goddess, who comes in her own good time. Still, she saves a few people from being sucked to death by the reptiles;[42] she gets them on their feet again while they are still breathing and sees to it that they get back home safely."

42. Apparently the "animals" mentioned in the previous paragraph, "whose bite is deadly and venomous."

ORATION 23

The Sophist

[282] Gentlemen, do you think that I still need the applause and cries of approval that you are accustomed to give me so generously every time I speak to you? Do you think that I need once again to gather an audience, to get up on the speaker's platform today, to be welcomed enthusiastically, and to savor whatever acclaim you may bestow on what I say [283]? Of course, I consider the sincere and genuine applause I always get from you—a spontaneous applause that no one commands you to provide—to be a sweet and highly cherished sound. But I would not so plainly have disturbed and troubled you just to get that applause. Whenever I come before you, I do so to give you advice or instruction, to put your leader [i.e., the emperor] before you in the hope of securing greater support for him, or to render an account of myself to you even though you do not demand it. But, because of your good humor and kindness, you turn these assemblies of mine into theatrical occasions. It will not be surprising, then, if you behave today as you always do. I have brought you together to judge whether or not I am guilty of the crimes I am accused of committing; but you will respond in your customary way, jumping up and shouting. You will forget that you have come here with the authority to make a decision. You will forget that this is not a festival. It is a law court, more diligent and wiser than the court of the thousand and one, and it has been en-

trusted with the task of deciding by vote what a person convicted of a crime must suffer or pay.[1]

First of all, do not be perplexed by the fact that I make you jurors and say that I will be involved in a legal battle even though I am neither a defendant nor a plaintiff, even though I have not been summoned to court by anyone and do not bring someone else before you myself. For you will see that it is not I but my accusers who are responsible for this very strange and unusual situation. They are so clever that not even I know who they are. They shoot their arrows at me unseen, just as the Plataeans once did at the Peloponnesians; on that occasion, the Plataeans were fleeing from the siege [of their city] at night, and the Peloponnesians were pursuing them in the dark with torches in their hands.[2] Yes, arrows of all kinds have come showering down around me from all directions—many arrows, one after another, and not from one quiver alone. But I do not know, and do not care to know, who are shooting them.

I am happy that they are such inept enemies and that no one of them has managed to touch my soul [**284**]. None of them has even grazed my body, and they have been unable to penetrate my defenses. On the contrary, the more arrows they shoot at me and the more intense those barrages get, the more they demonstrate how impervious and strong my metal armor is. That armor of mine was crafted, not by Hephaestus on Mt. Olympus, but by the gods who gave us philosophy and preside over it. Whomever they equip with defensive gear they make utterly invulnerable, even more so than they made Caeneus. The half-men or half-beasts [i.e., Centaurs] who combine against such a person and batter him with oak and fir trees accomplish nothing; he remains unharmed and unswerving. It is appropriate that such a person have a greater sense of accomplishment for putting up with the follies of his fellow men than did the famous [Caeneus], who did drive off [the Centaurs], for supporting on his shoulders a boulder weighing seven talents.[3]

1. "to put your leader [i.e., the emperor] before you": Themistius refers to his role as panegyrist of emperors, using the term ἀρχηγέτης for "emperor"; cf. *Orat.* 17.215d. "the court of the thousand and one": Themistius flatters his audience by telling them that they are superior to jurors of classical Athens. For the court of 1,001, see Dem., *Orat.* 24.9 with schol. 25 Dilts; MacDowell, *Law in Classical Athens,* 39–40. Cf. Them., *Orat.* 26.311c.

2. "not even I know who they are": cf. Socrates's anonymous "first" accusers (Pl., *Apol.* 18c–d). Plataeans: see Thuc. 3.23.

3. "the gods who gave us philosophy": for philosophy's divine origin, cf. Them., *Orat.* 34 [I] with n. 1 to my translation. Though the Lapith Caeneus was granted the gift

Those who are shooting arrows at me, then, do not want to come out into the open and stand in your midst, where they could be seen. They lie hidden somewhere, in secluded spots and caverns. What I do see is their arrows, falling and whirling down at my feet from I know not where. So let me pick them up from the ground and count them. Let me try to break them in two, if I can, and show how soft their barbs are and see if any of them have been smeared with poison. If I keep running my fingers along them and turning them round and round, perhaps I may find the name of the archer inscribed near the notches. This is how Philip of Macedon, when he was laying siege to Methone, learned the identity of the archer who shot from the wall. His name, Aster, had been branded on the arrow.[4] But enough of this. We must take leave of metaphor and really begin the trial.

I think that I should employ an introduction, just as rhetors do in structuring an oration. Let it be as follows: that these accusers of mine are doing nothing new on the present occasion. What has been customary for a long time and part of human nature since philosophy appeared on earth from the gods is now reappearing, once again, like a cyclically recurring disease. When it comes to things other than philosophy, this human trait [to which I am referring] certainly causes people [285] to envy, plot against and harass those who have more than they do, even if no injustice is done to them [by their more fortunate fellows]. It is not pleasant for a poor person to set eyes on someone glorying in his wealth, or for someone who cannot ride a horse to see someone who can, or for a weakling to look at a strong man. To the extent that wisdom [i.e., philosophy] is a greater and fuller blessing

---

of invulnerability, the Centaurs pummeled him with and buried him under trees, driving him into the ground while he was standing erect (note Themistius's "unswerving"). See, e.g., Pind., fr. 167 = *Thren.* 6 Snell[3]; Acusilaus F 22 (*FGrH* 2); Apoll. Rhod., *Argon.* 1.57–64 with schol.; Ovid, *Metamorph.* 12.171–72, 459–526; Apollod., *Epit.* 1.22; *Orph. Argon.* 170–74. Themistius's "boulder of seven talents" must be the "stone marker" that, according to Acusilaus, the Centaurs put over the buried Caeneus. Themistius's phrase "supporting on his shoulders" implies the persistence of life and sentience after Caeneus was buried (thus, e.g., Apoll. Rhod., loc. cit.; Agatharchides in Phot., *Bibl.* 250.443a). Other texts speak of his death upon burial (Acusilaus, loc. cit.; Palaephatus, *Περὶ ἀπίστων* 10 Festa). For modern debate about Caeneus's end, see Kakridis, *CR* 61 (1947): 78 ff., who does not take account of the implication of the Themistian passage. "who did drive off [the Centaurs]": the Greek is ὁ ἐξαμύνας, which the Teubner edition and Maisano, *Discorsi,* ad loc., judge corrupt. But Caeneus did initially drive off the Centaurs (cf. Apoll. Rhod., *Argon.* 1.60–61) before he was overwhelmed by them.

4. Philip II laid siege to Methone in 355–354 B.C. He was hit and blinded in one eye by an arrow, on which Aster had inscribed his name. See the exhaustive study of ancient testimonia on Philip's wounds by Riginos, *JHS* 114 (1994): 103–19.

than any other, it rouses and stirs up all the more people against the man who possesses or seems to possess it.

This situation first obtained back in the days of Pythagoras; and, like some legacy unavoidably transmitted to future generations, it continued to affect his [spiritual] descendants. As for the son of Mnesarchus himself [i.e., Pythagoras], he, of course, was so possessed of that much famed wisdom that he spent his whole life on the move because of those who envied and discredited him. He went from Samos to Croton because of Polycrates, and from Croton to Locri because of Cylon. At Locri, it was not one person but the whole citizen body who could not abide Pythagoras's virtue and consequently made him leave and sent him to Tarentum. The Tarentines again sent him off, this time to Metapontum, like an item of cargo; and there he died in the precinct of the Muses, having taken no food, as they tell it, for forty days. And why would one rehearse the story of Socrates? Our ears are full of the names Meletus, Anytus, and Lycon! Don't people even now inveigh against Plato, accusing him of having sailed to Sicily three times to get rich and enjoy its fine food? When could I ever easily draw up a list of the Cephisodoruses, Eubulideses, Timaeuses, Dicaearchuses, and the whole host of [other] individuals who attacked Aristotle the Stagirite? Their writings survive down to the present time, perpetuating their hostility and contentiousness.[5]

5. "This situation first obtained. . . . ": Themistius makes this assertion perhaps because he here thinks of Pythagoras as the first to call himself a philosopher (Diog. Laert. 1.12; Iambl., *Vita Pyth.* 12 [58]). For Pythagoras as a victim of envy (*phthonos*), cf. Diod. Sic. 10.10.2; Diog. Laert. 8.39; Porph., *Vita Pyth.* 54. For Pythagoras's movements as presented here, cf. esp. Porph., ibid. 9, 16, 54–57. According to both Diog. Laert. 8.3 and Porph., ibid. 9, 16, Pythagoras could not abide the Samian tyrant Polycrates; so too Iambl., ibid. 2 [11], but at 6 [28] he gives another motive for Pythagoras's leaving Samos. Cylon was a Crotoniate whom Pythagoras refused to allow into fellowship, and consequently he turned against the philosopher: Porph., ibid. 54; Iambl., ibid. 35 [248–49]. According to Porph., ibid. 56, a group of elders at Locri, representing the community, politely asked Pythagoras to leave because they did not want him to tamper with their laws. For Pythagoras's death, see, in addition to Porph., ibid. 57, Diog. Laert. 8.40. "Meletus, Anytus and Lycon": Socrates's accusers. For hostile and favorable explanations in antiquity of what motivated Plato to go to Sicily, see Riginos, *Platonica,* 70–74. "the Cephisodoruses" etc.: Cephisodorus was a pupil of Isocrates, Eubulides a philosopher of the Megarian School, and Timaeus the well-known historian from Tauromenium. For their invectives against Aristotle, see Düring, *Aristotle,* testimonia 58c, f, h; 59b; 60; 62–63; and his comments on pp. 384 ff. According to the Aristotelian Aristocles (in Euseb., *Praep. evang.* 15.2.11), their attacks were motivated by envy. Wehrli accepts ("wie es scheint"), on Themistius's authority, that Aristotle's pupil Dicaearchus took issue with his teacher in writing (*Die Schule des Aristoteles,* vol. 1, fr. 26 [Dicaearchus] and pp. 50–51). That supposition is perfectly plausible; but would Dicaearchus have written against Aristotle with the "hostility and contentiousness" that Themistius says characterized all four critics? It is this question that has led to the view

How, then, can I get angry, gentlemen, if, as a result of trying all my life to follow those illustrious men to the best of my ability, I have experienced things similar to what my guides once experienced? How can I get angry if I have hit the same reefs because I follow in the same tracks and have provoked and induced a swarm of drones equipped with stingers, as it were, to attack me? Not that I did this at all willingly or by choice; it is just that what I keep begging for and love and would be less willing to give up than my very soul naturally provokes such a response [286]. If I claimed to be a merchant, I would have to realize that the ocean is not always calm, that the winds are not always fair, that one does not always make money from one's cargo. One must reckon with storms, hidden rocks, and the need to jettison cargo, and sometimes with a band of pirates—another kind of storm, this one, more severe than rough waters. No, if the charges and verbal abuse that my contemporaries are leveling at me are no different from what the Telchines of old leveled at those famous and godlike philosophers, I must accept this abuse as a sign that I am walking close behind them and not wandering very far from them. For "sophist" and "impostor" and "innovator" were terms of reproach first used against Socrates, then against Plato, and next against Aristotle and Theophrastus.[6]

My defense must begin with this question: does this designation "sophist" [that my accusers give me] accord with reality, and is it applied to me because it represents the facts, or does the truth prove it to be a wrong designation despite the fact that it most certainly is applied to me? It would be the mark of a tasteless person to refer you to comic poets and prose writers and to remind you that long ago the title sophist was revered and highly regarded, or that the contemporaries of Solon and of Pythagoras used to call them sophists. It is not in this spirit, of course, that these accusers of mine would so designate me; they do not wish to honor me, but to vilify me. Protagoras, Prodicus of Ceos, and Gorgias of Leontini used to lay claim to the title sophist. They would advertise their wisdom as if it were just another thing for sale and would

---

that "Dicaearchus" is either a slip on Themistius's part or a textual corruption. The intended name might be Demochares, who is mentioned by Aristocles along with Timaeus, Eubulides, and Cephisodorus as an early vilifier of Aristotle (Euseb., ibid. 15.2.6). Cf. Zeller, *Die Philosophie der Griechen,* 2, 2: 889n; Düring, ibid., p. 388.

6. "if I have hit ... in the same tracks": cf. Pl., *Rep.* 8.553a–b? "drones ... stingers": cf. ibid. 552c–e. Themistius calls the maligners of the philosophers of classical Greece "Telchines," mythological beings known for their malice and envy (Herter, "Telchinen," *RE,* 5A, 1 [1934]: 205–7). The charge of being an innovator is taken up in *Orat.* 26.

charge their pupils much money for it. But since the value of the title sophist, like that of some coin, declined after their times, those who currently ridicule me would like to join the ranks of its debasers.[7]

Consider, then, how fairly I shall conduct the inquiry. You all know that there are established laws at your disposal—or perhaps I should say at the disposal of all human beings—according to which you must always act and address people appropriately. If you should disagree about something [287], you go to the laws and easily reach a decision on the basis of what they say. Philosophers too have written laws that clarify and explain whatever we may inquire about. Each philosopher has his own set of laws, which the founder of his philosophical system drafted. It is those that each of us follows and has taken as our norm. Just as Solon's laws are for the Athenian and Lycurgus's for the Spartan, the Platonist follows the laws that Plato wrote; the devotee of the Stoa, those written by Zeno of Citium; and he who is fond of the Garden, those drafted by Epicurus, the son of Neocles. So it often happens that the same man is guiltless under the laws of his city but is convicted by those of Plato or Zeno.

It is precisely a philosophical charge that they now bring against me. For our laws do not mention the sophist or say what sort of crime it is to be a sophist, nor do they call for the sophist's prosecution; in fact, they assume that being a sophist is in some sense honorable and not entirely unprofitable to the state.[8] On the other hand, the Academy and the Lyceum exclude the sophist and say that the man who is fond of that title and works to earn it does not befit [philosophy's] shrines. It is clear, then, that, since you have gathered here on my account, today you must examine, not the laws of Solon or Dracon or Cleisthenes or Lycurgus, but those of the philosophical schools. You must use as

7. "the mark of a tasteless person": Themistius seems to mean that it would be tasteless to assume that his audience was ignorant of the ancient meaning of "sophist." For the original, positive sense of the term "sophist," someone who possessed wisdom (*sophia*), and the negative connotations it acquired, see Guthrie, *History of Greek Philosophy*, 3: 27–34. For Pythagoras and Solon as sophists in a positive sense, see the prose writers Hdt. 4.95 and Isoc. 15.235, 313. For positive usage of the title in comic writers, Diog. Laert., prooem. 12 (Cratinus); Euphron, fr. 1.11–12 Kock. For the sale of wisdom by the sophists Protagoras, Prodicus, and Gorgias, cf., e.g., Pl., *Hipp. Maj.* 282b–d; Guthrie, op. cit. 35–40. "the value of the title ... declined": the word "sophist," however, continued to be used in Themistius's day, not simply as a term of abuse, but also as an honorable (or at least neutral) designation for a master or teacher of rhetoric. Note the pride that, according to Eunap., *Vitae phil.* 16.2.8 [496] Giangrande, Libanius took in the title.

8. Themistius is here thinking of publicly paid teachers of rhetoric and their immunities from public burdens (Kaster, *Guardians of Language*, 114–18, 223–30).

your test the signs and indications of sophistry that these philosophical laws provide. If I should seem guilty and liable under these laws, then seize me and hand me over to my accusers to do whatever they wish with their prey. But if those traces and marks point elsewhere than in the direction of my guilt, acquit me of the charge that I deserve the title sophist.

It is the divine Plato, then, who has a statute book filled with these [philosophical] laws. In him one finds, one after another, the many clear evidences [of sophistry] that have been discovered. Those who search for the sophist should rely on Plato's evidences in tracking him down. So we should put those evidences before us, it seems, and determine whether all or most or a few of them fit me **[288]**. Bear with me patiently, by the Graces, as I list every instance of this lawgiver's catching and netting his man, as if he were some hunter encircling a wild animal. He shows first that the sophist is a mercenary hunter of rich young men; secondly, that he is a merchant who sells items of knowledge for the soul; thirdly, that he is a retailer of these same items; fourthly, that he is self-employed and does the actual selling himself; fifthly, that he is a verbal competitor, skilled in eristic; and finally, that he forms opinions about the nonexistent, uses appearances to imitate reality, fashions phantasms of the truth, and is a verbal wonder-worker. This last point was the finishing touch that Plato attached and bound to his remarks. Plato, then, encircles the trueborn sophist with this whole chain of descriptions and epithets, in the hope that he might somehow, to the best of his ability, exhibit and make clear the sophist's multifaceted and cunning nature.[9]

So much for that. Let us now take up and examine each of these traits of the sophist separately, beginning with the first one. We shall see if any of them fits me, and if you can find that I exhibited any one of them, like some clearly visible footprint left in my wake.

You all know, I believe, that I have absolutely not hunted down any rich young man and have not charged a fee for my teaching. You all know that my pupils are neither young enough to be deceived easily

9. Plato's "statute book" is his *Sophist.* For the first five descriptions of the sophist, see Pl., *Soph.* 231d–e; for the sixth description, see ibid., esp. 233b–41b, 268c–d. For "hunting down" the sophist, cf. ibid., 218d, 226a–b, and esp. 235b–c. For putting on the "finishing touch" (κολοφῶνα), cf. Pl., *Theaet.* 153c; *Euthyd.* 301e; *Laws* 2.673d, 674c; *Epp.* 3.318b; Bühler, *Zenobii proverbia,* 4: 47–55. "the sophist's multifaceted and cunning nature" (τὸ πολυειδὲς καὶ πολύπλοκον): cf. Plato's description of the sophist and his art as "many-sided," ποικίλος (*Soph.* 223c, 226a), of the sophist as "many-headed," πολυκέφαλος (ibid. 240c).

nor such dolts that they would pay a fee for being duped. I am certainly not boasting about the fact that I do not charge for my teaching, nor am I of the opinion that it is a wonderful and sublime thing never to have accepted a fee. For if I needed money and help with my necessary expenses, be assured that, while I would not have agreed to or stipulated a fee, I would not have hesitated to make a Crito the storehouse of my necessities—a storehouse like the one Crito provided for [Socrates,] the son of Sophroniscus, filling a hollow pot with that man's daily allowance.[10]

But I am not in need. What I have suffices [289]. What my students do offer me is an adequate fee: propriety, respect, discretion, and moderation; their not being thickheaded, tiresome, foolish, or unpleasant; their not engaging in endless rounds of chatter; and their not being content with smugly fixating on one book and spending more time tearing it apart in the darkness of the night than the Greeks did in conducting their siege of Troy. None of my students follows me like some attendant or runs along beside me, clinging to my cloak; they do not give me the many "deep satisfactions" that sophists customarily get from their craft. In fact, I am so far from deriving profit of any kind from my flock of students that even those who call me a sophist do not dare to include that charge among their denunciations of me. On the contrary, what they say is that I attract my flock and keep them together by suffering financial loss myself, by feeding and paying *them!* It seems, then, that, according to these detractors, I would be a "mercenary hunter" in another sense, not by virtue of accepting pay, but because I spend money on others.[11]

Such, then, is my opinion, gentlemen, about this defamation (or compliment!), and it seems to me that it is much more fitting for a free and noble person simply to help and assist needy students financially than to torment, rack, and torture them by forcing them to pay when they are unable. Actually, neither behavior is inherently worthy of praise;[12] but to expect, when you are not in need, to be paid for [expli-

10. Themistius says that he would accept gifts (Kaster, *Guardians of Language*, 121), but not a fee. In refusing to charge a fee, he is like his model Socrates, of course (Pl., *Apol.* 31b–c). For Crito's tending to Socrates' needs, see Diog. Laert. 2.121 and note Pl., *Apol.* 38b; *Crito* 44b–45b. Petavius (in his comment ad loc. on Themistius) had already suspected that the detail of the hollow pot derives from the biography of Zeno of Citium (see Diog. Laert. 7.12).

11. For the buying of pupils, cf. Liban., *Orat.* 1.65, *Epp.* 405.8 Foerster.

12. Saying that neither helping students financially nor taking fees from them is praiseworthy per se is Themistius's way of avoiding boasting about the financial help he gives students (admitted to below) and of acknowledging that the average teacher does

cating] Demosthenes's forensic orations or Aristophanes's plays or all those verbs and nouns is never the mark of virtue. Nor is it ever the mark of virtue to be harsher than public exactors. Rather, these are the marks of a soul in love with gain and money, of an utterly sophistical and mercenary soul.

Because Prodicus and Protagoras the Abderite were paid, the one for teaching young men correct diction and word usage, the other for explicating the poems of Simonides and others, they both were sophists and were so designated.[13] For the first in the list of distinct definitions that Plato [*Soph.* 231d] worked out with reference to sophists says that to be a sophist is to charge the young and wealthy for any form of instruction [290]. Plato exempted neither Iccus the Tarentine gymnastic master nor Herodicus the Selymbrian physical trainer from this designation. He says [*Protag.* 316d–17a] that those two men used their skills as veils but really were quite fully sophists because they made money off of young men. And perhaps he would not even acquit a person who claims to be an interpreter of Aristotle[14] nor waiver in the case of such an individual if he charges a fee for his interpretation; he will seize him and contend that he is liable for his conduct. For even if a person offers a form [of instruction] that is highly revered and he is truly wise, still he must not stockpile his wisdom and advertise it as something purchasable. Rather, as I say, we shall regard the receipt of wages from young men for the teaching of any subject, however serious or trifling, as sophistical—if, that is, we follow the [Platonic] definition. On the other hand, suppose that a teacher should extend a helping hand and meet the needs of young men whose re-

---

not have his resources and must take fees. Cf., two paragraphs above, Themistius's assertion "I am certainly not boasting about the fact that I do not charge for my teaching."

13. One would expect "the one" to be Prodicus and "the other" to be Protagoras, but the opposite equation is possible. One wants to identify the explicator of poems with Protagoras, not only because in Pl., *Protag.* 339a–42a, Protagoras is found explicating Simonides, but also because he is made to assert there that mastery of the poets is the most important part of education. The teacher of correct diction (*ὀρθοέπειαν*) will then be Prodicus: cf. Pl., *Euthyd.* 277d, where *ὀνομάτων ὀρθότης* is a concern of Prodicus, and other texts in which precision in the use of *ὀνόματα* is variously ascribed to him (Pl., *Charmid.* 163d, *Cratyl.* 384b, *Laches* 197d; Arist., *Top.* 2.6 [112b25]; Marcell., *Vita Thuc.* 36). On the other hand, *ὀρθοέπεια* (as opposed to *ὀρθότης ὀνομάτων*) does seem to fit Protagoras better than Prodicus (Pl., *Phaedr.* 267c and *Protag.* 339a, despite *Cratyl.* 391a–c; Guthrie, *History of Greek Philosophy,* 3: 205). And we could identify Themistius's explicator of poems with Prodicus, since he too, as well as Protagoras, explicates Simonides in Pl., *Protag.* 339a–42a. But Themistius need not have felt any difference between *ὀρθοέπεια* and *ὀρθότης ὀνομάτων* "they both were . . . sophists": I have emended *ὅμως* ("nevertheless") of the editions to *ὁμῶς* ("both").

14. I.e., someone like Themistius himself.

sources are limited and, while improving their souls, should also help them materially; such an individual would be considered a perfect and ideal savior and benefactor. But if he should attend only to the body and plot against the mind, then he would be a sophist and an impostor, although more restrained than someone who does harm to both the body and the mind.

We must, then, examine and reconsider the nature of my own case. Let us first agree with our accusers that I have spent a great deal of money in hiring and buying students, and that many of them are paid a mina, some two minae, and some as much as a talent. What of it? I must make a small point very forthrightly, which is contrary to my nature. Do you know anyone who, after attending my classes—no, let me interrupt myself to say that I am not referring to some half-mad youth who let himself into my school for a while, yawning as he sat on the wooden seat, someone who could not even be driven away by a raving dog or a raised club. This young man did not associate and keep company with me, but only with my bench and my classroom. What I mean is this: of those students whom I select and regard highly, do you know of anyone who, after attending my classes, was corrupted or who degenerated from a better to a worse state? Do you know of anyone who, before his association with me, seemed gentle and mild but is now full of delusion <and> madness [291]? Do you know of anyone whom <the> multitude once approved of but now feel nothing but dislike and disgust for? Or have you heard any of those who associate with me boastfully and pretentiously carrying on about things univocally named [*συνωνύμοις*] or things equivocally named [*ὁμωνύμοις*] or things derivatively named [*παρωνύμοις*]?[15] Do I take men who are sober by nature and fill them with arrogance and conceit by testifying and guaranteeing to the whole world that [after having studied under me] they are smarter than Aristotle's own pupils? Do my students, as a result of the knowledge they have acquired, love and revere me all the more and fill my house abundantly with gold and silver, but treat the many people who make no demands on them badly and harshly? I could say many good things about each one of my students, but I do not think that someone who has a personal connection with them should be the one to speak on their behalf. For I see that it is not the athlete praised only by his own physical trainer and table companions who wins a crown and repute; those honors go to the athlete who has

15. Technical terms from Aristotle, *Cat.* 1a1 ff.; cf. Them., *Orat.* 21.247c.

been observed in the gymnasia by crowds of people as he effortlessly seizes his opponent by the neck or uses his weights. So, as for the man who does not charge for his services but instead provides grants of money and also gives virtue to those in need of it, let him be sharply distinguished from a sophist.

I have been telling you what other people imagine about me; and, gentlemen, do not believe what they fantasize about my treasures. They imagine that I have a chest brimming over with wealth, and that those who wish to draw from it do so without limit. Would that their fantasy were reality! For it would be no mean thing to display one's liberality and nobility in deed as well as in word, especially from justly acquired resources that one had inherited. The streams of justly acquired wealth—and they are so very translucent and gentle—flow far from their source, and nowhere does a rivulet whose waters are commingled with injustice pollute them. In any case, my inherited wealth is not great enough [to allow this level of liberality], nor am I a businessman or a money-maker.

Another thing my accusers say about me is also pure fantasy, that I give out and distribute to my students great amounts of imperial wheat **[292]**. I do give out imperial wheat, and it comes from the public granaries; and if this is a sign of being a sophist, then you would all be sophists—not only you who are seated together here, but also cobblers, bath attendants, leather cutters and all who, early in the morning, bring their tokens to the grain stalls.[16] But it is only fair that you take account of what I am now going to tell you. I was allowed by the emperor to avail myself not only of two hundred *medimnoi* of grain and two hundred *keramia* of olive oil—actually, my accusers do not yet know about the olive oil. Somehow that charge passed me by, so that my opponents could [later] have something to be even more upset and irritated about! As I was saying, I was allowed to avail myself not only of the grain and the oil, but also of that long list [of items] of luxury and comfort that go hand in hand with the hammered tablets. I obtained these prerogatives neither by begging for them nor through flattery nor by making use of a patron who had the emperor's ear, but because the emperor was present when I spoke and heard me in person not once or twice, but many times.[17] As a result, he deemed me worthy

16. If Themistius is a sophist for profiting from the *annona* (see Jones, *Later Roman Emp.*, 2: 696–97; Dagron, *Naissance,* 533–35) and then giving that wheat to his students, so is everyone else who profits from it. Themistius's accusers, though, did not fault him for accepting "imperial wheat" but for using it as bait to catch students.

17. Cf. Them., *Orat.* 18.224a–b, 31.353c, 34 [XIII].

of the greatest honors. Nevertheless, though I was permitted to enjoy these prerogatives, I did not agree or consent to them despite the fact that the emperor was very eager that I should do so.[18] Whether I acted correctly or not is for you to judge in common.

It seems to me very shameful and alien to a free man to lie to and deceive people about the most important aspect of one's person; and it is the mode of one's life and the character one assumes that are the most important aspect of our activities and conditions. Whoever lays claim to philosophy, then, and forcibly appropriates the title philosopher while weighing smoked hams and quarreling with stewards over the monetary value of wine and foodstuffs—well, this man is untrue to the philosopher's cloak, he desires a military belt and a military cloak, he is more vulgar than armed soldiers! Consequently, what I have availed myself of, in the share that is mine, is only an amount of support that met my daily needs and only the grain that the emperor distributes to the inhabitants of this city [Constantinople], not what he gives to soldiers. After all, I too am a citizen of this city, and I have preferred residing here to residing in my native city [293]. If I should permit myself to live in my native city, I would deserve to be scorned, of course, if I demanded grain in another city too.[19]

Whatever would have filled my wallet instead of relieving my slaves' hunger, whatever would have unfailingly caused an unfitting name to cling to my philosopher's cloak immediately upon accepting it, this I firmly refused. I did not dishonor my [spiritual] forebears, for I thought of the king and the philosopher in identical terms and believed that both alike dwell on the summits of human happiness and can go no further. He who thinks and imagines that there is something greater [than those summits] is still, in my opinion, wandering around somewhere in the lower regions and fails to climb up to that peak, which is most lofty and reaches high into the heavens. From that peak one can see not only the whole earth and ocean, but also the throne of Zeus himself and genuine high rank, streams of nectar and the meadow of

18. For the prerogatives Themistius refused to accept, which probably were attached to the Constantinopolitan proconsulship, see above, p. 19.

19. "while . . . quarreling with stewards over the monetary value" etc.: i.e., trying to commute grants in kind into monetary payments (see Carrié, *Mélanges de l'Ecole française* 87 [1975]: 1049–50). "only the grain that the emperor distributes to the inhabitants of this city": Themistius refers here, as at the beginning of 292a, to grain that is his due merely as a Constantinopolitan citizen and resident of the city. Dagron thinks that he is referring to professorial grain (*Naissance,* 534); he is more likely referring to the *annona popularis* (Jones, *Later Roman Emp.*, 2: 696–97). "if I should permit . . . in my native city": the Teubner edition has *ἐν ᾗ εἴπερ τις διάγειν ἐῴην*. Taking up a suggestion of Petavius, I delete *τις* and emend *ἐῴην* to *ἐῴμην*.

ambrosia.[20] You cannot be conveyed up to those summits on a tablet made of gold; you can get there only if you master and profit from the tablet on which Plato and Pythagoras wrote, an ancient tablet and one that has not been eaten away by worms.

So then, what granary do I empty out for my students? What heaps of grain do I pour over them, as if showering newly bought slaves with favors? Aristippus of Cyrene had Dionysius's grain ten times over, yet that did not make him a sophist; but I outdo even Gorgias, so it seems, because of the thirty choenixes![21]

All right, then, [suppose that they are prepared to concede that] I lock up my storehouse, and that I would be less likely to offer anyone a bronze coin than the whole of geometry and arithmetic. [Now they will claim that] I have beguiled one of the youths, a very fine fellow who was raised as an orphan; that he watches over things for me; that he sets out two tables, one laden with luxuries and the other with money; and that before long there cling and cleave to those tables not young men who have any need of Aristotle, but individuals who are seeking material sustinence and wish to fill their bellies. This worthless throng, this good-for-nothing mob escorts me, [they claim], as I rush into the agora **[294]**; they yell and shout out their approval at every word I utter and vie with one another to see who can better carry out

20. "an unfitting name": the Teubner editors rightly mark the transmitted adjective (οὐξοδαπόν) as corrupt, offering several possible emendations in their apparatus criticus. However one might attempt to restore the Greek, the general sense must be "a name that does not fit the philosopher." "for I thought . . . no further": with Smeal, "Themistios: The Twenty-Third Oration," 164–65, I accept Petavius's emendation ὅτι ("for") for οὐ, understanding Themistius to mean, in Smeal's words, that "because the philosopher already occupies the highest plateau of human happiness along with the [ideal] king, he is not in need of an extraordinary compensation from him." Themistius makes that highest plateau metaphorically approach the Olympian heaven. For the partnership of the ideal ruler and the philosopher, Smeal compares Them., *Orat.* 6.72a. "is still . . . wandering": "still" is Reiske's emendation (ἔτι) for the transmitted ἐστι.

21. "showering . . . with favors" (καταχύσματα): for the custom of showering new slaves with dried fruits, nuts, and other edibles, see Aristoph., *Plut.* 768, with schol.; Dem. 45.74; *Suda* K 877, 878 Adler. "Aristippus" etc.: "If the agricultural riches of the Syracusan court did not make the philosopher Aristippus a sophist, how could my relatively modest imperial grain allotment make me one?" For Aristippus at Dionysius's court, see Giannantoni, *Socraticorum reliquiae,* 1: 196–204. There was a tradition that Aristippus was a "sophist" who charged his pupils for his teaching (ibid. 185–88); if Themistius thinks of him as a sophist rather than as a philosopher, perhaps he means that it was the taking of fees, not the acceptance of Dionysius's generosity, that made Aristippus a sophist. For the important role of the sophist Gorgias of Leontini in the history of rhetoric, see, e.g., Diod. Sic. 12.53; Pausan. 6.17.8–9; Philostr., *Vitae soph.* 481, 492–93. "the thirty choenixes": what now are "the thirty choenixes [of grain]?" Are they a prerogative attached to a public chair of philosophy that Themistius is holding? Cf. the 30 *annonae* (= choenixes?) that rhetors at Trier got (*Cod. Theod.* 13.3.11 [A.D. 376]; Bonner, *AJP* 86 [1965]: 128n)?

the lowly function they perform. Well, if I actually had organized such a band of men with someone to act as its leader, I certainly would be a sophist and no less a one than Protagoras, who took advantage of the "pit-wealthy" Callias! But no one of my pupils is as famous as Callias or so extraordinarily given to extravagance. They come to me and love me, but without paying a fee or gaining anything themselves.[22]

By what means, then, do I hunt down and attract young men? What is the spell, what is the charm that causes many to abandon old Greece and neighboring Ionia, areas that both have great schools of philosophy, and come to the city [of Constantinople] to study under us? How is it that they are not prevented from coming by any of those things that make the city "great" and "fortunate"—her constant stream of pleasures, her clamorous festivals, the lack of leisure and quiet here, these sharp-sighted accusers themselves, who shake their spears at your flesh?[23] I hesitate to respond to my own questions, gentlemen, lest I really do appear to be boasting. But my accusers force me to report to this assembly the real inducements that I use on the young in response to the concocted and falsely reported ones. You do perceive well enough what these real inducements are; you have not utterly failed to notice them. Still, they need to be revealed and exposed even more.

When I was young, I wrote certain treatises in which I deposited and stored the legacy that I had received from my forefathers. These treatises have nothing original in them either from me or from anyone else. They only try to clarify what Aristotle means and to draw that meaning out of the words in which he restricted and confined it so that it would be unintelligible to the utterly uninitiated.[24] I never thought

22. "there cling ... to those tables": for "cling," I read Reiske's emendation προσίσχονται for the manuscript's προ-. Callias: In Pl., *Apol.* 20a, Socrates says that Callias spent more money on sophists than everyone else combined; cf. Xen., *Symp.* 1.5, who specifically mentions Protagoras as one of the sophists who were paid money by Callias. Callias is Protagoras's host in Plato's *Protagoras.* For Callias's prodigality and those who benefited from it, see Aristoph., *Av.* 284–86, *Eccles.* 810–11; Andocid. 1.131; Xen., *Symp.* 4.1–5; Athen. 4.169a, 12.537b–c; Philostr., *Vitae soph.* 610. For the epithet "pit-wealthy" (λακκόπλουτος), see Kirchner, *Prosopogr. Attica,* no. 7825; Beloch, *Griechische Geschichte,* 2, 2: 45.

23. Themistius, of course, is being ironic here, listing those features of Constantinopolitan life that should discourage people from coming there.

24. "certain treatises": i.e., apparently the *Paraphrases* of Aristotle. On this paragraph see Blumenthal, *Hermes* 107 (1979), esp. 176–77, responding to Steel, *Revue philosophique de Louvain* 71 (1973): 669–80. "my forefathers": apparently his philosopher father and his philosopher grandfather (Them., *Orat.* 5.63d; cf. 11.145b), on whom see Seeck, *Die Briefe,* 132, and Dagron, *T&MByz* 3 (1968): 6. Or is Themistius using the word "forefathers" figuratively to refer to philosophical predecessors in general? "the words in which he restricted" etc.: cf. Them., *Orat.* 20.235a, d; 26.319b–d.

that these treatises would be of any use to anyone else or would be taken seriously [295], for I knew that they were not works of sufficient richness or boldness to elicit that kind of response. They were merely an aide-mémoire for me alone, a depository for what I had heard, so that, if something should escape my memory, I could retrieve it, so to speak, from a safe storehouse, one that is unassailable by forgetfulness. So I feared for my treatises and kept watch over them lest they be spread abroad. But somehow or other these writings of mine escaped before I knew what was happening. They quickly passed from one person to another until they finally reached Sicyon.

At that time there lived in Sicyon a man who, of all the Greeks of my time, I would say was most truly and genuinely in possession of philosophy. He had been a disciple of the man of Chalcis [i.e., Iamblichus] when the latter was elderly. He was not, however, a devotee of the new song, but of the ancestral and ancient song of the Academy and the Lyceum.[25] He was not the sort of person who would stoop to vilification or become irritated or envious if someone else laid claim to some excellence. No, he was the kind who joined in encouraging and urging on anyone who he saw was inclined to be virtuous. Now after this man briefly familiarized himself with my serious writings—or should I say with my trifles?—he had almost the same experience as the philosopher Axiothea and Zeno of Citium and the Corinthian farmer. When Axiothea read one of the works written by Plato about the state, she left Arcadia and went to Athens. She listened to Plato, causing it to go unnoticed for quite some time that she was a woman, just as Achilles had concealed his sex in the house of Lycomedes. When the Corinthian farmer became acquainted with Gorgias—I do not mean the famous person of that name, but the work of that title that Plato wrote to refute the sophist—he immediately left his field and his vines and submitted his soul to Plato, becom-

25. The "new song" surely means Iamblichus's theurgic Neoplatonism, contrasted with a more conservative form of Platonism (cf. Fowden, *JHS* 102 [1982]: 44; Vanderspoel, *Historia* 36 [1987]: 383). Harduinus's identification of the philosopher of Sicyon with the Celsus (*PLRE,* vol. 1, under "Celsus 3") of Liban., *Epp.* 86 Foerster, was reprinted in Dindorf's edition of Themistius and reaffirmed by the Teubner editors, but Vanderspoel, loc. cit., shows that that identification cannot stand. He proposes instead an identification with Iamblichus's pupil Hierius (*PLRE,* vol. 1, under "Hierius 1"). Fowden, loc. cit., had suggested that Themistius's philosopher might be Iamblichus's pupil Euphrasius (*PLRE,* vol. 1, under "Euphrasius 1"). For Eunapius's lack of interest in Euphrasius as possible evidence of the latter's distance from Iamblichan Neoplatonism—a distance that is required for Themistius's anonymous—see my *Greek Philosophers and Sophists,* 62; for Iamblichus's Chalcis, ibid. 44.

ing a sower and planter of Platonic teachings. (This farmer is the person Aristotle honors in his Corinthian dialogue.) As for Zeno's experience, it is very well known and celebrated by many, I mean how [Plato's] *Apology of Socrates* brought him from Phoenicia to the Painted [Stoa in Athens].[26]

[**296**] The man of Sicyon himself did not need to be fed [by me], but he immediately urged the whole flock of students he was tending to go to the Bosporus [i.e., to Themistius in Constantinople]. And when these young men resisted, he sent them to the [temple of the] god [Apollo] to ask if that man's [i.e., Themistius's] understanding was better [than his own]. The god delivered the same judgment that he had given long ago regarding Socrates.[27] Please trust, gentlemen, by that very Apollo himself, that in reporting this to you I have not made up a story of the kind one would tell to children, nor am I trying to astonish you by the [fact that Apollo was the] judge, nor am I needlessly boasting and putting on airs. There is simply no other way to defend myself from those who malign and slander me than by showing that those who love and speak well of me are far superior to my maligners. For

26. "one of the works written by Plato about the state": or the Greek could mean "one of the books of Plato's *Republic*." Plato's pupil Axiothea wore men's clothing. In thinking of her as an Arcadian, Themistius seems to be confusing her with Lastheneia of Mantinea, another female pupil of Plato whom several ancient texts mention in connection with Axiothea. On Axiothea, see Riginos, *Platonica,* 183–84; Gaiser, *Philodems Academica,* 154–57, 358–59, 362–64. For Achilles disguised as a girl at the court of Lycomedes of Scyros, see, e.g., Stat., *Achill.* 1.198 ff.; Apollod., *Bibl.* 3.13.8; Philostr. Jr., *Imag.* 1 [392K]. "just as Achilles . . . Lycomedes": with Gasda, "Kritische Bemerkungen," 9, I read *ὥσπερ ὁ Ἀχιλλεὺς* <*ἐν*> *τοῦ Λυκομήδους*. Themistius's story about the Corinthian farmer has been taken to be a fragment—the sole fragment—of Aristotle's lost dialogue *Nerinthus,* the title of which is preserved in Diogenes Laertius's list of Aristotle's works (5.22). Those who accept this identification must attempt to explain why Themistius calls this work the "Corinthian dialogue." See Arist., fr. 64 Rose^3 = W. Ross, *Arist. fragmenta selecta* (Oxford, 1955), *Nerinthus,* fr. 1; Gaiser, *Platons ungeschriebene Lehre,* 449; Riginos, *Platonica,* 184–85; Laurenti, *Aristotele,* 1: 461 ff. More recently, and more prudently, O. Gigon keeps the *Nerinthus* and the "Corinthian dialogue" distinct (*Aristotelis opera,* ed. O. Gigon, vol. 3: *Librorum deperditorum fragmenta* [Berlin and New York, 1987], p. 275 and fr. 658). "[Plato's] *Apology*": the Greek has only *ἡ Σωκράτους ἀπολογία* and could have the more general sense "[the story of] Socrates' defense [of himself]." Themistius's anecdote about Zeno has been compared with the story in Diog. Laert. 7.2 (= *SVF,* vol. 1, Zeno, fr. 1) that, *after* coming to Athens, Zeno was converted to philosophy as a result of having read book two of Xenophon's *Memorabilia* (see Petavius and the Teubner editors, ad loc.; Riginos, *Platonica,* 185; Smeal, "Themistios: The Twenty-Third Oration," 173). More to the point is Diog. Laert. 7.31: according to Demetrius of Magnesia, writes Diogenes, Zeno's father brought him "many Socratic books" while he was still a boy at Citium in Cyprus. "Socratic books" (*Σωκρατικῶν βιβλίων*) could certainly include accounts of Socrates's self-defense. For Citium as part of "Greater Phoenicia," Diog. Laert. 7.1, cf. 7.25.

27. I.e., according to the Platonic *Apology* (21a), that there was no one wiser than Socrates; on this occasion, that there was no one wiser than Themistius!

the famous Socrates did not initially reveal the testimony of the Pythian [Apollo]; but when Lycon and Anytus were attacking him and Meletus had brought him to an impasse by charging that he was a sophist and a corrupter of the young, then he was forced to bring in the god as a witness before the jurors. Those jurors were immediately deceived by their own folly and bewitched by the speech composed by Polycrates and paid for by Anytus; for they were common citizens, and there was nothing hallowed about them.[28] But you have been specially selected from every quarter, and furthermore you are on trial with me. For you were the first to understand and to declare that my estate is something better than that of a sophist.

Yet it would not be remarkable, would it, if, by using my commentaries on Aristotle to help and assist me in the hunt, I had chased down a few young men and, by getting those men to act as hosts and paymasters on my behalf, had lured in hungry pupils? These are no mean nets and snares that I just alluded to, it seems! Having escaped from my house, they run around on their own, like Daedalus's statues, catching and tying up young men whose ears are not plugged up,[29] and they bring this quarry to me without my exerting myself greatly—or even slightly [297]! But here is something remarkable about my accusers. It is possible for them to knock these nets off their stakes[30]—these "nets" that go running around this way in their midst and that people are holding in their hands. Yes, it is possible for them to tear apart the joints of these nets and to show that their meshes are very loose and weak, and that people get caught in them only because of their ignorance. Yet my accusers either are unable to do this or choose not to do it. They are like bad hunting dogs who keep barking and

28. "[Socrates] was forced to bring in the god": see Pl., *Apol.* 20e ff. Socrates was indicted in 399 B.C. for corrupting the young and for disbelief in the state's gods, but not explicitly for "being a sophist": Pl., *Apol.* 24b–c; Xen., *Apol.* 10; id., *Mem.* 1.1.1; Diog. Laert. 2.38, 40. In saying that Socrates was indicted for being a sophist, Themistius either regards the actual indictment as tantamount to a charge of sophistry or is thinking of earlier charges against Socrates, such as those mentioned by Pl., *Apol.* 19b, 23d, with which cf. Eupolis, fr. 146b Kock, and Arist., *Rhet.* 2.24 [1402a20–30]. (For Socrates as sophist, see, e.g., Ehrenberg, *People of Aristophanes,* 273–78.) Themistius did not know that Polycrates's *κατηγορία* was written some years after Socrates's death: see Diog. Laert. 2.39; Chroust, *Socrates,* 69 ff., with the cautions of Dodds, *Plato, Gorgias,* 28–29.

29. Themistius imagines his commentaries not only to be running around, but also to be speaking. For Daedalus's "moving," "living" statues, see Morris, *Daidalos,* esp. 217–26; cf. Them., *Orat.* 26.316a–b, 28.342d.

30. "stakes": for the transmitted *χαλίδων*, read *σχαλίδων* (cf. Romano, *Κοινωνία* 4 [1980]: 117n). "[K]nock[ing] these nets off," etc. means, of course, successfully finding fault with Themistius's commentaries.

making a fuss: they derive no benefit from all that commotion and only end up scaring away the prey.

Very well, then. We have managed, even if with some difficulty, to work our way through [the charge of being] a mercenary sophist.[31] Let us next consider the labels "merchant," "retailer," and "seller of one's own goods" [cf. above, 288a] and see if any of them suits us. Now the divine Plato says that there is an art of exchange, which barters what it gives for what it receives. He says that people call the kind of interurban exchange that involves buying and selling and results in a transfer of goods "merchandising." As for intra-urban exchange of goods, if there is a sale of one's own handiwork or services, as in the cases of cooks and bath attendants, one would properly speak, according to Plato, of "an exchange of one's own goods"; but if one purchases goods made by others [and then resells them], the proper term for this would be "retailing" [cf. Pl., *Soph.* 223c–d].

Plato further says that merchandising, selling one's own goods and retailing, although they all fall under the single category of "exchange," are each differentiated into two subtypes by means of the same distinction by which the goods for sale themselves are differentiated. For, says Plato, there is a merchant who deals in foods, clothing, shoes—in a word, in all those things that our body requires—and there is a merchant who deals in the teachings and instruction by which the soul is nourished or flattered [Pl., *Soph.* 223e–24d, *Protag.* 313c–14b]. The same holds true for the retailer and for the man who sells his own goods. Anyone, then, who takes music or grammar or painting or anything else that benefits or soothes the soul and carries any such competence from city to city, buying in one place and selling in another, is no less a merchant than Lampis of Aegina. And if a person settles down right there in a city, purchasing some of his knowledge from others and putting together some of it on his own, and then sells that learning and exchanges it for money, he is a retailer or a seller of his own goods, and a somewhat more clever one than Sarambus or Thearion [**298**]. Thus Plato shows once again that the sophist is a three-headed monster like Geryon.[32]

31. Cf. Pl., *Rep.* 4.441c.

32. For the rich shipowner Lampis, see Dem. 23.211 (and note the comment of Volpis, *Demostene: L'orazione contro Aristocrate,* ad loc.); Plut., *Apophth. Lac.* 234f, *An seni res p. ger.* 787a; Clem. Alex., *Strom.* 7.16.101, p. 71 Stählin. Demosthenes 23.211 comments on Lampis's relationship with Aegina. "Sarambus or Thearion": cf. Pl., *Gorg.* 518b–c; Them., *Orat.* 21.251c. "Geryon": cf. Hes., *Theog.* 287; Palaephatus, *Περὶ ἀπίστων* 24 Festa. Plato, *Soph.* 240c, calls the sophist "many-headed."

For engaging in what kind of exchange, then, do my accusers indict me? Surely not for the kind that involves traveling abroad, nor for the kind that would require me to go only one stade. To be sure, I have visited and spent time in many cities, and I have traveled farther than Socrates, not just to Potidaea on military campaign. I actually have never borne arms on your behalf, but for your sake I have traversed much territory and have gone to many great and prosperous cities, including our mother city—and I do not mean ancient Megara, from where those who dwell along the Bosporus came, but the city [i.e., Rome] that rules over the other cities and co-rules with your city. If you benefited in some other [i.e., nonmilitary] way from that trip [to Rome], I would be reluctant to say so.[33]

In any case, I brought to the Romans the wares that belonged to me from the first as well as those I acquired here among you in the course of a full twenty years. Many of those wares I gathered together from the old treasures of memory, and some of them were my own handiwork. Well, those [Romans], who, as you know, look down on everything and are either unwilling or unable to admire anything that comes from abroad because there are so many things to admire in their own city—those Romans were nonetheless so captivated and overwhelmed by my wares that they offered me much land, both for tillage and for fruit-farming, to use and enjoy as I wished. They also offered me much silver and gold. They came every day to the place where I was staying and went to amazing ends to convince me to remain there for a while and to open up for them, as best as I could, the long closed precincts of Pythagoras and the temples of Plato and Aristotle and to reveal to them the statues therein.[34] When they were unable to persuade me [to stay], and I gave them my wares free of charge and then was hastening back to you, they tried to apply force and to call in the great emperor

33. "traveling abroad . . . only one stade": i.e., he can be indicted neither for interurban nor for intra-urban exchange. Note Pl., *Rep.* 2.371d. For Socrates at Potidaea, see Pl., *Apol.* 28e, *Charmid.* 153, *Symp.* 219e ff. Themistius is referring to his visit to Rome in 357 (Dagron, *T&MByz* 3 [1968]: 205–12). Rome, of course, is the spiritual mother city of Constantinople, the refounded Byzantium, in contrast to Megara, the literal mother city of Byzantium; see Dagron, *Naissance,* 15, 53. "if you benefited in some other way": Themistius apparently persuaded the emperor Constantius, while they were both in Rome, to augment Constantinople's dole. See Them., *Orat.* 34 [XIII] with n. 19 to my translation of that passage.

34. "a full twenty years": see above, p. 20. "wares . . . gathered . . . from the old treasures of memory, and some . . . my own handiwork": i.e., the intellectual property of others and some that he regards as his own. "to open up . . . precincts . . . and to reveal . . . statues": for this metaphorical manner of speaking about revealing philosophical truth, cf. Them., *Orat.* 20.235a–c.

[Constantius] to assist them with their passionate desire. What more trustworthy witness could I produce for you than the emperor himself, whose testimony has already been read to you in the senate? How, then, could I market my wisdom **[299]**, and to what other people would I go to do this, if the men to whom I could have most easily and readily sold my wares enjoyed them as a free gift?

I say nothing about the city of Antiochus [i.e., Antioch] and all the men I met there who craved and got hold of my merchandise. I say nothing of those I met in the Hellenized [parts of] Galatia. Those [Galatian] cities are not so great, nor can they contend with this greatest city [of ours], but you know that their citizens are sharp-minded and smart and quicker to learn than even the very Hellenic are. Once the philosopher's cloak appears among them, they immediately cling to it, as iron clings to a magnet. What would these men not give to be able to bring the teachings of Plato into their cities from abroad? These are men who, for Demosthenes's forensic orations or Thucydides's history, pay almost as much to experts in those classics as Xerxes did to Themistocles, son of Neocles![35] I know that many people from those cities are taking part in this assembly and judicial hearing. Ask them if what I say is true.

As to my not being a merchant who deals in any teachings, find out and inquire about that from others; but to determine that I am not a retailer or a seller of my own goods, direct your questions to yourselves.[36] Ask yourselves if I have settled here in a shop where I sell wretched speeches, either long or short ones. Ask yourselves if I proposed to make my living from some such business, and whether I have behaved like those very sophistical retailers who, as they hold out a measuring cup, yell and shout that that drink of theirs has the aroma of nectar, and that their half-pint is more capacious [than their rivals' is]. < . . . >

35. Antioch and Galatian cities: Themistius visited Antioch, which was wooing him, in 356 (Dagron, *T&MByz* 3 [1968]: 8–9). Galatian cities (esp. Ancyra?) would also have liked to have had his professional services. He had delivered *Orat.* 1 at Ancyra, probably early in 347, and Vanderspoel hypothesizes that he had taught for a while there in the 340s. See Dagron, ibid., 8–9; Vanderspoel, *Themistius,* 48–49, 73–77. "sharp-minded . . . quicker to learn": cf. Pl., *Rep.* 6.503c? "the very Hellenic": those in more fully Hellenized areas, those in the lands of classical Greece. Themistocles: it was actually Xerxes's son Artaxerxes who was generous to Themistocles, but the error already appears in Strabo 13.1.13 [587], 14.1.10 [636]; see Podlecki, *Life of Themistocles,* 41–42, 117–18.

36. "but to determine that I am not a retailer": Themistius now turns from interurban exchange (merchandising) to intra-urban exchange (retailing or selling one's own goods). Cf. Pl., *Soph.* 224d.

ORATION 24

An Exhortation to the Nicomedians

[300] When Prodicus and Gorgias were once living in Athens, there were people who paid serious attention to Socrates, the son of Sophroniscus. Yet Prodicus and Gorgias delivered orations that were extravagantly wrought and brimming with delight [301], and consequently they were able to charge their audience a fee to hear them; whereas Socrates's words were not fancy or clever, but he spoke in a simple, ordinary, casual manner and would gladly have paid someone for wanting to listen to him. Now I hope that you yourselves do not scorn one who is trying to present you with friendly offerings just because they are not extremely delightful or capable of enchanting your ears. You do often gather together to enjoy such presentations, and you love your banquet-givers because they are inventive, generous, and unstinting in their provisions, because they always set a Sicilian table and prepare many cunningly wrought [verbal] contrivances for you. Some of these men sing a native song, others sing a song that is Syrian and from the Lebanon. They beguile you with their music, whether it is domestic or imported.[1]

1. For Socrates's willingness to pay to be heard in contrast to the fee-taking of sophists such as Prodicus of Ceos and Gorgias of Leontini, cf. Pl., *Euthyphro* 3d. For the speaker as a banquet-giver, see also Them., *Orat.* 26.313a, 33.367a; cf. Pl., *Lysis* 211c, *Rep.* 1.352b, 354a–b, *Phaedr.* 227b, 236e, *Tim.* 27b; Liban., *Epp.* 241.4 Foerster. A Sicilian table is a lavish one: cf. Pl., *Epp.* 7.326b; Hor., *Carm.* 3.1.18; Athen. 12.518c; Them., *Orat.* 20.238b; Liban., *Orat.* 11.236; *CPG* 2.641. "prepare . . . for you": I read the variant "you" (ὑμῖν) instead of "us" (ἡμῖν), which is adopted in the

If you have come together here expecting any such performance from me, it is time for you to take your leave and not to trouble yourselves in vain. But if you can tolerate a Lycurgus as your banquet-giver,[2] then I would welcome you without hesitation—not with offerings as extravagant as those of others, but with what are perhaps more wholesome ones, offerings that it is possible not merely to admire, but also to derive some benefit from after the admiring is over. For the words I utter are born of Mnemosyne and Zeus.[3] Those elegant and playful utterances [of mere rhetors] have the same parentage, but there is a great difference between my utterances and those brother utterances of theirs. What that difference is I can tell you, if you want to hear about it. But please do not think me garrulous, a babbler who deviates aimlessly from his subject. For this is an important feature of my eloquence: it is free and independent, and, once it takes leave of its father, it is not compelled to stay on one course. If its pleasure is to take a course other than the one that lies before it, it makes a quick change and is not thereby led astray. What the difference is, then, between my utterances and their brother utterances you will easily learn from what I am about to tell you.

Teubner edition. "Some of these men sing" etc.: I translate *Ἀσσύριον* as "Syrian." Contending that Assyrian here means Christian and, on the inspiration of this passage, that the Neoplatonist Iamblichus was born at Chalcis ad Libanum rather than at Chalcis ad Belum, Vanderspoel, *Hermes* 116 (1988): 127–28, thinks that Themistius is polemicizing against "the normal pursuits of pagan education and . . . the popularity of rhetoric" (native song), against Christianity (Assyrian song) and against Iamblichan theurgy (song from the Lebanon); cf. id., *Themistius,* 18, 27, 44. I do not accept this interpretation. The notion that Themistius uses the word "Assyrian" to mean Christian perhaps originated in Petavius's note on this passage (cf. also Maisano, *Κοινωνία* 10 [1986]: 31). Themistius certainly uses the word to refer to the ancient Hebrews, specifically in quoting the Book of Proverbs (*Orat.* 7.89d, 11.147c, 19.229a), but "Assyrian" nowhere clearly means Christian in Themistius. For "Assyrian" meaning Syrian, note *Anth. gr.* 7.417.1–5; Dio Cass. 80.11.1–2; Nonnus, *Dionys.* 41.19. In the phrase "song that is Syrian and from the Lebanon" (*οἱ δὲ Ἀσσύριον καὶ ἐκ Λιβάνου* [*ᾄδοντες μέλος*]), the words "from the Lebanon" are a specification of what Themistius already has in mind in the more general word "(As)syrian." (Cf. Nonnus, loc. cit., "Assyrian Lebanon.") Despite the plural *οἱ δὲ* [*ᾄδοντες*], Themistius may have only one Lebanese sophist or rhetor at Nicomedia in mind. On my understanding, an allusion here to Libanius, proposed by a number of scholars (Brinkmann, *RhM* 64 [1909]: 639; Dagron, *T&MByz* 3 [1968]: 39; Teubner edition of Themistius's *Orations,* 2: 98; Maisano, *Κοινωνία* 10 [1986]: 31), is excluded: despite his name, Libanius was not from the Lebanon. In this passage, then, Themistius refers to sophists/rhetors at Nicomedia who are native (i.e., Nicomedian or at least Asianic), and he alludes to at least one rival at Nicomedia who is from the Lebanon.

2. A Lycurgan banquet would, of course, be a modest one: Xen., *Rep. Lac.* 2.5, 5.3–7; Plut., *Lycurg.* 10, 12.1, 13.4–7. Lycurgan speech is restrained: Plut., ibid. 19–20.

3. Mnemosyne and Zeus were the parents of the Muses (Hes., *Theog.* 52ff., 915 ff.).

We know that all things that are perishable and have a weak nature have two main needs: they need rest from constant toil, and they need to be cared for so that they do not deteriorate [302]. Let us therefore understand that the soul too needs both an eloquence that gives it rest and an eloquence that cares for it. Thus, there is one class of individuals who, when they come to the Muses' theater (and they do so regularly and often), smile at you and fawn upon you and greet the audience's leader with an embrace, whereas another class of individuals mainly stay at home and prefer to care for you away from the public arena.[4] If a god induces men of this latter class to address the people, they immediately become quite grave and make no effort to entertain; they are so uninterested in flattering their audience that often, once they become aware of some fault in them, they actually censure them. As for myself, since I am speaking to friends who are generally in healthy condition, I must imitate the wiser class of physicians, the ones who give their patients a bitter potion to drink only after having smeared the cup with honey. Perhaps you will let yourselves be more submissive to an oration that is therapeutic in a pleasurable way—an oration that one might liken to a skillful charioteer who uses the reins to control the chariot but does without a goad or whip. Now what can I say to benefit and, at the same time, to please you? I feel very obliged to favor this type of discourse in speaking to you. Let me tell you why.

The god who desired to attach me to this city and stirred up in me this genuine love for it does not allow me to remain here aimlessly and make no contribution to you, behaving as many of your admirers do. Nor does he allow me to treat you with bitter medicine,[5] lest, before I can cure you, I am unwittingly repudiated because of the unpleasantness of what I say. If I were the only person to have been enthralled by you, I could freely glory in the objects of my love without fearing that you might prefer a rival admirer. But as things are—for, as you can see, others have been moved to love you just as I have—it seems to me that the extreme tact and charm of my rivals will carry you away, and you will consequently slight me for being too solemn. And so I am compelled to tell you what for a long time I was resolved to keep to myself. The court of philosophy is not entirely devoid of Graces [303],

4. The two classes of individuals are sophists and philosophers who are disinclined to address the general public.

5. "Nor . . . medicine": an approximation for the Teubner's *οὔτε μὴν* [sc., *συγχωρεῖ*] *πικροτέροις φαρμάκοις πρὸς τὴν βοήθειαν †ἕλκεσθαι†*.

nor do those goddesses dwell far away from my classrooms. I would never organize a chorus [of students] for you that did not have its share of moderate pleasure. On the contrary, I shall be eager that Aphrodite always consort with the Muses; for she and they are sisters and delight in their relationship.[6]

In order that you may understand that this harmonious relationship of the goddesses is not an impossible thing, I want to share with you a piece of information that has hitherto not been revealed to you. A twofold race dwells within me, my friends. The two parts of the race have separate areas of residence, having divided between themselves the dwelling-places in my soul. Rhetoric nurses one part of the race, all-beautiful Philosophy the other. Now if you would like to acquaint yourselves with these two mothers of learning and to understand what the nature of each is, then listen as I tell you how they are represented.

Philosophy has a solemn appearance, a body of good size, and seemly garb. (Artists portray the virtues associated with her in identical garb.) Her hair is not let loose and allowed to become disheveled, nor is it braided in an intricately styled manner; it suffers neither from being given no attention nor from being given excessive attention. For since Philosophy has a marvelous natural beauty, she does not value or welcome artifice of any kind. Thus she does not use eye-liner or artificially redden her cheeks. A blush that is full of temperance appears on her face. Her glance brims with sobriety and is such that it also imparts sobriety to those who have beheld her. Looking upon this unadorned sight has already proved to be enough to cause a moral reform in the lives of some individuals. The Attic Polemo is a case in point. He had been accustomed to reveling in merrymaking, flute-playing, and drinking. But when he beheld Philosophy living with Xenocrates, that was the end of those flutes and parties and that vulgar passion of his; those things were driven out of his soul and no longer interested him. Instead, he latched on to the utter purity of Philosophy and, in his yearning for her [304], advanced so far that he received the honor of being initiated in the sacred rites of this goddess.[7]

6. "Graces . . . my classrooms [μουσείων]": Themistius seems to be alluding to the tradition that Speusippus, who succeeded Plato as head of the Academy, erected statues of the Graces in the Academy's μουσεῖον (Diog. Laert. 4.1). Zeus was the father of both Aphrodite and the Muses (Hom., *Il.* 5.312, 370–71; above, n. 3). Aphrodite, of course, represents the "charm" and "moderate pleasure" to which Themistius has just referred.

7. Cf. with this personification of the antithetical philosophy and rhetoric Them., *Orat.* 22.280a ff., and the examples of personified antitheses given in Waites, *HSCP* 23 (1912): 1–46. Polemo succeeded Xenocrates as head of the Academy in 315/14 B.C. For

As for Rhetoric—for I am sure that you yearn to know how she is represented too—she is a noble and very beautiful woman herself, but she is not content with her natural looks and often desires to beautify herself artificially. Her body is concealed by her many intricate adornments. She delights in the theaters of the Greeks and pushes her children into making public appearances from a very early age. They are such genuine offspring of this mother of theirs and so enamored of choral performance that they often manage to persuade their brothers [i.e., the offspring of Philosophy] to go with them to the theaters they frequent. The children have often persuaded the [two] mothers to go too and, all combined together, have ended up forming a wonderful united chorus, a Muses' chorus, so to speak. If they should be unwilling to take part in the chorus with one another, then each side is harmed by and harms the other in turn. The chorus of Philosophy's children, being full of solemnity, will have no share in pleasure and grace; the other chorus, lacking the restraint that comes from a sense of propriety, is often overtaken by a frenzy that leads to a lack of order at odds with what the Muses stand for. The best chorus is the one in which all the brothers join together with one another and blend pleasure with a sense of propriety—the very blend they keep promising you they will produce.

And for this zeal of theirs, they [i.e., the twofold race in Themistius's soul] ask for neither gold nor glory from you—for they are not mercenary or ambitious—but only for your genuine love and for a devotion as intense as that which they feel towards you. But they still do not believe me; they still do not think that they could ever be loved by you as much as they love you. They ask me to tell you a very old story, one that deserves your attention, and I shall do so. For our race has always loved tales; Greeks have an uncontrollable and insatiable thirst for the old stories and often seem to rattle on about them.

When Aphrodite gave birth to Eros, the child was beautiful and befitted his mother in every respect but one: he did not grow to a size appropriate to his beauty, nor did his body get larger [305], but for a very long time he remained just as he was when he was born. The baby's mother and the Graces, his nurses, did not know what to do when confronted with this situation. They went to Themis—for

---

his moral conversion, see the texts assembled in Gigante, *Rendiconti dell'Accad. di arch., lett. e belle arti di Napoli* 51 (1976): 107 ff. "that vulgar passion" (ἔρως ὁ πάνδημος): see Pl., *Symp.* 180e. "of this goddess": the Teubner edition adopts the transmitted τοῦ θεοῦ. I read Reiske's τῆς θεοῦ.

Apollo did not yet have possession of Delphi[8]—and asked her to find some means by which they might be delivered from their strange and astonishing misfortune. Themis said, "I shall put an end to your predicament. The problem is that you do not yet know the true nature of the baby. Eros, your genuine offspring, may perhaps have been born alone, Aphrodite, but he cannot grow alone in any part of his body: you need an Anteros if you want Eros to grow. These brothers will have the same nature; each will be responsible for the other's growth. For when they see each other, they will both shoot up equally; but if one of them is deprived of the other, they will both shrink in size." And so Aphrodite conceived Anteros, and Eros immediately had a spurt of growth and sprouted wings and was tall. Since this is Eros's fortune, he often endures strange transformations, now sprouting up, now shrinking, then growing again. He always needs his brother's presence. If he sees that his brother is of sizable stature, he is eager to appear bigger himself; but he often shrinks in size, against his own will, once he has discovered that his brother is shrunken and small.

Consider, then, that perhaps what I have told you has a serious meaning. I have welcomed the god [Eros] and given him a place in my soul and do not want to break my promise to him. From the moment he settled here I promised him that his brother [Anteros] would also be present and dwell here as one of the objects of my love.[9]

Now what do you think induces me to have such affection for you? This incredible, long sea-way? No, seamanship suits me no more than it does the soldiers of Arcadia. Then is it the kindly Phrygian river? But I also marvel at the Egyptian Nile—not because it fathers crops, but because it flows through the land where those wise Egyptians dwell. Well, is it the size of the nearby lake that attracts me to you? Then why did I not yearn for Lake Maeotis, with its circumference of 6,000 stadia [306]?[10]

8. For Themis's possession of the Delphic oracle before Apollo, cf., e.g., Aesch., *Eum.* 1 ff.; Pausan. 10.5.6. See on this consultation of the oracle the comments of Fontenrose, *Delphic Oracle,* 413.

9. "a serious meaning": i.e., not just an old mythological tale. The partnership of Eros and Anteros represents, of course, that of rhetoric and philosophy. For Eros and Anteros, see Merrill, *Speculum* 19 (1944), esp. 265–72.

10. "This incredible . . . sea-way": the Sinus Astacenus (Gulf of Izmit). Arcadia is landlocked. For seafaring as something alien to Arcadians, note Hom., *Il.* 2.614. "the . . . Phrygian river": the Sangari(u)s, which Themistius refers to by name below. Its sources are in Phrygia. "the nearby lake": Petavius and the Teubner editors, ad loc., identified it with Lake Ascania (Iznik), on the east side of which was located Nicomedia's rival Nicaea. It is more likely to be Lake Sunonensis (Sabanca), much closer to Nicomedia than Lake Ascania is (see Moore, *AJA* 54 [1950]: 97 ff.; Robert, *Documents d'Asie*

Now these attractions of your territory are great ones, and anyone who values such things will certainly be able to add more to the list—the extraordinary beauty of your baths, your theaters, your racecourses. But it is something else, my friends—for I must conceal nothing from you—that caused me to love you so passionately. I have a high-minded attraction to that "something else," a noble and inherited attraction. I could never love a man who does not have good qualities of soul in abundance but instead is enveloped by many cleverly fabricated externals. Such externals remind me of the feathers that the fable puts on the jackdaw: in the beauty contest he puts all his effort into trying to turn the good looks of others to his own advantage because he lacks a natural beauty of his own. I could not love a man who lacks good qualities of soul even if he lives in a house better than that of the Spartan king [i.e., Menelaus] and wears clothes more delicate than spiders' webs—delicate like the fetters of Hephaestus described by Homer [*Od.* 8.272 ff.]. (Those fetters of Hephaestus firmly bind the licentious and are unbreakable, even though they are invisible.)[11]

No, I could not love a man who lacks good qualities of soul, even if he bedecks himself in every other kind of adornment and reminds me of a picture I once saw: it was painted by a Persian and depicts one of the Persian kings, a handsome young man sitting on a royal throne. He has a tiara made of aquamarine and emerald and wears a wide collar made of the same gems and a purple cloak shot with gold. Suppose that someone should adorn the king himself even more lavishly than he is adorned in the painting. I shall certainly not think of the person as something more valuable than the painting. In fact, given that the person apparently shares in soul, what could be more odious than to compare him to the works of painters? Paintings aim and strive to open their eyes to everyone, just as if they were living and intelligent beings; but if you have a serious desire to learn from and ask questions of them, they are silent.[12]

As I said, I could never hold a person without good qualities of soul in high regard, nor could I think highly of a city in which men value theaters, baths, and racecourses for wretched ponies instead of

---

Mineure, 112–14). For ancient assessments of the size of Lake Maeotis (Sea of Azov), see Herrmann, "Maiotis 1," *RE,* 14, 1 (1928): 591–92.

11. "the jackdaw": cf. Aesop, *Fab.* 103 Hausrath-Hunger. The jackdaw covers himself with the plumage of other birds. "the Spartan king": cf. Them., *Orat.* 33.365b–c.

12. Cf. Pl., *Phaedr.* 275d. Themistius associates the mistaken valuing of body over soul with the even more fundamentally wrongheaded willingness to compare a human being to a soulless object.

the precincts of the Muses, Hermes, and Apollo. I would never have become so fond of you [307] if I had not known that you make some claim to virtue, not even if your bay [the Sinus Astacenus] brought in many more wonderful and unblemished things than it actually does, or if the Sangaris [River] brought in gold dust instead of grain. For virtue, according to Socrates, can belong to a city as well as to an individual man [cf. esp. Pl., *Rep.* 2.368e]. We do not call a person good because he owns many fields or houses or many items of clothing and pairs of shoes, or because he dines at a costly table and drinks from golden goblets, but because he has a sound intellect and cares about being educated. Similarly, we do not call that city good in which there is much for sale in a sumptuous marketplace, in which there are hordes of men drunk on wine and heaps of silver and gold casually stacked up on money changers' counters, in which the theaters' gates never close and horses are continuously racing—and I do not mean warhorses, although the horses I have in mind do stir up a truer war than warhorses.[13] For it is inevitable that such a city has festering sores and a deep-seated disease. Sometimes the swollenness caused by its diseased state is not noticed; the city might even appear to be very happy to those who see only what appears on the surface. But at other times the swelling suddenly shows and breaks out, allowing the city to listen, with a sense of appropriateness, to these words of Sophocles: "The city reeks with incense, it resounds with prayers and groans" [*Oed. Tyr.* 4–5].

Among other true words uttered by Phocylides are these: that a small city situated on a promontory and possessed of good judgment is superior to Nineveh in all her foolishness [*Sent.*, fr. 4 Diehl, *Anth. Lyr. Gr.*³]. I do want your land to be more productive than other lands; but I regard it as more important that your souls bear the fruits of learning, the learning that the Muses cull from Apollo's meadows and then hatch and bring to life in desirous souls that love what is good and beautiful. If souls graciously welcome this swarm of Muses, they immediately become winged and, with disregard for [the earth that is] at hand, traverse the heavens. These are the souls who, as the wise Euripides says, "do not hasten to share the troubles experienced by their fellow citizens or to commit unjust acts [308], but behold the ageless order of immortal nature" [fr. 910 Nauck]. For to look on true learning is really a soothing, serene, and placid experience. True learning is

13. "a truer war": i.e., a moral war within men's souls or in the body politic.

like something that is sheltered by a strong wall in a dust and windstorm.[14] No, it is what *gives* shelter to its devotees and protects them with a bulwark more unbreakable than any hard metal. Neither the powerful assault of insolence nor the tricky devices of pleasure could easily weaken this bulwark, and it is able to bear up against the unsteady moves of fortune. For this is the only wall that truly is the work of Apollo. The famous Trojan wall was not, I think, his work. For if it had been, it would not have easily given way to a single act of deceit. So do not let Homer tell us that Apollo and Poseidon built Troy's fortifications in service to Laomedon, nor let him make up a story about how the gods took wages for their service [*Il.* 7.452–53, cf. 21.441 ff.].[15] For only children will attend to him, believe him, and listen to him when he indulges in this sort of clever poetic invention.

Let us rather accept those passages in which Homer has represented the king of the Achaeans begging the gods to let him have, not ten warriors like Achilles, but ten counselors like Nestor [*Il.* 2.372]—the very old man Nestor, useless in battle, who Homer says was so burdened by old age that he could hardly cut through the attaching trace of a horse [*Il.* 8.87 ff.]. For Homer, I think, considers wisdom to be more worthy of honor than physical strength, and a good education more valuable than good birth. Thus everything Nestor says and does meets his highest expectations. But as for noble Achilles—although he brandished that famous ashen spear and was driven about by immortal horses and had sacked twenty-three cities, yet, since he was still suffering from a defective education, he did not pay full heed to Phoenix [*Il.* 9.328–29, 434–619; 16.140–54]. He cries because of a captive girl, he rolls about on the ground because of the fated death of a friend, and others forcibly restrain his hands, as if they belonged to a madman [*Il.* 1.349, 18.26–34; cf. 16.47, 849]. He releases a corpse only in exchange for gold and takes a payment for it [*Il.* 24.232, 468 ff.], and he is portrayed as being guilty of many other transgressions as well. The poet thereby shows that neither distinguished ancestors nor bodily strength [309], neither swiftness of foot nor extraordinary physical beauty is of much avail to one endowed with such things unless he also has good judgment. Now if these splendid and revered qualities are adorned by

14. "True learning is like" etc.: cf. Pl., *Rep.* 6.496d; Them., *Orat.* 8.104c, 26.326b.

15. "So do not let Homer" etc.: *Μή λεγέτω οὖν ἡμῖν Ὅμηρος ὅτι . . . ἐπυργώσαντο, μηδ' ὅτι διὰ πυρὸς ἐξειργάσθη καὶ ὕδατος, καταψευδέσθω δουλείαν ἔμμισθον τῶν θεῶν.* With Gasda, "Kritische Bemerkungen," 15, I delete *ὅτι διὰ . . . ὕδατος*.

learning, they would not seem entirely worthless; but in the absence of learning, they only make a person's iniquity all the more apparent.

Through his other poem and the second of his two philosophers [i.e., Nestor and Odysseus]—posted as this second philosopher was and boldly defending himself against the blows of fortune[16]—the poet seems to me to be saying nothing but this: that good judgment and the whole of virtue cannot be beaten or conquered by anything. And the man who uses virtue as his strong defense does not have an ignoble look on his face, the poet tells us, nor does he cast his eyes downward as he proceeds. Rather, he proceeds just as that great man [Odysseus] did when he walked towards Nausicaa [*Od.* 6.127 ff.]. Odysseus, having escaped the rough water, was naked and alone. Yet, since his raiment of virtue made up for his lack of clothing, he did not look like a beggar, the poet says, nor did he have the bearing of a cowering suppliant as he walked away from the surf and towards the king's daughter. Rather, the poet, being a maker of images that represent virtue, fashioned a simile and wrote [*Od.* 6.130] "he went along like a lion bred in the mountains, trusting in his strength." His "strength," of course, was reason. Of this alone heaven did not have the power to deprive him, even though it had deprived him of his wordly goods, his ships, his soldiers, and, at last, by Zeus, of the very shirt on his back. But Odysseus's power was not to be found in any of those things. And when he lost them, he put his trust in that which was his strength.[17]

16. Cf. Pl., *Rep.* 3.399b.

17. For Odysseus as a hero of wisdom and virtue, see Buffiere, *Les mythes d'Homère,* 372–91. For the sufficiency of his virtue, despite his lacking the gifts fortune gave to Achilles, cf. ps.-Plut., *De Homero* 2.136.

ORATION 25

In Reply to One Who Asked for an Extempore Oration

[309] Even if Phidias was extremely skilled at representing the divine or human form in gold and ivory, still he needed considerable time and leisure to execute his works. In fact [310], it is said that when he was working on his Athena, the base of the statue alone required much time and effort. So if someone had ordered him to demonstrate his talent by day's end, what would he have done? How would he have obeyed the command? Consider whether this would have been a proper response for him to make to an admirer: "Most excellent sir, you who love to behold my works, if you do not allow and concede me time to execute something new and original, you will simply have to gaze at my Athena [Parthenos] in the city [i.e., Athens] or my Zeus at Olympia until I finish sculpting something else; these works will be enough to nurture your admiration of Phidias." [1]

Since you yourself, my dear sir, think that you can wish a piece of my workmanship into existence on this very day, I too would urge you, my admirer, to direct your attention to something I have already crafted. You will not, I think, have to go to a place where one of these works is located. For I carry the products of my art within me; they are

1. The cult statues of Athena in the Parthenon and of Zeus in his temple at Olympia were Phidias's most famous works; see G. Lippold, "Pheidias 2," *RE,* 19, 2 (1938): 1920, 1925.

created in particular places but travel around from all those places with their craftsman.[2]

Allow me the time I need to fashion your image [in words]. I am not so clever and glib as to be able to improvise portraits at random, as the remarkable sophists do. Nor am I able to fashion a portrait of any official [ἄρχοντα], but only of one who can make ready this canvas of mine, which will have on it Justice as well as a physical likeness [of its subject], Mildness as well as power, and a host of many other gods and spirits; for it is not right for Socratic portraitists to fashion portraits that lack these features.

I do not undertake this kind of work very often, since I have very few models available to me. But the canvas you are setting up for me is a fine one and large, and the picture will not be cramped. On the right I shall put Law, which reared you from your boyhood and is now your partner. On the left I shall put Justice (may she never abandon you!) and whatever other attendants my model may indicate to be in order.[3] Such indications will be forthcoming, I am sure [311], and consequently no crucial features will be missing in my portrait.

But my time is limited. So now I must present to you an oration of mine, one selected from my hidden store.[4] The beauty of eloquence, of course, is not such that it blossoms forth in a newly fashioned oration only to fade away when the piece has become old; whatever shape eloquence takes at the outset, it retains forever.

2. The word I translate here as "products," ἀγάλματα, also means "cult statues" and thus sustains the comparison of Themistius's orations to Phidias's sculpture. Cf. Them., *Orat.* 20.235a–b, 27.332b; Liban., *Epp.* 77.1 Foerster, τὰ ἀγάλματα τῆς ψυχῆς. In the next paragraphs, Themistius works on a "canvas" (πίναξ); he produces a painted portrait (γραφή) or an image (εἰκών). The products that Themistius carries around with him are previously prepared orations (see the last paragraph of *Orat.* 25). "they . . . travel . . . with their craftsman": cf. Them., *Orat.* 27.336a.

3. "very few models available": Themistius must mean model individuals, not model orations. One "makes ready" (previous paragraph) or "sets up" (next sentence) a panegyrist's canvas by living an exemplary life. For officials enthroned beside Justice (and other political virtues), see Kantorowicz, *AJA* 57 (1953): 65–70. For "Law, which reared you from your boyhood," cf. Him., *Orat.* 46.10 Colonna, where the official in question is said to have been raised from infancy by Dike and Themis.

4. τί...τῶν ἀπορρήτων: "hidden" or secret because not published and therefore new to the person Themistius is addressing.

ORATION 26

<On Speaking, or, How the Philosopher Should Speak>[1]

PREFACE [*Προθεωρία*]

[311] Surely you do not think that I love theaters so much that I am unaware that a few discriminating men are more formidable to a speaker than the uninformed masses. Similarly, I think, a few select opponents make the leaders of armies more cautious than a huge mass of lightly armed men who have been thrown together, men off their guard and unmounted, shouting and clamoring in various languages. I am thinking of the kind of barbarian army described by Homer; he likens their shouting to that of birds who scream as they fly south to the Nile River because of the hard winter [*Il.* 2.804, 3.2 ff., 4.435 ff.]. As for my reaction to you, gentlemen, you know well that I am far more hesitant and timid in your presence than I was earlier before that large audience in the theater, who so readily shout their approval and so frequently jump up from their seats. At Athens, too, the Areopagus was a more respected court than the juries of one thousand and one men. But I suppose that you will not allow me to extend my introductory remarks any further; for the law did not permit that in the Areopagus either.[2]

1. The title has been supplied by editors (*Περὶ τοῦ λέγειν ἢ πῶς τῷ φιλοσόφῳ λεκτέον*). See Schenkl, *SAWW* 192, 1 (1919): 48, but note Kesters, *Plaidoyer*, 213–14.

2. "Surely . . . uninformed masses": cf. Pl., *Symp.* 194b–c. "At Athens, too," etc.: for the juries of 1,001, cf. Them., *Orat.* 23.283b, with n. 1 to my translation. For the respect accorded to the select Areopagus, see MacDowell, *Law in Classical Athens*, 116–17; Wallace, *Areopagos*, 126–27.

People do not give advice to carpenters on how to work wood, to cobblers on how to work leather, to weavers on wool or to lyre-players on the notes of the scale [312]. Laymen entrust each skill to the experts insofar as they can determine that these individuals actually are competent in their specialties. So why is it that virtually everyone gives advice to philosophers and tries to explain to them what they should say, and to whom, and when and where they should say it? Why is it that there is no one who does not consider himself a keen critic in this one area of knowledge, a critic both of what the philosopher says and of what he does? Now not everyone sets himself up as a judge of a poet's verses or of a rhetor's eloquence. And as for those young men who earlier offered you their first fruits in the theater and seemed so highly esteemed for each skill they displayed, you do not feel that you should be the ones to assess their performance; only those skilled in the composition of verse and prose should do so. But if a philosopher should summon you to this very same place and address you—I mean only after he had given much care and thought to his remarks, having "spent many sleepless nights" on them,[3] and having worked hard on the speech for many toilsome days, so that you might derive some benefit from it—in that case, his words would be judged and scrutinized, not only by philosophers, but also by rhetors and schoolteachers and physical trainers, by soldiers and former soldiers, and by just about everyone else. They would also pass judgment on the audience, saying that it was made up of common people, and on the place, pointing out that it was a theater. See, then, how philosophy is the one branch of knowledge that is so accessible to all, so easy to learn and master! Or perhaps I should call it a wondrous and bizarre branch of knowledge, if everyone will know precisely what suits it except the very persons who devote their whole lives to it!

But perhaps what I am saying is not quite correct or fair. After all, those who act as instructors to philosophers are not very many in number, nor have you all been extremely deluded by them. What is abominable about the situation, though, is that these few individuals, no better disposed than the masses and no closer to true knowledge than the crowd, appoint themselves lawgivers to philosophers and advise them to be silent, to keep what they know to themselves, and, like

3. "to assess their performance": the Greek has *κνισταρεύειν καὶ διασκοπεῖν*, and the first infinitive is corrupt. For emendations, see Petavius, Dindorf, and the Teubner editors ad loc.; Romano, *Κοινωνία* 6 (1982): 64. "spent many sleepless nights," etc.: cf. Hom., *Il.* 9.325–26.

those who hoard money, neither to make it public nor to share it [313]. Now if a philosopher should speak in defense of anything else, how much more should he do so in defense of the act of speaking itself? If he should come forward to speak publicly on any other subject, how much more so on this very one?

At any rate, I am here today, my dear fellow Greeks, for my benefit and yours, to provide an opportunity through this speech for me to have my say and for you to hear me. The proper thing for you to do is to share in my eagerness and to assist me and, as banqueters, to be no more indifferent to this feast than your host is. For my part, I tell you that it would be very hard to separate myself from you.[4] Whether you feel that way about philosophy is something that you know in your own hearts. As for your feelings towards me, let me say that it is good to love in return one who loves you.

Now here is the truth: everyone equally faces the danger that any connection between this city and philosophy has been precluded, and that philosophy will remain silent and the city unreceptive to what she says, as if the two were estranged from one another, unless I make thank offerings to both of them, on the one hand preserving and expressing philosophy's voice, and on the other hand making ready and unclogging the city's ears—all this after having shown that, being in good civic standing and not indebted <to the state>, I have access to both the [Constantinopolitan] senate and the assembly. Perhaps this is the task left to me from my previous ordeal; and if, after escaping that [earlier] column of mercenaries, I can also evade these lightly armed and unencumbered sophists, I may seem utterly untouched by that designation [i.e., "sophist"].

You must hear read to you again, as in a court of law, the sworn statement of accusation that these clever plaintiffs and artificers of silence lodge against me. "He is committing an injustice," they say in reference to me, "through his philosophical innovation and his 'introduction of new deities.' For he does not sit quietly in his room and converse solely with his pupils; instead, he comes out into the public arena, does not hesitate to appear in the very heart of the city, and ventures to speak before all sorts of people. And as serious as this is, still it is not the worst of it: now he even gathers audiences [314], for three successive days summons people to court, lets himself be commended,

4. For the "banquet" of an oration, cf. Them., *Orat.* 24.301a, 33.367a. "For my part, I tell you": cf. (?) Pl., *Rep.* 1.345a.

and canvasses his applauders.[5] What other indications and evidence could you possibly need that the gentleman is a sophist, since you see the chair and platform, the stolen goods that are proof of his crime?"

Alas! How persuasive my accusers are![6] What a good impression they make! I am very fearful that they may mislead you. For I cannot get a single one of my current associates to take the stand as a witness against them. Most of them help me and stand by me very commendably in other matters; but whenever this part of the accusation is brought up, they are horrified, become faint, and immediately go over to the side of my enemies. They leave me abandoned and without allies. Calling me a villain, one who is disdainful of the ancestral ways, they are harder on me than my original enemies. I understand why they are abandoning me, and I shall tell you. I must fight on all fronts at once, against those who desert me as well as against my enemies.

This fight is an unusually difficult one for me. I am being attacked by a host of men who are arrayed side by side in silence, who breathe forth silence instead of might and strength. So be patient, my friends, if I start by filling in the background and providing some introductory remarks. The ebbing of the water that was allotted to me does not hasten my speech; the amount was insufficient for this contest. It is the judges, after all, who are in charge of these proceedings—or the speaker himself, if he can speak so as to maintain a grip on his audience rather than drive it away.[7]

The aspect of my opponents' behavior at which I am utterly amazed and astonished is this: though they are annoyed at the introduction of any innovation or change and regard such a move as a wrongful act, they themselves are engaged in legal innovation in this indictment; and while bringing me to court as a sophist, they are themselves making a sophistical accusation. For in the judgment of the divine Plato, the lawgiver whom we have taken as our authority, the terms "statesman,"

5. "artificers of silence": i.e., they would like to silence Themistius. "his 'introduction of new deities'": this charge, intended metaphorically here, recalls the accused Socrates (Pl., *Apol.* 24b). So does the charge that Themistius does not keep quiet (ibid. 36b, 37e–38a). Cf. also the opening sentence of this paragraph with Pl., *Apol.* 19b. "summons people to court": i.e., metaphorically.

6. So were Socrates's (Pl., *Apol.* 17a).

7. "who breathe forth . . . strength": is this a play on Hom., *Il.* 3.8? "I start by filling in the background": the Teubner edition prints the transmitted *πόρρωθεν ἀγοίμην*. I would read Cobet's emendation *πόρρωθεν ἀρχοίμην* (*Mnemosyne* 11 [1862]: 429; cf. Gasda, "Kritische Bemerkungen," 15) or Kesters's *πόρρωθεν ἀναγοίμην*. "The ebbing of the water," etc.: a reference to the clepshydra (MacDowell, *Law in Classical Athens*, 249–50), by which Themistius refuses to be bound. Cf. Pl., *Theaet.* 172d–e.

"popular speaker," and "sophist" are not synonymous. If the person who appears before the masses and publicly addresses them at length does so out of concern for the welfare of his audience [315], Plato considers him a statesman and urges us to give him that designation. But if the only thing such a person desires is applause from the masses, then Plato regards him as a popular speaker and lover of the masses. A sophist, for Plato, is one who generally speaks briefly and is prepared to take on only one opponent at a time. This is the last of the definitions inscribed on the law-tablet. Because the definitions are so inscribed, my accusers could easily expose me if I am fraudulently tampering with the law.[8]

In this matter about which we are now meeting, then, my behavior was in no respect that of a sophist. You might assign me, though, to one of the other two classes, either to the honorable one [i.e., statesmen] or to the frivolous one [i.e., popular speakers]—to the honorable one if I am of any service to people, to the trifling one if I act only to enhance my own reputation. Now if there is anything beneficial in my words, you are the ones who would know, since you are my auditors. I would, of course, much more gladly address a lively audience, receptive to what I am saying, than to have you all yawning and bored sick with me. I do not desire applause for myself, applause merely for its own sake, but because I take it to be a sign that I am not saying what I am saying in vain, that I am not singing to you time and again to no purpose, but that I am touching the depths of your hearts. It is impossible for someone who is sympathetic to what is being said to sit still up there on that stone surface and be more motionless than the seat itself.

So in the use of the term that constitutes their accusation [i.e., "sophist"] these men are themselves innovating. They are misapplying the term, these guardians of custom! But in the facts of the case, there is no act of innovation. I am not the first to come up with the idea of forcing the eloquent not to restrict their speaking to their homes, where they are protected by doorkeepers and keys, but to be useful to the general public as well. But I am not yet arguing this point. I am not yet summoning my revered and ancient witnesses, men whom I am

8. "The aspect of my opponents' behavior," etc.: cf. Pl., *Apol.* 17a–b? For the Platonic definitions, see esp Pl., *Soph.* 268b. For the true statesman's concern for the general welfare, see, e.g., Pl., *Laws* 9.875a. For the term "lover of the masses" (δημεραστής), Pl., *Alcib. I* 132a. The "law-tablet" is, of course, the Platonic corpus.

sure you will believe once they take the stand. Let those witnesses wait for the appropriate moment for this in my speech.[9]

To the extent, though, that some innovation really *is* being ushered in, and I am the one who is introducing it and letting it loose on mankind, I do yield and concede the point to my accusers [316]. Now let them come forward and tell us whether every single innovation or new contrivance is criminal, or only bad innovations, which cause loss or damage. If everything that is not in accordance with custom is a crime, why don't they accuse and censure all the arts? For the arts have not been content to remain in the state they were in when first invented. They advance, still developing right down to the present and constantly creating something new to add to the old. Before Daedalus, all statues, not only herms, were square-cut. When Daedalus first spread apart the feet of statues, he was thought to be fashioning living beings. Consider the sea. Didn't raft-builders first prove to mankind that it is navigable? Then, when the builder Harmonides or someone before him came along, didn't merchant ships and trading vessels appear? Later still, the Corinthians built triremes at the Isthmus, and the Corinthian shipbuilder Ameinocles went to the Samians.[10] As for food and drink and all the rest of man's material life, did it become refined all at once? Didn't people at first feed on acorns and sleep in caves, without clothes, bedding or shoes? Only in the course of time, as men introduced one improvement after another, did our manner of life reach its current state of prosperity.

But could it be that, whereas the mechanical skills that are indispensible to us were receptive to innovation as they were being employed, those skills that are more refined and for our refreshment made their appearance in a complete and perfect form all at once? If you answer yes, then did Apelles contribute nothing to the art of painting, nor Terpander to lyre-playing, nor Timotheus to flute-playing? Did stately tragic drama enter the theater fully equipped at once with chorus and

9. Themistius is apparently alluding to Socrates, Plato, and Aristotle, to whose example he will refer below (318b, 318c, 319a, 319b–d).

10. On Daedalus, cf. Them., *Orat.* 23.296d, with n. 29 to my translation; see Donohue, "*Xoana*," 179–87; Morris, *Daidalos*, 237–56. For the early use of rafts, cf. Plin., *HN* 7.56 [206]. For Harmonides, see Hom., *Il.* 5.59 ff., with Kloesel, *RE*, 19, 2 (1938): 1984 s.v. "Phereklos 1"; cf. Plut., fr. 110 Sandbach and Them., fr. on "The Knowledge of Knowledges" 300b (Appendix 2). On the introduction of the trireme at Corinth, and on Ameinocles, see Thuc. 1.13. Ameinocles "went to the Samians" to build ships for them.

actors? Do we not pay heed to Aristotle? He tells us that first the chorus came forth and sang to the gods, then Thespis introduced the prologue and the spoken lines, thirdly Aeschylus introduced <two> actors and the buskins, and the further refinements of tragedy that we enjoyed were the work of Sophocles and Euripides.[11]

"Thus have we learned of the glorious deeds of our forebears" [Hom., *Il.* 9.524]. After philosophy had sprung up from obscure and frail seeds planted long ago, those forebears took it up [317]. But they did not passively abide the status quo; they kept adding something to philosophy. Consequently, there was nothing to which they did not eventually extend their investigations. They made both divine and human matters their domain.

At first there were a few sayings of Thales of Miletus and the other wise men in circulation. Even today walls and tablets are covered with these sayings. They are useful and quite sensible—as much as they could possibly be, consisting, as they do, of only two words—but they are lacking in argumentation, they resemble injunctions, and they give a very limited amount of ethical advice. Later, when Thales was approaching old age, he became the first person to devote himself to the study of nature. He directed his attention to the heavens and investigated the stars. He predicted publicly to all the Milesians that night

11. For the contributions of Apelles, Terpander, and Timotheus, cf. Plin., *HN* 35.36 [79 ff.]; [Plut.], *De mus.* 1135c, 1140f, 1141c; Clem. Alex., *Strom.* 1.16.78, p. 51 Stählin. "[Aristotle] tells us," etc.: assigned to Aristotle's lost *On Poets* by Laurenti, *Aristotele,* 1: 216–19, 255–58, and ("only by conjecture") by Janko, *Aristotle, "Poetics" I,* 65. See also Pickard-Cambridge, *Dramatic Festivals,* 130–32, 205; Garvie, *Aeschylus' Supplices,* 101n, 103–4, 117n, 120–21; Lesky, *Greek Tragic Poetry,* 28–29; Taplin, *Stagecraft,* 62; Colpi, *Die παιδεία,* 41–43; Garzya in Wissemann, *Roma Renascens,* 66–73. "sang to the gods": there is a textual variant "sang to the god [Dionysus?]." "thirdly . . . <two> actors": I reject the Teubner text's *Αἰσχύλος δὲ τρίτον ὑποκριτὴν* [sc., *ἐξεῦρεν*]. The tradition is divided between *τρίτον ὑποκριτάς* and *τρίτον ὑποκριτήν*. I opt for the former reading because its corruption to *τρίτον ὑποκριτήν* is an easier assumption than the reverse. Usener restores full sense by reading *τρίτον <δύο> ὑποκριτάς* (*Kl. Schriften,* 1: 163). Cf. Arist., *Poet.* 4.1449a16, where the introduction of the second actor is assigned to Aeschylus and that of the third to Sophocles. On the other hand, if the reading of the Teubner text is adopted, cf. *Vita Aesch.* 15 (ed. U. von Wilamowitz-Moellendorff in *Aesch. Tragoediae* [Berlin, 1914], 5), where the writer credits Aeschylus with the introduction of the third actor, while also recording the view of Dicaearchus of Messana that Sophocles was responsible for the innovation. Laurenti, op. cit., 255–57, tries to make tolerable the possibility that different things were said about the introduction of the third actor in the two Aristotelian works at issue. "the buskins" (*ὀκρίβαντας*): for my translation and parallel texts, see Pickard-Cambridge, op. cit., 205. If the Themistian passage actually is from Aristotle's *On Poets,* then apparently Themistius misrepresents his source, for "[t]here is no evidence at all of the use of . . . thick soles [by actors] until late in the Hellenistic age" (Pickard-Cambridge, op. cit., 204). Laurenti, op. cit., 219, wants to understand the plural *ὀκρίβαντας* here as *palcoscenico*. See also Garzya, op. cit., 70–71.

would come during the day, that the sun would set at the height of its course and the moon would move in front of it, so that its light and rays would be obscured.[12]

Although Thales made so many contributions, he did not commit his findings to writing. Neither did anyone else up to that time. Anaximander, the son of Praxiades, was a follower of Thales, but he did not follow him in every respect. He quickly innovated and deviated from Thales by being the first of the Greeks of whom we know to have dared to publish a written treatise on nature. Previously, writing treatises had brought reproach upon a person. It was not customary among the Greeks before Anaximander.[13]

I pass over Anaxagoras of Clazomenae and the extent of his innovations. He was the first to bring Mind and God into the creation of the world. He did not make everything depend solely on the nature of physical bodies.[14]

What about the excellent Socrates? Did he walk on the old and well-worn path? Did he follow in the footsteps of Archelaus? Didn't he have an even greater ambition and boldness than Archelaus? And his ambition was not merely to make some contribution to or improvement in philosophy, but to change and transform completely the subject of philosophical discourse [318]. For before his time almost everyone studied the heavens and the position and shape of the earth and tried to explain the generation of animals and the growth of plants. Socrates did not think that human beings could acquire this kind of knowledge; he felt that the pursuit of it wasted their lives and kept them from acquiring useful knowledge. He was the first one who considered and posed these questions: What should the basis of moral ex-

12. "Thales . . . and the other wise men": i.e., the so-called Seven Wise Men (cf. Them., *Orat.* 31.352c). "of only two words": one thinks immediately of *γνῶθι σαυτόν* and *μηδὲν ἄγαν* (Pl., *Protag.* 343a–b); see the Seven Wise Men 3 Diels-Kranz (= Stob., *Anth.* 3.1.172 Wachsmuth-Hense), passim, and cf. Them., *Orat.* 34 [IV]. For the claim that Thales was the first to study nature, see Diog. Laert. 1.24, Thales A 7 Diels-Kranz. Apuleius, *Flor.* 18, ascribes his theorizing on the sun to his *proclivis senectus*. For his prediction of an eclipse, see Hdt. 1.74 and the other texts given in Thales A 5 Diels-Kranz; Diog. Laert. 1.23. For his interest in the heavens more generally, see, e.g., Pl., *Theaet.* 174a; Arist., *Pol.* 1.11 [1259a11]; Diog. Laert. 1.23–24, 33–34.

13. The ancients were not in agreement on whether Thales had left any writings behind: Joseph., *Contra Ap.* 1.2 [14]; Plut., *De Pyth. orac.* 403a; Diog. Laert. 1.23, 34, 44. On Anaximander's innovation, see Kahn, *Anaximander,* 240; Conche, *Anaximandre,* 27, 48–50. For distrust of writing in classical Athens, see Harris, *Ancient Literacy,* 90–92.

14. "Mind and God": the word "and" is epexegetical. For Anaxagoras's Mind (*Nous*) as God, see ps.-Plut., *De plac. phil.* 1.7 (in H. Diels, *Doxographi graeci*[3] [Berlin, 1879], 299); Sext. Emp., *Adv. dogm.* 3.6; Lactant., *Instit. div.* 1.5.18.

cellence be? What is virtue in a human being and how may it be achieved? What is vice and how may one avoid it?[15]

If Socrates was forward in posing these questions, he was even more forward in that he did not speak about these issues confidentially and to his pupils alone, but to everyone without reserve, as he says somewhere [Pl., *Euthyph.* 3d], in banks, workshops, and wrestling schools. Modelers of figurines and smiths would surround him whenever he would vex people, which he did by testing them to see what they knew—what a general knew about courage, or what a popular political leader knew about good government, or what a rhetor understood about the factors by which the human soul is persuaded and led along, or whether a poet understood what kinds of poetry are beneficial. Thus it was that so much hatred was heaped upon him and that he reaped what benefits he did from his love of mankind.[16]

Well, then, did the very great Plato, because of Socrates's experience, confine himself quietly to his couch and room? Tell me, who was as active or innovative as Plato? He brought together and united for the first time the scattered settlements of philosophy, just as Theseus had made Athens a unified community; for until then philosophy had been broken up into three, or rather four, segments. In one place were the Italian Muses, in another the Sicilian Muses, in yet another the chorus of Ionian Muses. Some Muses investigated only divine matters, and some concerned themselves with nature. Encamped far away from these were the Muses who studied virtue and vice. And it was only in Egypt that mathematical studies felt at home. Plato, then, was the first to join together all these [pursuits], as if they had been the scattered members of a single living creature [319]. He caused them to breathe in unison and to have similar affections, and now one could not cut off one of their limbs without maiming and crippling the creature as a whole. In addition, Plato made many other contributions and innova-

15. Archelaus was Socrates's teacher. According to Diogenes Laertius (2.16), "physical philosophy ended with him, when Socrates introduced ethical philosophy." Diogenes adds, however, that Archelaus did not completely neglect ethics. Themistius's "almost" in "almost everyone studied" could be understood as a passing admission that some attention was given to ethics before Socrates. "the pursuit of it . . . useful knowledge": cf. Xen., *Mem.* 4.7.3. "What should the basis . . . be?": I emend the opening word ὅθεν to πόθεν; cf. Them., *Orat.* 34 [V]. For the "Socratic revolution," cf., e.g., Arist., *Metaph.* 1.6 [987b1]; Xen., *Mem.* 1.1.11–16; Cic., *Acad.* 1.4 [15–16]; id., *Tusc.* 5.4 [10–11]; Diog. Laert. 2.21; also Them., *Orat.* 34 [V].

16. For Socrates's habit of speaking in all sorts of public places, see, e.g., Pl., *Apol.* 17c; Xen., *Mem.* 1.1.10; cf. Them., *Orat.* 28.341d–42b. "what benefits he did [reap]": i.e., vilification and death.

tions. He created a type of discourse that is a blend of poetry and prose, with questioners, respondents, and narrators who captivate all of us human beings and lift us up off the earth![17]

In the face of all this, was not Aristotle clearly at a loss, incapable of devising something new himself? Not at all, for he was the first to separate philosophical treatises into distinct categories—those that focus on a single issue, those that aim at knowledge of existing things, and those that aim at virtue. Previously, everything had been combined in a disorderly way, like the army of the Medes before Cyaxares, son of Deioces, organized it into distinct sections.[18]

The notion that the same writings are not beneficial both to the general public and to philosophers is also distinctive of Aristotle, just as the same drugs and foods do not benefit both those who are perfectly healthy and those whose condition is precarious; the former should be given a regimen appropriate for the truly healthy, the latter a regimen that suits their particular bodily condition. And so Aristo-

17. For Theseus's synoecism see H. Herter, "Theseus," *RE,* suppl. 13 (1973): 1212 ff. "the Italian Muses . . . mathematical studies": cf. the Ionian and Sicilian philosophical Muses of Pl., *Soph.* 242d. The "Italian Muses" refer to Pythagoras and the Eleatics, the "Sicilian Muses" to Empedocles. Socrates may be thought of as being in the Ionian line (see Diog. Laert. 1.14), but he turned from physics to ethics, so "the Muses who studied virtue and vice" are distinctively Socratic Muses. The "four" segments of philosophy are therefore the Italian, the Sicilian, the pre-Socratic Ionian, and the Socratic. Cf. Kesters, *Antisthène,* 58. For Egypt as a source of mathematical knowledge, see Arist., *Metaph.* 1.1 [981b23], and the texts cited in Heath, *History of Greek Mathematics,* 1: 120–22, 128 (with Pl., *Rep.* 7.521c–31c, for the various branches of mathematics prescribed in Plato's educational scheme). For Plato's joining together of "scattered members" to form "a single living creature," cf. Atticus, fr. 1 des Places. "a blend of poetry and prose": I follow *LSJ* s.v. and the Petavius-Harduinus translation in translating ψιλομετρίας here as "prose." The only other occurrence of the word known to me is at Arist., *Poet.* 2.1448a11, where it seems to mean "verse unaccompanied by music" (see *LSJ* s.v. and the commentaries of Else and of Lucas on the *Poetics,* ad loc.). Kesters was surely wrong in transporting the Aristotelian sense into Themistius (*Antisthène,* 60n and his French trans. of this oration). According to Diogenes Laertius 3.37 (= Arist., fr. 73 Rose, 5 Laurenti [*De poetis*], 862 Gigon), Aristotle had already described Plato's style as "half-way between poetry and prose." See Walsdorff, *Die antiken Urteile über Platons Stil,* and Gaiser's treatment of the whole Themistian passage in *Philodems Academica,* 148, 321 ff. For the view that ψιλομετρίας in the Themistian manuscripts is corrupt, see, in addition to the Teubner apparatus criticus, Garzya, *Storia e interpretazione,* 20: 365–68.

18. "those that focus on a single issue" (πρὸς ἕνα ἀγῶνα): both Kesters, *Antisthène,* 50n, and Düring, *Aristotle,* 436, differently misunderstand the Greek. The three categories of writings must be sample categories. They are not intended to be a comprehensive scheme that will accommodate Aristotle's whole corpus, for the first category is of a different order from that of the other two. For Themistius's first category, cf. Ammon., *In Cat.*, prooem., p. 4 Busse, and Simplic., *In Cat.*, prooem., p. 4 Kalbfleisch (hypomnematic works of Aristotle that conduct an inquiry περὶ ἑνός τινος). On Cyaxares see Hdt. 1.102–3. But, according to Herodotus, Cyaxares was the grandson of Deioces.

tle called one class of writings "external" [θυραίους] and let them circulate without restraint, but the other class of writings he kept inside his school and shared, cautiously, only with a few. The bars that [when unfastened] give access to his teachings and [when fastened] deny access are in the hands of clarity and abstruseness; and to clarity and abstruseness, as if to the Hours, have been entrusted the tasks of making an opening in the cloud for his audience [i.e., in the "external" writings] and, contrarily, of placing that obstructing cloud above them [in the writings "kept inside his school"]. Those writings of Aristotle that are of general utility and were designed for a broad audience [i.e., the "external" writings] are truly full of light and radiance. They are useful without being boring or unpleasant at all. Aphrodite has been showered upon them, and the Graces make an appearance in them so that they will have an enticing quality. But as for the mystical part of Aristotle's corpus [i.e., that "kept inside his school"], in which the perfect rites are to be found, he saw to it that, even though the uninitiated have access to it, it is not really theirs. Therefore, although these mystical writings toss themselves at our feet, they are at the same time secured with more defenses than the royal palace at Ecbatana [320].[19]

Aristotle is also responsible for another innovation: he gave us an instrument [ὄργανον] for argumentation,[20] a supply of straightedges, so to speak, by means of which we would thereafter distinguish what is really true from what appears to be true because of its similarity to the truth. For we have the same experience in assessing arguments as we have in assessing people. Some people both are good and seem to be so; others seem to be good but actually are not. So it is with discourse.

19. Cf. with this paragraph Them., *Orat.* 20.235a–c, 23.294d; and see on it de Strycker, *Philologische Studiën* 7 (1935–36): 100–21. "one class of writings . . . the other class": i.e., the "exoteric" and the "acroa(ma)tic" or "esoteric" writings. When he writes of "external" (i.e., "exoteric") works, Themistius is probably thinking, or thinking mainly, of Aristotelian dialogues. See, e.g., the texts and discussions in Düring, *Aristotle,* 426–43; Laurenti, *Aristotele,* 1: 2–21, 74–88; also Guthrie, *History of Greek Philosophy,* 6: 53–59. "as if to the Hours" etc.: cf. Hom., *Il.* 5.749–51. "Aphrodite . . . the Graces": i.e., beauty and charm; cf. Them., *Orat.* 20.235b. For the attendance of Aphrodite and the Graces on Aristotle, cf. Elias, *In Arist. Cat.*, proem., p. 124 Busse; for the Graces alone, Olympiod., *Proleg.*, p. 11 Busse; note the comments of Kaibel, *Stil und Text,* 115–16. "the mystical part": according to Plut., *Alex.* 7.5, Aristotle's acroatic teachings were also called "epoptic," i.e., belonging properly to the mysteries and their initiates. "it is not really theirs": cf. the story in Plut., *Alex.* 7.6–9, and Aul. Gell. 20.5.7–12, about Aristotle's defense of his publication of acroatica; he said that they were "both published and unpublished," meaning that only those properly prepared could understand them. Ecbatana: see Hdt. 1.98.

20. The "instrument" is Aristotelian logic; see *LSJ,* s.v. ὄργανον III.

Some arguments both seem valid and are valid. But there are other arguments into which falsehood has insinuated itself, although this does not stop them from pretending to be valid and deceiving people. Aristotle was the first to devise an instrument that would detect these bewitchingly false arguments.

Now what is there that is new in what I am doing? I take philosophy—cooped up in her house, ill-humored, and avoiding gathering places, as the poets say Justice does[21]—and persuade her to come out into the open and not to deprive the multitude grudgingly of her beauty. Am I introducing some novelty in doing this? What I am doing is getting philosophy accustomed to not just benefiting one person at a time, as medicine does, but also to helping the people as a whole, to the best of her ability. The art of medicine may not be able to bring together to a single place everyone with similar physical conditions and maladies; it may have to visit separately every one of the houses of individuals who suffer from the same maladies. But philosophy does not minister to bodies, which generally have their own peculiar illnesses and require their own rooms and beds. Philosophy is the soul's helper. Souls generally have maladies in common, and the soul's nature is such that it can be treated anywhere. For this reason it is quite easy for philosophy to gather people together in an assembly without using a ruddled rope,[22] to get up on a high platform, and, like a god mechanically introduced on the tragic stage, to say:

"My good men, in what direction are you headed? Are you unaware that you are not at all acting as you should? You devote all your efforts to acquiring wealth, but you take no pains to ensure that the sons to whom you will leave your wealth will know how to use it justly. Nor, as a first step, did you cultivate a sense of justice in yourselves. You can see that you and your children learned your letters, verbs, and nouns quite well [321]—the things, that is, that you consider to be a perfect education in virtue—and yet subsequently used your wealth no less badly. How, then, can you fail to scorn the education that is currently in vogue here? How can you fail to seek out those who would put an end to this ignorance of yours? Yet it is because of this failure and indifference of yours—and not because of any lack of

21. Cf. Arat., *Phaen.* 96–136; Them., *Orat.* 3.46c.

22. A ruddled rope was used in classical Athens to move crowds from the agora to the place of assembly. The corralling rope was dyed red. Those who could not move fast enough to avoid getting red stains on their clothing were fined. See Aristoph., *Acharn.* 21–22, with scholia; Pollux 8.104.

understanding of conjunctions!—that your courtrooms are filled with people who fight and wage war with one another."[23]

<You are also right, philosophy,> when you say that people who exercise their bodies but have neglected their souls engage in another form of wrong behavior—that is, they neglect the part that was intended to rule and cultivate the part intended to be ruled.[24] You are right again when you say that, if a person does not know how to use something, it is better for him to forgo using it. If a person does not know how to use medications, it would be better for him not to use them, but to entrust them to a physician instead. If you do not know how to play a flute, you should entrust the instrument to a flute-player. If you are ignorant of the management of horses, it would be better to give the animals to someone skilled in horsemanship. And if a person does not know how to manage himself, there is no question that it is better for him to lead the life of a slave rather than that of a free man, giving over the rudder of his intellect, as if it were that of a ship, to someone else, to someone who has learned the art of piloting human beings.

These and all such pronouncements of Socrates and Plato are not the kind of prescriptions that would help one person while being harmful to another, as is the case with most medications administered to our bodies. On the contrary, these philosophical pronouncements would make anyone at all better and more courageous in the practice of virtue, whether a rhetor or an average citizen or a general, whether rich or poor, young or adult or elderly. For they are aids and benefits that are equally applicable to all. They are <no more> appropriate for *eupatridai* than they are for *pentakosiomedimnoi* or *zeugitai;* people should heed them regardless of their financial status.[25] If the law ordained that the whole citizenry, with their wives and children, should gather in assembly every year, then on that occasion the speaker who organizes the meeting should be obliged to set forth in his oration such principles for the people. For the larger and more inclusive the audi-

23. This paragraph is a textually close adaptation of Pl., *Cleitoph.* 407b–d, where Cleitophon is quoting Socrates. The comparison of philosophy, at the end of the previous paragraph, to "a god mechanically introduced on the tragic stage" is already from *Cleitoph.* 407a. For the use of the Platonic passage in other ancient texts, see Schenkl, *Wiener Studien* 21 (1899): 110.

24. This paragraph continues closely to adapt Pl., *Cleitoph.* 407e–408b. Some such supplement as I provide at the beginning of this sentence (cf. ibid. 407e) is needed.

25. The *eupatridai* were Athenian aristocrats, nobles by birth. The *pentakosiomedimnoi* and the *zeugitai* were the first and the third, in descending order, of the four Solonian economic classes. See Ober, *Mass and Elite,* 55–65.

ence is, the more effective and trustworthy the speaker will seem to them [322].[26]

When people are praised, they enjoy it less if they are praised as part of a large group. But the situation is different if they are being given injunctions or admonitions. In this case, being part of a crowd lessens much of the irritation and ill will that any words of censure or admonition naturally bring on. In armies, when the general gives a command to all the soldiers, each of them immediately devotes himself to the task at hand and strives to outdo his comrade. But if the command is given only to one or two soldiers, the general will have to use more words and explain the operation in detail and offer a considerable prize for the execution of the command. People react similarly when they are given advice. Suppose that you take aside one of those rich fellows who seem very happy, corner him, and then privately rebuke and admonish him as follows: "My good man, it is more fitting for a person to make his soul a thing of great worth than to enhance the value of his house. You cover your walls with many colorful decorations but neglectfully leave your soul blank, like a [freshly] waxed tablet.[27] In obedience to the poet Hesiod [*Op.* 746], you do not let yourself leave a room of your house in an unfinished state; but to carry around an unfinished mind you consider of no consequence." Now if you criticize just one person in this way, he will become suspicious and hostile and will regard your admonition as a reproach. If, on the other hand, you adapt these very same remarks for a mass audience and, with your hand extended, direct them to the people as a whole, that one person will be no less stung by them and will profit from them no less. But you will not have found fault with this or that individual; instead, you will have rebuked the offense.

There is something quite peculiar and strange about this verbal medication. The person who has ground or mixed it does not have to go up to those who are sick and apply it or rub it on. All he does is to bring it out and place it in the midst of the thousands of people sitting there. If anyone is seriously afflicted by a malady—even if his illness is hidden deep inside of him and does not manifest itself externally and no one knows about it—he reveals his condition by jumping up from the crowd and taking hold of the medication. If a person has some illness, he is happy to have the medication and profits from the treatment

26. For the reason explained in the next paragraph.
27. "[Freshly] waxed" and therefore not yet having anything written on it.

[323]. But if the illness should be irreversible and cannot be cured, then let the sick person be abusive and hateful, for such a man is quick to revile and to battle, not himself and his malady, but the one who, by his skill and out of his love of mankind, has prepared a remedy and made it available to the public. A physician should not refuse to treat people or avoid the sick just because there are a few sick individuals whom medicine cannot help. Nor should philosophers refuse to address the general public just because, in any mass audience, a Mammacythus and a Cyrebio derive no benefit from what they say.[28]

Let us proceed, by the Muses and Apollo, in this resolute fashion. Let us consider and examine how two [contrary] attitudes will coexist in us and seem to be two facets of a single view and conviction. On the one hand, we are pleased with and laud our common human nature and our love of our own kind, and we detail all the evidence that shows how God made us very open-hearted and well-disposed towards one another, far more so than is the case with all other creatures. But, at the same time, we have uncharitable and savage thoughts about people and try to evade our responsibilities to society (which is the front on which I have tried hard in my discourses to station virtue). We praise Prometheus, whomever one should understand him to be, because he did not make human beings solitaries and hermits, like wolves or leopards; yet we get dizzy at the sight of a crowd of people, just as the savages do in the play by that name that Pherecrates produced. We do, in fact, agree that the purpose behind our having a rich faculty of speech is that what we give to and receive from one another may extend beyond food, drink, clothing, and footwear and may also include the thoughts within our souls, thoughts that we exchange by means of the currency of words. Nonetheless, we remain silent, hidden away in our houses, and do not speak to the people with whom we form a single community. In some of our declarations, we say that those cities will be best governed and happy in which all the property of the inhabitants is held in common. We go further than that and, without hesitation, not only make land, houses, crops, vines, silver, and gold common property [324], but also arrange for children and wives to be held in common. Yet we also hide away what we make and produce in coffers. In theory we expel Epicurus, son of Neocles, and exclude him

28. "a Mammacythus and a Cyrebio": i.e., the thickheaded and the worthless or impudent. See Aristoph., *Ran.* 990, with schol.; Dem. 19.287 with schol. 503 and 504a Dilts, and cf. Athen. 6.242d.

from our list [of philosophers] because he approved of the injunction "live unnoticed" and was responsible for the doctrine that human beings are not sociable and civilized by nature; but in reality we approve of his opinion and turn a deaf ear to this very nature more openly than he did.[29]

If there is any possession or thing that should be shared by all, something that God designed to meet the most needs and provide the most benefit collectively, it is neither land or herds of cattle or sheep nor grain or wine or legumes; it is speech, which streams out from the soul. For it is not possible really to profit from those other things collectively; if people are to profit from them, you have to break up and dissolve a hitherto unified group into many individual units. But he who gave us a highly developed faculty of speech arranged that people's needs would be completely satisfied if they submit themselves to speech en masse, that speech would not be something people could benefit from only one at a time.[30] Consequently, we are not showing respect for the nature of the faculty of speech by remaining at home. Rather, we should fear that, if we confine and constrain speech, it will utterly perish and disappear; for speech is protected and safeguarded when exercised publicly.

Where speech has remained permanently confined and has not come forth from its confinement after its laborious birth, it is snuffed out along with the person who engendered it, even though it is immortal. Each thing reaches its full bloom and maturity provided that its natural drive and impulse are not thwarted and obstructed. Now if our faculty of speech is naturally disposed to mature and develop in darkness and obscurity, then let us not allow it to come into contact with even a few individuals nor permit it even to peep out at the world; instead, let us command it, well insulated in its den, to grow old and perish there [**325**]. But if it is inclined to grow wings and keep itself alive in the light of the sun, why will we not rescue it from darkness? Why

29. Prometheus as the maker of human beings: cf. Them., *Orat.* 27.338a–d, 32.359d; see L. Eckhart, "Prometheus," *RE*, 23, 1 (1957): 696–98. Pherecrates's play "The Savages": frs. 5 ff. Kock; cf. Pl., *Protag.* 327d. Common property, wives and children: one thinks, of course, of Plato's prescription of communism for his guardians in *Rep.* 3.416d–17b, 5.457c–d, although he strongly insists that they not even touch gold or silver. Plato, however, was not the only advocate of utopian communism in antiquity; see Dawson, *Cities of the Gods*. For Epicurus's "political quietism," against which Themistius warned Julian, see Aalders, *Political Thought*, 39–45; Jul., *Ep. ad Them.* 255b. For the exclusion of Epicurus "from our list," cf. Them., *Orat.* 20.236a. "to this very nature": i.e., to the nature that *has* made man sociable.

30. For an opposite view, see Ap. Ty., *Epp.* 10.

do we not open the door fully for it? Speech will know by its very nature, of course, towards whom it should proceed and when and how.[31]

We do not find fault with flute players for making music in public nor with orators for speaking in public, but only for playing pieces or saying things that are useless and unconducive to virtue.[32] We do censure and reproach men who expose to the wilderness the sons to whom their wives give birth. They wrong their city by depriving it of the citizens whom they have begotten. They fail to raise them or prepare them to be hoplites, say, or slingers or light-armed soldiers. But one's orations are better and more deserving of respect than one's children. So if a person buries his orations away in obscurity and locks them up, as if they were bastards begotten in adultery, and does not bring this fine progeny of his out to bestow upon the community, how could he be more ill-disposed towards his city and more deserving of public condemnation?[33]

We should do one of two things: either desist from writing for the whole body politic and actually ridicule Plato and Aristotle for their devotion to this kind of writing,[34] or adopt this kind of writing and then let our eloquence loose on the streets, content with whatever fortune it may encounter. Some of our orations may either die an immediate death because they were not given adequate attention and adornment, or they may be taken up by others and badly delivered, as happens when shepherds or cowherds come upon royal infants left in the wilderness and take them up, but then pass them off as their own and raise them in a way that is not worthy of their royal nature. This latter fate actually does befall those orations whose creator does not himself deliver them and nurse them along and present them just as he created them—that creator who shared every breath and pain with them during the throes of their birth. Instead, these orations are taken in hand by others, who recite them line by line but cannot infuse mean-

31. "Speech will know," etc.: cf. Pl., *Phaedr.* 275e–76a?

32. "things that are . . . virtue": for the text here, see Romano, *Κοινωνία* 2 (1978): 341–42.

33. In making a point about his orations, Themistius takes a position against child-exposure. For the practice and attitudes towards it in the Roman Empire, see, e.g., Harris, *JRS* 84 (1994): 1–22. "as if they were bastards": illegitimacy was one of several reasons for child-exposure. See Harris, art. cit., 12–13; Patterson, *TAPA* 115 (1985): 115–16.

34. "writing for the whole body politic": *γράφειν λόγους πολιτικούς*. With regard to Aristotle, Themistius is here thinking of his exoteric or "external" writings; see above, 319c.

ing into the words or make manifest the care with which their father engendered them.[35]

Let us imagine, by the gods, that the city should learn [326] that philosophy does not value keeping company with the general public and is even ashamed to do so because she regards such behavior as deserving of censure. Let us further imagine that the whole city, people and senate, were to assemble and select spokesmen. Many of you, no doubt, share in the madness and frenzy of philosophy.[36] Imagine the city choosing some of you as its representatives and, through you, speaking blunt and reproachful words to philosophy:

"Noble woman," the city would say, "how will you still be able to get irritated at us if you are considered useless in the lives of human beings? How will you continue to be able to insist that those who have no experience of you are to blame for your uselessness, and not you yourself? How can you abandon us to a half-deaf captain who has been lulled to sleep by wine and has handed over the rudder to men who cannot handle the helm, while you youself are unwilling to hold office, bear arms, or serve in the senate? You even begrudge us the one thing you could easily give [i.e., your spoken words], and you do not permit us to share in it en masse. Instead, you are always looking for walls and defenses behind which to hide out against the storm and the dust cloud, and you do not protect us or defend us as you can. It is just as if you were still living in Athens among the Athenian people at the time when they were supreme, and their power made them haughty and arrogant, and they were being led by Anytus rather than by Socrates. But my people are docile and compliant, the most easily managed of all and most readily won over by rational discourse.[37]

"As for the senate, in which I greatly delight and exult, whatever made you think that you should ignore it, and that it is shameful to address the senators publicly? Didn't they make you their equal in status precisely so that they might hear you address them? Don't they invite

35. The possibility that orations aimed at the general public may suffer various misfortunes is not, Themistius implies, an argument against addressing the general public. Besides, if care is taken, these misfortunes can be avoided. "when shepherds or cowherds . . . raise them": for this motif, see Redford, *Numen* 14 (1967): 209–28. "Instead, these orations" etc.: cf. Isoc. 5.26.

36. "the madness . . . philosophy": cf. Pl., *Symp.* 218b.

37. "considered useless . . . your uselessness": cf. Pl., *Rep.* 6.489b. "half-deaf . . . by wine": cf. ibid. 488b–c. "the storm . . . dustcloud": cf. Pl., *Rep.* 6.496d; Them., *Orat.* 8.104c, 24.308a. Anytus: one of Socrates's accusers.

you to their city from wherever you are on land or sea? Don't they persistently try to get you into their council chamber? They do this for one purpose: not so that you will put on horseraces or theatrical spectacles for them—for there are hordes of people who vie and contend with each other to do such things—but only so that you will be a source of order and a help to them and share with them the good qualities they believe you cultivate so well. But you say [327] that you will not associate with the assembled senate or regale them en masse. You will regale them only if each one of them comes separately to your house, without attracting attention—just as if you have prepared some bread and meat and drink that would be plenty for only one or two people but not enough for a larger number. But there is an abundant supply of discourse, and it is not used up by being lavished upon many people at once.[38]

"Why do you deceive people despite the great value you place on truth? You say that there are two parts to your wisdom, one that will come into play in matters involving the gods and the other in matters involving human beings. You have further divided and organized this second part of your wisdom into three parts, [each concerned with the execution of a distinct task]. The first task set for you involves the individual exclusively: to ensure that each human being be excellently and properly perfected as a discrete person. The second task is to ensure that the individual household is happy as a whole. The third and greatest task, towards which they say the other two are directed and guide us, is to teach how one <should> manage the whole city and its people. It is in the execution of this third task that you draft laws and constitutions (both those that transcend any assumption and those that start from an assumption) and other laws intended to improve [existing ones]; and you erect law tablets in the Painted Stoa, the precinct of Academus, and the Lyceum.[39]

38. "Didn't they make you their equal . . . ": here, of course, Themistius is thinking of his own adlection to the Constantinopolitan senate. "hordes . . . vie . . . to do such things": in fact, the praetorian and consular obligation to finance public entertainments at Constantinople was often burdensome: Jones, *Later Rom. Emp.*, 2: 532–33, 537–42; Dagron, *Naissance,* 150–52. "a source of order": the word is *kosmos;* cf. Pl., *Gorg.* 506e–507a. "regale": the Greek means, literally, to provide a banquet. For the metaphor, cf. 313a–b above with n. 4 to my translation. "just as if you have prepared . . . at once": cf. Them., *Orat.* 22.265c–d.

39. "two parts to your wisdom": cf. Pl., *Gorg.* 507a–b? "It is in the execution of this third task," etc.: i.e., Stoics, Academics, and Peripatetics engage in political philosophy and draft laws and constitutions that are more or less utopian ("transcending any assumption"), more or less practical. Cf. Arist., *Pol.* 4.1 (1288b10 ff.).

"Now we do not argue with you at all about the first part of your wisdom [i.e., that concerned with the gods]. Nor do we ask you to go to the trouble of explaining why the stars are not all carried along together, but why, instead, a few of them attempt to go in a direction opposite to that traveled by the majority. We do not ask you to explain why these great heavens themselves move in the direction they do, and why they did not decide to move in the opposite direction. Do not tell us what was made manifest to you about the region above the heavens, either. Nor do we ask you to discuss phenomena that are near us and associated with the earth and close at hand—thunder, lightning, winds, and rain. Do not tell us what snow undergoes that makes it so white, although it is only frozen water; or what conditions prevent hail from falling in the winter but cause it to do so frequently in the summer, even though hail is itself extremely cold. Do not explain to us whether a rainbow is a mirage and an illusion or its various colors are real; how the sea comes to be salty [328], though formed by water from rivers; or how the earth is pushed down by its weight yet remains positioned in midair. Let all these topics be reserved for the regular pupils in your school; we perhaps are too simpleminded or too old now for this 'higher' wisdom.

"Instead, why don't you get up on a high hill, if possible, and publicly proclaim how an individual and a whole household achieve happiness, and tell us what manner of life would ensure the well-being of a city? Wherever you speak, most of us will listen. We are not as arrogant as Thrasymachus, not as surly as Polus, not as shameless as Callicles, perhaps neither as roguish as Alcibiades nor as violent as Critias. And there is no one among our people who is as unlearned as Meno's slave, to whom you managed to explain a geometrical figure, although he hardly understood Greek.[40]

"You make use of the noble kind of rhetoric, and for no other purpose than to lead the masses wherever you think that you should. You call dialectic the counterpart to noble rhetoric and say that both rhetoric and dialectic belong to you and are your tools, one [i.e., di-

40. Thrasymachus is Socrates's challenger in the first book of Plato's *Republic,* Polus and Callicles challenge him in the *Gorgias.* For Alcibiades's character, see, e.g., Plutarch's biography of him (with *synkrisis*). For Critias's violence, see Xen., *Mem.* 1.2.12 ff., and his account of the Thirty in *Hell.* 2.3.15 ff.; Philostr., *Vitae soph.* 501–2. "to whom you managed to explain": philosophy, in the person of the Platonic Socrates, actually helped Meno's slave "recollect" knowledge he already had. See Pl., *Meno* 82b ff., and note *Meno* 85e. It is odd, in light of *Meno* 82b, that Themistius thinks of the slave as hardly understanding Greek (but for a different reaction, see Kesters, *Antisthène,* 127n).

alectic] to master individuals, the other to master the people en masse. In addition, you tell us why you need to concern yourself with discourse that has a persuasive force. The reason is that this is the kind of discourse by which the masses are led and charmed and to which they lend their ears; they are not readily receptive to discourse that presents the truth unless they have been mentally prepared for it in advance [i.e., by persuasive techniques]. In making these assertions, you deride Corax and Tisias and mock Theodorus of Byzantium because their contributions to the art of rhetoric were so minor and insignificant. You yourself, taking nothing for granted, explain how rhetoric can cause people to be persuaded **[329]**.[41]

"You have put as serious an effort into this art of rhetoric as you have into your investigation of nature. So why do you prepare these weapons for yourself only to lay them down as useless objects? Why do you make yourself skilled in doing something that you scorn and consider disgraceful? I am sure that you would not say that in your relationship with rhetors you tolerate what lyre-makers <and flute-makers> tolerate in their relationship with lyre-players and flutists: the former provide the instruments, but they entrust them to others to use, to those who play them. Nor would you tolerate the idea that the bridle-maker merely does the bidding of the horseman, the druggist of the physician, or the shipbuilder of the helmsman.[42]

"Why is it that, though you feel disgust for those whose business is controversy, you merely offer arguments [against them] without proposing an art of controversy yourself? Why do you disapprove of rhetoric yet, at the same time, fill the treasuries of memory with writings in defense of it? You teach that it is beneficial and useful, yet you do not practice it yourself, as though it were superfluous and vain. Have you so thoroughly forgotten the haughtiness you displayed long ago—and you were convinced that you were in the right—when you permitted no one but your initiates alone to lay claim to the art of

41. "dialectic the counterpart to . . . rhetoric": cf. the opening words of Aristotle's *Rhetoric,* with Grimaldi's comment ad loc. The Sicilians Corax and Tisias were said to have been the "earliest writers of [rhetorical] handbooks and the traditional founders of judicial rhetoric" (see Kennedy, *Art of Persuasion,* 58–61). Theodorus, mentioned by Plato, *Phaedr.* 266e ff., in conjunction with Tisias and other rhetoricians, also wrote a rhetorical handbook (Kennedy, op. cit., 70). "how rhetoric . . . persuaded" (*πῶς ἂν πειθὼ δημιουργοίη* [sc., *ῥητορική*]): cf. Pl., *Gorg.* 453a, with Dodds's comment ad loc. (on *πειθοῦς δημιοργός*).

42. Themistius has in mind the Platonic principle that what is needed is a knowledge that encompasses both how to make something and how to use it (*Euthyd.* 289). I have supplied "<and flute-makers>," i.e., *καὶ αὐλοποιοί.*

rhetoric? And at that time you were not apprehensive or fearful that anyone might consider you sophomoric in trying to rival Lysias and Thucydides, in repudiating them and nearly censuring Gorgias himself and Antiphon, and in praising only Pericles and Aspasia as accomplished and highminded rhetors because Pericles got these qualities of his rhetoric from his discussions with [the philosopher] Anaxagoras.[43]

"Consider what our sufferings will be and what difficulties you will cause us if you deliberately conceal the beneficial kind of rhetoric from us and hand us over to the fourth section of flattery, the reflected image of the <second> part of politics. This section of flattery you call the counterpart of cookery. Shall we attentively assemble only to hear people verbally shadowboxing on the speaker's platform in defense of Cimon or Nicias or Miltiades? Or to hear speakers twitter away in their prologues in praise of spring, swallows, and nightingales [330]? Shall we never benefit from a kind of discourse that is able to leave in us a goad to be virtuous? Or do you allow our love of listening to speakers unrestricted pasturage? Do you allow us to attend to speeches that, like the Sirens, enchant and bewitch? Will you not appear and counter those speeches with your shrill song? Do you fail to wake us up with your shout and stop us from being misled by reflected images and barren persuasion? Will you not, as the saying goes, wash and purify our briny ears with fresh water? Are you suspicious and disapproving of Homer's allure, since it instills absurd opinions about the gods, yet yourself unwilling to provide us with an antidote against the theater or to find us a moly like that which Homer [*Od.* 10.275 ff.] got for Odysseus from Hermes so that he could escape the witchery of Circe? And yet we hear that, when a young man asked Carneades whether a wise man too will fall in love with boys, he wittily answered that 'you beautiful young men would be suffering a terrible plight indeed, if only the unintelligent are interested in you.' But our plight will

43. Socrates "rivals" the orator Lysias in Plato's *Phaedrus,* and the funeral oration of Plato's *Menexenus* rivals Thucydides's Periclean funeral oration; cf. Dionys. Hal., *Ep. ad Pomp.* 1.10 Aujac; Anon., *Proleg. phil. Platon.* 9.22, p. 43 Westerink; Kesters, *Antisthène,* 135–36. "nearly censuring Gorgias himself": Themistius is here probably thinking especially of Socrates's and Gorgias's discussion in Pl., *Gorg.* 449c–61b; see Dodds's summary comments on Plato's representation of and quarrel with Gorgias in *Plato, "Gorgias,"* 9–10. The word "himself" points to Gorgias's special importance in the history of rhetoric. Antiphon of Rhamnus is described as a second-rate rhetorician in Pl., *Menex.* 236a. "Pericles . . . Anaxagoras": cf. esp. Pl., *Phaedr.* 269e–70a, where, however, Pericles's mistress Aspasia is not mentioned. But in Pl., *Menex.* 235e–36b, Socrates praises Aspasia's command of rhetoric, making her responsible for Pericles's success as an orator. "because Pericles got": the Greek has *προσειλκύσατο* and does not express the subject. There is a variant reading *προσειλκύσαντο* ("because Pericles and Aspasia got").

be even more wretched if we hear only the descendants of [Aelius] Aristides and no one will allow us to hear those of Plato.[44]

"Please, O noble woman, by the gods, do not grow weary, 'but come to our aid as fast as you can and save your faithful companions' [Hom., *Il.* 16.363; 21.311, 333]. 'Whatever benefits you bestow on us in our large numbers will not,' says Socrates, 'be a bad investment for you' [Pl., *Rep.* 1.345a]. Do not be intimidated by those who mock and ridicule you. For we who shall be grateful to you and helped by what you say are far more numerous. Pay no attention to those who mock you. Instead, imitate the Pythian Apollo. He, from his seat on the *omphalos* at the center of the earth, interprets not only for individuals, one at a time, but also for communities as a whole. The fact that his oracular responses will be heard in the Athenian assembly by the lampmaker Hyperbolus and the highwayman Diocles and the stupid Melitides as well as by Themistocles is not something that causes him to be overly selective in giving those responses.[45]

44. "the fourth section . . . cookery": Themistius is alluding to the scheme of Pl., *Gorg.* 464b–65e. The "fourth section of flattery" is rhetoric, a debased and unphilosophical rhetoric. Themistius is counting the sections of flattery in the order in which they are mentioned by Plato: (1) cookery, (2) self-adornment, (3) sophistry, (4) rhetoric. Kesters rightly adds "<second>". "in defense of . . . Miltiades": declamations on historical themes, of purely academic interest. "in praise of . . . nightingales": cf. Them., *Orat.* 27.336c; Jul., *Orat.* 7.236a. "like the Sirens": cf. Them., *Orat.* 28.341c. "your shrill song": the Greek has τὸν ὄρθιον νόμον, on which see Fleming, *CJ* 72 (1976–77), esp. 222–26; West, *Ancient Greek Music,* index s.vv. "nomos" and "orthios nomos." "wash . . . with fresh water": Pl., *Phaedr.* 243d; *CPG* 2.267; cf. also Liban., *Orat.* 18.18. "And yet we hear . . . interested in you'": though Carneades's remark puts the emphasis on the young men, Themistius is thinking first and foremost of the wise man: we need a moly to protect us from the allure of unprofitable, unphilosophical rhetoric, because that allure has a power comparable to the power that handsome young men have even over the wise. The Carneadean saying is not included in B. Wiśniewski, *Karneades: Fragmente, Text und Kommentar,* Archiwum Filologiczne 24 (Wrocław, 1970). "But our plight . . . of Plato": the "plight" is our vulnerability to the allure of unphilosophical rhetoric, like the vulnerability of even the wise to the allure of young men. Aelius Aristides, who had criticized Plato's criticisms of rhetoric, is here emblematic of unphilosophical rhetoric; see above, pp. 27–28.

45. "do not grow weary": cf. Pl., *Cratyl.* 428a, *Protag.* 333b, *Rep.* 5.450c. "from his seat . . . interprets": Pl., *Rep.* 4.427c. For the *omphalos* at Delphi, cf. Pausan. 10.16.3. For the individual and communal consultations of Apollo, see Fontenrose, *Delphic Oracle,* 244 ff. Hyperbolus: the maligned Athenian demagogue. "Lampmaker" was an aristocratic slur on the source of his wealth. See Kirchner, *Prosopogr. Att.*, no. 13910; Ostwald, *From Popular Sovereignty,* 201–3, 211–15, 328; Ober, *Mass and Elite,* 272–77. Diocles: apparently the villainous Diocles of Phlya of Isaeus, *Orat.* 8. Isaeus (8.3, 44) tells us that he was called "Orestes," apparently a nickname for persons prone to violence and theft (see Aristoph., *Acharn.* 1166, *Av.* 712, 1490–93). The scholiastic remarks on Aristophanes's "Orestes" (on *Acharn.* 1167; *Av.* 1487, 1490) call him a "highwayman" (λωποδύτης), the same term used by Themistius of Diocles, who was nicknamed Orestes. See Starkie on Aristoph., *Acharn.* 1166; Higham, *CQ* 26 (1932): 103–5. Melitides: the name was proverbial for a simpleton. See Aristoph., *Ran.* 991, with scholia to 990 and 991; *CPG* 1.244n, 251, 262n.

"But why am I speaking to you about Apollo? You see this Sun, Apollo's ancestor, don't you, and that the good resembles the Sun [331]? Doesn't this god seem to you to make display of his wisdom in public every day? He does not bring men together at the Pnyx in Athens, nor does he appear at Dionysus's theater there, as Gorgias did. Rather, he appears in this great and truly Olympic theater, where he summons and gathers all human beings, teaching and revealing to them when they should sow, when they should plant, when they should reap, when they should tend to their grapes, when it is the right time to set sail, and when to hang up the rudder over the smoke. The Sun also advises us about things of even smaller scale, more or less as philosophers exhort us in their treatises on what we should and should not do. All these things he explains to us from the heights of heaven, more radiantly and clearly than they do: he tells us when we should go to the agora and when we should return home, when it is better to be awake and when we should entrust ourselves to sleep. Human beings listen with pleasure to him when he reveals this wisdom to them, and they express their admiration for his teachings, not by what they say, but in their actions. For they comply with and dutifully carry out whatever he indicates and recommends. Nothing prevents the majority from obeying him or from standing up and acting as soon as he appears, even if a Sardanapalus and a Smindyrides sleep during the god's revelations. This is just what happens, I think, in the case of the sophists: some pay attention to them, but others do not."[46]

46. "this Sun, Apollo's ancestor": for this notion, see Jessen, "Helios 1," *RE,* 8, 1 (1912): 61–62, 82. (Soph., fr. 1017 Nauck, cited there is now fr. 752 Radt.) "the good resembles the Sun": if Themistius is thinking of the Platonic Good, cf. Pl., *Rep.* 6.508a–509b. "at the Pnyx": the hill where the Athenian assembly met. "in this great . . . Olympic theater": i.e., throughout the whole world, not just at Olympia, where the oratory of the just mentioned Gorgias had won him renown (Pausan. 6.17.8; Philostr., *Vitae soph.* 493). "where he . . . gathers all human beings": Kesters, *Plaidoyer,* 85, notes the Platonic derivation of the word "sun" in Doric (ἅλιος) from the verb ἁλίζειν, "to gather": Pl., *Cratyl.* 409a. "when they should sow . . . over the smoke": Themistius seems to have Hes., *Op.* 383 ff., in mind and echoes *Op.* 629 (cf. Kesters, *Antisthène,* 148n). Sardanapalus and Smindyrides: an Assyrian king and a Sybarite, both given to luxury and pleasure (Weissbach, *RE,* 1A, 2 [1920], s.v. "Sardanapal," esp. 2441–48; K. von Fritz, *RE,* suppl. 10 [1965], s.v. "Smindyrides"). Such carousers might well be asleep during daylight hours (Athen. 6.273c). On Sardanapalus's manner of life, cf. Them., *Orat.* 2.30d. Sardanapalus and Smindyrides are cited as a pair elsewhere too (Arist., *Eth. Eudem.* 1.5 [1216a17]; Theophrast. in Athen. 12.511c; Cleomedes, *Caelest.* 2.1 [168], p. 62 Todd). "during the god's revelations": ἐν μέσῳ ὄντος τοῦ θεοῦ τῇ ἐπιδείξει (Teubner edition). For μέσῳ I read Reiske's emendation μέσῃ.

ORATION 27

On the Need to Give Thought, Not to Where [We Study] but to the Men [Who Will Teach Us]

[331] Why is it only in the case of what we call learning that men care about being instructed in a revered and famous city rather than by a teacher who is a master of his subject? One wants to be taught metal working, for example, by a person who really knows that art, or flute and lyre playing by expert musicians, wherever in the world they may happen to be [332]. So why is it that men do not give learning the same consideration? Why do they seek out a place rather than a teacher, paying no heed to eloquence itself? Why do they investigate whether or not the city under consideration is old and rich in ancient legends? Why do they regard this as a matter of great importance? After all, nothing prevents you from making the same pair of shoes in an obscure city that you would make in a highly regarded one, nor does anything keep you from writing the same letters of the alphabet in either kind of city; the situation is no different when it comes to acquiring the art of eloquence. Yet, whereas men try to practice carpentry, build houses, and weave in a uniform manner everywhere, when it comes to eloquence, they select one place or city for themselves and malign speakers in other cities, as if the latter were betrayers of the goddesses' mysteries. I see that men have built temples to Hermes in every country district and city, yet they think it inappropriate to regard schools of rhetoric as the truer temples of Hermes. If someone should fashion a gold or silver or ivory statue [ἄγαλμα] of Hermes here, people reverence and venerate it as much as they would anywhere else;

yet they scorn and dishonor the works [ἀγάλματα] of eloquence fashioned from the rhetorical art of this place.[1]

I have an urge to address all of you; but, by Zeus, I am not a babbler, nor do I want to speak to no purpose or on a matter of no significance. Unlike the lucky sophists, I am not clever or glib enough for that. I am addressing you because a certain individual considers the schools here to be of poor quality and has no respect for them. He apparently offers no other specific criticisms and is unable to do so. He therefore seems to be one of those who pass judgment on cities rather than on the eloquence to be found therein. Do you want me to persuade him, then, if I can somehow find a way to do so, that locale should not displease him or make him unhappy, so long as he knows in his heart what truly counts?

Most excellent young man, I myself reaped the fruits of rhetorical study in a place far more obscure than this one, not a refined Greek place, but one on the outskirts of Pontus near [the river] Phasis. There, as the poets have told us in amazement, the *Argo* arrived safely from Thessaly, and there she was taken up into heaven. There too one finds the river Thermodon, the lands of the Amazons, and the plain of Themiscyra [333].[2] Yet even though the place was so barbaric and unrefined, one wise and virtuous man was able to convert it to Hellenism and make it a shrine of the Muses. Settling in the midst of Colchians and Armenians, he did not teach what the neighboring barbarians thought an educated man should know—how to use the bow and the javelin and mount a horse. Rather, he taught how one becomes adept at rhetoric and distinguishes oneself [as a speaker] at festal as-

1. "whether . . . the city . . . is old . . . ": cf. Pl., *Hipp. Maj.* 285d. "Why do they regard . . . great importance?": for the transmitted μεταποιοῦνται I read K. Kontos's conjecture μέγα ποιοῦνται ("Φιλολογικαὶ παρατηρήσεις," Ἀθηνᾶ 6 [1894]: 177–78). "the goddesses' mysteries": i.e., those of Demeter and Persephone at Eleusis. "I see that men have built," etc: people reverence statues of Hermes equally everywhere. But rhetorical schools are truer shrines of Hermes, the god of eloquence, than are his temples. Therefore what issues from the schools should be equally reverenced everywhere. ἀγάλματα: for the play on its two senses, cf. Them., *Orat.* 20.235a–b, 25.310b.

2. "in a place . . . on the outskirts of Pontus": Seeck, *Die Briefe*, 292, oddly conjectured that it was Paphlagonian Sinope, "obgleich die geographische Bestimmung nur mangelhaft dazu passt." Vanderspoel, *Themistius*, 34, has argued for Neocaesarea. "[the river] Phasis": the text has Φάσιδος, which could mean either the river or the city. "as the poets have told": cf. Apoll. Rhod., *Argon.* 2.1260 ff.; *Orph. Argon.* 750 ff. For the transformation of the Argo into a constellation, cf. Arat., *Phaen.* 342 ff.; Maass, *Commentariorum in Aratum reliquiae*, 255–56; Val. Flacc., *Argon.* 1.1–4. For Amazons at Themiscyra on the Thermodon, see P. Devambez, "Amazones," *LIMC*, 1, 1 (1981): 586. I take τὰ Ἀμαζόνων ἔργα to mean "[tilled] lands" (see *LSJ*, s.v. ἔργον I, 2a). For Amazonian farming, see Strabo 11.5.1 [504].

semblies. If I am telling the truth about him, it should be immediately apparent when I speak. I did not go to his school on my own initiative or by my own decision; I was sent there by [my father], a man who loved me as only a father could, and who put me through the right kind of test as only a philosopher could. Yet, [young man], you will doubtless include that [teacher] too among the objects of your scorn, because he too acquired his much-discussed love of wisdom in this region. And I suppose that you will scorn me even more than him because I received my very first initiation into wisdom's mysteries without even leaving my hearth and home.[3]

Come, then, let us examine what it is that is distressing me—although I myself cannot at all understand why I am so upset. If we had bodily ailments and needed the help of the god [Asclepius], and he were present here in his temple on the acropolis and revealed himself to the sick, as they say he does, would we have to go to Tricca or sail to Epidaurus because of its ancient renown, or could we be relieved of our ailment merely by taking a short walk [to your acropolis]? And what if we had had need of this god's father [Apollo] a short time ago, when he was displaying his prophetic powers among your neighbors? Would the name Paphlagonia have seemed dishonorable and unworthy of consideration in comparison with that of Delphi? Apparently, we would have had to rush off to Castalia and to places that have august names. I suppose that we would have had to hasten off to Pytho and delight in ancient Mt. Parnassus and see the silent prophetess.[4] I sup-

3. "one wise and virtuous man": Vanderspoel, *Themistius,* 34–35, conjectures that he was Basil, father of the homonymous church father. "If I am telling the truth" etc.: i.e., if he was adept at rhetoric, I, his pupil, should also be adept. "sent . . . by [my father], a man," etc.: i.e., I take Themistius to be referring to his father, not to a fatherly friend (*pace* Seeck, *Die Briefe,* 292; Schemmel, *Neue Jahrbücher für Pädagogik* 11 [1908]: 154). "who put me through the right kind of test": cf. Them., *Orat.* 20.240c. "that [teacher]": the Greek has *κἀκείνου*, which I take to refer to Themistius's teacher, not to his father (*pace* Wilhelm, *Byzantinisch-neugriechische Jahrbücher* 6 [1927–28]: 457–58; Stegemann, *RE,* 5A, 2 [1934]: 1643). "my first initiation": i.e., from his father.

4. "Tricca . . . Epidaurus": The shrines of Asclepius at Tricca and especially at Epidaurus were famous (Edelstein and Edelstein, *Asclepius,* 2: 232 ff.). "this god's father . . . among your neighbors": Vanderspoel, *Themistius,* 32, n. 7, and Maisano, *Discorsi,* 896, n. 7, agree with Harduinus and the Teubner edition of Themistius's *Orations,* ad loc., that the recently silenced oracle of this neighboring locale was that of Abonutichus, best known from Lucian's *Alexander.* But that cannot be correct because, even though Apollo had some connections with the Abonutichan shrine (Lucian, *Alex.* 10, 13–14, 38–39), the oracular god there was Asclepius-Glycon. Others have thought that the city in which Themistius was speaking was Abonutichus (Wilhelm, *Byzantinisch-neugriechische Jahrbücher* 6 [1927–28]: 451–52; Ballériaux, *AC* 65 [1996]: 143–45). Apollo's Delphi—its older name was Pytho—sits on the slopes of Mt. Parnassus. Castalia was Delphi's sacred spring.

pose that we would have had to say goodbye to the very Apollo whose prophetic powers we needed and to get angry at him because he preferred the heart of Paphlagonia to that of Greece [334]! But we would seem ridiculous if we failed to honor a place because of its god and instead dishonored the god because of the place. I marvel at Miletus and Colophon because Apollo has been present in those places from ancient times on. But if he should establish himself somewhere closer to me and there make manifest his prophetic powers, I shall go to that city—or, by Zeus, to that village or field or grove or tree, if it be a tree that Apollo should fancy, just as they say Zeus fancied the oak tree at Dodona. You surely notice, [young man], that those who worship the sun extend their hands towards it wherever it appears in the sky, even though the east is more revered than the other regions and we see the sun there before we see it anywhere else.[5]

You say that you are a lover of learning and eloquence. Will you not, then, seek them out and be content to remain wherever you find them and to have your fill of them there, whether the place is Athens or the Peloponnesus or Boeotia? Boeotia, of course, was thought to be a boorish place, and they would call it swine land, in mockery, I think, of the Boeotians' lack of learning. Yet Pindar and Corinna and Hesiod were not defiled by that swine land. And you have surely heard that Anacharsis the Scythian was a wise man as well as a Scythian. For a man involved in politics, I think, it is of primary importance, as the poet says, that his city be highly regarded. But eloquence does not need a famous homeland. It is held in equal honor everywhere—and the eloquence that flourishes in an isolated area is perhaps more honored than that found in big cities. Homer, in fact, prefers a general reared in Salamis [i.e., Ajax] to one from Mycenae [Agamemnon]. He prefers the man from Phthia [Achilles], even though he was raised in the mountains, to all the other Greeks and barbarians [Hom. *Il.* 2.768–69, 7.161 ff.; Pind., *Pyth.* 6.21]. I myself prefer Homer's poetry, whether he composed it in Chios or in Smyrna, to anything ever produced at Athens and would want to read it at whatever cost.[6] For in his poetry,

5. "Miletus and Colophon": Themistius is referring to the oracles of Didyma (Branchidae) near Miletus and of Claros near Colophon. For Zeus's oracular oak at Dodona, mentioned below, see, e.g., Hom., *Od.* 14.327–28; Pl., *Phaedr.* 275b; Pausan. 1.17.5, 7.21.2. "the east is more revered": cf. Liban., *Orat.* 11.16.

6. For Boeotian swine, cf. Pind., *Ol.* 6.90 with schol.; Cratin., fr. 310 Kock; *Suda* 583 B Adler. Pindar, Corinna, and Hesiod were Boeotian poets; cf. how Galen, *Protrep.* 15, adduces Pindar against the proverbial characterization of Boeotians as swine. For Anacharsis's wisdom despite his barbarian origins, cf. Menander, fr. 612 Koerte-

I believe, I shall learn this lesson: that nothing prevents a man educated in Ithaca [i.e., Odysseus] from being wily, and nothing prevents a man of Pylos [Nestor] from having a voice sweeter than honey [cf. Hom., *Il.* 3.216, *Od.* 2.173 etc.; *Il.* 1.249].

Consider, [young man], whether I am right in saying [335] that one who loves something truly and genuinely should not give the impression of loving it only in certain places, but of being attached to it everywhere. One who loves gold, as we observe, does not esteem it in Athens and scorn it in Megara. He does not value it highly in Corinth and disdain it in Sicyon. Whether you give him bits of gold from the Pactolus—with which they say the river flowed in the days of Croesus—or gold from the Thracian mines, which have been worked for a long time, he will take it with equal pleasure and enthusiasm.[7] And what about the horse lover? You surely realize that he fancies all horses equally, regardless of where they come from. Whenever he sees a horse up for sale in the marketplace, he considers, first and foremost, its size and beauty and whether it runs fast and very far. When he learns that it has excellent qualities, only then will he find out, as a matter of secondary interest, whether it comes from Thessaly or Sicily or Cappadocia. To the man who loves dogs, both Celtic and Laconian puppies are pleasant to own. He is "bitten" by Castorians, by Arcadians and by Cretans, which instinctively ferret out the lairs of wild animals by following in their tracks. The dog lover will not reject home-bred pups either, so long as they are as good-looking and swift of foot as the imported breeds.

Shall we not say, then, that the lover of eloquence desires not the eloquence of this place or of that place, but eloquence pure and simple, and the whole of it?[8] The person who is possessed of eloquence but belittles it because of the city [in which it is found] is not really a lover of knowledge and eloquence; we shall have to say instead that he is a lover of Corinth or of Argos or of some other city, not a lover of the learning that he claims to have acquired.

Thierfelder; Galen, *Protrep.* 13–14; Lucian, *Anachars.* 17; SHA, *Aurel.* 3. Boeotian swine, Pindar and Anacharsis appear in Galen in a discussion of the unimportance of familial and geographical origins, as does Anacharsis in the SHA. "as the poet says": a similar sentiment is ascribed to Simonides by Amm. Marc. 14.6.7, to "Euripides (according to the prevailing view) or someone else" by Plut., *Dem.* 1.1. "Chios . . . Smyrna": Chios and Smyrna were not the only claimants of Homer (see Raddatz, "Homeros 1," *RE,* 8 [1913]: 2194–99); below (337c), Themistius opts for Chios.

7. The Pactolus: see J. Keil, "Paktolos," *RE,* 18, 2 (1942): 2439. Thracian gold: Casson, *Macedonia, Thrace and Illyria,* 59 ff.

8. Cf. Pl., *Rep.* 5.475b.

A Median horse has a prouder bearing than a Sarmatian horse. Castorian dogs have one kind of beauty, and vulpines have another, and the polymath Xenophon will explain to you the differing ideal types for each breed [336]. People differentiate Dorian, Phrygian, and Ionian melodies. But I know of no differences of kind or race in the manifestations of eloquence. I am aware that there are individual stylistic qualities and types (for example, Plato's harmonious style of composition and Demosthenes's intensity and various other distinctive qualities). But you can acquire these through practice and take them with you everywhere, whether you are traveling by land or by sea, even if you have no ship or beast of burden.[9] For it is the human soul that will shoulder and have charge of the stylistic modes, if you wish it to do so; and there is no need to fear that they will burden the soul like some heavy cargo. Have you not heard Homer call words "winged" [*Il.* 1.201 etc.]? The more "wings" there are, the lighter and loftier they will make the soul. But let not my verbal wings pass by you in vain. Consider this, [my friend], if you will: if eloquence was supposed to be established in only one place, the god would not have given it wings. Why would it have needed them if it were about to root itself down like a plant? A wing has a natural affinity with music: all creatures that have no wings are unmusical, whereas those that are musical, such as the nightingale, the swan, and the cicada, do have wings. And do not think that I invoke the swan and the nightingale for adornment and to no purpose, as do the clever sophists, who have used these birds like a rouge to beautify their orations. Rather, by referring to these birds I am trying to explain to you that music is not something fixed or motionless, nor is its power restricted to a particular locale, as is the power of mantic waters and exhalations.[10]

9. For the excellence of Median (or Nisaean) horses, cf. Them., *Orat.* 22.266a; see Amm. Marc. 23.6.30; R. Hanslik, "*Νισαῖον πεδίον*," *RE,* 17, 1 (1936): 712. For the Sarmatian horse and ancient breeds of horse in general, see Keller, *Die antike Tierwelt,* 1: 218 ff.; Hyland, *Equus,* 11 ff. "Castorian dogs," etc.: Themistius is alluding to Xen., *Cyneg.* 3.1 ff. For dogs in antiquity, see Keller, op. cit., 1: 91 ff.; Merlen, *De Canibus,* a book written by a veterinarian, but without scholarly apparatus. The Laconian Castorian was named after the mythological Castor (Xen., *Cyneg.* 3.1); the Laconian vulpine (*ἀλωπεκίδες*) was thought to have been a hybrid between the dog and the fox (Keller, op. cit., 1: 120–21; Merlen, op. cit., 28–29, 36–38). For Demosthenic intensity (*τόνου*), cf. Dion. Hal., *Dem.* 13; [Lucian], *Encom. Dem.* 32. "you can . . . take them with you": cf. Them., *Orat.* 25.310b–c.

10. "The more wings . . . the soul": one might compare the Platonic image of the winged philosopher, *Phaedr.* 248c ff. "the god . . . wings": Hermes *logios?* "sophists . . . have used these birds": cf. Them., *Orat.* 26.329d. "mantic . . . exhalations": cf. Ael. Arist., *Orat.* 1.46 Lenz-Behr.

[Young man], do you think that the city where eloquence [λόγοι] first made its appearance [i.e., Athens] is the only fitting place to be educated? Well, wheat and vines do not grow only where grain and wine first appeared [i.e., in Attica]; you will note that grain dealers sail to Egypt and Thrace and the Bosporus and the Chersonese [to procure grain]. You should know that the Athenians themselves imported grain from other places, even though Triptolemus belonged to them, and though it was from their midst that his serpent chariot once took wing [337]. It is said that horses were first hitched to a chariot by Erechtheus [in Athens], but nowadays countless Illyrians, Egyptians, and Thracians drive them in almost every city. According to legend, weapons first appeared in Attica—how could it be otherwise, since human beings first appeared there too? So it is high time, I suppose, for you to scorn and belittle people from places other than Attica![11]

But nothing, I think, prevents something that had its origin among one people from receiving an even more enthusiastic reception from another people. After all, comedy originated a long time ago in Sicily, the home of Epicharmus and Phormus, but developed into something more splendid at Athens. The originators of the tragic genre were Sicyonians, but Attic poets perfected it. Upon seeing Phidias's Zeus at Olympia, surely you will not need Attica to be able to admire Phidias, will you? You have Plato's handiwork right here; you will not make your regard for the man who fashioned such works contingent upon knowing where he was born and lived, will you? If you do, then you should be educated in Chios because of Homer, in Ascra because of Hesiod, in Boeotia because of Pindar. How, knowing the Stagirite [i.e., Aristotle], will you ever dishonor Stagira? How will you ever dishonor Cyprus, the land of Zeno of Citium?[12]

11. Cf. the priority of Athens/Attica in Aelius Aristides's *Panathenaicus, Orat.* 1 Lenz-Behr: 2, 6, 43 (eloquence: *μαθήμασι καὶ λόγοις, τῶν λόγων, λόγους*); 32–34, 37 (crops); 43 (chariot yoked, weapons); 25, 33 (human beings). See also Pl., *Menex.* 237d–238b; id., *Laws* 6.782b; Isoc., 4.26–33, 38–40, 47–48; Aelian, *Var. hist.* 3.38. Triptolemus, an agricultural hero associated with Eleusis and Demeter, scattered seed from his air-borne chariot, drawn by serpents: e.g., Ovid, *Metamorph.* 5.642 ff.; Apollod., *Bibl.* 1.5.2; Liban., *Laudat.* 7.14. Erechtheus was also called Erichthonius (Ael., *Var. hist.* 3.38). Verg., *Georg.* 3.113–14, and Plin., *HN* 7.56 [202], specify that he introduced the four-horse chariot. See Schroeder, *De laudibus Athenarum,* for traditional praises of Athens (esp. pp. 19–24, 66–67).

12. On Themistius's remarks here on comedy and tragedy, see Garzya in *Roma Renascens,* ed. Wissemann, 65–66; Bettarini, *Κοινωνία* 19 (1995): 125–34. Janko, *Aristotle, "Poetics" I,* 65, assigns them conjecturally to Aristotle's lost *On Poets.* See also Colpi, *Die παιδεία,* 41–43, 53. "Upon seeing Phidias's Zeus . . . ": Phidias was an Athenian. "the Stagirite": cf. the adducing of Aristotle to illustrate the unimportance of place

If I am accomplishing nothing by all the fine things I have been saying and you have a strong desire for tales about foreign places, then you should not only sail about in the Greek world, but also go to Egypt and Ethiopia and India. You can come back and tell us about serpents and elephants instead of relating trifling tales with which everyone is familiar. You will encounter the Indian ant, a big creature—and a big story! The Brahmans will not let you come up off the ground with them; they will hurl thunder and lightning down at you![13]

But if you really thirst for water from the Muses' fount and are not merely posturing, draw from the spring whose waters flow right by you. This water is fresh and clear. Stop seeking out the fountains of Pirene and Arethusa.[14] The matters whereof I speak were settled long ago, from the very beginning, and are an ordinance of the gods [338]. Therefore, in seeking out eloquence, look to men, not to places.

To convince you, [my friend], I shall tell you a brief but old story.[15] Once the earth was unadorned and lacking in beauty. Then the gods decided to attend to it. So they sent the two sons of Iapetus [Epimetheus and Prometheus] to the earth. They charged them with the task of adorning the earth and gave them various good things for this purpose, including permission to create all the living creatures who were to live off the earth and adorn it. Epimetheus and Prometheus divided the work. One of them [Prometheus] fashioned and, at the same time, supervised the living creatures, forming them from a mixture of earth, fire, and their cognates.[16] The other [Epimetheus] bedecked the land itself, apportioning to each part of it what the gods had provided for this purpose. Dispensing what he was given, he made the earth rich in crops, he adorned her with vines, with Athena's fruit [the olive], one area with an abundance of fruit trees, another area with thriving woodlands—hair for the earth, as it were. He implanted gold here, copper there, silver elsewhere, and other such things in other places, giving as equal a share of these adornments as he could to each part of the earth.

---

of origin in Galen, *Protrep.* 14, and SHA, *Aurel.* 3. The latter text also adduces a Zeno—but the Eleatic rather than the Stoic of Citium.

13. "the Indian ant": see Hdt. 3.102. The Indian Brahmans levitated: see Philostr., *Vita Apoll.* 3.15, 17. For their control over thunder, see ibid. 3.13.

14. Pirene (in Corinth) and Arethusa are cited as examples of famous fountains; Arethusa is undoubtedly the fountain in Syracuse (cf. Them., *Orat.* 11.151d, with *RE,* 2 [1896]: 680–81, s.vv. "Arethusa" 11 and 14).

15. Cf. the story in Pl., *Protag.* 320c ff., although it differs significantly from Themistius's version.

16. "their cognates": cf. Pl., *Protag.* 320d, "from earth, fire and substances compounded with fire and earth."

After he had distributed all of these so-called goods, Father Zeus felt pity for the earth and desired to give it a share of divinity. So he gave it a second mixing bowl, one brimming with intellection and good judgment.[17] But he gave this gift on the condition that the whole earth partake of it. Epimetheus had no idea how to implement this injunction of Zeus. But Prometheus understood that good judgment and reason cannot grow in the earth like other seeds, that only the soul of a living being can contain and nurture this kind of seed. So he took the second mixing bowl and poured its contents into human beings, and therefore one finds reason wherever one finds human beings. Humans, it seems, are the only receptacle for and site of learning and reason [*λόγου*]. Thus, for raising leguminous and other plants, one place is better than another; but eloquence [*οἱ λόγοι*] is the fruit of human souls, and it is in souls that one must search for good or defective eloquence.

A certain competence, though, is required for eloquence, just as a knowledge of agriculture is required to grow things. Consider how very similar both endeavors are. First of all, you have to work the soul thoroughly [339] and make it fit to be sown.[18] This you will do by being ready to learn and attentive. If you let the soul get hard and compacted, the sower will waste the seeds, and the soul itself will yield not good judgment and virtue, but the thorny growths of vice and ignorance. Then, when the soul is sown and planted, you must hoe it and renew, through your memory, what was sown, and keep the soul free of weeds so that the good, cultivated sprouts will not be choked by a profusion of overpowering growths. Most important, you should avoid sowing indiscriminately and planting things from which you will get no useful fruit. For expressions of eloquence, like flora, are often pleasingly lush, but fruitless and without benefit. For example, groves of plane trees and poplars are not highly regarded by farmers; they are valued only by playful girls and the tired traveler and the king of the Persians, who had a golden plane tree.[19] So be selective and fix your attention on those seeds from which you will derive benefit.

Now if you have your sights set on money and assess what is beneficial on that basis, then you should pursue the kind of eloquence

17. Cf. Them., *Orat.* 6.77d–78a.

18. For the agricultural metaphor, cf., e.g., Pl., *Rep.* 6.492a, *Phaedr.* 276b ff.; Plut., *De lib. educ.* 2b, e; Arr., *Epict. Diss.* 4.8.36–40.

19. On tree-planting, cf. Them., *Orat.* 20.237c–d. On the golden plane tree, see Hdt. 7.27; Xen., *Hell.* 7.1.38; cf. Them., *Orat.* 13.166b. Perhaps Themistius is thinking of the "playful girls" of Pl., *Phaedr.* 229a–b.

that will yield wealth for you. The seed for this is very much at hand in the law courts and public assemblies. It reaches full bloom in the agora and around the public speaker's platform. [Young man], I could tell you the names of people who have made much money in these places. If you should approach them and pay court to them, they will quickly make your tongue great and extraordinary. In speaking, you will overtake orators from other cities by ten or perhaps twenty feet—or maybe by a whole stade! That's how clever our sophists are![20]

If, however, you set your sights, not on gain, but on your own self and on how you may become a better person, then you must seek out another kind of plant—not an earthly one, but a heavenly one. Kept in your soul, it will be of much worth to you in and of itself, even if no one derives profit from it or admires it. This type of plant is rare; it is found in few men only, for people do not admire it much. It does not secure gold or silver [340], but actually disdains wealth and regards it as utterly insignificant. For this reason, people disdain this heavenly plant. But if they had ever seen and tasted its fruit, believe me, they themselves would have uttered that well-known maxim, that all the gold on and under the earth does not equal the value of virtue. As things are, in their ignorance and inexperience of the gain to be derived from this heavenly plant, people concern themselves only with its foliage; they marvel at it and believe that the plant consists entirely of it. But it was the root of this plant that Homer, or rather Hermes, gave to Odysseus when he went to Circe to free his companions from the folly of pleasure. You yourself can obtain this plant from the god if you make the effort, and he will reveal its nature to you as he did to the son of Laertes. Do not think that it will be useless to possess this plant just because you will not be sailing by Circe's famous island or will never see her or drink her potion. Know well, my good young man, that, if you do not have a full supply of this remedy, not one but many Circes will mix up a potion for you—not Circes who live so far away that one has to go a great distance to reach them, but Circes who are continuously with you and surround you and summon you to themselves.[21]

20. "In speaking . . . stade!": cf. Eupolis, *Demes,* fr. 94 Kock. "That's how . . . are!": cf. Pl., *Menex.* 235c.

21. "not an earthly [plant]": cf. Pl., *Tim.* 90a; Them., *Orat.* 13.170b. Themistius has two distinct criticisms of the masses: they do not appreciate the heavenly plant of virtue, and they do not understand that virtue's foliage depends on virtue's root. "all the gold . . . virtue": cf. Pl., *Laws* 5.728a; Them., *Orat.* 21.261c. For the story of the sorceress Circe, see Hom., *Od.* 10.203 ff. She had given some of Odysseus's companions a

Now does Egypt or some distant Homeric island produce this root, and do you have to travel far again to obtain it? Well, if you want to understand the words of the epic, you will be able to dig up the remedy right here. For the line "It was dark of root and had a flower like unto milk" [Hom., *Od.* 10.304] gives the keys to and indications of the remedy's identification. If you cannot determine the sense of the line, do you want me to remind you of another utterance, one that you learned in school when you were still a boy? It will seem quite clear to you and will explain the epic line. The utterance is that the root of genuine learning is bitter, but its fruit is sweet and pleasant.[22] Now if you substitute "dark" for "bitter" and "white" [i.e., milky] for "sweet" and furthermore understand a god to be the giver of the herb, then the poet's intention will be apparent to you. And you would find that Hesiod supports Homer by putting the work of achieving virtue in first place but assuring us that there will be rest at the end [*Op.* 289–92]. Consequently, if it is possible to train oneself in virtue everywhere, then it is also possible to dig up that remedy everywhere. I believe that Homer is making this point when he has Hermes, after exhorting Odysseus, provide him with the herb, neither by importing it from some other locale nor by traveling to some far-off place to get it, but by pulling it up out of the very ground on which he stood [*Od.* 10.302–303]. What else is he saying except that, for one capable of taking it, this herb is always at hand and near by?[23]

---

drugged potion and then turned them into swine. The root or herb that Hermes gave to their rescuer, Odysseus, son of Laertes, protected him from Circe's magic; the gods called this herb "moly." For the allegorical interpretation of it, see Buffiere, *Les mythes d'Homère,* 150, 292, 512–15; Eustathius on Hom., *Od.* 10, p. 381 Stallbaum. In Dio Chrys. *Orat.* 7 (8).21–26, Circe's potion is compared to pleasure's temptations.

22. This utterance, often but not always attributed to Isocrates, was the subject of a school exercise, the *chreia;* see Hock and O'Neil, *Chreia,* 1: 325–26.

23. Eustathius cites Themistius's thesis in his comments on Hom., *Od.* 10, p. 381 Stallbaum.

ORATION 28

The Disquisition on Speaking

[341] It is not only philosophers who produce so many words; so do poets and rhetors. But the latter [i.e., rhetors] are vain, showy, and boastful about this learning of theirs and broadcast it to the whole human race. They often bring their eloquence out to theaters and festive assemblies, where it is arrayed in gold and purple, reeking of perfume, painted and smeared with cosmetics, and crowned with garlands of flowers. In addition to being so splendidly and lavishly adorned themselves, what they say is designed to be ingratiating. They are exceedingly courteous and gracious. They honor, extol, and salute those who gaze upon them. They emit a whole range of sounds and, like Sirens, sing songs full of pleasure. And since they are so courteous and agreeable to their audiences, their audiences salute and praise them in turn, and consequently the earth and the sea are teeming with these men.[1]

As for the descendants of Socrates [i.e., philosophers], in our day they have vanished and become nonentities—understandably and deservingly so. For they are fearful (I know not why) and wary of public assemblies, where the poet says men become famous [Hom., *Il.* 9.441], and they cannot bear to look away from their couches and secluded corners. They have completely forgotten that their forebears used to speak to crowds of people in workshops [342], porticoes, baths, and

1. "like Sirens": cf. Them., *Orat.* 26.330a. "the earth . . . these men": an echo of Hesiod, *Op.* 101, where earth and sea are said to be teeming with *evils*.

theaters. Consequently, those forebears not only used to win over and secure the allegiance of the people who came to their schools; they would also draw the cobbler away from his leather, the money lender away from his counter, and the fornicator away from his brothel. Urged on by the warm feelings they had for their fellow men, they would go to Olympia and the Isthmus, to Aegina and to Eleusis. They themselves, along with the gods [of those places], came to be reckoned <among those well known> to the masses. But since that time the descendants of Socrates, as if they were thieves and robbers, have been avoiding hubs of activity < . . . > and they are distrusted—unless it is their very wisdom that is causing them to lose their tongues![2]

Gentlemen, I am trying, and I am eager, to restore Socrates's descendants to their ancient condition. But I fear and suspect that, in making the effort to speak to you about this matter, I may appear to be even stranger than these silent philosophers themselves.[3] I am fully aware that they have a stubborn, willful, and unyielding disposition. They do not allow themselves to speak freely to people. In their boorishness, they are more sparing of words than they are of gold, and they strictly determine and take care to say neither more nor less than is fitting to anyone. Because they are so closemouthed, they do not win the friendship or goodwill of many people at all. And, as if that were not enough, they are also as self-important as can be: they believe and assure others that the praise they themselves bestow on a person really belongs to him, whereas the praise bestowed by those "refined and extravagant gentlemen" [i.e., rhetors] is wrongly ascribed and inappropriate. If this were so, one would not be able to determine whom public speakers are praising unless the lauded man's name were explicitly recorded in their words of flattery. This is the situation we encounter when portraits are painted by poor artists: their subjects cannot be identified by looking at the paintings, but only by reading the names of the subjects inscribed on them. True praise, though, is so vibrant, so

2. "they would also draw the cobbler," etc.: cf. Them., *Orat.* 26.318b. "They themselves . . . came to be reckoned," etc.: i.e., they became as well-known as the gods and goddesses honored at the Olympic Games (Zeus), the Isthmian Games (Poseidon), Aegina (Hecate Enodia [see Lucian, *Navig.* 15; Pausan. 2.30.2; Liban., *Orat.* 14.5]) and Eleusis (Demeter and Persephone). I tentatively fill the conjectured first lacuna with something like *εἰς τοὺς γνωρίμους* (i.e., *ἐτέλουν* . . . <*εἰς τοὺς γνωρίμους*> *τοῖς πολλοῖς ἀνθρώποις*). "hubs of activity": *τὰ μέσα* < . . . >. Perhaps the first words in this conjectured lacuna should be *τῆς πόλεως*; cf. Them., *Orat.* 22.265c. I leave the words immediately after this conjectured lacuna (*τοῦ ὀργάνου οὐκ ἀπεικότως*) untranslated.

3. Because Themistius advocates a public role for silent philosophers who currently have the unpleasant qualities that he goes on to detail.

much more alive than any of Daedalus's fabrications,[4] that, even if it is tossed out, as is done by speakers, into the midst of a crowd, it leaps forth and attaches itself to the person to whom it belongs. So if a speaker who is bestowing praise should turn his gaze away from the lauded person and look somewhere else [343], the audience always fastens its eyes without hesitation upon the man who is the natural recipient and fitting object of the words that have rolled off the speaker's tongue.

Look, I myself direct words of praise to the assembly because that official [ἄρχων] of yours seems to me to be truly living up to the title of his office. He is beyond the reach of bribery, open to reason, and a lover of freedom. Although he approves of high-mindedness, he guards against the self-importance that is akin to that quality. I do not name the person to whom I am referring. I do not look at him or smile at him. I do not point to him or get up and embrace him. Nonetheless, [as soon as I began praising him], you immediately understood whom I meant, and your eyes turned from me to him. The truth, of course, is so compelling that you cannot stop shouting and clamoring and jumping up from your seats. Yet the words I uttered were plain ones—quite casual remarks and very much in the ancient style—and they were not too dressed up or too embellished. But, of course, it is not my words that you appear to admire; it is the man with reference to whom my words issued forth and were clearly heard. I am sure that you will swear an oath in defense of my speech and affirm that it was neither an act of deceit nor of flattery. Rather, it was like someone shouting down from his seat to an accomplished competitor, following his every move and pointing out what he must guard against and encouraging him to remain undaunted.

4. "Daedalus's fabrications": i.e., artistic representations. Cf. Them., *Orat.* 23.296d, with n. 29 to my translation.

In Reply to Those Who Interpret [His Oration] "The Sophist" Incorrectly

[343] How wretched and very strange is philosophy's fortune if, instead of being able to clear herself easily of charges brought against her, the actions that she alone undertakes and decides upon have an effect opposite to that intended. In showing that abusive remarks made against her are false, she appears to be abusive herself. In defending herself against an accusation, she herself appears to be leveling an accusation [344]. Why, compared to philosophy, Autolycus's cleverness amounts to nothing! Autolycus used to alter the color of cattle, but he could <not> turn them into wolves and leopards.[1] The magic of the spoken word, though, is much more amazing than this cleverness of

1. Autolycus, Odysseus's grandfather, was a thief (Hom., *Il.* 10.266–67; *Od.* 19.394–96). He altered what he stole to avoid detection. "but he could <not> turn them into . . .": the context seems to demand that we accept Harduinus's conjectural "not" despite the resistance of Dindorf, the Teubner editors, and Maisano, *Discorsi,* ad loc. Themistius elsewhere (*Orat.* 7.96d, 21.251c) refers to the μεταμόρφωσις that Autolycus effected upon what he stole—which suggests more than an alteration of color, but need not imply transformation into other species. Cf. two passages in the Homeric commentator Eustathius: on *Od.* 19 (p. 209 Stallbaum), Eustathius says that Autolycus altered the colors of his stolen animals; on *Il.* 10 (vol. 3, p. 65 van der Valk), he writes of an alteration of their ἰδέας. According to Hyginus (*Fab.* 201), Autolycus converted what he stole "in quamcunque effigiem uellet," from white to black, from horned to unhorned—or vice versa. See also Hes., fr. 67b Merkelbach-West, with the comments from the *Etymologicum magnum* and from Tzetzes quoted there: commenting on Hesiod's assertion that Autolycus made everything ἀείδελα, the *Etymologicum* says that the Homeric thief altered the colors of his stolen animals; Tzetzes says that he altered their markings or brands.

his was! For it transforms what is said into its opposite! While seeming to be defending itself, it prosecutes. While shielding itself to avoid injury, it stabs and injures. Some of the arms that soldiers bear are for repelling blows, and others, it seems, for hitting and striking at the enemy; but speech, the most ingenious thing in the world, is more resourceful than iron, and the only choice one has is to employ it as both armor and dagger![2]

No, I would put it this way: speech does have some single intended effect, but a person who does not hear it correctly dragoons and forces it into a position that it neither intended nor aimed at initially. Such a person takes unfair advantage of speech's natural disposition, which is accommodating and open to having countless meanings imposed on it. When those meanings are fitting even to a small degree, the one who leads the argument astray may be forgiven for his meddling. But when a meaning entirely opposite to what was intended is imposed on an oration, this is something portentous and monstrous. And I do not know any pair of things in oratory that are more opposite than accusation and defense—just as there are no two things more opposite than praise and censure or bad advice and good advice.

Tell me, then, you most wise explicators[3] of the unexpected meanings of my utterances, why do you go so far in meddling with and assessing my recent oration [i.e., *Orat.* 23]? If you say that it is an accusatory oration because it argued that those who bring charges against me are false accusers and liars, you would be quite correct; and the exposing of a lie is indeed a harsh accusation against the liar. But if you examine the matter further, the malice is not to be found in my oration, but in those who understand the oration as they do. For the oration does not even claim to know the individuals who deride me as a sophist. Rather, it tries to show that they are far from hitting the mark with their gibe [345]. It calls upon Plato the Athenian as a reliable witness, and it accurately lists, in

2. "more amazing . . . most ingenious": the tone, of course, is ironic. The irony is dropped in the next paragraph. "speech . . . more resourceful than iron": the transmitted text is *ὁ πάντων εὐμηχανώτατος πράγμα ἀπορώτερόν ἐστι τοῦ σιδήρου*. I emend *ἀπορώτερον* to *εὐπορώτερον*. The only meaning one could get from the transmitted reading is "harder to oppose." But the sense is better served by my emendation: speech can both defend itself and attack, unlike arms of iron that are made for only one of these two purposes. Cf. John Chrys., *Expos. in Ps.* 137 2 [*PG* 55.410], *εὔπορος . . . καὶ εὐμήχανος* (also id., *Ad pop. Antioch. homil.* 11.2 [*PG* 49.122]; *In Genes. homil.* 26.5 [*PG* 53.238]); [Lucian], *Halc.* 6, *ἄπορος . . . καὶ ἀμήχανος*.

3. Themistius uses a word (*χρησμολόγοι*) meaning "diviners" or "expounders of oracles."

Plato's own words and language, in the manner of those who read from a code of law, all the traces and signs of the sophist to which Plato alerts us. But, [sir], if those laws are such as to irritate and vex you, you refrain from censuring them and, instead, you harass me—I who have taken refuge in them like those who are driven to the gods' shrines.[4]

If the individuals who brought charges against me were harassing me with some other accusation, the remarks I made to those who sat and listened to me would have been different. I would not have said the same things, nor would I have spoken in the same manner, because a person who [allegedly] does such and such is responsible for answering a charge connected with that particular activity. (If I do [always] respond to accusations in the same manner, gentlemen, then punish me; if not, then let me go.) So if someone had stood up while I was delivering those remarks of mine and had shouted out that "you have entered this place to make an accusation against so-and-so—for we all know that man who does the things you say he does"—I would have said to him: My good sir, that man and I have no involvement with one another. Do not set us at variance with one another. Do not add to my words what you may imagine is there, and do not interpret what I say as you understand it, but as I intend it. For I consider only that part of an issue that pertains to me, and it was to set that straight that I summoned jurors.[5] This and this alone—what pertains to me—is the subject of my present remarks.

I say that those who call me a sophist give me an incorrect title, for I am not sufficiently versed in the things to which sophists owe their reputation. The divine Plato says that Hippias gives evidence of such accomplishments, and that the other sophists are skilled in them too. (He [i.e., Socrates] makes these remarks in the *Lesser Hippias,* in what he says to the famous Hippias, and elsewhere.) The words of an apparently marveling and wonder-struck Socrates in the *Lesser Hippias* [368b ff.] are along these lines: that Hippias once came to Olympia and gave evidence of an incredible number of accomplishments, and that these included epic, tragic and dithyrambic poems, the composition of a wide range of treatises, works on the harmony of rhythms

4. The Teubner editors print ὥσπερ οἱ διωκόμενοι ἐπὶ τὰ ἱερὰ πρὸ θεῶν but suggest that πρὸ θεῶν should perhaps be emended to προθέοντες ("like pursued men who run to the gods' shrines"). I have adopted Reiske's emendation of πρὸ θεῶν to τῶν θεῶν.

5. I.e., the "jurors" before whom Themistius delivered *Orat.* 23; see *Orat.* 23.283b–c.

and on orthography, a knowledge of astronomy, geometry and music, and the study of nature.[6]

Gentlemen, such a heap and swarm of wisdom was never mine **[346]**, nor could it ever be—and I also declare that it could never belong to anyone else in this city [i.e., Constantinople] either. Perhaps it is actually beyond the capacities of human nature that such an abundance and treasure of almost uncountable blessings be stored up in a single human soul. If you, [sir], think that any one of our fellow citizens is so blessed, happy is he for his good fortune, happy are his pupils! As for me, my admirable fellow, I am far removed from enjoying such happiness; and I do not reject the title sophist because there is anything wrongful in it, nor because it is something that warrants a penalty of exile or death, but—and I tell you this over and over—because I am far removed from sophistic accomplishments.

Why, then, would anyone be annoyed at me for admitting publicly that I am poor in wisdom and that the areas of my knowledge are quite few in number—and this despite the fact that I have been studying hard and have been frantically immersed in my work over a long period of time? Because I am boastful and arrogant, perhaps, about those few areas of knowledge that I have mastered? Because Socrates would have silenced me for bragging about my limited knowledge, since he did not think or agree that he himself was wise, even though the god [Apollo] declared him to be the wisest of all?[7] No, [sir], you are just trying to frighten me and are being quarrelsome. For I know that all in this city who are now called sophists are courteous and kind, and none of them lays claim to Hippias's boastfulness. And so none of them is at war with me or ill-disposed towards me because of the fact that I do not declare myself to be a sophist. Neither is any physician going to be ill-disposed towards me for declaring myself to be a lyre player. For if all whose areas of competence are different from mine were my enemies, my situation would long ago have become untenable.

As for that person, whoever he is, whom you are dreaming up, [sir], and imagining, my oration [*Orat.* 23] does not have reference to him.

6. On Hippias's accomplishments, cf. Pl., *Hipp. maj.* 285b–86b; *Protag.* 315c, 347a. "on the harmony of rhythms": *περὶ ῥυθμῶν ἁρμονίας*. Is this what Themistius wrote, or should we emend to *περὶ ῥυθμῶν καὶ ἁρμονίας* (or *ἀρμονιῶν*)—"works on rhythms, on harmony (-ies) . . . "? Cf. Pl., *Hipp. maj.* 285d, *Hipp. min.* 368d.

7. Cf. Pl., *Apol.* 19d–23b.

Why would he be annoyed and irritated by it? If it is quite clear to you, [sir], that he is incensed, he should not be incensed at what I said, but at what it actually was that made my oration seem to refer to him. For words do not create realities for us that were not already there [347]; if they did, human happiness would be the easiest thing to achieve! Rather, when the reality obtains, then the account of the reality follows upon it. One must therefore do away with the reality, and the shadow is then driven off along with what is solid.[8]

But, as I previously said, I do not find anyone in our city who is so wise that this claim of being learned in a long list of subjects could be appropriately made of him; all are stunted and only half-formed in comparison to Hippias. If there is someone here who can write a tragedy, epic verse or dithyrambs, like the young man from Egypt who recently visited us, such a person admits that, when it comes to the higher wisdom, he is ignorant.[9] If, on the other hand, a person considers himself supreme and unrivaled in that higher wisdom, then he feels it beneath his dignity to pursue these petty and mundane skills; he will not even write a short clause or a line of verse. Consequently, no one could have any reason for taking offense at my oration [*Orat.* 23]. . . .[10]

That sophists charm the young by going to large cities and there persuading them to abandon ties with others, with fellow citizens and foreigners, with younger and older people, and instead to associate only with themselves and wait at their doors and even to give up interest in marriage and child-rearing—this is not my assertion, but the wise Plato's, openly made in the very words I just used. And this is not vilification. On the contrary, Plato calls such [youths] excellent, and I myself termed them good men in my oration. When a youth spends money and endures physical hardship on account of a person he thinks will make him a better man, that is truly evidence of the young man's distinction and a sign of his virtue. No one finds fault with Callias because he revered and honored, not only Protagoras, but Antimoerus of Mende and the other pupils of Protagoras as well. No one finds fault with him for emptying his coffers to make a guest room for the

8. "the shadow": cf. Democritus B 145 Diels-Kranz, "a word is a shadow of a deed," cited at Them., *Orat.* 11.143b, 16.200d.

9. For the Egyptian poet, see above, p. 20, n. 75.

10. I leave the relative clause at the end of this sentence untranslated (*ἐπὶ τῷ λόγῳ οὗ εἴσω κάμπτει* [corrected, according to Harduinus, from the manuscript's *εἰσωκάππει*] *καὶ ὁλοκλήρου οὐκ ἐξικνεῖται*) because I can make no good sense of it. Maisano translates the sentence "Nessuno quindi può prendersela con me per quel discorso che non lo tocca e che non arriva a comprendere per intero."

sophists; for this was the sign of a noble mind, one in love with learning.[11] But it was, perhaps, not a very fortunate aspect of Callias's love of instruction that he never looked to Socrates, the son of Sophroniscus, that he never felt the smart of Socrates's words, although it was the latter's habit to speak often to all the Athenians [**348**]. Plato does not deride Alcibiades, son of Cleinias, though, when he confessed to his fellow drinkers at the banquet that he was prepared to oblige his teacher [Socrates] in every way. No, Alcibiades's speech [Pl., *Symp.* 218a ff.] is splendid praise of both Socrates and himself—of himself because he was captivated by <Socrates> alone, and of Socrates because he was the only one who was not captivated by Alcibiades.[12] But if Alcibiades submitted himself to Socrates in every respect and Socrates made Alcibiades a better man in no respect, then commendation would go to Alcibiades and censure to Socrates.

11. The opening of this paragraph (i.e., "the very words I just used") echoes Pl., *Protag.* 316c; cf. also 315a. "this is not my assertion, but . . . ": cf. Pl., *Symp.* 177a, with Eur., fr. 484 Nauck. "Plato calls such [youths] excellent (βελτίστους)": cf. Pl., *Protag.* 316c, *τῶν νέων τοὺς βελτίστους*. "I myself termed them good men (χρηστούς) in my oration": apparently in the lost portion of *Orat.* 23. In the *Protagoras,* Protagoras is staying at the house of the wealthy Callias; Protagoras's most highly reputed pupil Antimoerus is there, also listening to the great sophist (314e–15a). For Callias's guest room, see *Protag.* 315d.

12. "Plato does not deride," etc.: i.e., it is better to be passionately devoted to philosophy than to neglect it utterly. "Socrates . . . not captivated by Alcibiades": Themistius is referring to Socrates's disdainful reaction to Alcibiades's sexual advances.

ORATION 30

Should One Engage in Farming?

[348] Hesiod of Ascra, who is said to have received from the Muses themselves the gift of song as well as the laurel [*Theog.* 29–34, *Op.* 662], used his poetic skill in praise of heroes and the Muses. He also included agriculture among the objects of his praise [i.e., in *Works and Days*]. He praised the whole of its nature and made us students of its techniques. He combined his discussion of agriculture with what he had to say about virtue, on the grounds that they are one and the same thing, and that we master agriculture and virtue by learning one from the other and studying both together.[1]

But now, being the follower of Hesiod and the Muses that I am, I must show at some length that Hesiod was not considered wise without reason, and that he became very famous because of what he said about farming—so much so that, when he competed with Homer in wisdom and song at the tomb of Amphidamas, the judges awarded him the crown and the victory. For Homer sang of wars and battles, of the two Ajaxes fighting together [*Il.* 13.701 ff.], and of other such things; but Hesiod hymned the earth's works and days—the days in the course of which earth's works are augmented [349]. And so Hesiod won the support of all the judges.[2]

1. In his *Works and Days,* Hesiod advocates and gives advice on both moral behavior and agriculture.

2. For the contest, see Hes., *Op.* 654–57, and the *Hom. et Hes. Certamen.* According to the *Certamen* (pp. 247–48 Rzach[3]), after Hesiod sang of the agricultural year

Let the gods who oversee agriculture be summoned to help me with my oration. I also summon whatever is best in all that the Muses preside over, and I call upon the leader of the Muses himself [i.e., Apollo]. For it is from the fruits of agriculture that they receive yearly recompense—drink-offerings, sacrifices, banquets, and all that the Hours cause to spring up from the earth—and they receive this recompense not only for helping mankind in oratory, but for everything that human beings have from on high. If we should also summon Dionysus, the nymphs, Demeter's daughter [Persephone], the rain-bringing Zeus, and nourishing Poseidon, then we shall be within short range of the rites and add a dose of Prodicus's wisdom to our eloquence.[3] Prodicus makes all of mankind's religious ceremonies, mysteries, festivals, and rites dependent on the blessings of agriculture. He thinks that even the idea of gods came to human beings through agriculture, and he makes agriculture the guarantee of all piety.[4] Not even Orphic rites and mystic ceremonies are unconnected with agriculture. In saying that Orpheus bewitches and charms everything, the myth hints that it was through the cultivated [ἡμέρων] fruits provided by agriculture that Orpheus tamed [ἡμερῶσαι] the whole of nature and the behavior of wild creatures and eradicated and tamed the wild element in souls. It was also believed that Orpheus bewitched the wild creatures by means of

---

(from his *Works and Days*) and Homer sang of war and the two Ajaxes (from his *Iliad*), Amphidamas's brother, King Paneides, gave Hesiod the prize, valuing peace and agriculture over war.

3. Dionysus is associated with the vine and vegetation (A. Veneri, "Dionysos," *LIMC*, 3, 1 [1986]: 414–15), and Demeter and her daughter with vegetation and particularly with grain (Burkert, *Greek Religion*, 159–61). Themistius is probably thinking of the nymphs as attendants of Dionysus (H. Herter, "Nymphai 1," *RE*, 17, 2 [1937]: 1573). Note that he calls on Zeus and Poseidon with epithets (ὑέτιος, φυτάλμιος) that suit the agricultural theme (for Zeus, see Jessen, "Hyetios," *RE*, 9, 1 [1914]: 89–90, and J. Schmidt, "Ombrios 1," *RE*, 18, 1 [1939]: 350; for Poseidon, see J. Schmidt, "Phytalmios 2," *RE*, 20, 1 [1941]: 1175, and E. Wüst, "Poseidon," *RE*, 22, 1 [1953]: 504). Cf., in an appreciation of agriculture at Plut., *Sept. sap. conviv.* 158e, the juxtaposition of Dionysus, Demeter, Zeus ὄμβριος and Poseidon φυτάλμιος. "within short range of the rites": "rites" is meant metaphorically here (i.e., we shall be ready to launch into the encomium).

4. See Prodicus B 5 Diels-Kranz; Kalbfleisch in *Festschrift Theodor Gomperz*, 94–96; Nestle, *Vom Mythos zum Logos*, 351 ff.; Guthrie, *History of Greek Philosophy*, 3: 238–42; Henrichs, *HSCP* 79 (1975): 107 ff., with *Cronache ercolanesi* 6 (1976): 15–21. I adopt Diels's conjectural emendation ἔννοιαν ("the idea of gods") with Kalbfleisch and Guthrie against the manuscripts' εὔνοιαν ("the goodwill of [the] gods"), which is read by the Teubner editors of Themistius's *Orations* and by Nestle. "The idea of gods came to human beings through agriculture" in that religion was born when human beings deified the fruits of the earth (as well as other beneficial things). Themistius "add[s] a dose of Prodicus's wisdom" to his oration by invoking agricultural deities or deities who are called by agriculturally pertinent epithets, thereby alluding to the Prodican linkage of agriculture and religion reported here.

his music, while using the fruits of agriculture for all his sacrifices and rites in honor of the gods.[5]

Orpheus's reputation reached all peoples, and everyone accepted agriculture. Whether you visit the Ethiopians, who stretch from east to west in the southerly regions, or the Celts, who inhabit the northerly regions, or the peoples who are located between the Ethiopians and the Celts, you will find farmers, plowmen, and diggers. The more advanced men are in agriculture, the happier they are. If some inhospitable Scythian, who lives an uncultivated life, has chosen to be a vagrant instead of a farmer, then he pays the price for his mistake—he is without hearth, a vagrant, patterning his life on that of the wild beasts.[6] And so agriculture is rather remarkable in that those peoples, if there really are any [350], who have failed to honor the tilling of the soil are the harshest and most savage. They say that, even if such men do not work the land, they survive only by importing the fruits of agriculture from abroad. A certain poet [Dionys. Perieg. 186–94] laments such men because they are innocent of the ear of wheat and know nothing of sowing or of the harvest; and he quickly adds that, without agriculture and fixed dwellings, their lives are like those of wild animals.

Those who lived a civilized life and had houses were the first, after having been relieved of preoccupation with their need for food, to look up to heaven and honor the gods and live by a system of justice and laws. They no longer had to spend all their time on life's bare necessities; since they could easily meet life's needs, they became adepts at wisdom. They built cities for themselves, erected temples, lived by a system of justice, and made laws. Consequently, agriculture is a greater source of laws than anything else is. It was she who allowed us to be human beings, to write legal codes and, once we had written them, to ratify them. And lawmakers have given more attention to agriculture than to anything else. Desiring peace and confronting the inevitability of war, some of them ban war by law; some decided on war so that no

5. Themistius links Orpheus with agriculture in two ways. First, exploiting the common root of the Greek adjective "cultivated" and the verb "tame," he has Orpheus taming through agriculture. Secondly, he contends that, even when taming through music, Orpheus used the fruits of the earth to honor the gods. See Linforth, *Arts of Orpheus,* 69–70, 255–57; Guthrie, *Orpheus,* 40–41; Graf, *Eleusis,* 35–36.

6. For nomadic, nonagricultural Scythians, cf., e.g., Aesch., *Prom.* 707–10; Hdt. 4.19, 46; Amm. Marc. 22.8.42. "[T]he pastoral nomad remained till the end of antiquity a synonym for barbarism, savagery, and utter alienation from the world of civilized men" (Shaw, *Ancient Society* 13–14 [1982–83]: 5–31 at 24).

one would devastate their own farmers' fields; and others safeguarded peace so that the digger and the plowman would be free from fear and able to raise their plants and crops in the proper seasons of the year. Also, the intention of commercial legislation is to allow those who do not have enough of the earth's produce and those who have a surplus of her various fruits to traffic safely with one another.

Through their laws, human beings achieved justice, and, having achieved it, they safeguard it. So it is reasonable [to say] that justice in human society is very much a result of agriculture. For farmers have no free time to be unjust. They are not compelled to commit acts of injustice because of poverty; on the contrary, they live a life of abundance. City dwellers and others (apart from farmers) who revere slander and injustice are the people who find time away from their occupations to commit acts of injustice. The farmer knows only one simple and noble good, the good that he gets from the earth as he tends to his business over the course of the year. He is convinced that injustice arises from meddling in other matters, and, from his safe distance, he avoids such meddling [351]. He is, by nature, so completely a stranger to injustice that, when it is present, wars and civil strife and the ruination of agriculture immediately result, but when justice and observance of law prevail, the fruits of the earth abound. One might compare the relationship between the farmer and injustice to that of naturally opposed elements, such as water and fire, which cannot mix with each other: when they come together, one of them is utterly destroyed.[7]

Homer and Hesiod say that even the weather is kind to the deserving and favors them.[8] For whereas the unjust are struck by hailstorms, by heavy rains that do not enhance the earth's fertility, and by plagues, the agricultural efforts of the just are rewarded. Gentle rains from Zeus fall down on their lands, and their oaks produce not only their proper fruit, but honey as well, since swarms of bees fill the trees' barren cavities with honeycombs.

From all this, it should no longer be difficult to understand that there is nothing that brings more profit to human beings than to engage in farming and live one's life pursuing this occupation. If you value self-sufficiency, farming will provide you with an abundance of

7. Cf. Theagenes of Rhegium 2 Diels-Kranz.

8. Hom., *Od.* 19.109–14; Hes., *Op.* 225–37. Plato uses both of these passages together in *Rep.* 2.363a–c.

life's necessities. If it is affluence that you want from your efforts, [remember that] the poets sing of Plutus [i.e., Wealth] as the child of Demeter[9] because the blessings of agriculture increase a person's resources in a way that nothing else does. All other occupations need agriculture.[10] Those engaged in skilled occupations and other pursuits, as well as people who have power and men who acquire a royal scepter, put their hopes for their reign or their power <or> their pursuits and occupations in the blessings of agriculture. Agriculture, from its abundant resources, supplies everyone else. So not even a king has any advantage—whether he is an Achaemenid or a Heraclid or whoever he may boast to be—unless the interests of those who nourish the community take precedence over the whole military establishment.[11] Whether a person is a painter or a sculptor, whether we are talking about merchants or sailors—well, why do I need to go through every occupational category? There is simply no one who does not need agriculture. If we have agriculture and it bestows its bounty on us, then everyone's endeavors flourish, and each person brings his efforts to a happy conclusion. But if the fruits of agriculture are inadequate, then nothing is left to sustain life.

9. According to Hesiod, *Theog.* 969–74, the grain goddess Demeter was the mother of Plutus.

10. "agriculture": I tentatively adopt Harduinus's emendation *γηπονίας* here instead of the transmitted *ἐπινοίας*, which is accepted in the Teubner edition.

11. "Achaemenid . . . Heraclid": i.e., a member of the old Persian dynasty descended from Achaemenes, or a ruler (e.g., the kings of Sparta) who boasts descent from Heracles. "unless . . . establishment": *εἰ μὴ τοῖς ὅπλοις τὰ τῶν τροφῶν τῆς παρασκευῆς ἁπάσης ἡγοῖτο*. Taking *τὰ τῶν τροφῶν* as the subject and *τῆς παρασκευῆς ἁπάσης* as the complement of the verb, I would suggest that we delete the words *τοῖς ὅπλοις*.

ORATION 31

Concerning His Presidency [of the Senate], Addressed to the Senate [of Constantinople]

[352] I have often wished to speak to you publicly, conscript fathers, about the grievances that certain individuals are expressing against me in private, and I feel that this is a most suitable time to do so, during the sacred month of the year, when the law grants a truce even to those who are very suspicious of one another.[1] Perhaps those who are annoyed at me will be kinder to me after they learn where I stand on the issues about which they now think that I am in disagreement with them. I shall speak as briefly as I can and try to keep my remarks within the proper bounds.

I followed the most highly regarded of the ancient philosophers, who explain that there are two philosophical paths, one that is more concerned with divine matters, and a second that is more useful in public affairs. I chose the kind of philosophy that is beneficial to you over that which investigates only what concerns me personally. I elected the kind of philosophy that operates in the public arena. In so doing, I followed the example of Socrates and Aristotle and their predecessors the celebrated Seven Wise Men, who, by combining deeds

1. "the sacred month (τὴν ἱερομηνίαν) . . . when the law grants a truce": commentators have seen an allusion here to the beginning of the calendar year, to Lent or to Easter time (i.e., Holy Week and Easter Week). See Bouchery, *AC* 5 (1936): 207–8; Schneider, *Die 34. Rede,* 50; Dagron, *T&MByz* 3 (1968): 26; Vanderspoel, *Themistius,* 209–10. Themistius was urban prefect when he delivered this oration. He held office for "<a few> months" (*Orat.* 34 [XI]). We cannot be sure which months, or how many, these were; cf. above, p. 35.

with their words, showed us a kind of philosophy that is neither inactive nor useless to society. For nearly forty years now I have followed all these philosophers, putting my learning to work in your service and going on a series of embassies for you, sometimes by myself and at other times in company with the best of you.[2] You yourselves know that on those embassies my service was neither dishonorable nor disreputable nor unworthy of your appointment of me.

Perhaps it is good for you to remember the most important of those good deeds of mine, while I myself let them slip from my mind [353]. I did graciously accept, both from you and from the emperors, appropriate honors—prizes of a sort—for all my services. I did this, though, not for my own sake, nor to better myself, but because I had in mind what Plato says and I wanted many of your fellow citizens to perform similar services for you. For "what is honored," Plato says, "is always practiced, and what is not honored is disregarded." For this reason I did not put up a fight about these two bronze statues. I did not resist when the emperor thought that I should ride beside him in his chariot nor when he gave me the much discussed tablets [of office]. I conceded that emperors could bestow such honors on philosophers, but I did not completely transfer or reassign my time from greater to lesser concerns.[3]

Next, it is said that the tablets [of office] are a delusion. I agree that they are a delusion if one relies on them to reach a high level of virtue. But let me respond, briefly and frankly, to this assertion. I consider an honor to be delusive if a person has bought it for a sum of money, has made many requests for it and waited in anticipation of it, or has received it as compensation for a service at court. But if a person should

2. "two philosophical paths": cf. Them., *Orat.* 8.104a–d. "Socrates" etc.: cf. Them., *Orat.* 34 [III] ff., where however Themistius refers to early Greek wise men, but not to the "Seven." "a kind of philosophy . . . useless to society": cf. Them., *Orat.* 34 [XXVII]; *Demeg. Const.* 20a, 22b. "For nearly forty years now": Themistius must be referring to the oratorical and philosophical services that began before his adlection to the senate in 355 as well as to the various political services that were made possible by his adlection. "embassies": cf. Them., *Orat.* 17.214b, 34 [XXIX].

3. "Perhaps it is good . . . from my mind": i.e., his good deeds should be remembered so that others may emulate them, but he does not want to boast about them himself. Cf. the reference to Adrasteia below (354c), with my note there. The Platonic quote: Pl., *Rep.* 8.551a; cf. Them., *Orat.* 4.54d, 15.195d, 16.204a. "two bronze statues": cf. Them., *Orat.* 34 [XIII] with n. 20 to my translation. "tablets [of office]": by which he was appointed urban prefect. See Chastagnol, *La préfecture urbaine,* 191–92; and for the "delusive tablets" of the next paragraph, Schneider, *Die 34. Rede,* 15–16; Dagron, *T&MByz* 3 (1968): 50. "I did not completely transfer" etc.: i.e., philosophy still remained important to him.

win it as a reward for his virtue and learning without having deliberately sought it out or requested it—a reward whose bestowers find it impossible to give to anyone but that individual—I say that such an honor actually falls short of his merits and is not at all delusive—unless one maintains that honors bestowed on the Deity are also delusive because they are less than what is due to Him.[4]

To me, the office I hold as a result of my learning [i.e., the "office" of philosopher] is loftier than any carriages overlaid with silver or any loud-voiced heralds. It is an office that emperors can neither bestow nor take away. Whether I sit on a golden chair, a wooden chair, or a low stool, I take this office around with me, and it alone endures when I leave this mortal body behind. The son of Ariston [i.e., Plato], Aristotle, Speusippus, and Xenocrates have been holding this office down to the present day.[5] After all, don't lawmakers seem to you to rule over those who obey their laws, and teachers over learners, and those who persuade people to pursue virtue [i.e., philosophers] over the ones who are persuaded **[354]**? Those philosophers have been holding office for more than 700 years and will continue to do so year after year, so long as the men born into this world are superior to swine and the other animals. They have held this office longer than the Persians ruled in succession to the Assyrians, longer than the nearby Macedonians ruled, and longer than the Romans have yet ruled.

Yet why should we compare Philip [II of Macedonia] to Plato or Alexander [the Great of Macedonia] to Aristotle with reference to length of office? No one pays heed today to Philip or Alexander. Their opinions and laws have no weight today among men. But Plato's and Aristotle's opinions are still vibrant and pure. In the course of so many changes of emperors and sovereigns, those opinions have remained unchanged, unmoved, unshaken. Who now names his way of life after Alexander, as people do after Plato? Who now lays claim to Philip's name, as they do to that of Aristotle? It is a noble thing to be numbered with Plato and Aristotle, to take a seat with them. It is a lofty

4. "if one relies on them . . . virtue": i.e., as is made clear below, an office/honor should be a reward for virtue, not a road to virtue. "without having deliberately sought it out": cf. Them., *Orat.* 18.224a–b, 23.292b, 34 [XIII].

5. "carriages . . . heralds . . . chair": distinguishing marks of the urban prefecture. See Chastagnol, *La préfecture urbaine,* 199, 203–5; Robert and Robert, *REG* 74 (1961): 220; Schäfer, *Imperii Insignia,* 51–52. The epigram of Palladas that is critical of Themistius's acceptance of the urban prefecture alludes to the silver that adorned his official carriage (*Anth. gr.* 11.292). The headship of Plato's Academy passed first to Speusippus, then to Xenocrates.

and magnificent thing to be empowered as their successor by tablets of office given by them. Because of those tablets I can say proudly, after having invoked Adrasteia, that I have no "need" of human "honor; I consider myself honored by Zeus's decree."[6]

If I should also need honor from human beings, I would beg you, whom I regard so highly, to be just judges of my virtue. Otherwise, "I have others who will honor me, especially" [Hom., *Il.* 1.174–75] your fathers and founders, the Romans. I made known to you what those contenders for heaven said about me, including how they admitted that they need my good qualities. In addition to the Romans, the emperors honor me. Constantius is enough for me, he who often called my philosophical learning an adornment of his reign. Julian is enough for me, he who was compelled to call me a worthy ambassador, not only of the fair city, but also of the whole world, and who acknowledged in writing that the first prize in philosophy belonged to me. Valens is enough for me, he who was often overcome by my words. Gratian suffices for me, boasting as he does to the Romans that he was responsible for my visit to them [355]. I value more than the most stately thrones the remarks of the most godlike Theodosius that were recently read to you.[7] If you should pattern your lives after those remarks and welcome philosophy in a fitting manner, then no decree would make me happier than one issued by you. But if some of you are persuaded to prefer those who depend on fortune over those who put their confidence in virtue—well, I would wish to have no part in a chorus in which singing out of tune with the Muses seems more highly regarded than singing in harmony with them.

I mention the Muses, and this is no small matter. You do well in having made the senate-house a temple in their honor and in having

6. One invokes the retributive goddess Adrasteia (or Nemesis) in propitiation, to avert her jealous punishment of a boastful or bold remark. Cf. Aesch., *Prom.* 936; Eur., *Rhes.* 342–43, 468; Pl., *Rep.* 5.451a; Alciphr., *Epp.* 4.6 Schepers; Them., *Orat.* 34 [X]; Amm. Marc. 14.11.25–26. The quotation is from Hom., *Il.* 9.607–8; Achilles is speaking and telling Phoenix, who is urging him to fight, that he does not need the honor of gifts.

7. "the Romans": in this paragraph, Themistius is alluding to his visit to Rome in 376 (Vanderspoel, *Themistius,* 179–82). Cf. Them., *Orat.* 34 [XXIX]. Themistius's "good qualities" had already been appreciated at Rome during his visit of 357: Them., *Orat.* 23.298a–d. "Constantius . . . who . . . called my philosophical learning an adornment of his reign": the emperor certainly implies this in the *Demeg. Const.* "a worthy ambassador . . . whole world": cf. *Demeg. Const.* 22c, "an extraordinary citizen of our city [Constantinople], whom one would have every reason to call a citizen of the whole cosmos." "the fair city": i.e., Constantinople. See Dagron, *Naissance,* 52. "the remarks of . . . Theodosius": they must have been in praise of Themistius and philosophy.

erected statues of these goddesses on both sides of their precinct. For one chorus of Muses was not enough for you. Homer has a total of nine Muses in heaven; but among you hospitality is extended to twice that number, and Helicon has transferred itself to the Bosporus.[8] You adorn your senate better than the old Romans adorn theirs.

Yet I trust now that your purpose in giving the goddesses a home here, in this place where no one may enter except the elect, was not to make a display of their beautiful statues, but to show those who are on this body's roll the appropriate way for a senator to excel over others: not by having the prize of wealth or carriages or rods or axes, but by winning the goodwill of the Muses. For you have heard the name that is given to this temple: it is not called a general's headquarters or a theater or a treasury, but a body of elders and a council-chamber, and in it preside [the Muse] Calliope and any man "whom the daughters of great Zeus will honor."[9]

8. For the Constantinopolitan senate-house as a temple of the Muses, cf. Them., *Orat.* 17.215d, 19.228a–b; see Dagron, *Naissance,* 139–40, and Paschoud on Zos. 5.24.8 (n. 50, p. 186). Homer's nine Muses: *Od.* 24.60. Mt. Helicon was the Muses' haunt in Boeotia.

9. "carriages . . . axes": for carriages, cf. section 353c above. The rods (*fasces*) and axes were ancient Roman symbols of power. The urban prefect was entitled to the *fasces:* see Chastagnol, *La préfecture urbaine,* 198; Schäfer, *Imperii Insignia,* 212–13. "and in it preside" etc.: Hes., *Theog.* 75 ff. In this passage Calliope is said to be preeminent among the Muses. The daughters of Zeus (i.e., the Muses) are said to make rulers whom they honor eloquent and wise judges. *Orat.* 17 also ends with an exhortation to the senate.

ORATION 32

On Moderation of One's Emotions [*Μετριοπαθής*], or, On Love of One's Children

[355] I would say that the human race is endowed with two kinds of reproduction and offspring; one kind issues from the body, and the other from the soul itself. Nature devised both kinds of reproduction, thereby providing our race with an immortality of her own contrivance [356]; but with each kind her goal is reached in a different way.[1]

The weakness or strength of what the soul conceives derives from the reserve of virtue in it when giving birth. The offspring of a good soul and of good [psychic] seed are hardy and manly enough to withstand any destructive pressure exerted against them from without. They are in full bloom as soon as they are born, and they remain at their peak forever. The offspring of a base and weak soul, however, are barren and not viable. Memory receives them but does not preserve them; instead, quickly excluded from memory's domain, they are taken into the bosom of oblivion.[2]

Contrast now the offspring of the body. They are neither saved by their parents' virtue nor destroyed by their parents' vice; the Fates and

1. For bodily and psychic reproduction, cf. Pl., *Symp.* 206c, *Theaet.* 150b ff. Themistius and Libanius play in their correspondence on the two senses of "offspring": see the scholion to Liban., *Epp.* 241 Foerster (printed ad loc. in Foerster's edition). "an immortality ... contrivance": Pl., *Polit.* 270a (ἀθανασίαν ἐπισκευαστήν), cf. *Symp.* 207c–208b. In translating the Platonic phrase I follow J. B. Skemp in his translation of the *Politicus* (New Haven, Conn., 1952).

2. "not viable": literally "wind-eggs" (ἀνεμιαῖα). Cf. Pl., *Theaet.* 151e, 157d, 161a, 210b. "Memory," etc.: Themistius means that, for example, a literary work of poor quality will not be remembered for very long, if at all.

Necessity and the indissoluble and unalterable destinies that they spin rule over this kind of offspring. For if children were at all affected [by the virtue or vice] of their parents, Socrates's son Lamprocles would not have died prematurely, nor would Pisistratus's son Hippias have succeeded to his father's tyranny.[3] No, it is Clotho, Atropos, and Lachesis [i.e., the Fates], the daughters of Necessity, as I said, who were allotted the authority and power over the body's offspring. If these goddesses twirled a person's spindle to the right, his children, even though they are weak, become strong and flourish, and they reproduce themselves in turn, just as bees produce swarms of their own kind. All these progeny give a number of names to their source—"father," "grandfather," and, as time goes on, titles celebrating his happy old age. But if the Fates twirled a person's spindle to the left and with an uneven motion, he is a very wretched individual. He is burdened by his fate, which is to have children who are born blind and unable to reproduce themselves. Worse off still is the person for whom the Fates spun a delicate thread of fine quality around the spindle's whorl, then, after a while, cut it and broke it off.[4] For after having a taste of pleasure for a short while—a painful pleasure with disease festering beneath its surface—such individuals soon see the worthlessness of their offspring and understand that such deceptions of nature are not unlike dreams. But the offspring of souls, those whom the Muses raise and nurse, in the first place always ensure that their fathers suffer no pain on their own account; and, secondly, they equip their fathers [357] to endure very courageously any misfortunes involving their own brothers [i.e., the offspring of bodies].[5] If you would like to hear where they get the ability to equip their fathers in this way, I can tell you.

A mighty and powerful herb grows in the meadows of philosophy, an herb like the one that Homer says Helen, the daughter of Zeus, got from the Egyptian woman Polydamna [*Od.* 4.219 ff.]. The [soul's] children gather in the herb from this grassland. They collect an ample supply of it from the precincts of Plato and from those of Aristotle, son

3. Plutarch, *De gen. Socr.* 590a, also makes Lamprocles die young and, erroneously, before his father (contrast Pl., *Phaedo* 116b, Diog. Laert. 2.26). In light of the previous sentence, the point seems to be that Socrates's virtue did not save Lamprocles from a premature death, nor did the vice of Pisistratus's tyranny (cf. Them., *Orat.* 34 [XV]) cause Hippias to perish before he too became a tyrant.

4. "Worse off still" (*συμφορώτερος*): the context demands the meaning that I give to the adjective (cf. Ballériaux, *Byzantion* 58 [1988]: 24), even though this is not a meaning to be found in the standard lexica. Cf. *συμφορά* = "misfortune."

5. The "offspring of souls" here will be insights, convictions, etc. that help a person endure misfortunes suffered by his children.

of Nicomachus.[6] Then they pound it, mix it in memory's mixing bowl, and smear and rub their father with it. The application quickly works its way in, seizes and takes hold of the heart without delay, and works to cast out the distress that is firmly lodged there and has worked its way into the very depths of the soul. It is now that the power and the vigor of the herb really manifest themselves. The herb strikes and assails from every direction. The pain refuses to relent or yield and will not even withdraw under truce; instead, pointing the irresistible sharp ends of its own nature at its opponent, it defends itself boldly and repels the assaults of reason. When this happens, the herb barricades and walls in the pain. It encloses the pain on all sides and puts unbreakable bars on the exits. The result is that, when the pain shouts out, it cannot be heard, nor can it be seen when it leaps up.

The father tends to his exterior, making it peaceful and calm, so that no perceptible evidence of the siege taking place within is provided to anyone. Thus his distress remains confined within, where it reels to and fro and howls out things that no one can hear, while outside all is peaceful and unimpeded. Outside, the baths are not closed to this person, nor is he barred from banquets and the usual gatherings. Sometimes he even breaks out in laughter—a light, superficial, shallow laughter. Consequently, you would not believe that any part of such a person is not full of joy; such a dim idea do his porticoes [i.e., his exterior] give, with their fortitude and high-spiritedness, of [the activity of] this herb. Nevertheless, these words from comedy apply to such a person: "In the agora this man is thought to be happy, but when he opens," [358] not "his door," but his soul, he is found to be "wretched three times over" [cf. Menander, fr. 251 Koerte-Thierfelde]. Actually, a man's [bad] fortune should never force the designation "wretched" on him if he is a true philosopher. But neither does this mean that he is happy or fortunate. For virtue and wisdom do not suffice to ensure him pleasing epithets; it is enough that they keep disgraceful ones at bay.[7]

All philosophers admit the truth of what I say[8] in practice, even though it is only adherents of the Lyceum who assent to it in theory. Those who do accept what I have been saying avoid bringing on themselves the ridicule that Persaeus of Citium once suffered from Anti-

6. Cf. "the meadows of Plato and Aristotle" in Them., *Orat.* 4.54b, 15.185a.

7. I.e., a philosopher will escape the shame of being unable to endure misfortune, but not necessarily misfortune itself.

8. I.e., that the philosopher is affected by emotions but knows how to moderate them.

gonus [Gonatas of Macedon]. Persaeus, a pupil of Zeno, was living with King Antigonus. The king would hear Persaeus constantly speaking in an overly confident tone and often harping on those nice-sounding Stoic phrases, the kind of thing that comes out of the mouths of smug young men. The wise man, Persaeus would say, cannot be conquered by fortune or enslaved; he is unassailable and unaffected by emotion [ἀπαθής]. So the king decided that he would try to refute all of Persaeus's pretentious claims by putting him to a practical test. He arranged for some merchants from Cyprus and Phoenicia to visit him, having instructed them ahead of time on what they should say to cause Persaeus to be put to the test. He then proceeded to question them, inquiring first about their ships and the navy and the soldiers in Cyprus[9] and other such things that one would expect a king to ask. Calmly continuing in his conversation, he next asked them about the state of Persaeus's domestic affairs back in Citium. When these merchants heard Persaeus's name, they were suddenly saddened and lowered their heads. It was apparent to Persaeus that, in response, they were going to report some bad news. All of his confidence left him. He pressed hard and earnestly begged them for information. When they replied, with reluctance, that his wife had been seized by some Egyptian pirates while she was walking out to a field with her favorite slaves and then had been sold into slavery, that his beloved young son had been murdered, and that his slaves and other possessions were gone forever, thenceforth Zeno no longer existed for Persaeus, nor did Cleanthes. Nature had refuted their fine sayings because in fact they were empty and weak sayings, not supported by experience.[10]

Gentlemen, I admire many other things about Aristotle [359], but I especially admire and esteem the wisdom revealed in the fact that his teachings do not distance themselves from the creature about which they are put forth. Rather, they bring help to its weakness and rectify what is deficient in it and provide all possible means by which creatures may reach their best condition. Aristotle's teachings neither over-

9. The king deliberately mentioned Cyprus to pave the way for a question about Cypriote Citium.

10. Cf. the very short version of this anecdote about the Stoic Persaeus in Diog. Laert. 7.36. Diogenes makes it explicit that Antigonus made up the story of the assault on Persaeus's family and property. For Persaeus at Antigonus's court and for his life in general, one may pursue the bibliography recently given by Dorandi, *Filodemo, Storia dei filosofi: La Stoà,* 10, n. 53. Like Persaeus, Cleanthes was a pupil of the founder of Stoicism, Zeno, and he succeeded Zeno as head of the school (Diog. Laert. 7.174). For another story about Persaeus's being disabused of a doctrine of Zeno, see Plut., *Arat.* 23.5–6.

reach nor slight a creature's mean; nor are they so extremely clever that they forget, because of that cleverness, that the living being who is the object of their concern has much of the earthly and terrestrial in it, but only a small portion of the divine and heavenly. His teachings are content if they can thoroughly drive off and clear away the many unessential things by which the immortal part of a mortal being is burdened. As for what cannot be made to fade away or be washed out, what is deeply impressed and embedded, his teachings are happy if they can at least adorn and beautify these features of mortal beings and suppress their excessive manifestation.

For Aesop the storyteller says that those who try to suppress and do away utterly with what cannot be washed out of a mortal being will likely have the same experience as the man who bought the Indian slave [cf. Aesop, *Fab.* 274 Hausrath-Hunger]. Aesop says that the man who bought that Indian was displeased with the color of his skin. So he tried to wash him clean and wipe the color off of him. He went around to springs and rivers and used soap and detergent on him. When the slave's skin began to suffer from abrasion while his color remained unaffected, his obstinate master reluctantly came to the conclusion that the Indian's skin color was part of his nature and that it would be easier to remove his soul from him than his dark coloring. So too, pleasure, pain and all the other emotions are inevitably engrained in human beings, and pain is more pronounced and more abiding than the other emotions. Aesop makes this point a second time, too; for, in his telling, Prometheus did not mix the clay out of which he fashioned man with water, but with tears.[11]

Therefore, we must not try to eradicate the emotions, for this is impossible. Rather, we should, if possible, trim them back, tame them, put them to rest as far as we can, and admonish them; for they gladly submit to this kind of management. And if you guide them in this way, they will seem useful and beneficial rather than useless and harmful. For God did not make the emotions a component of human beings [360] in order to inflict harm and disgrace on us; he interwove them into the soul and added them to its design for the survival and protection of the human race—anger so that we may ward off what is injurious to us, and desire for food and drink in anticipation of the body's

11. "the ... emotions are ... engrained": cf. Arist., *Eth. Nic.* 2.3 [1105a3]. "Prometheus" etc.: this is Aesop, *Fab. gr.* 430, in Perry, *Aesopica,* 1: 491; cf. *Sent.* 27 (Perry, ibid., 254).

natural and necessary excretion. Thus one emotion has been assigned the task of responding to one bodily crisis, and another to another.

Each emotion must remain within proper bounds, and this measured state [μέτρον] of each is its virtue. The virtue for spiritedness is courage, that for appetite is temperance, and the virtue for love of money and of gain is generosity and munificence. As for the feelings excited by office, power, and authority, their measured state is high-mindedness.[12]

Now if the emotions should be left in a disorderly state and untreated by reason, they quickly become wild and get out of control, like cultivated and useful plantings that have been neglected by a farmer. They sprout vices, comparable to thistles, which are dangerous and a poison to others and especially to the proprietor himself. But there are also cases in which emotions that are in peak condition wither away and are snuffed out.[13] People thus afflicted need reason, too—not a reason that checks and stifles the emotions, but one that, keeping them well watered, guides and coaxes them back up to an appropriate level of growth.

So, then, every virtue is beseiged, on this side and that, by two vices, the vice of opting for an insufficient expression of emotion and that of being given to emotional excess. One must not, as a result of focusing on base and perverted emotions, be uniformly suspicious of all of them and drive them all out;[14] instead, one must investigate nature's purpose and the reason why she implanted and impressed each of the emotions in the soul.

Take, for example, the issue at hand: if we were not extremely attached and bound to our children by feelings of delight, but neglected them as soon as they were born, leaving them naked, deserted, weak, and unable to keep themselves alive, would not the human race have vanished and perished a long time ago [361]? In fact, that attraction to our children, naturally implanted and cultivated in us, compels us to curry the favor of midwives; to call in caretakers, wet nurses, slaves to accompany our children to school, and physical trainers; to require the services of rhetors and schoolteachers; to spend and also to make money. We sow and plant, go to war and set sail, and subject ourselves

12. Cf. Arist., *Eth. Nic.* 2.7 [1107b].

13. "like cultivated ... plantings": for the simile in this context, cf. Plut., *De virt. mor.* 451c. "But there are also cases ... snuffed out": *ἔστι δὲ ἐφ' ὧν ἔμπαλιν καταφθίνει καὶ ἀπομαραίνεται εἴσω τῆς ἀκμῆς*. Add a *τὰ* (i.e. *παθήματα*) before *εἴσω*.

14. I read Stobaeus's *ἐξελαύνειν* here instead of the Teubner edition's *διεξελαύνειν*.

with unbelievable zeal to every sort of hardship—and all so that, when we die, we do not leave our offspring in want of anything. In a word, because we are enchanted by our children, we put up with rearing them, a troublesome and painful responsibility. I shall give you a good example of just how troublesome it is: if a child has been struck by an ailment, the child himself feels pain in his head, eye, or hand, but his father feels it in his whole body and soul.

I have expatiated on these matters, my good men, because I suspect that, whenever you see philosophers just as attached to their sons and daughters as the masses are, you ridicule and look down on them. So I tell you that this feeling of theirs is very philosophic. If many men experience it, they experience it only because nature has implanted it in every human being as a trace of philosophy. By the gods, is it not philosophic and entirely divine to strive for immortality?[15] Understand that, in this, a philosopher is not *like* the masses; he is much *superior* to them and *better* than they are for it. I shall say something quite the opposite of what you expect: he is superior and better because he *outdoes* the masses in his love of his children.

One can readily observe shoemakers, bath-keepers, carpenters, and smiths slighting nature and easily breaking the bonds by which she bound them to their offspring. Now bitches take care of their puppies as long as they need their mothers' teats; but shortly after that need passes, they start biting and tearing at them and stop providing them nourishment. Their behavior clearly shows that, when they were taking care of their puppies, they were not acting on their own;[16] rather it was nature who was looking after the weak newborn creatures. The majority of human beings treat their children just as bitches treat their puppies. As long as children are very young and their speech is halting and confused [362], parents dote on them and value them not only more than material wealth, but even more than their very own souls. But when children take leave of youth, their parents simultaneously take leave of their intense love for them. As soon as they enroll them in the ranks of adult men, they make them their enemies. Then they put a higher value on their land, their silver, and their gold than they do on a son—indeed, they even regard a cook, a maidservant, and maybe even a horse and a coat as things worth more than a son. This is still not

15. Here, the immortality of the human race through procreation.
16. "they were not acting on their own": οὐκ αὐτοὶ ἐθεράπευον. Maisano, *Discorsi*, ad loc., corrects αὐτοί to αὐταί.

hardhearted compared to what happens if a son offends or irritates his father, even in some small way: the father takes his son to court and demands that he be put to death and is not afraid to applaud the imposition of that penalty!

If it does not seem dignified to you to say that philosophers are better than merchants and fullers, then I shall speak of satraps and tyrants, of Ariobarzanes, son of Mithridates, and of Periander, son of Cypselus. Ariobarzanes banished his son and was delighted to rid himself of him. Periander barred [his son] Lycophron from fire and water. Now if satrap and tyrant are still not grand enough titles for us, then take this illustrious and grand title: king and despot of half the earth. I am referring to Artaxerxes, son of Darius and Parysatis. Surely you know that this Artaxerxes slaughtered one of his sons and forced the other to perish by his own hand.[17] You hear Euripides telling in his tragedies that Theseus begged his father Poseidon to bring down a curse on his own son Hippolytus, and you also hear that this curse was the punishment for the son's temperance and justice [*Hippol.* 887 ff., 1100–1101, 1298–99]. And the excellent Amyntor must be very excellent indeed, since he was provoked to utter a curse of sterility and childlessness on [his son] Phoenix! He prayed that Phoenix have no children, that Phoenix not give him any grandchildren. And he was provoked to utter this curse by such a terrible transgression on Phoenix's part: in deference to his mother, Phoenix had daringly tried to set Amyntor and his concubine at odds with one another [Hom., *Il.* 9.448 ff.]!

I cannot imagine, then, that you would still say that I am wasting words over nothing if I should praise philosophers because they are

17. "If it does not seem dignified to you to say": i.e., if the comparison is ipso facto insulting to philosophers. Themistius will now compare the philosopher with individuals of higher standing, only to show that the latter are even more unloving towards their grown children than are men of lower standing. "to rid himself of him": literally, if Jacobs's conjecture *κατακναίων* is accepted, "to scrape himself clean of him" (*pace LSJ*, s.v. *κατακναίω*). Ariobarzanes, a satrap of Dascylium in the fourth century B.C. (Judeich, "Ariobarzanes 1," *RE*, 2 [1896]: 832), was betrayed by his son Mithridates (Xen., *Cyropaed.* 8.8.4; Val. Max. 9.11 ext. 2); but I know of no other ancient evidence that the son was ever banished by his father. Ariobarzanes did drive his predecessor Pharnabazus's son into exile (Beloch, *Griechische Geschichte,* 3, 2: 146–47). Has Themistius confused the facts? For Periander, tyrant of Corinth in the late seventh and early sixth centuries, and his son, see Hdt. 3.50 ff. Artaxerxes II, king of Persia, 404–358 B.C.: Themistius is referring to Artaxerxes's sons Darius and Ariaspes (Plut., *Artax.* 26 ff.; Justin. 10). Cf. esp. Ael., *Var. hist.* 9.42. But Darius had been plotting against his father. Aelian makes Artaxerxes demand or at least approve of Ariaspes's suicide; but, according to Plutarch, Ariaspes's suicide was caused by false reports, generated by his brother Ochus, that Artaxerxes wanted him eliminated, and Artaxerxes lamented the suicide.

not guilty of the kind of transgression that private citizens, dynasts, kings, heroes, and sons of gods seem to fall into—I mean that some of the latter value money, others honors, others tyrannical power, and others unbridled pleasure more than they value their own sons [363].

I am reluctant to believe the poets completely, since they do not even exempt the gods themselves from moral weakness, not even the eldest of the gods [i.e., *Κρόνος*]. Clearly, you yourselves are full of Hesiod and of what he says about Cronus—that he devoured most of the offspring he begot, and that Rhea just barely managed to raise [their son] Zeus [*Theog.* 453 ff.]. But if this is what Hesiod sings about the gods, let us be rid of him—unless Cronus means something else to him, and he is telling a simple and ancient tale that he is hiding behind a strange curtain. Now this tale (for I shall not permit you to be deceived by the poets) contains nothing solemn or grand. Its substance is simply that time [*χρόνος*]—I mean this time in which I and you and the other animals and plants find ourselves enmeshed—is the eldest of all things and, with its ceaseless flow, does away with everything that exists in this world except reason. Reason alone prevails over time and remains unaffected by it and, by means of memory, restores what time has destroyed. But if poets should generally be allowed to make up fictions such as these, Homer's fictitious tale about Sarpedon is much more beneficial to mankind. Although he made Zeus the father of Sarpedon, nonetheless he says that Zeus was upset and distressed when his son was about to be slain by Patroclus; and Zeus was unable to undo what fate had already determined [Hom., *Il.* 16.419 ff.].[18]

Understand well, then, gentlemen—lest I become long-winded—that the man who loves his children experiences a praiseworthy emotion. He does not resemble the lover of wealth or the lover of money. People understandably call those epithets disgraceful, and that indeed is what they are. For it is our own depravity, not nature, that causes us

18. "the eldest of the gods": Themistius calls Cronus the eldest of the gods because he identifies him with time (*χρόνος*), which is the first of all things (Scythinus *apud* Stob., *Anth.* 1.8.43 Wachsmuth-Hense; cf. Apul., *De mundo* 37 [371]). *Orphic Hymn* 13, which makes Cronus the begetter of time, calls him father of gods and men (see also McCartney, *CP* 23 [1928]: 187–88). For the identification of *Κρόνος* with *χρόνος*, see Roscher, *Ausführl. Lex.*, 2, 1 (1890–97): 1495–97, 1546–47; Pease on Cic., *De nat. deor.* 2.25 [64] (2: 709–10). "time . . . does away with everything . . . except reason": cf. Cic., *De nat. deor.* 2.25 [64]; Sallust., *De deis* 4.2 Rochefort. In the myth, Zeus represents reason. "Homer's fictitious tale is much more beneficial": because it does not require an allegorical interpretation to make it into something edifying. "Although he made Zeus" etc.: i.e., although Zeus is a god like Cronus, he does not respond to Sarpedon in an unfatherly way, as Cronus had done.

to love wealth and money. But love of children has been bound onto nature from heaven above; it is fastened to that truly golden and unbreakable chain,[19] through which nature continuously stitches and binds together what is being generated [i.e., children] and what is decaying [i.e., parents] and does not permit the latter to slip into nonexistence.

Therefore, the philosopher is not ashamed of loving his children any more than he is ashamed of loving wisdom or the written and spoken word. For he loves best those writings and orations **[364]** that he himself produces and rears, and the procreation of children is the same sort of legitimate productivity on his part, just as Zeus's procreation of Athena was.[20]

19. For this image of Homeric origin (*Il.* 8.19), see Lévêque, *Aurea Catena Homeri* (with a comment on this Themistian passage on p. 30). Note also Them., *Orat.* 2.32d.

20. Athena was born from the head of Zeus. The Stoic Chrysippus understood the birth of Athena, goddess of wisdom, to symbolize the fact that "things pertaining to the arts and sciences come into being inside . . . men and come out by way of the head [i.e., the mouth]" (*apud* Galen, *De plac. Hipp. et Pl.* 3.8.19, trans. P. de Lacy).

ORATION 33

[Title Lost]

[364] The musical theorist Aristoxenus tried to restore the vigor of music after it had already begun to lose its potency. He liked the more masculine melodies himself, and he urged his pupils to reject the soft and zealously to pursue the manly in song. Once someone in his circle asked him, "How would it profit me if I turned my back on the pleasing musical idiom that is now in vogue and devoted myself to an old musical style?" "You will sing less frequently in the theaters," Aristoxenus replied; for it is not possible both to please the masses and to be faithful to the standards of the past in one's field of endeavor.[1] Thus, even though Aristoxenus was engaged in a pursuit that has broad appeal, he regarded the disdain of the people and of the theater's throng as a matter of no significance. If he could not remain faithful to the principles of his art and simultaneously sing in a way that delighted the masses, he would opt for art over popularity.

Now why have I made Aristoxenus's retort the introduction to my oration? I have thought [about that retort], my dear Greeks, ever since I came here to speak to you in these assemblies, and I suspected that you would ask me why—maybe all of you, maybe none of you. The answer to my question would have to be that I love you, dear friends, and value you very highly and would most gladly address you day af-

1. Aristoxenus, fr. 70 in Wehrli, *Die Schule des Aristoteles,* 2: 29, and see Wehrli's comments on pp. 68–69; West, *Ancient Greek Music,* 165, 370–71.

ter day as you sit here en masse, but that these theaters do not completely welcome the knowledge to which I am so passionately devoted. For that knowledge does not seek to be the epitome of delight or to say what it says to give pleasure. Consequently, it sometimes injures and pains an audience, making people feel dejected and causing them to leave.

Suppose that a self-important and exultant individual should come to a public gathering [365]. His bearing is such as it is for a number of reasons: because he owns many houses and fields, many flocks of sheep and herds of horses, and even has droves of people at his disposal; because he feasts on delicacies that he gathers in from land, sea, and sky; and because the people of this very city that rules the empire [i.e., Constantinople] watch for him on the streets,[2] applaud him as soon as he appears, and shout out from every direction that he is happy, prosperous, and blessed. Now when such a person, convinced as he is by the masses of the blessedness of his state, comes to a public gathering and is taken hold of by philosophy and, unless he has been completely corrupted, is fairly easily reeducated by her through the words of the speaker, it becomes clear that his fellow human beings, themselves already misled, are misleading him. For happiness and blessedness are not found in silver or in food and drink. Many people have storerooms filled with these things, treasuries loaded with them, and yet are more unhappy than those who have been cast out into the streets.

Do you fail to pay heed to Menelaus, the king of Sparta? The walls of his palace were made of gold, as was the roof above the walls. His court gleamed with electrum. Silver was the least of his possessions. Do you fail to pay heed to that man as he laments, "I have no joy, no delight, in being master of this wealth"? What more do you seek, you blessed king? You live in a house of gold, your partner [Helen] is the most beautiful woman in the world, you are considered to be Zeus's son-in-law, and you rule over great Lacedaemon![3] Yet the fact is that, however much fortune stands by those whom she favors, she cannot escape being thought of as deficient unless she is accompanied by art. For prosperity is not found in unbridled wealth, but in a bridled soul and in education; and the function of education is to cause the owner

2. Contrast Them., *Orat.* 23.298b, where Rome and Constantinople are said to *co-rule*. See Dagron, *Naissance,* 52–53.

3. For the precious metals of Menelaus's palace, see Hom., *Od.* 4.71–76. His quoted lament is *Od.* 4.93 with the supplementary phrase οὐδ' ἐπιτερπόμενος. His wife, the beautiful Helen, was the daughter of Zeus (Hom., *Il.* 3.426, *Od.* 4.184).

[of mere material goods] to become possessed of the goods of the soul. For the more precarious the instruments are, the more one needs a surer knowledge.[4]

Philosophy, then, makes such assertions. She takes away from a person the happiness he thought he was in full possession of and even[5] subjects the very word "happiness" [εὐδαιμονία] to examination and investigation, assuming it to be derived from *τὸ εὖ τὸν δαίμονα ἔχειν* [366] [that "one's divine spirit," that is, one's soul, "is in good order"] or from *τὴν δαημοσύνην καὶ τὴν ἐπιστήμην* ["skill" and knowledge].[6] When philosophy speaks in this manner [through us], do we not act very beneficially in discomforting that so-called "happy" individual and, no less than him, the people who favor him with the word "happy"? All those people sit there upset and annoyed by what they hear. Will they not be permitted, they wonder, to favor certain individuals as they please by describing them with the words [they want to use]? Will someone try to rob them of this freedom? Will one person try to stand in the way of the masses—a weak-voiced person, perhaps, standing up to a loudly clamoring audience? The audience bears up as the speaker lays bare and cleanses their language and explains each and every word to them. He does just what genealogists do, explaining the distant origin of each word and the reason why the ancient fathers and creators [of words] linked them to the things they signify; and he shows how later, through the passage of time, words lost their original signification and were applied inappropriately to other things.

To spare you from also being subjected to the same experience that other audiences have had to endure, and to avoid needlessly discomforting men who have never ceased being friendly [to me] and gathering to listen [to me], I stay home much of the time. I sing and work at the Muses' art for myself and for the Muses, as they say. And instead

4. For "art"—here tantamount to "the art of living," or "a correct sense of values"—cooperating with fortune, see Pl., *Laws* 4.709b ff. In his letter to Themistius (257d), Julian quotes this Platonic passage and says that Themistius taught it to him. For wealth as an "instrument" (*ὄργανον*), cf. Arist., *Eth. Nic.* 1.7 [1097a27], 1.8 [1099b1]; *Pol.* 1.4 [1253b32], 1.8 [1256b37].

5. The word "even" is *προσέτι*, Harduinus's conjecture for the transmitted *πρὸς τί*, which the Teubner edition marks as a crux.

6. Themistius's first etymology, including his explanation of "divine spirit," is ascribed to Plato by Clem. Alex., *Strom.* 2.22.131, p. 185 Stählin. Clement was apparently thinking of Pl., *Tim.* 90c. See also Isnardi Parente, *Senocrate-Ermodoro,* 141–42 (Xenocr., frs. 236–39), 421–22; Arist. fr. 57 Rose[3]; Alcinoos ["Albinus"], *Didaskal.* 28 [182] Whittaker-Louis, with the editors' comments. It is *δαημοσύνην* that is offered as the second etymology, *καὶ τὴν ἐπιστήμην* being a gloss on that poetic word; for this etymology, cf. Pl., *Cratyl.* 398b.

of thousands and thousands of people jumping up out of their seats and shouting, I have all these young men giving me their full attention in the quiet setting [of my private quarters].[7] Do not be surprised then if, in keeping company with the divine Plato, in consorting with Aristotle, in being stubbornly bound to my Homer, I do not often ascend the speaker's platform and address these gatherings. For I must either attend to those writers and consequently deprive you of the freedom to use words as you like; or I must simply allow you your indiscriminate use of language and, in so allowing, find myself undoing the ordinances of our [linguistic] fathers.

I want you to agree to something today, though, before I begin to speak: that you will not become irritated or raise a clamor if I put some very celebrated and well-known words to the test and show you what meaning they had when they first gained currency in Greek, and then how most people who had made these words their own put false and thoughtless usages of them into circulation [367]. If you will not agree to control your tempers, if your intention in meeting with me is anything other than to submit yourselves quietly to my oration until its mission is accomplished, then I shall abandon the whole lot of you and take my leave, giving no thought to the fact that you came here by my invitation. For you are here to listen to what *I* want to say, not to what *you* are craving to have me say. The most courteous guests at banquets do not force their hosts to serve something other than what the latter choose to prepare for the meal![8]

So what do you say? Will you be patient? What shall I do? Listen to the argument for a while, right from its beginning. Perhaps the prelude to my oration will make you more amenable.

The words that we humans use often suffer the same fate as our coins: they do not always retain, through the whole course of time, the same value or as high a value as they had initially—precisely what has happened to those coins of the recent past that were driven out of the marketplace a short time ago. Or don't you remember that, right after the first of those bronze coins went into circulation, they were well regarded and had a high value, and they would have brought you quite a

7. The word I translate as "stay home" (οἰκουρῶ) is commonly applied to the confinement of women; see *LSJ*, s.v. II. "I sing . . . for myself and for the Muses": see Dio Chrys. 60/61 (77/78).18; Julian, *Misopog.* 338a; cf. Val. Max. 3.7, ext. 2. "all these young men": perhaps Themistius points here to a group of young men in the audience who have attended his private lectures.

8. For the speaker as a provider of a banquet, cf. Them., *Orat.* 24.301a–b, 26.313a.

good return for a modest outlay; but that in the course of being offered as tender—and I mean after only a short while—they did not maintain their value < . . . and> are utterly useless when they turn up in shops? The very famous and celebrated words *βασιλεύς* and *ὕπατος* have suffered just such a fate, although we may be glad that, for so many years, they allowed us to designate one and the same person in two ways.[9]

And now that these two words have been put before you, my oration has reached the point at which its task is to reveal and explain to you[10] what kind of person would enjoy the hard-won distinction of having both terms applied to him in their true sense and without any hint of flattery. My oration must also inform you that it is rarer to encounter such a person than to see the phoenix, a bird that, according to the storyteller Herodotus [2.73], appears among the Egyptians every five hundred years in the temple. . . .

9. "but that in the course . . . in shops?": the text is *προϊὸν δέ, καὶ ταῦτα ἐν οὐ πολλῷ χρόνῳ οὐδ' ἰσαρίθμως, οὕτως ἀχρείως εἰς τὰ πωλητήρια ἀφικνεῖται*. But, with Seeck, *Die Briefe*, 293, I assume a lacuna after *ἰσαρίθμως*. For the coins referred to here, see above, p. 44. "The very famous and celebrated words," etc.: Themistius seems to mean that the use of the word *βασιλεύς* to designate any king (or emperor) at all and of the word *ὕπατος* as an equivalent of Latin "consul" are linguistic debasements. (Cf. Them., *Orat.* 23.286c–d, where the negative sense of the term "sophist" is explained as a debasement of its original positive sense, and the process is again compared to a coin's decline in value.) Themistius presumably means that, before its debasement, the term *βασιλεύς* was reserved for a philosopher-king or a morally supreme ruler (cf. Arist., *Pol.* 3.13 [1284b25–34], 3.17 [1288a15–29]). (Does he believe that there actually was a time in history when *βασιλεύς* was used only in its undebased sense?) *Ὕπατος* meant "highest" or "best" before meaning "consul." Before their debasement, "king" and "highest" / "best" were synonyms. One may surmise that, in what followed, Themistius lauded the current emperor, in passing, as *βασιλεύς* and *ὕπατος* in the "original" sense of those words (cf. Them., *Orat.* 11.153c). Perhaps the emperor was also *ὕπατος* in the "debased" sense (i.e., consul) when this oration was delivered; if so, one can well imagine that Themistius would have noted the coincidence (cf. Maisano, *Discorsi*, 977, 987, although I do not think that he fully understands Themistius's *ὕπατος*; Vanderspoel, *Themistius*, 49n). "to designate," etc.: *ἡ διπλῆ τοῦ αὐτοῦ ἐπωνυμία*. I restore the transmitted *αὐτοῦ*, as does Maisano, *Discorsi*, ad loc., in place of Cobet's conjecture *ἐνιαυτοῦ* (*Mnemosyne* 11 [1862]: 434), which was regrettably accepted by the Teubner editors. Cf., in the next paragraph, "the . . . distinction of having both terms applied to him." Maisano has the typographical error, *διπλῆτου*.

10. *ἥκει ὁ λόγος ἐκκαλύψαι τε καὶ ἑρμηνεῦσαι*. Gasda questioned the text ("Kritische Bemerkungen," 20). Perhaps simply supply *εἰς τὸ* after *λόγος*.

ORATION 34

In Reply to Those Who Found Fault with Him for Accepting Public Office

[I] I have much praise and the warmest feelings for those who consider philosophy to be worth so much that they regard even the highest public office as falling short of it. For to think so well of the most divine of human endeavors is, in my estimation, a sign of no base nature.[1] But suppose that such individuals express this view of theirs without ever having investigated or thought it worth learning what activities actually do befit philosophical learning? Well, I regard this attitude to be unworthy of the opinion such people claim to have of philosophy.

Now if this recent criticism of theirs [i.e., that public office does not befit philosophy] were directed at me alone, it would have been sufficient for me to argue with them elsewhere. But since it must be judged inappropriate that the man who has bestowed [an office] be a joint target of their accusation along with the man who accepted it, you [i.e., Theodosius] must be the judge before whom I refute the shared charge.[2] For in bringing philosophy from the sphere of words to that of deeds, we have either both lifted her up or both cast her down.

1. For philosophy's divine origin, cf., e.g., Pl., *Tim.* 47b; Arist., *Metaph.* 1.2 [982b28–983a11]; Arist. (?), *De mundo* 1.391a1; Sen., *Epp.* 90.1–2; Them., *Orat.* 23.284a, d.

2. "you must be the judge": "you" surely means Theodosius and not the unnamed critic whom Themistius addresses later in the oration. Since Theodosius cannot rightly be a co-defendant, he must be the judge. See above, p. 38, and Schneider, *Die 34. Rede*, ad loc. "[E]lsewhere" in the first sentence of this paragraph means "somewhere other than in the emperor's presence."

Before anything else, I must make a number of things clear both to all of you who are now listening to me and to those who will subsequently come upon this oration. I must explain what it is proper to consider philosophy's work to be, with what purpose she has come into the lives of us humans, how she was initially exalted and esteemed, and how she is tied and related to true kingship but estanged from tyranny. Only then will you more easily be able to determine whether in accepting office I was keeping within ancestral bounds or going beyond them.

[II] If someone should ask all of you what it is that especially distinguishes a human being from the rest of the animal kingdom, and why humans rule and prevail over other animals, who is so far removed from reason that he would fail to see that it is precisely reason that is the special prerogative of human nature? It is certainly not strength or speed of body or keenness of perception; it is impossible to say just how inferior we are to beasts and birds in all these qualities. Now if reason, this asset of human beings, gets a good training, it produces a living being of divine pedigree on earth. If it gets a bad training, the end product is a beast who is harder to contend with than bears or boars; for when reason is in the service of vice, it is a weapon that is very hard to resist.[3] It was to ensure this good training that people sought out law and the special competence by which law might be introduced among men. And if you go back as far as possible to the first beginnings of philosophy, like those who go in search of the sources of rivers, you will find that philosophy's source was nothing other than this legislative competence. You will find that, as soon as this competence made its appearance, those who distinguished themselves and were successful in this first and exclusive [philosophical] activity became celebrated and well-known.

[III] The famous Solon, Lycurgus, Pittacus, Bias, and Cleobulus were given the title "wise men" by the people who lived in those times. These wise men did not twist syllogisms this way and that, nor did they talk about the forms. They did not expose the fallacy in the arguments about the veiled figure and the horned figure—troublemaking and mischievous sophisms that are not easy to come up with, but knowledge of which is a useless possession. Solon and the others did

3. "If someone should ask ... in all these qualities": cf., e.g., Isoc. 3.5–6; Sen., *Epp.* 124.21–23; Plut., *De fortuna* 98c–f. All remark on the combination in humans of mental superiority to other animals and inferiority to them in other respects. "Now if reason ... hard to resist": cf. Pl., *Laws* 6.766a; Arist., *Pol.* 1.2 [1253a31–37].

not try to measure the sun. They did not try to determine the moon's course. No such activities were the basis for their renown as wise men. They were called wise because they drafted laws and taught what people should and should not do, what it is fitting to opt for and what to shun. They were called wise because they explained that this human animal is not a hermit or self-contained, but a social and political creature, and it is therefore fitting that he attend to his country and its laws and constitution. And these wise men were themselves as quick to act as they were to instruct others. Consequently, you will find that, while there are powerful sayings in the writings of each of them, they were also men of countless deeds—embassies and military commands, the liberation of their cities, the acquisition of new territory.[4]

[IV] Such were the first beginnings of philosophy. But as time went on, philosophy experienced the same thing that the other arts did. Although it was need that introduced those other arts, they did not rest content with [meeting] need. Architecture did not stop at walls and a roof. Weaving did not stop at the mere covering of the body. These arts advanced further, making beautiful as well as merely necessary things and seeing to it that adornment was added to their works. So, too, philosophy came to a point at which she was not content with "know yourself," "know the moment," and "nothing in excess" and was not

4. "Solon . . . Cleobulus": Solon, Pittacus, Bias and Cleobulus—but not the Spartan lawgiver Lycurgus—were commonly listed among the traditional Seven Wise Men (see Barkowski, "Sieben Weise," *RE,* 2A, 2 [1923]: 2242–47). But note how Cic., *Tusc.* 5.3 [7] associates Lycurgus with the Seven, and cf. the group "Solon, Lycurgus and Pittacus" at Jul., *Ep. ad Them.* 262d. "twist syllogisms . . . useless possession": cf. Them., *Orat.* 2.30b. "the forms": Themistius is thinking of the Platonic forms. For the "veiled figure" and the "horned figure," see Lucian, *Vit. auct.* 22–23; Diog. Laert. 7.187; Hamblin, *Fallacies,* 89–91. "to measure the sun . . . to determine the moon's course": Themistius is thinking of Thales, one of the traditional Seven Wise Men (C. J. Classen, "Thales 1," *RE,* suppl. 10 [1965]: 943 ff.)—and would exclude him from the wise men highlighted here. For Thales's differentiation from other wise men due to his attention to matters other than ethics and politics, cf. Cic., *De orat.* 3.34 [137]; Plut., *Solon* 3.6–8; August., *De civ. Dei* 8.2. "not a hermit (μονῆρες)": again Themistius is implicitly contrasting Thales with the wise men he has in mind here: Thales, according to Heraclides Ponticus, called himself a hermit (μονήρη) and a recluse (Diog. Laert. 1.25). "a social and political creature": one thinks especially of Arist., *Pol.* 1.2 [1253a3], 3.6 [1278b19 ff.]; see also *Eth. Eudem.* 7.10 [1242a25]. "men of countless deeds": for the representation of early Greek wise men as given to action rather than to theory, see *RE,* 2A, 2 (1923): 2261–62, 2263; *RE,* suppl. 10 (1965): 934 *sub fine;* Snell, *Leben und Meinungen der Sieben Weisen,* 70–83; and, for Lycurgus, Plut., *Lycurg.* 31.2–4. "embassies" etc.: note, e.g., Bias's service to his native Priene as ambassador to Samos (Plut., *Quaest. gr.* 296a), Pittacus's command of his city's army in the war against Athens over land in the Troad (Diog. Laert. 1.74), Pittacus's liberation of his native land from the tyrant Melanchrus (Diod. Sic. 9.11.1, Diog. Laert. 1.74), and the tradition of Solon's acquisition of the island of Salamis from the Megarians (Plut., *Solon* 8–10, with *CAH*², 3, 3: 373).

satisfied with providing services and admonitions that met merely the basic needs of human life. So she has put on much external adornment—the investigation of nature and the refinement of discourse.[5] Similarly, a house might have, in front of the men's hall and the women's chamber, a gateway and an entrance and embroidery and statues; these do not meet a basic need but are an adornment and beautification of the basic necessity.

[V] And so that famous Socrates of old, whom one could call father and founder of a richer wisdom, fully examined problems of good and evil, but he did not think that he should investigate other questions, which he felt either make no difference to us or go beyond the limits of our knowledge. His sole concern was how a human being, a household, and a state could be happy. He used to praise Homer above everyone else for considering it important to examine "what evil and what good has been done in your house" [*Od.* 4.392]. Socrates's genuine chorus—Cebes, Phaedo, Aristippus, Aeschines—stayed within the bounds he set.[6]

The divine Plato alone, since he had such a noble nature and was a man of such majesty, was the first to adorn philosophy with its many embellishments. He included in it special fields of knowledge such as arithmetic, music, and astronomy. But he advanced further than that, going beyond the bounds of the heavens themselves. He dared to investigate whether there isn't <something> higher than nature herself. His purpose was not to reveal a superfluous realm that contributes nothing to this polity of ours. Quite the contrary: it is a very distinctive feature of Plato's penetrating mind that he links human good to divine good and fashions the human polity, as much as possible, with reference to the polity of the All. This is the purpose of works of his such as the *Republic,* the famous *Laws,* the *Phaedrus,* and the *Gorgias.* This is his purpose in all the works in which he vigorously contends to outdo himself in demonstrating that we should choose justice for what it is

5. "know yourself" etc.: cf. Them., *Orat.* 26.317a. "the refinement of discourse": i.e., rhetoric.

6. "either make no difference . . . our knowledge": cf., e.g., Cic., *Acad.* 1.4 [15]; Euseb., *Praep. evang.* 15.62.10. For Socrates's use of the Homeric quotation in describing his investigations, see, e.g., Muson. Rufus, fr. 3 Lutz; Aul. Gell. 14.6.5; Diog. Laert. 2.21. Themistius here sees Socrates advancing beyond certain early Greek wise men ("a richer wisdom," "*fully* examined"), but also continuous with them in his focus on ethics, society, and polity. So, too, Plato and Aristotle (below), while not restricting themselves to these ethico-political concerns, will remain true to them. Contrast the different rhetorical context of the survey of the history of philosophy in *Orat.* 26.317a ff., where Themistius draws a sharp line between Socrates and his predecessors.

and avoid evil for what it is, even if no reward is offered for the former and the latter escapes all punishment.[7]

[VI] Now does Aristotle differ from Plato in all this? He has a greater curiosity and love of detail than Plato, but still there is no part of his philosophical project and system that neglects the question of human good; in fact, his whole philosophy is directed towards the good and has the good as its point of reference. For the essence of human happiness, in his view, is our practice of virtue over the whole course of life and the soul's acting in accordance with virtue in formulating its guiding principles. We philosophize, he says, not to know justice, but to do justice as far as we can. He has portioned out the good to the soul, to the body and to externals, and he makes human happiness complete by drawing from the first, the second, and the third mixing bowls. He says that, although happiness in an individual person is something desirable, it is greater and fuller when found in the whole city. He therefore calls his method "political."[8] He says that it is impossible to fare well [εὖ πράττειν] without engaging in action [πράττειν], and that the god who guides this whole cosmos and those [divinities] who make the rounds with him are devotees of a practical and political philosophy, who keep the whole of nature steady and unharmed through the course of time.

Such are the many great works and projects that this art of philosophy undertook on behalf of humanity and of human happiness. Yet the masses are ignorant of all this and do not choose to inform themselves about it. They have marveled at philosophy's antechambers, walls, enclosures, groves, and meadows; but they do not prize the fact that the house of philosophy has apartments that can withstand the wind and are not easily affected by the blasts of fortune.[9]

[VII] But our most godlike emperor does not share this widespread attitude. As a follower of those famous men [whose contributions to philosophy I have been discussing], he brought philosophy, which was

7. "arithmetic . . . astronomy": e.g., Pl., *Rep.* 7.521c ff. "beyond the bounds of the heavens": i.e., to the forms. "we should choose justice for what it is": cf., e.g., Pl., *Rep.* 4.441c–45b, 9.588b–92b.

8. "For the essence . . . guiding principles": cf. Arist., *Eth. Nic.* 1.7 [1098a11–20]. "not to know . . . but to do justice": cf. Arist., *Eth. Nic.* 2.2 [1103b26–31], 2.4 [1105b9–18]; Them., *Orat.* 2.31c. "He has portioned . . . externals": cf. Arist., *Eth. Nic.* 1.8 [1098b12–14, 1099a31–1099b8], 10.8 [1178b33–35]. "happiness complete . . . mixing bowls": the three bowls contain goods of the soul, goods of the body, and external goods. "although happiness in an individual . . . 'political'": cf. Arist., *Eth. Nic.* 1.2 [1094b7–11].

9. "apartments," etc.: i.e., ethics and its application in social and political action.

cooped up at home for some time, out into her ancestral arena of public conflicts. Like someone who possesses a statue that is the product of ancient craftsmanship, he has put philosophy on display before the public instead of merely enjoying it himself in private. If anyone should be called the heir of the divine Plato's teachings, it should not be Speusippus or Xenocrates, but the person who made Plato's vision prevail—something that the famous philosopher himself would have done more than anything else, had he been able. It was a vision of political power and philosophy coming together, not of good judgment and secular authority going their separate ways. The emperor has shown those who are now alive something they no longer expected to see: philosophy passing judgment in union with the highest power, philosophy broadcasting inspired and action-oriented precepts that up to now she has merely been proposing in her writings. Future generations will sing the praises of Theodosius for his summoning of philosophy to the public sphere, just as they will praise Hadrian, Marcus [Aurelius], and Antoninus [Pius], who are his ancestors, his fellow citizens, founders of his line. Theodosius was not content merely to inherit the purple from them; he also brought them back into the palace as exemplars after a long lapse of time and set philosophy by his side, just as they had done.[10]

[VIII] Neither the Persian Cyrus nor Alexander the Great could reach this level of distinction. Alexander deemed his guide Aristotle worthy of many great honors and peopled Stagira for him, but he did not give the philosopher a role in the exercise of that massive power of

10. "he brought philosophy . . . out": i.e., by appointing the philosopher Themistius to public office. Cf. Them., *Orat.* 17.213c–14a. "Speusippus or Xenocrates": Speusippus headed the Academy after Plato's death and was succeeded by Xenocrates. "It was a vision . . . in her writings": Themistius is thinking, of course, of the philosopher-king (cf. Pl., *Rep.* 5.473d). Compare what he says of Theodosius in *Orat.* 17.214a–b. "Hadrian, Marcus [Aurelius], and Antoninus [Pius]": listed in the same order, with Trajan preceding them, in Them., *Orat.* 17.215a (cf. 19.229c, "neither Trajan nor Marcus nor Antoninus"). At 19.229c, Marcus and Antoninus, this time with Trajan, are again called Theodosius's fellow citizens and founders of his line. Themistius thinks of all five emperors as Spaniards. Antoninus could be thought of in this way only if one were to imagine that he became a Spaniard through his adoption by Hadrian. Cf. Mai in Dindorf, ad loc., and Schneider, *Die 34. Rede,* 110; and for Antoninus's origins, see Hüttl, *Antoninus,* 1: 27–28. For Marcus's Spanish connections, see Birley, *Marcus,* 28. "founders of his line" (ἀρχηγέτας): cf. *Epit. de Caes.* 48.1, "Theodosius . . . originem a Traiano principe trahens"; Syme, *Emperors and Biography,* 101–2. Themistius extends the notion to include Trajan's immediate three successors, all "good" emperors like him. Hadrian, Pius, and Marcus each became the adopted son of his predecessor. "brought them back . . . as exemplars": τὰς εἰκόνας αὐτῶν ἐπαναγαγών. With Schneider, *Die 34. Rede,* ad loc., I do not take εἰκόνας literally. See Lampe, *Patristic Greek Lex.*, s.v. εἰκών II C.

his. Neither did Augustus give Arius such a role, nor Scipio Panaetius, nor Tiberius Thrasyllus. In these individuals the three statesmen had only observers of their private struggles: even though they might have greatly desired to drag them into the stadium's dust, they were unable to do so.[11]

But this was not the experience of our current emperor's fathers and the founders of his line [Hadrian, Antoninus Pius, and Marcus Aurelius], whose names are great. They pulled Arrian and Rusticus away from their books, refusing to let them be mere pen-and-ink philosophers. They did not let them write about courage and stay at home, or compose legal treatises while avoiding the public domain that is law's concern, or decide what form of government is best while abstaining from any participation in government. The emperors to whom I am now alluding consequently escorted these men to the general's tent as well as to the speaker's platform. In their role as Roman generals, these men passed through the Caspian Gates, drove the Alani out of Armenia, and established boundaries for the Iberians and the Albani. For all these accomplishments, they reaped the fruits of the eponymous consulship, governed the great city [of Rome], and presided over the ancient senate.[12] For the emperors [who thus employed them] knew that it is proper that public office, like the body, be cleansed, and that the greater and more noble the office is, the more cleansing it needs. These

11. Stagira: destroyed by Alexander's father Philip and, according to Plut., *Alex.* 7.3, repeopled by him. Other texts agree with Themistius in ascribing the repeopling to Alexander (Plin., *HN* 7.29 [109]; Ael., *Var. hist.* 12.54; *Vita Aristotelis Marciana* in O. Gigon's ed. [Berlin, 1962], p. 3). Hamilton, in his comment on Plut., loc. cit., suggests that "Alexander interceded with Philip." See also Gigon, op. cit., 56–57. Arius: philosopher and friend of Augustus. Julian, *Ep. ad Them.* 265c–66a, notes his refusal of an office in Egypt, but he did serve as procurator in Sicily. See *PIR*² A 1035; Bowersock, *Augustus,* 33–34, 39–41. For the Stoic philosopher Panaetius's friendship with Scipio Aemilianus and an assessment of that relationship, see Astin, *Scipio Aemilianus,* 296 ff. Thrasyllus: the emperor Tiberius's friend and astrologer, he was also a man of philosophical learning (W. Gundel, "Thrasyllos 7," *RE,* 6A, 1 [1936]: 581–84). Julian, *Ep. ad Them.* 265c, also remarks on his lack of involvement in public affairs. "into the stadium's dust": cf. Them., *Orat.* 17.213d–14a; Jul., *Ep. ad Them.* 263a.

12. "They pulled Arrian and Rusticus away from their books": cf. Them., *Orat.* 17.215a. The senatorial career of Arrian, pupil of Epictetus and himself deemed worthy of the title "philosopher," culminated under Hadrian. Q. Iunius Rusticus, the Stoic teacher of Marcus Aurelius, was ordinary consul and urban prefect under Marcus but had already held the suffect consulship under Hadrian. So far as we know, only Arrian fought the Alani. Only Rusticus held an "eponymous" (i.e., ordinary) consulship and "governed the great city [of Rome]" (i.e., was urban prefect). Precisely what office or function Themistius is alluding to in the words "presided over (*προήδρευον*) the ancient senate" is unclear. For more details and comment on this passage, see *PIR*², 1: 814; Bosworth, *CQ* 22 (1972): 164–67; id., *HSCP* 81 (1977): 229–32; Stadter, *Arrian,* passim. "pen-and-ink philosophers": cf. Them., *Orat.* 2.31c.

emperors understood that <the same> opinion was held by the ancient Romans, who saw the learned Cato hold the quaestorship, Brutus the praetorship, Favonius the plebeian tribunate, Varro the office with six axes and Rutilius the consulship. I pass over Priscus, Thrasea, and others of the same sort; writers will sate you with them if you should choose to consult their accounts.[13]

Nor was Marcus [Aurelius] himself anything but a philosopher in the purple. The same can be said for Hadrian, Antoninus [Pius], and, of course, for our current ruler Theodosius. [IX] If you should look at his belt and cloak, you will number him with the vast majority of emperors; but if you cast your eyes on his soul and his intellect, you will class him with that famous triad [of philosophical emperors].[14] For surely he should be placed among those who are similarly minded, not among those who are similarly garbed.

This emperor, then, needed no help in challenging me to pursue virtue—and I do not mean a virtue that is idle and inactive and that explicates the meaning of words and logical propositions, but one that daily <spurs us on to> action as it instructs us in the precepts of the

13. "that public office ... be cleansed": by entrusting it to philosophers. "<the same> opinion was held": cf. Them., *Orat.* 17.215a–b, adducing "Varros, Catos" and Favonius (cf. below). For the philosophical credentials of the five late Republican senators, see, in addition to Schneider's comments in *Die 34. Rede,* ad loc., Arnold, *Roman Stoicism,* esp. 386–88; Rawson, *Intellectual Life,* 95, 283–87 and passim (see index). P. Rutilius Rufus was consul in 105 B.C., M. Porcius Cato (surely Uticensis) was quaestor in 64 (?), and M. Iunius Brutus was urban praetor in 44; for the date of Cato's quaestorship, see *MRR,* 3: 170–71. Themistius's assertion that Cato's admirer M. Favonius held the plebeian tribunate is not elsewhere confirmed. For the bearing of the problematic Cic., *Ad Att.* 2.1.9, and for reaction to Themistius's testimony, see Ryan, *Athenaeum* 82 (1994): 505–21. "[T]he office with six axes" should be M. Terentius Varro's praetorship, the date of which is uncertain. The periphrastic expression for the praetorship is used for *variatio,* the routine term ἐστρατήγει having just been employed for Brutus. For the date of Varro's praetorship, see *MRR,* 2: 466; Gruen, *Last Generation,* 165n. For the periphrastic expression, see Mommsen, *Römisches Staatsrecht,* 1: 384–85; Samter, "Fasces," *RE,* 6 [1909]: 2003–4. Themistius sees Thrasea Paetus and Helvidius Priscus—doubtless the elder Priscus, Thrasea's son-in-law—as men who combined philosophy and political action. These senators were part of the so-called "philosophic opposition" to emperors in the first century. Cf. Them., *Orat.* 17.215b, and see Dudley, *History of Cynicism,* 125–42; Griffin, *Seneca,* passim (see index).

14. "Nor was Marcus," etc.: the exemplary emperors did not merely employ philosophers but were also philosophers themselves. Marcus, author of the *Meditations,* is well known as philosopher-emperor. The notion that Hadrian and Pius were philosophers has its seeds in the intellectual culture and philhellenism of the former (Boatwright, *Hadrian,* 202–12) and the upright character of the latter (Dio Cass. 70.3.1; Eutrop. 8.8; Aur. Vict. 15; *Epit. de Caes.* 15; SHA, *Pius* 13.3–4 and passim). Cf. Them., *Orat.* 13.166b. "his belt and cloak": the ζώνη (*cingulum*) and the χλάμυς (*paludamentum*), the imperial military garb; see H. Sauer, "Paludamentum," *RE,* 18, 3 (1949): 281–86; Alföldi, *Die monarchische Repräsentation,* 161–69, 175–76, 182–83.

Academy. Do you say, then, that it was ambition that caused me to accept the task of presiding over the fair city [of Constantinople], and that in so doing I went from a higher to a lower position? Yes, I did "descend to a lower position" if I did anything in violation of the Academy's precepts; but if I observed the laws we get from the Academy in everything I did, then I did not "descend," my friend, but, while staying in the same place, have moved up to a higher station. **[X]** The famous Socrates did not descend from the heights of philosophy in serving as a *prytanis,* for he opposed the Thirty. Nor did the most excellent Xenophon descend from philosophy in commanding the Ten Thousand, for he saved the Greeks from extreme dangers. Parmenides did not descend from philosophy in giving laws to the Greeks of Italy, for he filled the whole of Magna Graecia, as it is called, with good order.[15]

Now if there was anything meritorious in my tenure of office, it was not my own doing; it was something impressed on me from the example of [Theodosius]. If I did not succumb to gain, it was because I took as my model the person who gives money to others every day. If I kept my anger under control, it was because I had my eye on the person who appointed me. If I was the protector of orphans, it was because I was imitating the common father of all. If I allowed nothing to go wrong with the public dole, this too was a concern that I got from the very same source. If I judged cases in accordance with the laws, it was because I had the living law in sight. Therefore, bent as I was on this emulation of my model—and I invoke Adrasteia and call your own judgment of me to witness before saying what I am going to say—**[XI]** I did not make <a few> months any the less honorable than many

15. "This emperor, then, needed no help," etc.: the manuscript has *καὶ οὗτος οὖν μόνος ἤρκει σοι ὁ βασιλεὺς ζῆλον ἀρετῆς προκαλέσασθαι.* With Schneider, *Die 34. Rede,* ad loc., I emend *σοι* to *μοι.* "<spurs us on to>": some such supplement is needed here. "the fair city": cf. Them., *Orat.* 31.354d, with n. 7 to my translation. "I went from a higher," etc.: in his epigram critical of Themistius's acceptance of the urban prefecture (*Anth. Pal.* 11.292), Palladas also employed the imagery of "descent" from and "ascent" to what is truly lofty. "while staying in the same place": i.e., while being true to the Academy's principles. Socrates: i.e., he did his public duty in serving as *prytanis,* but in fidelity to his principles he later opposed the tyrannical Thirty. Principle also caused him to take issue with his fellow *prytaneis.* See Pl., *Apol.* 32b–d; cf. Them., *Orat.* 20.239a–b. Xenophon played a major role in leading a Greek corps of ca. 10,000, recruited for the Persian Cyrus the Younger, back to safety from Persia. The Socratic Xenophon could easily be called a philosopher: e.g., Philo, *De vita contempl.* 7.57; Plut., *Quaest. conviv.* 1.612d; Athen. 9.368a; Eunap., *Vitae phil. et soph.* I 1, 453 Giangrande. Cf. the adducing of Socrates and Xenophon in Them., *Orat.* 17.215b. Parmenides legislated for his native city, Elea, not for the whole of Magna Graecia (Plut., *Adv. Colot.* 1126b; Diog. Laert. 9.23; cf. Strabo 6.1.1 [252]).

years.[16] I did not leave those over whom I had authority feeling oppressed by my tenure of office, but thirsting for me to remain in office. It is not the lapse of time that creates goodwill in one's charges; it is forethought, devotion to one's work, and putting nothing ahead of the common good—not love of glory, not political power, not what one might be inclined towards out of personal enmity or favoritism. Anyone who remains faithful to these norms does not need many years; in fact, he shrinks from a long tenure of office. For it is difficult for a human being to preserve moral beauty unsullied for a long time, whereas a few months and days suffice for a show of virtue. In no other art do we look for the number of works produced. What we look for are beauty and precision of craftsmanship. I admire Phidias for his Pisaean Zeus, Polygnotus for his hall [at Delphi], and Myron for one heifer. How many more works Pauson produced than Zeuxis or Apelles! But who does not prefer one painting of Zeuxis or Apelles over the whole oeuvre of Pauson?[17]

[XII] But if you, [sir], feel strongly that length of service is something to be proud of and sought after, then I can also take pride in how long I have played a role in the political life of the fair city [of Constantinople]. For right from the beginning, when I was young, I chose not to practice philosophy in secluded corners. No, as I passed from childhood to adolescence, from adolescence to adulthood, and from adulthood to this old age of mine, I have always loved this city. It was not with unwashed hands, as the saying goes, that I took up her reins [as urban prefect].[18] No, [in accepting that office] I was bringing this long-standing and uninterrupted effort of mine to its consummation; I have steadily climbed from the lower elevations of civic virtue to its summit. **[XIII]** I first attained this position of leadership when all of you selected me as an ambassador to glorious Rome and sent me [there] to the son of Constantine [i.e., Constantius]. I first began to

16. "the living law" (τὸν ἔμψυχον νόμον): for this well-established idea in monarchical theory, see Aalders in Steinmetz, *Politeia und Res Publica*, 315–29. For the invocation of Adrasteia, cf. Them., *Orat.* 31.354c, with n. 6 to my translation. "<a few> months": see above, p. 35.

17. "his Pisaean Zeus": the statue that Themistius elsewhere calls Phidias's "Olympian" Zeus: see *Orat.* 25.310b, with n. 1 to my translation, and 27.337b. For the paintings by Polygnotus in the Cnidians' hall at Delphi, see Pausan. 10.25–31. Myron's bronze statue of a heifer is the subject of *Anth. gr.* 9.713–42, 793–98, and Auson., *Epigramm.* 68–75. See Plin., *HN* 34.19.57. Aristotle notes that Pauson depicted morally base characters (*Poet.* 2.1448a5, *Pol.* 8.5 [1340a36]). An anecdote about a trick picture of his could have been understood as an indication of artistic insincerity (see esp. Ael., *Var. hist.* 14.15).

18. "with unwashed hands": Hom., *Il.* 6.266; *CPG* 1.187, 383; ibid. 2.4.

look after the people of this city when I restored its dole. I first began to provide for its senate when I was augmenting the list of men of common background [who are its members] from barely three hundred to two thousand.[19] As a result of these services, I was awarded these two bronze statues by two emperors, received extraordinary written tributes, and was invited to assume this office [i.e., the urban prefecture] not once or twice, but often.[20] Now add to all of this the circumstances

19. "ambassador to . . . Rome": the reference is to Themistius's embassy to Rome in the spring of 357. See Dagron, *T&MByz* 3 (1968): 205–12. "I restored its dole": Themistius apparently took advantage of his embassy to Rome and his contact with Constantius there to convince the emperor to restore the grain dole at Constantinople to its former higher level. Constantius had punitively reduced it, roughly by half, in 342. See Dagron, ibid., 55, 208–9; Them., *Orat.* 23.298b with n. 33 to my translation. "I was augmenting . . . to two thousand": Themistius recruited new Constantinopolitan senators in the late 350s. See Petit, *AC* 26 (1957): 349–50; Dagron, *Naissance,* 129–30; Chastagnol, *Acta Antiqua Acad. Scient. Hungar.* 24 (1976): 350–53. Jones, *Later Rom. Emp.*, 2: 527, understands Themistius to be referring not to a rapid enlargement of the Constantinopolitan senatorial order from 300 to 2,000 in the late 350s, but to a much slower growth that stretched from the late 350s to the date of this oration; that, however, is not the natural sense of the Greek. The figure 2,000 is easier to accept if we understand it to include *clarissimi* in the East who were being transferred from the Roman to the Constantinopolitan senate (thus Dagron, Chastagnol) and the ever-increasing number of functionaries to whom that senate was being opened (thus Dagron). The exaggeration, as Dagron notes (*Naissance,* 130, n. 3), is not in the figure 2,000, but in Themistius's representation of the enlargement of the senate as his own one-man show. Themistius would have been in office as proconsul of Constantinople at least by the time he was enlarging the senate, if not already at the time of his embassy to Rome; see above, pp. 1–2. There is good rhetorical reason why Themistius does not explicitly mention the proconsulship, held some twenty-five years earlier, in *Orat.* 34: he does not want to appear unduly interested in officeholding per se, and he wants to stress the special, almost unique, imperative of accepting office from Theodosius.

20. "two bronze statues": the first was awarded by Constantius in 356 (Vanderspoel, *Themistius,* 96), the second by a later emperor prior to Theodosius; cf. Them., *Orat.* 17.214b, 31.353a. "written tributes": e.g., the extant tribute of Constantius in the so-called *Demegoria Constantii,* the written tribute of Constantius alluded to in Them., *Orat.* 23.298d–99a (see Dagron, *T&MByz* 3 [1968]: 210–11), the written tributes of Julian and of Theodosius alluded to in Them., *Orat.* 31.354d–55a. "not once or twice, but often": it is clear from what follows that Themistius is referring to the multiple requests of a *single* emperor. Who that emperor was has been a vexed question. Dagron, *T&MByz* 3 (1968): 56–59, and Vanderspoel, *Themistius,* 111–12, argue for Constantius. Neither scholar believes that Themistius held the Constantinopolitan proconsulship in the late 350s. Indeed, Dagron believes that Themistius might have refused an offer of the proconsulship rather than the urban prefecture, which replaced the Constantinopolitan proconsulship in 359. That cannot be right, because in *Orat.* 34 [XIII] Themistius says that what he refused earlier in his life was "this office," i.e., the urban prefecture that he did hold under Theodosius. But the notion that Themistius refused Constantius's offer of the new urban prefecture—after serving as the last proconsul of the city, as I am inclined to believe—is plausible. Daly has thoroughly argued the old position that the emperor whom Themistius turned down was Julian (*Byzantion* 53 [1983]: 164–212). Brauch has raised a significant objection to this position (*Byzantion* 63 [1993]: 50): Themistius's remark in *Orat.* 34 [XIV] that the unnamed emperor "often made me . . . his traveling companion" does not appear to fit Julian. Brauch himself argues that the unnamed emperor of *Orat.* 34 [XIII–XIV] was Valens.

and the time [of those invitations]. I did not beg [for what was offered]. It was offered to me only because of my eloquence, when the beans were not yet ready to be harvested, and by a man who had anything but an easy manner. In writing to the senate, he explicitly conceded that, although he had managed with great difficulty to win me over in part, <I> had not been completely enlightened. He also wrote that I have given far more than I have taken and have made the word "office" more honorable through my holding office.[21]

[XIV] If someone should ask me why I shrunk from [accepting the urban prefecture] in the past but did not hesitate to accept it at this stage of my life, I will tell him without holding anything back or wavering. That emperor [to whom I said no] deserves high regard from me. He merits every laudatory thing that could be said about him, for he has left nothing small or large undone that lifts philosophy on high. In fact, he often took advice from me in council while I was wearing my philosopher's cloak, and he also often made me his dinner guest and his traveling companion. He gently endured it when I admonished him and did not take it badly when I rebuked him, because he was <not> merely considering what I was personally saying to him, but also < . . . > and he was reticent and contained, and he preferred the common good to what might please a single person. But oftentimes, you know, the circumstances surrounding human actions cause those actions to be assessed incorrectly. Who, though, is so much harder than steel that he could resist the gentleness and mildness of our current emperor or his enveloping persuasiveness? Who could fail to believe that it was philosophy herself, seated before him, who offered the tablets of office? It was from this very hand that I accepted the tablets, a hand that has inflicted a sentence of death on no one, a hand from which streams of good flow day after day, a hand that checks evil.[22]

21. "I did not beg . . . my eloquence": cf. Them., *Orat.* 18.224a–b, 23.292b, 31.353b–c. "It was offered . . . my holding office": text and interpretation here are very problematic, and what I offer must be regarded as tentative. Cf. Schneider, *Die 34. Rede,* 70–73, 123–24; Dagron, *T&MByz* 3 (1968): 56. "when the beans . . . harvested": I find it difficult to take this literally. Perhaps Themistius means, metaphorically, that *he* was not ripe for the urban prefecture when it was first offered to him; that office would be a culmination of his career, to be held under Theodosius. "<I> had not been completely enlightened": i.e., not persuaded to accept the urban prefecture. If the emperor offering the urban prefecture was Constantius, then "win[ning Themistius] over in part" could mean having convinced him to accept the Constantinopolitan proconsulship before offering him the new urban prefecture. "through my holding office": i.e., the Constantinopolitan proconsulship.

22. "because he was <not> . . . single person": the text is uncertain. The Teubner edition has ὡς <οὐ> τἀμὰ ἴδια μόνον, ἀλλὰ καὶ στεγανὸς κτλ. With Schneider, *Die 34.*

[XV] Plato rightly refused to cooperate with Dionysius, for he was enslaving Sicily. Solon rightly fled from Pisistratus, for he was robbing the citizens [of Athens] of their freedom. Musonius rightly turned away from the lyre-playing Nero, and Demetrius rightly avoided the mad Domitian.[23] But how would I have defended myself against my accusers if I had not yielded to our emperor? Could I have said that he who was summoning me to office was hard to deal with? That he was stubborn? That he put up a fight against reason? That he resisted the bridle of admonition? That he prohibited people from speaking frankly to him? Or, if I could not have made these assertions, could I have said that he was malicious or envious or money-hungry? By the gods, what could I have said of him?

[XVI] How could I still demand that the uselessness of philosophers be blamed on those who fail to make use of them, if I myself had not sallied forth in a spirit of cooperation when I was summoned by a man smitten by a divine love of philosophy to lead the city that nurtured me? I shall bring Plato forward to testify to you, [sir], that, in saying yes to the emperor, I was following that famous philosopher's prescriptions. For when in his writings he demands from the gods a young, smart, high-minded, and generous king for the human race, he means this emperor of ours, even if he does not name him. It is this emperor

---

Rede, ad loc., I posit a lacuna after *ἀλλὰ καί*. For *τοῦ καθ' ἕκαστον κοινῇ κεχαρισμένου τὸ συμφέρον προσεξετάζων*, I read (tentatively) with Cobet, *Mnemosyne* 11 (1862): 100–101, *τοῦ καθ' ἕκαστον κεχαρισμένου τὸ κοινῇ συμφέρον προεξετάζων* ("preferred the common good to what might please a single person"). "But oftentimes . . . incorrectly": Themistius's promise to explain his past refusal of office "without holding anything back or wavering" amounts to nothing more than invoking "circumstances" and adding that his refusal was misunderstood. "a sentence of death on no one": cf. Them., *Orat.* 15.190b.

23. For Plato's rupture with the empire-building tyrant Dionysius I, see Plut., *Dion* 5.1–7; Diog. Laert. 3.18–19. Like Themistius, Diogenes Laertius 1.49–54, 65–67 has Solon flee from Athens in opposition to the tyranny of Pisistratus (cf. ps.-Dio Chrys., *Orat.* 20 [37].4; Aul. Gell. 17.21.5); contrast Plut., *Solon* 30–32, who has Solon remain in Athens. The Stoic Musonius Rufus was persona non grata and exiled under Nero; see *PIR*² M 753, where however the Themistian remark is misconstrued. The tradition that Demetrius the Cynic was persona non grata under Domitian is found in Philostratus's *Vita Apollonii;* in that work (7.10), Apollonius finds him living boldly near Rome, but outside of the city to avoid the tyrannical emperor. This tradition may not be historical, but it is unnecessary to suggest with Schneider ad loc. that Themistius has mistakenly substituted Domitian for Vespasian, under whom Demetrius had also been persona non grata (see *PIR*² D 39 and my comments in *Letters of Apollonius,* 132–33); Themistius may simply be following the Philostratean tradition. What Themistius is saying in this paragraph is that it is just as right to cooperate with an ideal ruler as it is wrong to cooperate with a tyrant. But we need not take him to be implying that the emperor of *Orat.* 34 [XIII–XIV], from whom he would not accept an urban prefecture, was himself a tyrant (*pace* Dagron, *T&MByz* 3 [1968]: 57, n. 140; 58).

of ours for whose appearance he prays. The marks [by which we are to recognize Plato's ideal ruler] belong to Theodosius more than to anyone else. So this emperor is the ruler Plato prays for; and if his prayer had been fulfilled [during his lifetime], would he not have seized the opportunity to work with such a ruler? Would it not have been alien to Plato to fail to embrace the ruler he intently sought if such a ruler had appeared? For what purpose would he have endorsed more fully the laws he wrote [other than to cooperate with an ideal ruler]? For what [other] purpose would he have shown more plainly how well put are the injunctions that one who holds the highest office should rely on persuasion rather than on intimidation, and that one should take up the sword as rarely as possible?[24]

It is precisely these injunctions that we see carried out and hear uttered every day. Hasn't wailing been banned from governmental buildings? Isn't "public executioner" an obsolete title? "Giving information," "charging," and "denouncing" are unintelligible words now. **[XVII]** No one fears the abominable *curator*, the wicked tax collector, the cursed informants, or the "eyes" that are up to no good in their seeing. Our ears ring with good news: this fellow has returned from exile, this fellow the emperor saved, although the law sentenced him to death, here's someone who got his property back, here's someone whom the emperor supported for a year, this man got financial help from him in marrying off his daughters, here's a man whom he helped pay off a debt that had to be settled. Among the Persians of old, a prize was offered to anyone who invented a new pleasure, but [in our time] the emperor will offer rewards to the person who provides new funds for benevolent purposes. What, though, could be more novel than the return of gold from the imperial treasury, by the very same route on which it came there, to the individual from whom it was unjustly exacted? No such thing was ever heard of throughout time's long course; the money lost by those who had been wronged was never restored to them. Consider also that, to those who have asked for a loan, our em-

24. "How could I still . . . use of them": cf. Pl., *Rep.* 6.489b. "the city that nurtured me": cf. Them., *Orat.* 17.214b–c. "a young . . . generous king": cf. Pl., *Rep.* 6.487a with 485b ff.; *Laws* 4.709e–10d. See also Them., *Orat.* 3.46a; 4.62a; 8.105b–c, 119d; and esp. 17.215b–c. "this emperor is the ruler Plato prays for": hence "Theodosius," i.e., "God-given." Cf. n. 6 to my translation of *Orat.* 17. "the injunctions that . . . as possible": Themistius may have in mind here Plato's critical description of the tyrant's use of force against his own people (*Rep.* 8.566d–69c) or the critique of war-oriented constitutions in *Laws* 1.625c–32d (cf. 7.803d–e). Themistius regularly preaches against the ruler's use of force and the instilling of fear (*Orat.* 1.10c–d; 3.45b, 48b; 5.67b–c; 7.96b–c; 9.122b; 16.207c–208a).

peror gives an outright gift of money; that his gift to a person amounts to more money than the individual asked for; and that, in addition, he covers up the fact that the money was requested, so that it may be thought to be a spontaneous gift. In so acting, what Alcibiades does he not outdo? What Cimon does he not show to be a Smicrines?[25]

[XVIII] But my eyes now fall on these young people, and I cannot pass by them in silence, even if the theme of my oration does not allow me to dwell on them individually. Imagine orphaned sons and daughters of a family famous on the father's side who lose even their family house, although they are not being punished for anything! They were deprived of all their property and spent so many years gaping at strangers' doors that misfortune was their lot right into adulthood. Then our emperor was manifested to them, as if mechanically introduced onto a stage, and all their woes disappeared. They were no longer fatherless, no longer in need, no longer private citizens. Our emperor made it possible for them to recover their patrimonies and to live comfortably. But did he permit those whom he deprived of the property he restored to the orphans to be discomforted? Not at all! For it cost him money to be generous; he paid a price to be pious.[26] He

25. "Hasn't wailing" etc.: cf. Them., *Orat.* 13.175c. "*curator*" (λογιστήν): i.e., *curator civitatis,* an imperial urban official with "wide powers of interference in most departments of civic life" (Jones, *Later Rom. Emp.*, 2: 726 ff.). "tax collector" (ἐκλογέα): does Themistius mean the *exactor civitatis* (Jones, op. cit., 1: 456–57, 2: 727 ff.)? "eyes": i.e., spies. Cf. Them., *Orat.* 21.255d, with n. 33 to my translation. Note *Cod. Th.* 10.10.12 and 13 (A.D. 380) and 9.39.2 (385), edicts of Theodosius and colleagues against unjust and habitual informers. "this fellow has returned ... be settled": cf. Them., *Orat.* 15.192d. "the emperor saved ... to death": cf. Them., *Orat.* 19.227d–28a. "Among the Persians ... a new pleasure": cf. Cic., *Tusc.* 5.7 [20]; Val. Max. 9.1, ext. 3; Athen. 4.144e–f, 12.539b, 12.545d. Plut., *Quaest. conviv.* 622b, makes it an Assyrian practice. "to the person who provides new funds for benevolent purposes" (καινὴν εὐεργεσίας ἀφορμήν): or does the Greek mean "to the person who provides him with a new opportunity to exercise his benevolence"? "the return of gold ... unjustly exacted": cf. Them., *Orat.* 13.174b, 16.212c, 19.227d. For Alcibiades's and Cimon's liberality, see Theopomp., *FGrH* 115 F 89; Nepos, *Alcib.* 1.3, 3.4; id., *Cimon* 2.1, 4.1–4; Plut., *Alcib.* 16.4; id., *Cimon* 10. Smicrines: a comic miser (Goldberg, *Making of Menander's Comedy,* index, s.v. "stock characters").

26. For Theodosius's concern for orphans, cf. Them., *Orat.* 15.194c, 16.212c, 17.216a. "not being punished": but their fathers had been punished. In *Orat.* 15.194d, Themistius tells Theodosius that "you let children inherit everything that belonged to their parents except the accusations leveled against them." "mechanically introduced": like a god, a deus ex machina. "no longer private citizens": i.e., they have become, figuratively, the emperor's children. Cf. Them., *Orat.* 15.194c, 17.216a. "to be generous": the Greek is φιλανθρωπίαν. This Theodosian virtue is mentioned again below with reference to his treatment of the Goths (XX, XXIV, "kindness"; XXV, "lover of humanity"). For the importance of φιλανθρωπία in the ideal Themistian ruler, see Valdenberg, *Byzantion* 1 (1924): 562–66; Downey, *Historia* 4 (1955), esp. 201–3, 207–8; id., *HTR* 50 (1957): 268–73; Daly, *Historia* 21 (1972): passim; id., *Byzantion* 45 (1975): 22–40.

bought back the orphans' property from those who possessed it, as if he were a private citizen; and then, as emperor, he presented it as a gift to those who had lost it. So now both parties enjoy a blameless wealth. One side has got back what belongs to it, and the other side has justly acquired a good sum of money in compensation for the property that was unjustly in their hands.

[XIX] I know many people who, in failing to reciprocate fully the emperor's goodwill, seemed ungrateful to him for benefits received. And it certainly is very painful to a benefactor to be treated inconsiderately by the person who has profited from his benefaction. Nevertheless, this utterly invulnerable ruler of ours was not wounded by such delinquency; rather he just keeps pouring from that same urn [of benefactions].[27]

But, as I was saying, one point after another gets hold of me and diverts me from the theme of my oration. I have not come here intending to enumerate all the praiseworthy actions of our ruler. My purpose in praising him is to show that I myself am a man of good judgment, that, in associating with such an emperor in such an office [i.e., the urban prefecture], I did not bring philosophy down, but lifted her up. [XX] I leave aside the case of Socrates's service as *prytanis,* since it was the lot that gave him that office and not anyone's considered judgment. I should instead compete boldly with Arrian and Rusticus over the relative value of our appointments to office. When I see that the emperor's gentleness has been more powerful than all the arms of the Roman empire, that these Scythians [i.e., Goths] did not yield to the eastern and the western armies that were assaulting them, nor to armies from the Tigris and from Arabia that had swiftly marched in as reinforcements, but decided to bow down only to the emperor's kindness [XXI]—when I see all this, I praise Euripides for preferring good counsel to masses of troops, and I congratulate those emperors who will have this kind of trophy inscribed in their honor, a trophy in the securing of which not a single soldier will have been involved.[28]

27. "from that same urn": a reference to the Homeric Zeus's urn of benefactions (*Il.* 24.527–28). Homer also gave Zeus an urn of woes. But Plato, criticizing Homer, denied that woes come from the gods (*Rep.* 2.379c–d). Themistius accepts Plato's critique and panegyrically assigns the emperor, too, only an urn of benefactions (*Orat.* 6.79c, 15.194a–b, 19.228d–29a). The sentence ends with the words *καὶ τοῖς ἔτεσι μὴ δυνάμενος*, which the Teubner edition marks as a crux and I omit from my translation. For emendations, see the Teubner's apparatus criticus.

28. "as I was saying": cf. the opening sentence of section XVIII of this oration. Socrates: see section X. Arrian and Rusticus: the point is that it was better to serve Theodosius than Hadrian, Antoninus, or Marcus Aurelius. The latter emperors, according to

I also enter the arena against Antoninus: while that emperor did procure water from heaven when his infantry were hard pressed by thirst, you, [Theodosius], extinguished a fire that had spread over a great portion of the earth. The clouds also submitted once to a king of the Lydians after he had offered prayers, but the barbarians at the height of their power were never made subject to anyone. They behaved boldly against our infantry, yet they were captured by our emperor's virtue and offer themselves voluntarily as prisoners of war despite their recent confidence in their weapons. You alone, [Theodosius], have proved yourself equal to everyone and everything—to Thracians, Celts, and Illyrians, to weapons, horses, and everything else needed to fight wars, and to impassible rivers.[29]

[XXII] All that [military] ingenuity of ours has proved useless; only your advice and your judgment provided an invincible resistance, and the victory you won through these inner resources of yours was finer than it would have been had you prevailed by arms. For you have not destroyed those who wronged us, but appropriated them. You did not punish them by seizing their land, but have acquired more farmers for us. You did not slaughter them like wild beasts, but charmed away their savagery—just as if someone, after trapping a lion or a leopard in nets, were not to kill it but to accustom it to being a beast of burden. These fire-breathers, harder on the Romans than Hannibal was, have now come over to our side. Tame and submissive, they entrust their persons and their arms to us, whether the emperor wants to employ them as farmers or as soldiers.[30] They are conscious of how many and

---

Themistius, "escorted [Arrian and Rusticus] to the general's tent" and sent them east, where they "drove the Alani out of Armenia" (section VIII); but Theodosius relies on "gentleness" and "kindness" (below). Themistius is referring in this paragraph to the peace treaty Theodosius signed with the Visigoths in 382. The terms were favorable to the Visigoths, settling them within the empire as federates of Rome. See Jones, *Later Rom. Emp.*, 1: 156–58; Nixon and Rodgers, *In Praise of Later Roman Emperors,* 473–74n. Daly, *Historia* 21 (1972): 351–79, gives a positive assessment of Themistius's advocacy of peace-making and clemency and of his support of the Theodosian policy of accommodating and assimilating northern "barbarians." Euripides: fr. 200 Nauck; cf. Them., *Orat.* 15.191a, 16.207d.

29. "I also enter the arena against Antoninus": i.e., on behalf of Theodosius. As in *Orat.* 15.191b ("Antoninus . . . who was called Pius") Themistius misattributes Marcus Aurelius's rain miracle to his predecessor. For the rain miracle, see Birley, *Marcus,* 172–74. "you . . . extinguished a fire": cf. Them., *Orat.* 14.181b, 16.206d, 18.219b. "a king of the Lydians": i.e., Croesus. See Hdt. 1.86–87. "You alone" etc.: cf. Them., *Orat* 14.181a. "Thracians, Celts, and Illyrians": i.e., in the Roman army.

30. "For you have not destroyed . . . or as soldiers": cf. Them., *Orat.* 16.210d–11b; Pacatus, *Panegyr. Lat.* 2.22.3 Mynors. The Visigoths were given land in the diocese of Thrace and served as federates in the Roman army. "These fire-breathers (*οἱ πῦρ πνέοντες*) . . . than Hannibal was": cf. Them., *Orat.* 7.87a, "these fire-breathers, harder on the

how serious the injustices are that they have committed, but this does not frighten them. Consciousness of what they have done does not cause them to disbelieve that they will be spared and treated kindly by those who have suffered the worst injustices from them. But it is the emperor's mildness that is their real guarantee that they will not suffer for what they have acknowledged that they did.

[XXIII] We may compare what the poets say about the Giants. Those creatures rose up against and resisted Ares, Enyo, Zeus's thunderbolt, and the <other> gods for a long time. But when the young, handsome, and enchanting gods Apollo and Hermes appeared, bows <and> arrows were no longer needed; the Giants were charmed by the young gods' wand and lyre. Such are the victories of piety: they do not destroy the vanquished, but improve him.[31]

[XXIV] Come here, you Thracians and Macedonians, and fill yourselves with this incredible sight: Scythians dwelling under the same roof with us, bound to us by treaty, sharing in the celebration of our victory over them. They apparently did not know what a gracious person they would find [in Theodosius], in whose nets they would be caught. Men who thought that they could take from the Romans the once impregnable Haemus [range] and the Hebrus River, and the rough terrain of Thessaly were caught without much of a struggle in the divine defenses of piety, justice, mildness, and kindness. So come out now with confidence from behind your walls. It is time to leave your battlements and to tend to your cattle and plows. It is time to sharpen your sickles instead of your swords and javelins. The land has now been opened to wayfarers; one does not have to sail the seas now that it is safe to go by land. Road stations, stables, and lodging houses are back in business and are springing up everywhere with the effortlessness that characterized past times. A great cloud of hail has suddenly turned into a clear sky, a stormy swell has become a calm sea, and this has happened so gently and quietly that it seems puzzling.[32]

Romans than Mithridates was." For "fire-breathers," see *LSJ,* s.vv. *πνέω* V, *πυριπνέων*, *πυρίπνοος*, *πύρπνοος*.

31. "the <other> gods": with Schneider, *Die 34. Rede,* ad loc., I supply "<other>," *ἄλλοις*. "wand and lyre": i.e., Hermes's wand and Apollo's lyre. "Such are," etc.: cf. Them., *Orat.* 16.211a. F. Vian, "Gigantes," *LIMC,* 4, 1 (1988): 195, comments on Themistius's version of the Gigantomachy, with its nonviolent resolution, in his discussion of the myth in ancient literature. Cf. Them., *Orat.* 13.176d–77a, 16.208a.

32. "sharing in the celebration . . . over them": cf. Them., *Orat.* 16.210d. "a gracious person": The manuscript has *λεῶ*. I read *ἵλεῳ* with Mai (1816 ed.), not the conjectural emendation *Ἰόλεῳ*, adopted in the Teubner text and in Schneider's edition. If "Iolaus" were read, it would refer to Fl. Saturninus (*PLRE,* vol. 1, under "Saturninus

For those whom we did not overcome in battle, we brought to terms after laying aside our arms. For a while we were counting the number of people against whom we would be drawn up in battle; now we are counting how many there are over whom we shall have authority. In days gone by, we were distressed by the prospect that there might be many Scythians, but now we are distressed by the thought that there may be too few.

[XXV] Consider next how much more kingly Theodosius has been in his dealings with men who caused him grief than Homer's wide-ruling Agamemnon, son of Atreus and grandson of Pelops. Agamemnon rebukes his brother [Menelaus], who is beginning to yield to the suppliant [Adrastus]. He also expresses a very harsh and barbaric wish: that none of the Trojans may escape, that not even "the boy whose mother carries him in her womb" may escape, but that even those Trojans not yet brought to term may perish before being born.[33] But we, <in our mildness> to suppliants, raise their sons and their unmarried daughters. We do not hate them for being Scythians, but deem them worthy, as human beings, of being spared.

This is how things are: if a ruler continually attacks the arrogant barbarians, he makes himself emperor of the Romans alone. But if he spares as well as conquers, he knows that he is emperor of all peoples. Such a ruler could rightly and truly be called a lover of humanity. As for other rulers, you might call Cyrus a lover of the Persians, but not of humanity. You might call Alexander a lover of the Macedonians, but not of humanity. You might call Agesilaus a lover of the Greeks, and Augustus a lover of the Romans, and others lovers of the races or peoples over whom they were thought to rule. But the "lover of humanity" without qualification and the "king" without qualification is he who asks only if he has before him a human being who needs to be

---

10"), who made peace with the Goths in 382 as Theodosius's lieutenant, i.e., playing Iolaus to Theodosius's Heracles. But *ἵλεῳ* is the palaeographically easier emendation (cf. the corruption of *ἵλεῳ* to *λεώ* at Them., *Orat.* 4.53c), and one wants a reference to Theodosius here, not a sudden acknowledgment of his lieutenant. Themistius will describe *himself* as Theodosius's Iolaus below (section XXVIII). "Men who . . . Thessaly": a corrupt passage, marked as a crux in the Teubner edition. I very tentatively follow earlier emendators and read *ἀλλ' <οἵτινες ἁλωτά σφισι> τὰ ἄμαχά ποτε Ῥωμαίων τὸν Αἷμον ὑπελάμβανον καὶ τὸν Ἕβρον καὶ τὰς Θετταλικὰς δυσχωρίας* [ἃς δικάζονται]. . . . See the apparatus criticus of the Teubner text and of Schneider's edition. Cf. Them., *Orat.* 14.181b. "sickles . . . javelins": cf. Them., *Orat.* 16.211b. "Road stations . . . past times": cf. ibid. 212b. "a stormy swell . . . sea": cf. ibid. 212a.

33. "wide-ruling Agamemnon": *εὐρυκρείων*, the Homeric epithet (e.g., *Il.* 1.102). "Agamemnon . . . before being born": see Hom., *Il.* 6.37–60, and the nearly identically phrased passage in Them., *Orat.* 10.132a.

treated fairly. Such a ruler does not ask if this person is a Scythian or a Massagete, or whether he previously committed this or that act of injustice. Even if it is perfectly legitimate to make such inquiries, it is not godlike to do so, nor is it in line with the great divine appellation by which all of you designate emperors. To make such inquiries is the mark of rulers who walk upon the earth, who do not consider it reprehensible to be hostile or unfriendly to someone.[34] For such rulers, if one party causes injury and the affected party then inflicts injury in return, if someone suffers something and then acts in response, this is all a pardonable pattern of behavior, since it keeps fortune and power in balance. [XXVI] But for the ruler who is so superior to the rest of mankind that the divine appellation he enjoys does not appear to be at odds with his behavior, it is not right to be hostile or unfriendly to fellow human beings, any more than it would be right for a shepherd or a keeper of horses or a cowherd to be hostile to sheep or horses or cattle.

Socrates, the son of Sophroniscus, showed that this [benevolent] kind of rule was much more naturally suited to the governed. This very Socrates took up the much repeated assertion about the just man and justice—namely, that one should treat one's friends well and do harm to one's enemies—but he retained only half of it, correcting the other half. He agreed that one should treat friends well; the correction he made was that one should not harm one's enemies, but make them one's friends.[35]

[XXVII] Now if we know that someone who wears the philosopher's cloak subscribes to this corrected assertion about justice, we shall praise and admire him, especially in light of the fact that Socrates

34. "This is how . . . of all peoples": cf. the nearly identical Them., *Orat.* 10.131d–32a. "As for other rulers . . . to be treated fairly": cf. Them., *Orat.* 10.132a–c, with some of the phrasing nearly identical to what we find here. A lacuna in *Orat.* 10.132c can be filled from this passage; see Schneider, *Die 34. Rede,* ad loc. "a Scythian or a Massagete": Massagete, like Scythian (= Goth), is a classicizing term for a northern people—but not the Alans (*pace* Maisano ad loc.) as in Amm. Marc. 23.5.16 because at *Orat.* 16.207c Themistius differentiates Alans from Massagetes. "the great divine appellation," ὀνόματι τῆς θειότητος (cf. XXVI below): a Christian ruler could understand θειότης to betoken virtue or doing good, as Themistius explains to Theodosius elsewhere (*Orat.* 15.189a, 192b, 193d; 19.225c–26d, 229b). "rulers who walk upon the earth": i.e., who are not godlike. The expression is Homeric (*Il.* 5.442).

35. "Socrates took up the . . . assertion": the Teubner text has ἀπεδέχετο καινῶς τὸν...λόγον, καινῶς being the editor's emendation of the transmitted καὶ πρὸς. I leave καινῶς untranslated. For other emendations of the passage, see the Teubner apparatus criticus. For Socrates's opposition to harming one's enemies, see Pl., *Rep.* 1.335b–36a; *Crito* 49a–d; cf. Them., *Orat.* 7.95a. A Christian emperor would doubtless think of the Christian injunction to love one's enemies. Libanius, *Epp.* 62.2 Foerster, compliments Themistius himself for treating his enemies with kindness.

himself was unable to profit from his own opinion and could not bring Meletus, Anytus, or Lycon over to his side. In fact, what we know and see is an emperor who daily and hourly treats his friends well and also caused his enemies—whole groups and tribes of them—to abandon their ill-will and become favorably disposed towards us. So, summoned by this emperor to the public sphere, I did what Socrates praises and Plato admires: I played my part there with him. I did not stoop low, my good sir, in presiding over one of the earth's two eyes.[36] I have not cast off philosophy; rather I have added action to thought.

[XXVIII] You hear, [sir], that Heracles, the son of Zeus, was so great, not because he had a precise knowledge of conclusive and inconclusive arguments, but because he put a stop to lawlessness and did not permit beastlike people to act in accordance with their nature. Well, what I did was to imitate Iolaus; I served for a time as an assistant to the gloriously victorious [Heracles] and tended to our common hearth [Constantinople]. This was not a waste of my time, and it is not fitting that I should be more diminished by having played this role than if I had spent the whole time at the dice board. Plato did not descend [from the heights of philosophy] in crossing the Ionian Sea three times on behalf of Dion, nor did Aristotle in the concern he showed for Stagira, nor did Carneades or Critolaus in serving as ambassadors on behalf of Attica. [XXIX] Yet, in the opinion of some, I was "rolling around on the ground" some time ago, when I traversed the West and the East, already carrying around with me this city's high opinion [of my activities].[37]

36. "Socrates ... favorably disposed towards us": Themistius lauds Theodosius for being unaffected by the fact that Socrates's unwillingness to harm his accusers Meletus, Anytus, and Lycon was not reciprocated. "the earth's two eyes": i.e., Rome and Constantinople. For the expression, see Schneider's comment in *Die 34. Rede,* ad loc.

37. "conclusive and inconclusive arguments": Diogenes Laertius 7.77–78 explains these terms in a discussion of Stoic logic. Cf. Them., *Orat.* 2.33a. For Heracles's opponents, see the article on him by J. Boardman et al. in *LIMC,* 4, 1 (1988): 728 ff.; 5, 1 (1990): 1 ff. Iolaus was Heracles's companion and assistant (M. Pipili, "Iolaos," *LIMC,* 5, 1 [1990]: 686 ff.). For "gloriously victorious" (καλλινίκῳ) as an epithet for Heracles, see Adler, "Kallinikos 6," *RE,* 10, 2 (1919): 1650–52. In assuming the urban prefecture of Constantinople, their "common hearth," Themistius played Iolaus to Theodosius's Heracles. Plato: Dion can be said to have motivated only the second and third journeys to Sicily (Pl., *Epp.* 7.326b–29b, 337e–40a). Cf. Them., *Orat.* 17.215c. Aristotle: the philosopher played a key role as advocate for the restoration of Stagira after its destruction by Philip. Cf. Them., *Orat.* 34 [VIII], with my n. 11 and see Val. Max. 5.6, ext. 5; Dio Chrys. 30 (47).9; Diog. Laert. 5.4; *Vita Arist. Marc.*, p. 3 Gigon. Carneades and Critolaus: the Academic Carneades, the Peripatetic Critolaus, and the Stoic Diogenes came to Rome in 155 B.C. to seek to relieve Athens from a fine that had been imposed on the city (Plut., *Cato Maj.* 22; Aul Gell. 6.14.8–10; Macrob., *Sat.* 1.5.13–16). We need not assume with Schneider, in his comment on this passage of Themistius, that the Stoic

I would not exclude from the number of my embassies my recent visit to glorious Rome.[38] On that occasion I went as ambassador to your fathers [i.e., the Romans], ensuring that our two cities would be in harmony and causing all of you to be honored and revered by them. For the resolution they passed on your behalf and sent to the emperors [Gratian and Valens] lends dignity to all inhabitants of your city. And if I would not tire you by enumerating the praises I received there—this, after all, is the most burdensome sort of thing one has to listen to—I would already have read out to you the acclamations of the Roman senate. Through them you would all have profitably learned by how much the Romans outstrip others in exalting and honoring virtue.

[XXX] Do not, then, be a literalist, [my good man]. Just because Plato in the *Republic* [7.520c; cf. 519d] uses the word "descend" when he coaxingly addresses those who are moving from the divine to the human sphere of vision, do not imagine that holding public office is something trifling. Realize, [sir], that "up" and "down" are not simple concepts. Epicurus is certainly trifling, as is anyone who admires him and has become enamored of bodily pleasure. Plato, on the other hand, is always in the upper sphere, as is anyone who follows Plato and seeks to become like God. But I stand between these two men, being content to be sometimes "up" and sometimes "down." For me, being in the lower sphere does not mean being there completely; for when I am there, I depend on the upper sphere and take my directions from on high.[39]

Diogenes's name was deliberately omitted here. In referring to this philosophic embassy, Aelian too mentions only Carneades and Critolaus (*Var. hist.* 3.17). Other texts mention only Carneades and Diogenes (Cic., *Acad.* 2.45 [137] and *Tusc.* 4.3 [5], with which contrast Cic., *De orat.* 2.37–38 [155 ff.]; Plut., loc. cit.). "rolling around on the ground": the extreme to which "walking upon the earth" (see above, section XXV) or "stooping low" (above, XXVII) can lead. "when I traversed the West and the East": cf. the references to his embassies in *Orat.* 17.214b, 31.352d and 34 [XIII], and see Vanderspoel, *Themistius,* 179–80.

38. Surely the visit of 376 (see Vanderspoel, *Themistius,* 179–82; *pace* Schneider, *Die 34. Rede,* 143, and Maisano, *Discorsi,* p. 1024, n. 107). Cf. Them., *Orat.* 31.354c–d. The word "number" (ἀριθμοῦ) is a conjectural emendation of "numbers" (ἀριθμῶν); see Schneider, op. cit., 92.

39. "as is anyone who admires [Epicurus]": this has been seen as a hit at the "dissolute" or Epicurean Palladas, who criticized Themistius for accepting the urban prefecture. (See above, p. 38; Mai in Dindorf, *Themistii Orationes,* 471; Dagron, *T&MByz* 3 [1968]: 50, n. 94; and for Palladas's "Epicureanism," Luck, *HSCP* 63 [1958]: 456–57.) But note Cameron, *CQ* 15 (1965): 222n. "to become like God": cf. Pl., *Theaet.* 176b.

APPENDIX I

Oration 17

ON HIS APPOINTMENT TO THE URBAN PREFECTURE [OF CONSTANTINOPLE]

[213] Our most godlike ruler [Theodosius] has brought philosophy back to the arena of public administration again after a long lapse of time, and he has brought her back more conspicuously than his recent predecessors did. For they would give philosophy only verbal honors. It is not that they disapproved of philosophy, which time and again preferred to return to the life of action;[1] but under them philosophy's role in public affairs and service to the common fatherland was restricted to going on embassies. In contrast, our current emperor bestows office on her as well and bids her tend in her own right to business that he hitherto thought should be entrusted to others. Long ago it was possible for philosophy to act as a guide to those engaged in the fray without doing anything more herself than observing public contests in quiet detachment. But our emperor has put an end to philosophy's mere observing and restores her to the arena [214]. He makes it possible to convince the human race that reason was not intended to operate apart from the realm of action, but that actions guided by reason are what one wants to display to the world. He

1. "has brought philosophy back . . . again": "philosophy," at least in the first sentence, means Themistius. "Again" alludes to Themistius's earlier holding of office, namely, the Constantinopolitan proconsulship in the late 350s under Constantius (see above, pp. 1–2). "not that they disapproved . . . life of action:" *εἰς δὲ τὰ ἔργα προελομένην [φιλοσοφίαν] πολλάκις κατελθεῖν οὐκ ἐδυσώπησαν*. With Maisano, *Discorsi*, ad loc., I read the conjecture *προελομένην* for the manuscripts' *προελόμενοι*, although my understanding of the Greek differs from his. If my understanding of the Greek is correct, note that Themistius does not here address the question why he once refused office; he will take that issue up in *Orat.* 34 [XIII–XIV].

shows human beings that philosophy does not teach ancient precepts in safe detachment, but that she acts on the precepts she teaches.

Our times have produced a reign that is attuned to the views of the ancients, who understood that things would go well for cities when the authority to act and the ability to speak well were found together and when political power and philosophy were united. Our most philosophical ruler shows us that power and philosophy are in fact found together for the first time in himself. He also urges me, in this old age of mine, to be true to my philosophical youth and gives me as my own this august and distinguished urban prefecture, the most independent of the offices that are his to confer. This prefecture follows on my ten embassies and my trips abroad, which I undertook on your behalf whenever possible, from my youth right to the present time of my life.[2] I believe that I carried out these missions in a manner that was not unworthy of your appointment of me and was of some benefit to the city.

Our ruler outdoes his predecessors. For, instead of honoring me with two statues and frequent invitations to attend on him, he adorns me with a very great and busy office. He also causes the office to be adorned by my tenure of it, for he selects as head of the royal city, not a foreigner or a stranger, but a native, one who was raised and advanced and dwells in your midst, so that any good that comes from this office, held right here [in the city], will be seen to be to the common advantage of all of us.[3]

You can see, then, that it would have been wrong for me to refuse to accept appointment to this office. For a philosopher who resists when a philosophical emperor selects him to serve the state straightway demonstrates that the title "philosopher" does not truly belong to him—unless we think that philosophy is to be found only on the tongue and not much more in the soul. A philosopher wrongly resists an imperial appointment when the emperor in question has his temper calmed and his anger bridled by reason, when greed is banished from his soul and cruelty dwells far away from him, when law, justice, and right preside all around him. He who does not consider such an emperor to be a philosopher is not only deaf to Plato and Pythagoras **[215]**; he also does not understand the obvious fact that all yearning for virtue is philosophy. He reduces the most divine of sciences to long hair, perhaps, and to a beard and the philosopher's cloak.[4]

2. "power and philosophy": cf. Them., *Orat.* 34 [VII]. "[F]or the first time" is sheer flattery; Themistius had called Constantius and Julian philosopher-kings (Them., *Orat.* 2.40a–b; Jul., *Ep. ad Them.* 253c). "the most independent of the offices": a fair description only if taken to mean "l'autorité suprême à *l'intérieur de la ville* [de Constantinople]." See Dagron, *Naissance,* 230 (emphasis mine); and for the urban prefecture vis-à-vis the praetorian prefecture, see ibid. 286–87. "ten embassies": cf. Them., *Orat.* 31.352d, 34 [XXIX].

3. "two statues": cf. Them., *Orat.* 34 [XIII] with n. 20 to my translation. "a native": it is clear from *Demeg. Constantii* 21d that Themistius was not born in Byzantium/Constantinople, so "native" (ἐγγενῆ) here cannot be understood literally. He was a native only in spirit. Note esp. Schemmel, *Neue Jahrbücher* 11 (1908): 153–54, and see Vanderspoel, *Themistius,* 31, who misrepresents the view of Stegemann, *RE,* 5A, 2 (1934): 1642.

4. "long hair" etc.: i.e., external marks of a philosopher, which do not guarantee that their wearers are genuine philosophers (see my comments in *Letters of Apollonius,* 92 [*Epp.* 3], 127 [*Epp.* 70] and esp. 134 [*Epp.* 79]).

So let the times in which we live enjoy the return of the days of Trajan and those of Hadrian, Marcus [Aurelius], and Antoninus [Pius], who pulled Arrian and Rusticus away from their books and made them participants and assistants in the administration of public affairs. In so acting, these emperors were doing nothing new, nor were they introducing an unusual practice into the political arena. They were merely emulating the ancient Romans, in whose time philosophical Scipios, Varros, and Catos took part in public affairs and held the highest offices. In those days Thrasea, Priscus, Bib<ul>us, and Favonius also took part in public affairs, alternating between the philosopher's cloak and the toga in the manner of Xenophon and Socrates among the Greeks, the former serving as general and the latter as *prytanis*.[5] I pass over the divine Plato, who prayed that he would find the kind of king with whom he could share his concerns about the public sphere but failed to have his prayers fulfilled. Seeking, as he himself says somewhere, a young, temperate, mild, gentle, high-minded, and generous king, none other than a Theodosius, he went off three times to Dionysius and to Sicily and, because he yearned for true monarchy, he was forced into association with a tyrannical regime. I also pass over Pittacus, Bias and Cleobulus, and Archytas of Tarentum as well, men who were more devoted to action than to their writings.[6]

In light of both the person who bestows the office [of urban prefect] and the person who accepts it, the present age is no less worthy of commemoration than all those bygone times. It is essential, conscript fathers, that you assist the bestower and the holder of the office. There is nothing great or honorable in the fact that you outdo the masses in your residences, your gold and your silver. But if everyone sees that we are serious about honoring philosophy and putting virtue in first place, then we shall not be untrue to the title "fathers." Then the senate will be preeminent, then it will be a temple of the Muses, not filled with [mere] bronze statues, but [truly] permeated by those [divine] models.[7]

Let us imitate our leader, you guardians of the inhabited world. Let us follow the God-given decree [that put him on the throne] **[216]**. Let us seem more and more precious to him each day. It is neither stores of wealth that this young man considers precious nor much-esteemed gems nor richly embroidered garments.[8] He gladly divests himself of such resources and gives them

5. For details in this paragraph up to this point, cf. Them., *Orat.* 34 [VII *sub fine,* VIII, X *init.*], with the notes to my translation. "Bib<ul>us" is Harduinus's correction of the transmitted "Bibus" (*Βίβος*). Themistius probably means M. Calpurnius Bibulus, Caesar's consular colleague in 59 B.C. Bibulus was the son-in-law of Cato Uticensis, whom Themistius doubtless has in mind in his reference to "Catos."

6. "Seeking ... generous king": cf. Them., *Orat.* 34 [XVI], with n. 24 to my translation. "a Theodosius": i.e., "God-given" and therefore the eventual answer to Plato's prayers—although in *Orat.* 3.46a–c and 4.62a–d it is Constantius who was the answer to Plato's prayers, and in *Orat.* 8.105b–c it is Valens. Themistius is also playing on the emperor's name below (215d), when he speaks of "the God-given (*θεοσδότῳ*) decree." "[Plato] went off three times": cf. Them., *Orat.* 34 [XXVIII]. "Pittacus ... Cleobulus": three of the traditional Seven Wise Men. Cf. Them., *Orat.* 34 [III]. Archytas: Pythagorean, statesman and friend of Plato (see Guthrie, *History of Greek Philosophy,* 1: 333–36).

7. For the senate as a temple of the Muses, cf. Them., *Orat.* 31.355a ff. *Orat.* 31 ends as *Orat.* 17 does, urging the senators to let their values be shaped by philosophy.

8. "this young man": i.e., Plato's "young" king (see 215c above). Theodosius was 37 or 38 years old when *Orat.* 17 was delivered.

away. The only thing he considers precious and is unable to resist is virtue and the qualities virtue presides over: love of humanity, mildness, forbearance. Because of him no one has clothed himself in black, no one is fatherless, no one at all is an orphan. If some unfortunate fate allotted the hardship of orphanage to individuals while they were still young children, they got an emperor in lieu of their own fathers.[9] It is the treasuries and the store of these good deeds that our emperor wants to see growing and increasing. Having laid up such treasure in himself first, he thinks it right that we too should abound in such resources. For only if we have resources of this kind will he view us as highly valued for goods we possess.

You must restore good order and behavior to the senate, then. From your leaders you must demand an honorable tenure of the office that they adorn, and from the masses you must demand ready obedience.[10] You should realize that the great senate is not unlike a healthy living being. It is appropriate, in the case of such a creature, that the rest of the body follow the eyes, that the hands and the feet not take first place away from the eyes. When each part of the body is content to play its own limited role, then the whole living being necessarily thrives.

9. For Theodosius's concern for orphans, cf. Them., *Orat.* 15.194c, 16.212c, 34 [XVIII].

10. "From your leaders": Themistius means senators like himself, not emperors (*pace* Méridier, *Le philosophe Thémistios,* 91).

APPENDIX 2

Fragment on "The Knowledge of Knowledges"

[299] . . . [a higher order of knowledge] that understands well what it speaks of and takes up no topic unless it comprehends the issues involved better than they are comprehended by the [areas of knowledge that are of a lower order], all lined up, as the latter are, one after another. Indeed, when those [lesser] areas of knowledge leave matters in doubt because of their inability to deal with them, this higher order of knowledge takes them up and examines them from every angle, bringing a clarity and solid footing to them. It is thus well said that there is a "knowledge of knowledges" [300]. By this we do not mean that there is a [higher order of] knowledge that considers it important to consort with angles or to become absorbed in numbers, but that the cables of areas of knowledge [that are of a lower order] are attached to a [higher order of] knowledge, and the latter knowledge, as director of the former areas of knowledge, presides over them and explains how they should approach individual problems.[1]

The supervision that this higher order of knowledge exercises over the arts and its authority over them are rather kingly. It seeks to look down from on high, so to speak, at arts that walk on the ground and to judge each one of them. Its intention is to determine whether a given art will benefit a correctly ordered polity[2] or is harmful and dangerous. It will decide which art should be fully admitted as something healthy and which should be utterly banished as a

1. "angles . . . numbers": i.e., the higher order of knowledge does not concern itself with, for example, the details of geometry or of arithmetic, but guides and monitors such branches of knowledge in the manner indicated in this fragment. Cf. Them., *Orat.* 21.251a, "philosophers should supervise [rhetors and grammarians] . . . but should not themselves do the work of rhetors or grammarians."

2. "correctly ordered" (ὀρθῇ): i.e., a polity aimed at the common good (Arist., *Pol.* 3.6 [1279a18]).

disease that would disgrace the city. For every art is certainly capable of handling what has been assigned to it and of doing what it does for all who have need of its services, but it is unable to make a judgment about its own utility or harmfulness.

Another unfortunate and defective thing about the arts is that they perform their services for the good and the bad alike. The knife-maker cannot determine whether he will be giving a knife to a murderer; the shipbuilder cannot judge whether he will be building a ship for a robber, as Harmonides did for Paris; and the helmsman who saves someone on his ship cannot decide whether it would have been better to let him drown. But if good judgment and wisdom guide and order what the arts do, they will make up for what is lacking in them and will not permit them to offer their goods to [all] who come their way.[3]

This, then, is what is meant when we say that there is a "knowledge of knowledges" and an "art of arts": that a [higher order of] knowledge establishes the first principles of areas of knowledge [that are of a lower order] or monitors how those areas of knowledge are put to use.[4]

3. For Harmonides, see Hom., *Il.* 5.59 ff., and cf. Them., *Orat.* 26.316b, with n. 10 to my translation. "good judgment and wisdom" (φρόνησις καὶ σοφία): another way of speaking of the "knowledge of knowledges" that is the subject of this fragment.

4. "knowledge of knowledges" (ἐπιστήμη ἐπιστημῶν): one might note the terminological parallels ἐπιστημῶν ἐπιστήμη in Pl., *Charm.* 170c (and see 166b–76d), and "philosophiam artem esse artium et disciplinam disciplinarum" in Macrob., *Sat.* 7.15.14 (cf. 1.24.21), but the manner in which these passages elaborate on the terminology makes them conceptually unparallel to Themistius. Cf. Jul., *Orat.* 9.183a Rochefort.

APPENDIX 3

The *Demegoria Constantii*[1]

[18] If you and yours are in good health, it is well; I and the army are in good health.[2]

Your rejoicing is reasonable, conscript fathers, as you take pleasure in the number of our victories and enjoy the current peace in safety. In my concern about such matters, I am always trying either to add some new sphere of command to the Roman Empire by force of arms or to be of some help to subject peoples through legal enactments. On this occasion, too, I am sure that you have assembled expecting, as you are accustomed to do, either news of military successes or some munificent peacetime boon. But I consider it to be my duty not merely to ensure through public blessings that you are all joyful, but also to display, to the extent that I am able, an appropriate care and concern for you individually. For it is when people enjoy a public benefaction as individuals that its effects are especially felt [19]. Consequently, if the individual is the end of public concerns, then it is the individual who must first and foremost be

1. The *Demegoria Constantii* is transmitted with Themistius's orations. The full title in codices A and *Π* is "The Emperor Constantius's Oration [*Δημηγορία*] to the [Constantinopolitan] Senate concerning Themistius." Codices *Ψ* and u preserve the following note: "This letter [*ἐπιστολή*] concerning the most illustrious philosopher Themistius was delivered and read in the senate on the Kalends of September when Arepio and Lollianus were consuls. The most illustrious proconsul [of Constantinople] Justinus read it." "Arepio" is a corruption of "Arbetio," and the year is 355. This document, translated from the original Latin (see Liban., *Epp.* 434.2 Foerster), announces and justifies Themistius's adlection to the Constantinopolitan senate. For such *orationes/epistulae* to the senate, note Millar, *Emperor,* 277. Themistius thanked Constantius in his *Orat.* 2.

2. This opening sentence is found in codices *Ψ* and u, but not in A and *Π*. Dindorf and the Teubner edition of the *Orations* bracket it. But the formulaic expression (see Millar, *Emperor,* 353–54) fits Constantius's situation (in the West) well in the year 355; see Barnes, *Athanasius,* 221–22.

in my thoughts. Rather, if the truth is to be told, when I judge an individual man worthy of an appropriate honor, I am giving a public gift. For no favor conferred with reason and judgment belongs to its recipient alone; it is offered to everyone as a common prize for similar toils.

The philosopher Themistius's repute, the subject of many a conversation, brought word of him to me, and I felt that it was in line with both a kingly mentality and your mentality to reward his virtue with an appropriate honor. So what I did was to adlect him to the order of the most illustrious senators, this man who prides himself on what it is fitting to pride oneself on. For I believe that, by this favor, I not only honor Themistius, but also the senate no less than him—and, in my view, it is fitting that the senate share in a gift that befits philosophy. So in giving honor you [senators] will receive it in turn, and in receiving it you will give it.[3] People achieve honor and are made famous by a variety of things, some by the glory of wealth, some by the amount of property they own, some by their efforts on behalf of the state, and others by their rhetorical skills. All men of intelligence struggle to reach one and the same summit of good repute by various and sundry paths. But of life's many roads, only that of virtue is safe and secure; the others are winding and dangerous. So whenever someone is about to be adlected to your ranks, the one question you should ask before all others is whether he walks on the path of virtue. Do not regard any other mark of the order of most illustrious men to be as important as right judgment and good thinking. These are things that philosophy especially seeks to achieve.

Themistius's learning was enough for him to be deemed worthy of the greatest honor, whether he was philosophizing in seclusion or perhaps not saying a word; for a person who possesses virtue is just as worthy of honor as one who displays it [20]. And it is fitting that recompense come to the worthy, even if they themselves are not eager to appear to be worthy. But the fact is that this man, whom the present oration heralds, does not pursue a philosophy that refuses to be shared with others.[4] The good that with effort he has brought together he shares, with even greater effort, with those who wish to partake of it. He has become a spokesman of the ancient men of wisdom, a hierophant of

3. "Themistius's repute . . . brought word of him to me": Themistius had also delivered the panegyrical *Orat.* 1 before Constantius in Ancyra probably early in 347 (Vanderspoel, *Themistius,* 73–77; Ballériaux, *Byzantion* 66 [1996]: 319–34). "your mentality": read "your" (*ὑμετέρας*) with Dindorf instead of "our" (*ἡμετέρας*) with the Teubner editors. "[W]ith both a kingly mentality and your mentality" means, of course, "with my and your mentality." "the most illustrious senators": here and below the superlative English adjective represents *λαμπρότατος*, the Greek equivalent of the Latin senatorial title *clarissimus.* "this man who prides himself" etc.: *τὰ εἰκότα σεμνυνόμενον δι' ἀλλήλων*. I delete *δι' ἀλλήλων*. See the Teubner apparatus criticus. "and, in my view . . . in a gift": something is not quite right about the text printed by the Teubner editors (*ἧν τὸ μετασχεῖν δωρεᾶς ἄξιον νενόμικα*). See the Teubner apparatus criticus. I have simply deleted *τό*. Both here and below, Constantius speaks of *adlectio* as both an imperial and a senatorial act. "[L]a proposition impériale précédait le vote de cooptation de l'Assemblée" (Chastagnol, *Acta Antiqua Acad. Scient. Hungar.* 24 [1976]: 348).

4. For Themistius's "sharing" of philosophy, cf. *Orat.* 26.320 ff., 28.341d–42c, 31.352c.

the sanctuaries and shrines of philosophy. He does not permit the old doctrines to perish; he causes them to flourish forever and to become new [again]. It is he who personally ensures that all human beings live in accordance with reason and have regard for learning.

You yourselves see, conscript fathers, that in human life nothing very fine and excellent can be achieved, either in a household or in a city, without virtue. Those who are deservedly the leading philosophers would be regarded as the common fathers of all precisely because they exercise and train young men in virtue. These philosophers teach how sons should honor their own fathers and what sort of care children should receive from their fathers. In a word, the philosopher is really the judge and overseer of us all. From him we learn how the people should be managed and how the senate should be honored. He is, quite simply, a proven and accurate standard for the whole body politic. If it were possible for all human beings to be philosophers, baseness would be removed from human life, every excuse for injustice would be banished, and there would be no need of legal compulsion. The things that people are restrained from doing by fear they would hate by choice.

I am all the more enthusiastically drawn to the matter under discussion because, eager as I am for philosophy's light to shine throughout the whole world, I especially wish for philosophy to thrive in this city of ours. And this is what I understand is happening because of Themistius's efforts.[5] [Constantinople] is priding herself on the gatherings of young men studying philosophy in her streets and is becoming the common abode of learning [21], with the result that all men from everywhere have unanimously conceded that she is supreme in philosophy, and the teachings of virtue proceed from our city, as if from some undefiled fount, to all parts of the earth. Consequently, as I said at the beginning of my statement, I am giving a common honor to both you and Themistius. For while receiving Roman rank [ἀξιώματος] from us, he in turn gives us his Hellenic wisdom [σοφίαν],[6] so that he thereby shows that our city is the summit of both good fortune and virtue. Being supreme in all other blessings, she now obtains the most prized blessing as well. If it is the mark of a loving emperor to fortify the city with walls, to adorn the walled area with buildings and to fill it with a large number of citizens, how much more so is it to augment the senate with the addition of this sort of person, a person who will improve the inhabitants' souls and will erect, along with the city's other buildings, a gymnasium of virtue? So the one who provides everything else for the city [i.e., the emperor] [now] gives it the first of all blessings; he who cares for the city's intellectual and educational well-being obtains for it what is most important, what many desire but very few achieve.

I know that to offer reasons why Themistius would be worthy of the greatest honor other [than his achievement as a philosopher] is not something that those who appreciate the greatness of philosophy would do. Philosophy is in and of itself the most sufficient of things. If you fail to adduce it alone [as the

5. For Themistius himself on his own drawing power, see *Orat.* 23.294b–96a.

6. Cf. *Cod. Theod.* 6.4.12 (A.D. 361), where the *scientia* of *Themistius philosophus* is said to enhance his *dignitatem.*

reason to honor someone] and instead enumerate a person's other qualities along with his distinction in philosophy, you do not augment philosophy by what you add to it; rather you make it seem deficient by the assumption that it is in need of something. Still, let us be patient with this oration if it wants to show that, even if his achievement as a philosopher is discounted, this man is worthy to join your ranks. If it is right to coopt and love in return those who love you, consider that Themistius, who of his own free will has become deeply attached to us, by his own choice preferred our city to his native city and became a citizen [of Constantinople] by his own decision before citizenship was officially granted to him.[7] Consider what a great thing it is to show people from other cities who are otherwise happy that the place where we reside is worthy of love [22]! For Themistius has not taken refuge in the prosperity of this city because of domestic poverty. He is not hard-pressed financially, but he has no interest in becoming rich either.[8] In our midst he turned his mind to marriage and to the rearing of children, which ensures the continuity of our race. Marriage and child-rearing are praised when entered upon by someone other than a philosopher; but the assuming of these responsibilities by a philosopher is most beneficial. For the philosopher's life should be set before all other people as a standard and a goal; if he honors our city, concerns himself with the continuity of our race [that is ensured by marriage] and interests himself in the accumulation of money only to the extent necessary to satisfy his basic needs, he will induce many people to emulate him. For you must not think that true philosophy completely removes itself from communal life or absolutely refuses to concern itself with the community's affairs. Know that he who is much concerned with the city and transforms people into the very best human beings always makes them the very best citizens as well. Behold Themistius's many good qualities, then—qualities that have adorned this most illustrious man for you. He is rich in learning, he is not in financial straits, he willingly chose this city, he does not reside here by necessity, but necessity alone would separate him from you. Why should I say any more? In this unique philosopher I have given you a most illustrious man, an extraordinary citizen of our city, whom one would have every reason to call a citizen of the whole cosmos.

But I know well that Themistius does not hear all his praiseworthy attributes enumerated with equal pleasure. He regards only the praises of his philosophical achievement as appropriate, and he wants other praises to be voiced with restraint or not even to be voiced at all. But if perhaps I enumerated all his qualities, I have not spoken at length with the intention of pleasing the man; I have done so to show you that, when things are done by my judgment, I leave nothing unexamined or untested. And if one should tell the truth, Themistius is not known to me [only] in his present condition; I also know

7. Themistius was probably made a citizen of Constantinople and adlected to its senate simultaneously. Cf. above, p. 1.

8. Cf. Liban., *Epp.* 434 Foerster (A.D. 355), to Themistius: "[W]hile not disdaining the means whereby you became a member of the Senate, you have deliberately repulsed all that brings financial gain" (trans. A. F. Norman). For Themistius himself on his lack of interest in financial gain and his (relatively) limited resources, see *Orat.* 23.289a–94a.

about his past and about his lineage. I have such a wealth of information about the man that I could list his more distant forebears, who are mentioned in old writings, but I deliberately refrain from doing so [23]. For his father [Eugenius] is at hand, and because of him it is superfluous to mention other ancestors. Not even you are unaware of who his father is. For a person who utters this man's name, it is enough to point to consummate philosophy. There is no region, no people, and no city that has not heard of Eugenius's renown. You yourselves would all testify that this man has been possessed by philosophy throughout his whole life. None of the ancient teachings and subjects of study has escaped him. This man has been his own intellectual and moral rival; and in both spheres, although he is supreme, he continues to be surpassed by himself. So this man, the best of all men, the most preeminent of all, is considered to be equaled only by his son, and only Themistius can succeed him in their family and in philosophy.

For all the stated reasons, then, you must co-opt this excellent man [Themistius] and make him a member of your assembly. By this act we can also please my most divine father [Constantine], seeing to it, as we do, that the deliberative body named after him flower and bloom with the greatest of blessings. We must bestow a fitting dignity upon the spoken and written word more than upon everything else. We must give wisdom a suitable honor, learning an appropriate reward, and virtue the prize that is owed to it. The most excellent of the fields of knowledge—and I am referring to philosophy—must shine forth from all quarters and in the midst of everyone. For when the first and best art gets its proper honor, the other arts will also receive more attention.

From all of what I have said, then, it is clear that what I have presented to Themistius I have presented to you. I am sure that, in consecrating a good man rather than a religious shrine or a gymnasium in the name of my most divine father, I am offering a great gift to him as well.

Bibliography

THEMISTIAN EDITIONS AND TRANSLATIONS

Dindorf, W., ed. *Themistii Orationes.* Leipzig, 1832. Includes the Petavius-Harduinus annotations (*Orats.* 1–33) and the notes to *Orat.* 34 from A. Mai's 1816 edition.

Downey, G. "Themistius' First Oration." *Greek and Byzantine Studies* 1 (1958): 49–69. An English translation.

Gildemeister, J., and F. Bücheler. "Themistios *Περὶ ἀρετῆς*." *RhM* 27 (1872) 438–62. A German translation of the Syriac.

Harduinus, J. See under "Petavius" below.

Kesters, H. *Plaidoyer d'un Socratique contre le Phèdre de Platon, XXVI*[e] *Discours de Themistius: Introduction, texte établi et traduit.* Louvain and Paris, 1959.

Mai, A. *Classicorum auctorum e Vaticanis codicibus editorum Tomus IV.* Rome, 1831. Includes Greek text and Latin translation of *Orat.* 34 and the *θεωρία* of *Orat.* 20, with notes.

———. *Themistii philosophi Oratio in eos a quibus ob praefecturam susceptam fuerat vituperatus.* Milan, 1816. Greek text and Latin translation of *Orat.* 34 and the *θεωρία* of *Orat.* 20, with notes.

Maisano, R. *Discorsi di Temistio.* Turin, 1995. A revised version of the Teubner text with Italian translation, introduction, and annotations.

Oppermann, S. "*ΘΕΜΙΣΤΙΟΣ* I. *ΕΙΣ ΤΟΝ ΑΥΤΟΥ ΠΑΤΕΡΑ* II. *ΒΑΣΑΝΙΣΤΗΣ Η ΦΙΛΟΣΟΦΟΣ* (20. und 21. Rede): Ueberlieferung, Text und Uebersetzung." Diss., Göttingen, 1962.

Petavius, D., and J. Harduinus, eds. *Themistii Orationes XXXIII.* Paris, 1684. Greek text, Latin translation and annotations, which were reprinted in the Dindorf edition. *Orat.* 34 and the *θεωρία* of *Orat.* 20 would not be published till the nineteenth century, by Angelo Mai.

Schenkl, H., G. Downey, and A. F. Norman, eds. *Themistii Orationes.* 3 vols. Bibliotheca Teubneriana. Leipzig, 1965–74.

Schneider, H. *Die 34. Rede des Themistios (περὶ τῆς ἀρχῆς): Einleitung, Uebersetzung und Kommentar.* Winterthur, 1966. Includes a revised version of Dindorf's Greek text.

Schroeder, F. M., and R. B. Todd, trans. *Two Greek Aristotelian Commentators on the Intellect: The "De Intellectu" Attributed to Alexander of Aphrodisias and Themistius' Paraphrase of Aristotle "De Anima" 3.4–8.* Toronto, 1990.

Smeal, J. "Themistios: The Twenty-Third Oration." Diss., Vanderbilt University, Nashville, Tenn., 1989. Introduction, translation, and commentary.

Todd, R. B., trans. *Themistius On Aristotle's "On the Soul."* Ithaca, N.Y., 1996.

OTHER WORKS CONSULTED

This bibliography is almost entirely restricted to works cited by abbreviated title. With the exception of Stegemann's *RE* article on Themistius, dictionary and encyclopedia articles are not included.

Aalders, G. J. D. "*ΝΟΜΟΣ ΕΜΨΥΧΟΣ.*" In *Politeia und Res Publica,* ed. P. Steinmetz, pp. 315–29. Palingenesia 4. Wiesbaden, 1969.

———. *Political Thought in Hellenistic Times.* Amsterdam, 1975.

Adam, J. *The Republic of Plato. Edited with Critical Notes, Commentary and Appendices.* 2 vols. 2d ed. Cambridge, 1963.

Albini, U. "Appunti di lettura." *SIFC* 4 (1986): 272–73.

Alföldi, A. *Die monarchische Repräsentation im römischen Kaiserreiche.* 2d ed. Darmstadt, 1977.

Amouretti, M.-C. *Le Pain et l'huile dans la Grèce antique.* Centre de Recherche d'Histoire ancienne, vol. 67. Paris, 1986.

Arnold, E. V. *Roman Stoicism.* Cambridge, 1911.

Astin, A. E. *Scipio Aemilianus.* Oxford, 1967.

Athanassiadi, P. *Julian: An Intellectual Biography.* London and New York, 1992. Reprint of P. Athanassiadi-Fowden, *Julian and Hellenism: An Intellectual Biography* (Oxford, 1981).

Ballériaux, O. "Le *ΜΕΤΡΙΟΠΑΘΗΣ Η ΦΙΛΟΤΕΚΝΟΣ* (Discours XXXII) de Thémistius." *Byzantion* 58 (1988): 22–35.

———. "Thémistius et l'exégèse de la noétique aristotélicienne." *Revue de philosophie ancienne* 7 (1989): 199–233.

———. Review of *Greek Philosophers and Sophists in the Fourth Century A.D.: Studies in Eunapius of Sardis,* by R. J. Penella (Leeds, 1990). *AC* 61 (1992): 464–66.

———. "La Date du *ΠΕΡΙ ΦΙΛΑΝΘΡΩΠΙΑΣ Ἢ ΚΩΝΣΤΑΝΤΙΟΣ* (*Discours I*) de Thémistios." *Byzantion* 66 (1996): 319–34.

———. "Eugénios, père de Thémistios et philosophe néoplatonicien." *AC* 65 (1996): 135–60.

Barnes, T. D. *Athanasius and Constantius: Theology and Politics in the Constantinian Empire.* Cambridge, Mass., 1993.

Becchi, F. "L'ideale della *Metriopatheia* nei testi pseudopitagorici: A proposito di una contraddizione nello ps.-Archita." *Prometheus* 18 (1992): 102–20.
Behr, C. *Aelius Aristides and the Sacred Tales.* Amsterdam, 1968.
———. "Citations of Porphyry's *Against Aristides* Preserved in Olympiodorus." *AJP* 89 (1968): 186–99.
Beloch, K. J. *Griechische Geschichte.* 4 vols. in 8. 2nd ed. Strassburg and Berlin/Leipzig, 1912–31.
Bettarini, L. "Temistio, Sicione e l'origine della tragedia." *Κοινωνία* 19 (1995): 125–34.
Bevegni, C. "Un codice inesplorato dell'or. 24 di Temistio." *SIFC* 80 (1987): 62–63.
Birley, A. *Marcus Aurelius: A Biography.* 2d ed. New Haven, Conn., 1987.
Blumenthal, H. J. "Photius on Themistius (Cod. 74): Did Themistius Write Commentaries on Aristotle?" *Hermes* 107 (1979): 168–82.
———. *Aristotle and Neoplatonism in Late Antiquity: Interpretations of the "De Anima."* Ithaca, N.Y., 1996.
Boatwright, M. T. *Hadrian and the City of Rome.* Princeton, N.J., 1987.
Bohnenblust, G. *Beiträge zum Topos Περὶ φιλίας.* Berlin, 1905.
Bonner, S. F. "The Edict of Gratian on the Remuneration of Teachers." *AJP* 86 (1965): 113–37.
Bosworth, A. B. "Arrian's Literary Development." *CQ* 22 (1972): 163–85.
———. "Arrian and the Alani." *HSCP* 81 (1977): 217–55.
Bouchery, H. F. "Contribution a l'étude de la chronologie des discours de Themistius." *AC* 5 (1936): 191–208.
———. *Themistius in Libanius' Brieven.* Antwerp, 1936.
Bouyges, M. "Notes sur des traductions arabes d'auteurs grecs." *Archives de philosophie* 2, 3 (1924): 1–23.
Bowersock, G. W. *Augustus and the Greek World.* Oxford, 1965.
———. *Julian the Apostate.* Cambridge, Mass., 1978.
Brauch, T. "The Prefect of Constantinople for 362 A.D.: Themistius." *Byzantion* 63 (1993): 37–78.
———. "Themistius and the Emperor Julian." *Byzantion* 63 (1993): 79–115.
Brinkmann, A. "Lückenbüsser." *RhM* 64 (1909): 637–40.
Brown, P. *Power and Persuasion in Late Antiquity: Towards a Christian Empire.* Madison, Wis., 1992.
Bühler, W., ed. *Zenobii Athoi proverbia.* 6 vols. Göttingen, 1982-.
Buffiere, F. *Les Mythes d'Homère et la pensée grecque.* Paris, 1956.
Burkert, W. *Greek Religion.* Translated by J. Raffan. Cambridge, Mass., 1985.
Callu, J.-P. "Denier et nummus (300–354)." In *Les "Dévaluations" à Rome: Epoque républicaine et impériale,* pp. 107–21. Collection de L'Ecole française de Rome, 37. Rome, 1978.
———. "Analyses métalliques et inflation: L'orient romain de 295 à 361/368." In *Hommes et richesses dans l'empire byzantin,* 1: 223–33. Paris, 1989.
Callu, J.-P., and J.-N. Barrandon. "L'inflazione nel IV secolo (295–361): Il contributo delle analisi." In *Società romana e impero tardoantico: Istituzioni, ceti, economie,* ed. A. Giardina, 1: 559–99. Rome and Bari, 1986.
Cameron, Alan. "Notes on Palladas." *CQ* 15 (1965): 215–29.

———. "Wandering Poets: A Literary Movement in Byzantine Egypt." *Historia* 14 (1965): 470–509.

———. *Porphyrius the Charioteer.* Oxford, 1973.

Carrié, J.-M. "Les Distributions alimentaires dans les cités de l'empire roman tardif." *Mélanges de l'Ecole française de Rome, Antiquité* 87 (1975): 995–1101.

Casson, S. *Macedonia, Thrace and Illyria: Their Relations to Greece from the Earliest Times down to the Time of Philip, Son of Amyntas.* Oxford, 1926.

Chambry, E., ed. *Esope, Fables.* 2d ed. Paris, 1960.

Chastagnol, A. *La Préfecture urbaine à Rome sous le bas-empire.* Paris, 1960.

———. "Remarques sur les sénateurs orientaux au IVe siècle." *Acta Antiqua Academiae Scientiarum Hungaricae* 24 (1976): 341–56.

Chroust, A.-H. *Socrates, Man and Myth: The Two Socratic Apologies of Xenophon.* Notre Dame, Ind., 1957.

Cobet, C. G. "Ad Themistii Orationem XXXIV." *Mnemosyne* 11 (1862): 97–109.

———. "Annotationes criticae ad Themistii Orationes." *Mnemosyne* 11 (1862): 222–66, 394–434.

Colpi, B. *Die παιδεία des Themistios: Ein Beitrag zur Geschichte der Bildung im vierten Jahrhundert nach Christus.* Europäische Hochschulschriften, ser. 15, vol. 36. Bern, 1987.

Conche, M. *Anaximandre: Fragments et témoignages.* Paris, 1991.

Cook, A. B. "The Gong at Dodona." *JHS* 22 (1902): 5–28.

Cracco Ruggini, L. "Sofisti greci nell'Impero romano." *Athenaeum* 49 (1971): 402–25.

Croissant, J. "Un Nouveau Discours de Thémistius." *Serta Leodiensia,* Bibliothèquc de la Faculté de Philosophie et Lettres de l'Université de Liége 44 (1930): 7–30.

Dagron, G. "L'Empire romain d'Orient au IVe siècle et les traditions politiques de l'hellénisme: Le témoignage de Thémistios." *T&MByz* 3 (1968): 1–242.

———. *Naissance d'une capitale: Constantinople et ses institutions de 330 à 451.* Bibliothèque byzantine, Etudes, 7. Paris, 1974.

Daly, L. J. "Themistius' Plea for Religious Tolerance." *GRBS* 12 (1971): 65–79.

———. "The Mandarin and the Barbarian: The Response of Themistius to the Gothic Challenge." *Historia* 21 (1972): 351–79.

———. "Themistius' Concept of φιλανθρωπία." *Byzantion* 45 (1975): 22–40.

———. "'In a Borderland': Themistius' Ambivalence Toward Julian." *Byzantinische Zeitschrift* 73 (1980): 1–11.

———. "Themistius' Refusal of a Magistracy (*Or.* 34, cc. xiii–xv)." *Byzantion* 53 (1983): 164–212.

Dawson, D. *Cities of the Gods: Communist Utopias in Greek Thought.* New York, 1992.

Denniston, J. D. *The Greek Particles.* 2d ed., corr. Oxford, 1966.

Diehl, E., ed. *Anthologia lyrica graeca.* 3 vols. 3d ed. Leipzig, 1949–52.

Dillon, J. "'Metriopatheia and Apatheia': Some Reflections on a Controversy in Later Greek Ethics." In *Essays in Ancient Greek Philosophy,* vol. 2, ed. J. P. Anton and A. Preus (Albany, N.Y., 1983) = J. Dillon, *The Golden*

Chain: Studies in the Development of Platonism and Christianity (Brookfield, Vt., 1990), ch. 8.
Dodds, E. R. *Plato, "Gorgias." A Revised Text with Introduction and Commentary.* Oxford, 1959.
———. *Euripides, "Bacchae." Edited with Introduction and Commentary.* 2d ed. Oxford, 1960.
Donohue, A. A. *"Xoana" and the Origins of Greek Sculpture.* American Classical Studies, 15. Atlanta, Ga., 1988.
Dorandi, T., ed. *Filodemo, Storia dei filosofi: La Stoà da Zenone a Panezio (PHerc. 1018).* Philosophia Antiqua, 60. Leiden, 1994.
Downey, G. "Philanthropia in Religion and Statecraft in the Fourth Century after Christ." *Historia* 4 (1955): 199–208.
———. "Themistius and the Defense of Hellenism in the Fourth Century." *HTR* 50 (1957): 259–74.
———. "Themistius and the Classical Tradition." *Classical Bulletin* 34 (1958): 49–51.
———. "Allusions to Christianity in Themistius' Orations." *Studia Patristica* 5 (1962): 480–88.
Dudley, D. R. *A History of Cynicism.* London, 1937.
Düring, I. *Aristotle in the Ancient Biographical Tradition.* Acta Universitatis Gothoburgensis, 53. Göteborg, 1957.
Edelstein, E. J., and L. Edelstein. *Asclepius: A Collection and Interpretation of the Testimonies.* 2 vols. Baltimore, 1945.
Ehrenberg, V. *The People of Aristophanes.* 2d ed., rev. New York, 1962.
Else, G. F. *Aristotle's Poetics: The Argument.* Cambridge, Mass., 1957.
Fasce, S. *Eros, la figura e il culto.* Genoa, 1977.
Fleming, T. J. "The Musical Nomos in Aeschylus' *Oresteia.*" *CJ* 72 (1976–77): 222–33.
Foerster, R. "Andreas Dudith und die zwölfte Rede des Themistios." *Neue Jahrbücher für Pädagogik* 3 (1900): 74–93.
Fontenrose, J. *The Delphic Oracle: Its Responses and Operations with a Catalogue of Responses.* Berkeley and Los Angeles, 1978.
Fowden, G. "The Pagan Holy Man in Late Antique Society." *JHS* 102 (1982): 33–59.
Fraisse, J.-Cl. *Philia: La Notion d'amitié dans la philosophie antique.* Paris, 1974.
Gaiser, K. *Platons ungeschriebene Lehre.* 2d ed. Stuttgart, 1968.
———. *Philodems Academica: Die Berichte über Platon und die Alte Akademie in zwei herkulanensischen Papyri.* Supplementum Platonicum, 1. Stuttgart–Bad Cannstatt, 1988.
Garvie, A. *Aeschylus' "Supplices": Play and Trilogy.* Cambridge, 1969.
Garzya, A. *Storia e interpretazione di testi bizantini: Saggi e ricerche.* London, 1974.
———. "Temistio e i primordi della tragedia." In *Roma Renascens,* ed. M. Wissemann, pp. 65–77. Frankfurt am Main and New York, 1988.
Garzya, A., et al., eds. *In Themistii Orationes index auctus.* Hellenica et Byzantina Neapolitana, Collana di studi e testi, 11. Naples, 1989.

Gasda, A. "Kritische Bemerkungen zu Themistios (Fortsetzung)." *Städtisches Evangelisches Gymnasium zu Lauban, LX. Jahresbericht* (1887): 1–20.

Geffcken, J. *The Last Days of Greco-Roman Paganism*. Europe in the Middle Ages, Selected Studies, 8. Translated by S. MacCormack. Amsterdam, 1978.

Giannantoni, G. *Socraticorum reliquiae*. 4 vols. Naples, 1983–85.

Gigante, M. "I frammenti di Polemone academico." *Rendiconti dell'Accademia di archeologia, lettere e belle arti di Napoli* 51 (1976): 91–144.

Goldberg, S. M. *The Making of Menander's Comedy*. Berkeley and Los Angeles, 1980.

Gomme, A. W., and F. H. Sandbach. *Menander: A Commentary*. Oxford, 1973.

Gow, A. S. F. *Theocritus. Edited with a Translation and Commentary*. 2 vols. 2d ed. Cambridge, 1952.

Graf, F. *Eleusis und die orphische Dichtung Athens in vorhellenistischer Zeit*. Religionsgeschichtliche Versuche und Vorarbeiten, 33. Berlin and New York, 1974.

Griffin, M. T. *Seneca: A Philosopher in Politics*. Oxford, 1976.

Grimaldi, W. M. A., S.J. *Aristotle, "Rhetoric" I: A Commentary*. New York, 1980.

Gruen, E. S. *The Last Generation of the Roman Republic*. Berkeley and Los Angeles, 1974.

Guthrie, W. K. C. *Orpheus and Greek Religion*. 2d ed. London, 1952.

———. *A History of Greek Philosophy*. 6 vols. Cambridge, 1962–81.

Hamblin, C. L. *Fallacies*. London, 1970.

Hamilton, J. R. *Plutarch, "Alexander": A Commentary*. Oxford, 1969.

Hansen, G. Ch. Review of *Themistii Orationes quae supersunt*, ed. H. Schenkl and G. Downey, vol. 1 (Leipzig, 1965). *Gnomon* 38 (1966): 662–66.

———. "Nachlese zu Themistios." *Philologus* 111 (1967): 110–18.

Harris, W. V. *Ancient Literacy*. Cambridge, Mass., 1989.

———. "Child-Exposure in the Roman Empire." *JRS* 84 (1994): 1–22.

Heath, T. *A History of Greek Mathematics*. 2 vols. Oxford, 1921.

Hebert, B. *Schriftquellen zur hellenistischen Kunst: Plastik, Malerei und Kunsthandwerk der Griechen vom vierten bis zum zweiten Jahrhundert*. Grazer Beiträge, suppl. vol. 4. Graz, 1989.

Henrichs, A. "Two Doxographical Notes: Democritus and Prodicus on Religion." *HSCP* 79 (1975): 93–123.

———. "The Atheism of Prodicus." *Cronache ercolanesi* 6 (1976): 15–21.

Higham, T. F. "Two Notes on Aristophanes' *Birds*." *CQ* 26 (1932): 103–115.

Hock, R. F., and E. N. O'Neil. *The Chreia in Ancient Rhetoric*. Vol. 1: *The Progymnasmata*. Society of Biblical Literature, Texts and Translations, 27, Graeco-Roman Religion, ser. 9. Atlanta, Ga., 1986.

Hüttl, W. *Antoninus Pius*, 2 vols. Prague, 1933–36.

Hultsch, F. *Griechische und römische Metrologie*. 2d ed. Berlin, 1882.

Huss, W. "Der Name der Byrsa von Karthago." *Klio* 64 (1982): 403–6.

Hyland, A. *Equus: The Horse in the Roman World*. New Haven, Conn., 1990.

Isnardi Parente, M. *Speusippo: Frammenti*. La scuola di Platone, 1. Naples, 1980.

———. *Senocrate-Ermodoro: Frammenti.* La scuola di Platone, 3. Naples, 1982.

Janko, R., trans. *Aristotle, "Poetics" I, with the "Tractatus Coislinianus," a Hypothetical Reconstruction of "Poetics" II, the Fragments of the "On Poets."* Indianapolis, 1987.

Jones, A. H. M. *The Later Roman Empire, 284–602: A Social, Economic and Administrative Survey.* 3 vols. and map suppl. Oxford, 1964.

———. *Sparta.* Oxford, 1967.

Jones, C. P. "Themistius and the Speech *To the King.*" *CP* 92 (1997): 149–52.

Kagan, D. *The Fall of the Athenian Empire.* Ithaca, N.Y., 1987.

Kahn, C. H. *Anaximander and the Origins of Greek Cosmology.* New York, 1960.

Kaibel, G. *Stil und Text der ΠΟΛΙΤΕΙΑ ΑΘΗΝΑΙΩΝ des Aristoteles.* Berlin, 1893.

Kakridis, J. T. "Caeneus." *CR* 61 (1947): 77–80.

Kalbfleisch, K. "Griechische Miscellen I." In *Festschrift Theodor Gomperz,* pp. 94–96. Vienna, 1902.

Kantorowicz, E. H. "*Σύνθρονος Δίκη.*" *AJA* 57 (1953): 65–70.

Kaster, R. A. *Guardians of Language: The Grammarian and Society in Late Antiquity.* The Transformation of the Classical Heritage, 11. Berkeley and Los Angeles, 1988.

Keller, O. *Die antike Tierwelt.* 2 vols. Leipzig, 1909–13.

Kennedy, G. *The Art of Persuasion in Greece.* Princeton, N.J., 1963.

———. *Greek Rhetoric under Christian Emperors.* Princeton, N.J., 1983.

Kennell, N. M. *The Gymnasium of Virtue: Education and Culture in Ancient Sparta.* Chapel Hill, N.C., 1995.

Kent, J. P. C. *The Roman Imperial Coinage.* Vol. 8: *The Family of Constantine I,* A.D. 337–364. London, 1981.

Kertsch, M. "Ein bildhafter Vergleich bei Seneca, Themistios, Gregor von Nazianz und sein kynisch-stoischer Hintergrund." *VChr* 30 (1976): 241–57.

Kesters, H. *Antisthène, "De la dialectique": Etude critique et exégétique sur le XXVI*[e] *discours de Thémistius.* Louvain, 1935.

Kier, H. *De laudibus vitae rusticae.* Marburg, 1933.

Kindstrand, J. F. *Homer in der Zweiten Sophistik.* Studia Graeca Upsaliensia, 7. Uppsala, 1973.

Kirchner, J. *Prosopographia Attica.* 2 vols. Berlin, 1901–3.

Kneale, W., and M. Kneale. *The Development of Logic.* Oxford, 1962.

Konstan, D. "Friendship, Frankness and Flattery." In *Friendship, Flattery, and Frankness of Speech: Studies on Friendship in the New Testament World,* ed. J. T. Fitzgerald. Supplements to *Novum Testamentum,* 82. Leiden, 1996.

Lamberton, R. *Homer the Theologian: Neoplatonist Allegorical Reading and the Growth of the Epic Tradition.* Transformation of the Classical Heritage, 9. Berkeley and Los Angeles, 1986.

Lampe, G. W. H., ed. *A Patristic Greek Lexicon.* Oxford, 1961.

Laurenti, R. *Aristotele: I frammenti dei dialoghi.* 2 vols. Collana di filosofi antichi, 8–9. Naples, 1987.

Legrand, P. *The New Greek Comedy.* Translated by J. Loeb. London and New York, 1917.

Lenz, F. W. *The Aristeides Prolegomena. Mnemosyne* Supplements, 5. Leiden, 1959.

Lesky, A. *Greek Tragic Poetry.* Translated by M. Dillon. New Haven, Conn., 1983.

Lévêque, P. *Aurea catena Homeri: Une étude sur l'allégorie grecque.* Annales littéraires de l'Université de Besançon, 27. Paris, 1959.

Linforth, I. M. *The Arts of Orpheus.* Berkeley, 1941.

Lloyd, A. C. "Emotion and Decision in Stoic Psychology." In *The Stoics,* ed. J. M. Rist. Berkeley and Los Angeles, 1978.

Lucas, D. W. *Aristotle, "Poetics": Introduction, Commentary and Appendixes.* Oxford, 1968.

Luck, G. "Palladas—Christian or Pagan?" *HSCP* 63 (1958): 455–71.

Maas, M., and J. Snyder. *Stringed Instruments of Ancient Greece.* New Haven, Conn., 1989.

Maass, E., ed. *Commentariorum in Aratum reliquiae.* Berlin, 1898.

MacDowell, D. M. *The Law in Classical Athens.* Ithaca, N.Y., 1978.

MacMullen, R. *Soldier and Civilian in the Later Roman Empire.* Cambridge, Mass., 1967.

Maisano, R. "La critica filologica di Petau e Hardouin e l'edizione parigina del 1684 delle Orazioni di Temistio." *Archivum Historicum Societatis Jesu* 43 (1974): 267–99.

———. "Per una riedizione dei *Discorsi* di Temistio."*Κοινωνία* 2 (1978): 93–116.

———. "Postilla Temistiana." *Κοινωνία* 5 (1981): 97–88.

———. "La *paideia* del *logos* nell'opera oratoria di Temistio." *Κοινωνία* 10 (1986): 29–47.

Martin, J., ed., and P. Petit, trans. *Libanios, "Discours,"* vol. 1: *Autobiographie (Discours I).* Paris, 1979.

Masaracchia, A. "Note agli Ἐπιτρέποντες di Menandro." *Helikon* 8 (1968): 364–69.

Mason, H. J. *Greek Terms for Roman Institutions.* American Studies in Papyrology, 13. Toronto, 1974.

Matino, G. "L'uso delle preposizioni nei Discorsi di Temistio." *Annali della Facoltà di Lettere e Filosofia dell' Università di Napoli* 19 (1976–77): 63–107.

Mayor, J. E. B., ed. *Thirteen Satires of Juvenal.* 2 vols. London, 1900–1901. Reprint, Hildesheim, 1966.

McCartney, E. S. "Father Time." *CP* 23 (1928): 187–88.

Méridier, L. *Le Philosophe Thémistios devant l'opinion de ses contemporains.* Rennes, 1906.

Merlen, R. H. A. *De Canibus: Dog and Hound in Antiquity.* London, 1971.

Merrill, R. V. "Eros and Anteros." *Speculum* 19 (1944): 265–84.

Mesk, J. "Dion und Themistios." *Philologische Wochenschrift* 54 (1934): 556–58.

Michaelis, A. "Sarapis Standing on a Xanthian Marble in the British Museum." *JHS* 6 (1885): 287–318.

Michell, H. *Sparta*. Cambridge, 1952.

Millar, F. *The Emperor in the Roman World (31 B.C.–A.D. 337)*. Ithaca, N.Y., 1977.

Mommsen, Th. *Römisches Staatsrecht*. 3 vols. in 5. 3d ed. Leipzig, 1887–88.

Moore, F. G. "Three Canal Projects, Roman and Byzantine." *AJA* 54 (1950): 97–111.

Moraux, P. *Der Aristotelismus bei den Griechen*. 2 vols. Berlin, 1973–84.

Morris, S. P. *Daidalos and the Origins of Greek Art*. Princeton, N.J., 1992.

Morrow, G. R. *Plato's Cretan City: A Historical Interpretation of the Laws*. Princeton, N.J., 1960.

Nestle, W. *Vom Mythos zum Logos: Die Selbstentfaltung des griechischen Denkens von Homer bis auf die Sophistik und Sokrates*. 2d ed. Stuttgart, 1942.

Nissen, H. "Griechische und römische Metrologie." In *Einleitende und Hilfs-Disziplinen*. Handbuch der klassischen Altertumswissenschaft, 1. 2d ed. Munich, 1892.

Nixon, C. E. V., and B. S. Rodgers. *In Praise of Later Roman Emperors: The Panegyrici Latini*. Berkeley and Los Angeles, 1994.

Ober, J. *Mass and Elite in Democratic Athens: Rhetoric, Ideology and the Power of the People*. Princeton, N.J., 1989.

Ostwald, M. *From Popular Sovereignty to the Sovereignty of Law: Law, Society, and Politics in Fifth-Century Athens*. Berkeley and Los Angeles, 1986.

Paschoud, F., ed. *Zosime, "Histoire nouvelle."* 3 vols. in 5. Paris, 1971–89.

Patterson, C. " 'Not Worth the Rearing': The Causes of Infant Exposure in Ancient Greece." *TAPA* 115 (1985): 103–23.

Pease, A. S., ed. *M. Tulli Ciceronis, "De Natura Deorum."* 2 vols. Cambridge, Mass., 1955–58.

Penella, R. J. *The Letters of Apollonius of Tyana: A Critical Text with Prolegomena, Translation and Commentary*. *Mnemosyne* Supplements, 56. Leiden, 1979.

———. *Greek Philosophers and Sophists in the Fourth Century A.D.: Studies in Eunapius of Sardis*. ARCA: Classical and Medieval Texts, Papers and Monographs, 28. Leeds, 1990.

Perry, B. E., ed. *Aesopica: A Series of Texts Relating to Aesop or Ascribed to Him or Closely Connected with the Literary Tradition That Bears His Name*. Vol. 1. Urbana, Ill., 1952.

Petit, P. *Les Étudiants de Libanius*. Paris, 1957.

———. "Les Sénateurs de Constantinople dans l'oeuvre de Libanius." *AC* 26 (1957): 347–82.

Pfeiffer, R., ed. *Callimachus*. 2 vols. Oxford, 1949–53.

Pickard-Cambridge, A. *The Dramatic Festivals of Athens*. 2d ed. Revised by J. Gould and D. Lewis. Oxford, 1968.

Pizzolato, L. *L'idea di amicizia nel mondo antico classico e cristiano*. Turin, 1993.

Podlecki, A. J. *The Life of Themistocles: A Critical Survey of the Literary and Archaeological Evidence.* Montreal and London, 1975.

Powell, J. G. F. *Cicero, "Cato Maior de Senectute." Edited with Introduction and Commentary.* Cambridge, 1988.

Primmer, A. "Karion in den Epitrepontes." *Wiener Studien* 20 (1986): 123–41.

Rawson, E. *Intellectual Life in the Late Roman Republic.* Baltimore, 1985.

Redford, D. B. "The Literary Motif of the Exposed Child." *Numen* 14 (1967): 209–28.

Riginos, A. Swift. *Platonica: The Anecdotes concerning the Life and Writings of Plato.* Columbia Studies in the Classical Tradition, 3. Leiden, 1976.

———. "The Wounding of Philip II of Macedon: Fact and Fabrication." *JHS* 114 (1994): 103–19.

Rist, J. M. *Stoic Philosophy.* Cambridge, 1969.

———. "The Stoic Concept of Detachment." In *The Stoics,* ed. id. Berkeley and Los Angeles, 1978.

Robert, J., and L. Robert. "Bulletin épigraphique." *REG* 74 (1961): 119–268.

Robert, L. "Epigrammes relatives à des gouverneurs." *Hellenica* 4 (1948): 35–114.

———. "Documents d'Asie Mineure." *Bulletin de correspondance hellénique* 102 (1978): 395–543 = *Documents d'Asie Mineure,* Bibliothèque des écoles françaises d'Athènes et de Rome 239 *bis* (Athens and Paris, 1987), 91–239.

Robin, L. Review of *Antisthène "De la dialectique": Etude critique et exégétique sur le XXVIe discours de Thémistius,* by H. Kesters (Louvain, 1935). *REG* 49 (1936): 315–20.

Romano, R. "Themistiana I." *Κοινωνία* 2 (1978): 339–42.

———. "Themistiana II." *Κοινωνία* 4 (1980): 115–17.

———. "Themistiana III." *Κοινωνία* 6 (1982): 61–66.

Roscher, W. H., et al. *Ausführliches Lexikon der griechischen und römischen Mythologie.* 6 vols. in 9. Leipzig, 1884–1937.

Ryan, F. X. "The Quaestorship of Favonius and the Tribunate of Metellus Scipio." *Athenaeum* 82 (1994): 505–21.

Schaefer, A. "Historisches aus den neuen Scholien zu Aeschines." *Jahrbücher für classische Philologie* 93 (1866): 26–29.

Schäfer, T. *Imperii Insignia, Sella Curulis und Fasces: Zur Repräsentation römischer Magistrate.* Mitteilungen des Deutschen Archaeologischen Instituts, Römische Abteilung, Suppl. 29. Mainz, 1989.

Scharold, J. *Dio Chrysostomus und Themistius.* Burghausen, 1912.

Schemmel, F. "Die Hochschule von Konstantinopel im IV. Jahrhundert p. Ch. n." *Neue Jahrbücher für Pädagogik* 11 (1908): 147–68.

Schenkl, H. "Die handschriftliche Ueberlieferung der Reden des Themistius." *Wiener Studien* 20 (1898): 205–43.

———. "Die handschriftliche Ueberlieferung der Reden des Themistius." *Wiener Studien* 21 (1899): 80–115, 225–63.

———. "Beiträge zur Textgeschichte der Reden des Themistios." *SAWW* 192, 1 (1919): 3–89.

Schlange-Schöningen, H. *Kaisertum und Bildungswesen im spätantiken Konstantinopel.* Historia Einzelschriften, 94. Stuttgart, 1995.

Schmid, W., and O. Stählin. *Wilhelm von Christs Geschichte der griechischen Litteratur,* 2.2. 6th ed. Munich, 1924.

Scholze, H. *De temporibus librorum Themistii.* Göttingen, 1911.

Schroeder, O. *De laudibus Athenarum a poetis tragicis et ab oratoribus epidicticis excultis.* Göttingen, 1914.

Seeck, O. *Die Briefe des Libanius.* Leipzig, 1906.

Seeck, O., and H. Schenkl. "Eine verlorene Rede des Themistius." *RhM* 61 (1906): 554–66.

Shackleton Bailey, D. R. *Cicero's Letters to Atticus.* 7 vols. Cambridge, 1965–70.

Shaw, B. D. "'Eaters of Flesh, Drinkers of Milk': The Ancient Mediterranean Ideology of the Pastoral Nomad." *Ancient Society* 13–14 (1982–83): 5–31.

Smyth, H. W. *Greek Grammar.* Revised by G. M. Messing. Cambridge, Mass., 1966.

Snell, B. *Leben und Meinungen der Sieben Weisen.* 3d ed. Munich, 1952.

Stadter, P. A. *Arrian of Nicomedia.* Chapel Hill, N.C., 1980.

Starkie, W. J. M., ed. *The Acharnians of Aristophanes.* London, 1909.

Steel, C. "Des commentaires d'Aristote par Themistius?" *Revue philosophique de Louvain* 71 (1973): 669–80.

Stegemann, W. "Themistios 2." *RE,* 5A, 2 (1934): 1642–80.

de Strycker, E. "Themistios' getuigenis over de exoterische en akroamatische werken van Aristoteles." *Philologische Studiën* 7 (1935–36): 100–121.

———. "Antisthène ou Thémistius?" *Archives de philosophie* 12 (1936): 475–500.

Syme, R. *Emperors and Biography: Studies in the Historia Augusta.* Oxford, 1971.

Taplin, O. *The Stagecraft of Aeschylus.* Oxford, 1977.

Tarán, L. *Speusippus of Athens: A Critical Study with a Collection of the Related Texts and Commentary.* Philosophia Antiqua, 39. Leiden, 1981.

Tigerstedt, E. N. *The Legend of Sparta in Classical Antiquity.* 3 vols. Stockholm, 1965–78.

Usener, H. "Lectiones graecae." *RhM* 25 (1870): 574–616 = *Kleine Schriften* (Leipzig, 1912–13), 1: 156–203.

Valdenberg, V. "Discours politiques de Thémistius dans leur rapport avec l'antiquité." *Byzantion* 1 (1924): 557–80.

Vanderspoel, J. "The Fourth Century Philosopher Maximus of Byzantium." *Ancient History Bulletin* 1, 3 (1987): 71–74.

———. "Themistios and a Philosopher at Sikyon." *Historia* 36 (1987): 383–84.

———. "Themistios and the Origin of Iamblichos." *Hermes* 116 (1988): 125–28.

———. *Themistius and the Imperial Court: Oratory, Civic Duty, and Paideia from Constantius to Theodosius.* Ann Arbor, Mich., 1995.

Volpis, L., ed. *Demostene: L'orazione contro Aristocrate.* Milan, 1936.

Waites, M. C. "Some Features of the Allegorical Debate in Greek Literature." *HSCP* 23 (1912): 1–46.

Walden, J. W. H. *The Universities of Ancient Greece.* New York, 1909.

Wallace, R. W. *The Areopagos Council, to 307 B.C.* Baltimore, 1985.

Wallis, R. T. *Neoplatonism.* New York, 1972.

Walsdorff, F. *Die antiken Urteile über Platons Stil.* Bonn, 1927.

Webster, T. B. L. *Studies in Later Greek Comedy.* 2d ed. Manchester, 1970.

Wehrli, F., ed. *Die Schule des Aristoteles,* 10 vols. 2d ed. and 2 suppl. vols. Basel and Stuttgart, 1967–78.

West, M. L. *Ancient Greek Music.* Oxford, 1992.

von Wilamowitz-Moellendorff, U. *Menander, "Das Schiedsgericht" (Epitrepontes).* Berlin, 1925.

Wilhelm, F. "Zu Themistios Or. 27 (p. 400 Dindorf)." *Byzantinisch-neugriechische Jahrbücher* 6 (1927–28): 451–89.

———. "Zu Themistios Or. 27D." *Philologische Wochenschrift* 50 (1930): 1003–1004.

Zeller, E. *Die Philosophie der Griechen in ihrer geschichtlichen Entwicklung.* 3 vols. in 6. 4th ed. (II, 2). 5th ed. (II, 1; III, 1; III, 2). 6th ed. (I, 1; I, 2). Leipzig, 1919–23.

Zonta, M. "*Hebraica veritas:* Temistio, *Parafrasi* del *De coelo*. Tradizione e critica del testo." *Athenaeum* 82 (1994): 403–28.

Index

For exhaustive coverage of the text of Themistius, see the index nominum in the third volume of the Teubner edition of Themistius's *Orations* and *In Themistii Orationes index auctus* by Garzya et al. The text of Themistius's *Orations* and *Paraphrases* is available for word searches on "Thesaurus Linguae Graecae CD ROM D" (1992).

Text:	10/13 Sabon
Display:	Sabon
Composition:	Impressions Book and Journal Services, Inc.
Printing and Binding:	Edwards Brothers, Inc.